C000008722

SPEAKING IN THE PAST TENSE
Canadian Novelists on Writing
Historical Fiction

Herb Wyile

Wilfrid Laurier University Press
WLU

We acknowledge the support of the Canada Council for the Arts for our publishing program. We acknowledge the financial support of the Government of Canada through the Book Publishing Industry Development Program for our publishing activities.

Canada Council for the Arts Conseil des Arts du Canada

ONTARIO ARTS COUNCIL
CONSEIL DES ARTS DE L'ONTARIO

Library and Archives Canada Cataloguing in Publication

Wyile, Herb, 1961–
    Speaking in the past tense : Canadian novelists on writing historical fiction / Herb Wyile.

Includes bibliographical references.
ISBN-13: 978-0-88920-511-6
ISBN-10: 0-88920-511-6

    1. Historical fiction, Canadian—History and criticism. 2. Historical fiction, Canadian—Authorship. 3. Novelists, Canadian—Interviews. I. Title.

PS8191.H5W935 2007   C813'.081   C2006-906460-1

© 2007 Wilfrid Laurier University Press
Waterloo, Ontario, Canada
www.wlupress.wlu.ca

Cover design by P.J. Woodland. Cover image by Frances Anne Hopkins, detail from *Canoes in a Fog, Lake Superior* (1869, oil on canvas), courtesy of the Glenbow Museum Collection. Text design by Catharine Bonas-Taylor.

∞

This book is printed on Ancient Forest Friendly paper (100% post-consumer recycled).

Printed in Canada

Every reasonable effort has been made to acquire permission for copyright material used in this text, and to acknowledge all such indebtedness accurately. Any errors and omissions called to the publisher's attention will be corrected in future printings.

No part of this publication may be reproduced, stored in a retrieval system or transmitted, in any form or by any means, without the prior written consent of the publisher or a licence from The Canadian Copyright Licensing Agency (Access Copyright). For an Access Copyright licence, visit www.accesscopyright.ca or call toll free to 1-800-893-5777.

Contents

Illustrations

Author Photos

Guy Vanderhaeghe photo (p. 25) by Margaret Vanderhaeghe, courtesy of McClelland & Stewart.

Rudy Wiebe photo (p. 53) by J.D. Sloan, courtesy of Random House of Canada.

Jane Urquhart photo (p. 79) by Elsa Trillit, courtesy of McClelland & Stewart.

Wayne Johnston photo (p. 105) by Neil Graham, courtesy of Random House of Canada.

George Elliott Clarke photo (p. 133) by Geeta Paray-Clarke, courtesy of George Elliott Clarke.

Margaret Sweatman photo (p. 165) by Brian Hydesmith, courtesy of Random House of Canada.

Fred Stenson photo (p. 189) by Greg Garrard, courtesy of Greg Garrard.

Joseph Boyden photo (p. 219) by Stephanie Beeley Photography, courtesy of Penguin Canada.

Heather Robertson photo (p. 241) courtesy of Heartland Books.

Thomas Wharton photo (p. 269) courtesy of Thomas Wharton.

Michael Crummey photo (p. 295) by Holly Hogan, courtesy of Michael Crummey.

Acknowledgements

This project was largely made possible by a series of Acadia University Research Fund grants, which paid for the travel costs of the majority of these interviews and funded the illustrations for the book. I am also extremely grateful to a number of people for playing host to me while I was criss-crossing the country or for otherwise helping to facilitate the interviews; my thanks to Cliff Lobe and Gloria Borrows, Geraldine and Hugh Hind, David Buchanan, Pamela Banting, John Mahon and Shelagh Wildsmith, Cameron Malcolm and Dianne Willisko, Doris Wolf and Paul DiPasquale for their hospitality and aid. I would also like to express my gratitude to Sharon Klein at Knopf Canada for helping to organize the interview with Wayne Johnston. Thanks go also to Wanda Campbell and Eszter Schwenke for their feedback on the interview with Jane Urquhart, and I am particularly indebted to Cynthia Sugars for her invaluable advice on the introduction. Tom Scott, Bill King, and T.D. McGee also played a crucial role in bringing about this project. I would like to give special thanks to Jacqueline Larson at Wilfrid Laurier University Press for her enthusiasm for the project from the get-go and thanks to the rest of staff at WLUP for shepherding the manuscript through the publication process.

Interviews, I discovered, are a lot of work (go figure!), and I am extremely grateful to the Acadia students who helped prepare and transcribe some of these interviews. Thanks go first of all to Katherine Lusk for her help on the interviews with Heather Robertson and Jane Urquhart, and likewise to Erin Demings for her help with the latter. Thanks go also to Mpho Marupeng for her work on the interviews with Margaret Sweatman and Guy Vanderhaege, and to Daniel Kyte for helping with the interview with Wayne Johnston. Finally, I am grateful to Amy Heffernan for her work on the interviews with Rudy Wiebe and Fred Stenson and to Robyn Lippett for helping to proofread the manuscript.

Tracking down the illustrations for *Speaking in the Past Tense* was a challenge in itself, and I am very grateful for the assistance of staff at Library and Archives Canada, "The Rooms" (Archives Division, Newfoundland and Labrador), the Glenbow Museum, the Whyte Museum of the Canadian Rockies, the Provincial Archives of Alberta, the Frederick Cook Society, Veterans Affairs Canada, the Provincial Archives of Manitoba, and the Mathers Museum at Indiana University.

"The Iceman Cometh Across: An Interview with Thomas Wharton" was previously published in *Past Matters/Choses du Passé: History in Canadian Fiction,* a special issue of *Studies in Canadian Literature* (27.1) that I co-edited with Jennifer Andrews and Robert Viau in 2002. "Confessions of a Historical Geographer: An Interview with Jane Urquhart" appeared in *Essays on Canadian Writing* 81 (2004). Both interviews are reprinted here with the kind permission of those journals.

Last and foremost, I would like to express my extreme gratitude to Heather Robertson, Thomas Wharton, Jane Urquhart, Margaret Sweatman, Guy Vanderhaeghe, Wayne Johnston, Fred Stenson, Rudy Wiebe, Michael Crummey, George Elliott Clarke, and Joseph Boyden for the enthusiasm, time, and effort they put into helping to make this collection of conversations happen.

Introduction

Anyone concerned with the current state of Canadian history can be forgiven for being confused by what seem to be conflicting readings of its vital signs. On the one hand, there are those who suggest that history in this country is in a palliative condition—that it is suffering, in other words, from fatal neglect. On the other hand, there are those who see rumours of the demise of Canadian history as being highly exaggerated, and even some who see it as being in fine form. How to account for this wide and seemingly paradoxical divergence of views? Much of it has to do with broader developments in the discipline of history. Particularly over the last three decades, the discipline of history, in Canada as elsewhere, has experienced a profound upheaval, the result of a sustained challenge to traditional notions of what constitutes history and what it means to write history. Part of the fallout of these ideological and professional differences among historians has been intense public debates about the erosion of Canadians' knowledge of their own history and about the importance of that erosion to a sense of national identity. Many historians committed to a more traditional political and military history are anxious about Canadians' declining historical knowledge and declining adherence to a unifying historical narrative. Other historians, while skeptical about such monolithic narratives about Canada's past and more committed to a pluralistic social history, are often nonetheless concerned by a declining sense of historical consciousness and an increasing tendency to appreciate the past only in commodified, dehistoricized form. Just as in health care, the fact that the patient is getting a lot of attention doesn't necessarily mean that she or he is well.

While concern about the growing irrelevance of history is to a degree echoed in the field of Canadian literature, Canadian literature seems to be one forum in which there is undeniable evidence of a renewed interest in and revitalization of Canadian history. Indeed, for Canadian writers at the turn of the twenty-first century, history has indisputably become a central preoccupation. Since the appearance of ground-breaking, self-consciously historiographical novels by Rudy Wiebe and Timothy Findley, such as *The Temptations of Big Bear* and *The Wars* in the 1970s, historical fiction has grown to be one of the most popular and substantial literary genres in Canada. Many of the most notable novels published since that time—such as Joy Kogawa's *Obasan* (1981), Susan Swan's *The Biggest Modern Woman of the World* (1983), Michael Ondaatje's *In the Skin of a Lion* (1987), Daphne Marlatt's *Ana Historic* (1988), and more recently Margaret Atwood's *The Blind Assassin* (2000)—have been concerned with history. Of the current generation of novelists making a mark both nationally and internationally, a conspicuous proportion write about the past, whether those fictions are set in Canada or elsewhere: Joseph Boyden, George Elliott Clarke, Michael Crummey, Wayne Johnston, Sky Lee, Ann-Marie MacDonald, Anne Michaels, Rohinton Mistry, Fred Stenson, Margaret Sweatman, Jane Urquhart, Guy Vanderhaeghe, Thomas Wharton, and others. Canadian readers are increasingly eager to delve into the country's past, and Canadian writers have played a huge role in cultivating and feeding that interest.

Representations of Canadian history and, in particular, the genre of historical fiction have also become of increasing concern to Canadian literary critics and scholars. Since Dennis Duffy published a short overview of the genre, *Sounding the Iceberg: An Essay on Canadian Historical Novels*, in 1986, the body of critical commentary on contemporary Canadian historical novels has grown considerably. Along with Linda Hutcheon's seminal chapter on historiographic metafiction in *The Canadian Postmodern* (1988), key studies include Martin Kuester's *Framing Truths: Parodic Structures in Contemporary English-Canadian Historical Novels* (1992), Manina Jones's *That Art of Difference: 'Documentary-Collage' and English-Canadian Writing* (1993), and Marie Vautier's *New World Myth: Postmodernism and Postcolonialism in Canadian Fic-*

tion (1998). The journals *Studies in Canadian Literature* and *Canadian Literature* have recently published special issues on history in Canadian literature, *Past Matters: History and Canadian Fiction* (2002) and *Archives and History* (2003), respectively.

This present collection is a follow-up to my own contribution to this burgeoning area, *Speculative Fictions: Contemporary Canadian Novelists and the Writing of History* (2002), a critical study of the themes and textual strategies of twenty contemporary English-Canadian historical novels. While conducting research for *Speculative Fictions*, I started to appreciate that English-Canadian writers' interest in, and knowledge of, history went well beyond their novels. I thus resolved to provide a forum for reflections on Canadian history by people who have invested a great deal of time and effort in studying Canada's past and, through their writing, have raised Canadians' consciousness of the importance of that past. *Speaking in the Past Tense* is that forum. This collection contains interviews with eleven writers, practically, but not quite, from coast to coast: veteran writers such as Rudy Wiebe, who has published many historical novels dealing with Native people and his own Mennonite background, most notably *The Temptations of Big Bear* (1973) and *The Scorched-Wood People* (1977); Heather Robertson, who published *The King Years*, a trilogy of historical novels about William Lyon MacKenzie King, in the 1980s; and Fred Stenson, a journeyman Alberta writer who has been writing fiction since the 1970s but has most recently made a distinct mark with his historical novels *The Trade* (2000) and *Lightning* (2003). It includes conversations with established writers such as Jane Urquhart, whose lyrical novels set predominantly in rural southern Ontario tend to touch on watershed moments in Canadian history; Guy Vanderhaeghe, whose last two novels, *The Englishman's Boy* (1996) and *The Last Crossing* (2002), are set in "Whoop-Up Country," the border territory of the southwestern prairies at the end of the nineteenth century; Wayne Johnston, (in)famous for his rollicking portrait of Newfoundland premier Joey Smallwood in *The Colony of Unrequited Dreams* (1998); and George Elliott Clarke, winner of a Governor General's award for poetry, whose first novel, *George and Rue* (2005), deals with the execution of two of his cousins for killing a taxi driver in Fredericton in 1949. Finally, there are interviews with writers who have more recently established a presence on the literary scene in Canada: Thomas Wharton, whose novel *Icefields* (1995) is a lyrical chronicle of exploration and development in the Rockies; Margaret Sweatman, who has written about the history of Winnipeg and the Winnipeg General Strike in her novels *Fox* (1991) and *When Alice Lay Down with Peter* (2001); Michael Crummey, whose *River Thieves* (2001) is set against the background of the extinction of the Beothuk of Newfoundland at the beginning of the nineteenth century; and Joseph Boyden, whose first novel *Three Day Road* (2005) revolves around two young Cree men who serve as snipers with the Second Canadian Division in Belgium and France during World War I.

The roster of Canadian writers who write about history is, of course, a long one, and there are many others who might have been part of this collection. The majority of these writers are those whose work was the focus of *Speculative Fictions*, and Michael Crummey, Fred Stenson, George Elliott Clarke, and Joseph Boyden have published important novels since the work on *Speculative Fictions* was completed. The governing principle behind the selection of these writers is that they all focus on public history—that is, key episodes in Canadian history, particularly episodes whose representation involves engagement with historical documents and sources (Smallwood and Confederation, The Winnipeg General Strike, the Riel uprisings) but also involves elements such as class, race, ethnicity, gender, and postcolonial considerations. Certainly, one can say that much, if not most, Canadian fiction is historical, but there are different degrees and different kinds of history. The traditional historical novel usually revolves around some pivotal historical incident, or era, or figure, and my principal concern here, as in *Speculative Fictions*, is with contemporary writers whose work in some ways engages in a dialogue with the public historical record and identifiable historical figures but has also started to push the boundaries of that definition and of the definition of history.

This dialogue is particularly important in the case of those whom the historical record has tended to exclude—women, the working class, and racial(ized) minorities—and one obvious fact about this collection is that the latter seem underrepresented. At the same time, however, the resulting predominance here of writers of European heritage is arguably an accurate reflection of the state of Canadian historical fiction. Historical novels by Native Canadian writers or by Canadian writers of Asian, South Asian, Middle Eastern, or African heritage are relatively scarce, something which may have to do with their historical exclusion from (albeit recent embrace by) the Canadian literary scene and with their exclusion from dominant narratives about Canada's past. In the interview included in this collection, George Elliott Clarke makes the compelling argument that the current generation of writers from minority groups may be the first to feel secure enough about their place in Canadian society to write about their histories, and Joseph Boyden suggests that the relative absence of such novels by Aboriginal writers may largely be attributed to the cataclysmic break with the past effected by the residential school system. These groups of writers, furthermore, have arguably had different priorities than addressing in fiction public figures and episodes from Canada's past. Even where this is not the case, the genre of historical fiction itself—as the experience of women writers has shown—poses difficulties to non-dominant groups because of the very exclusiveness of the historical record, which tends to be preoccupied with the activities of white, upper-class English males. The reasons for this relative absence are too complex to explore here, but certainly one consideration is that it's easier to engage the historical record in fiction when the historical resources are there in the first place. Somewhat paradoxically, perhaps one of the most important conclusions to be drawn from *Speaking in the Past Tense* is that a genuine literary engagement with the history of this country requires going well beyond the confines of the historical novel.

The conversations in *Speaking in the Past Tense* concentrate on various aspects of the writing of historical fiction—its attraction, its challenges, its significance. These interviews explore the writers' engagement with the history behind and around their novels, contributing to an understanding of the historical contexts and sources that inform their work. This understanding is especially important because the majority of these writers have enjoyed little sustained critical attention.[1] In that sense, *Speaking in the Past Tense* seeks to make a useful contribution to existing scholarship on contemporary English-Canadian fiction. But these conversations also address the nature of historical fiction as a genre and various aesthetic, epistemological, and political questions about the writing of history. In that respect, the collection also participates in an expanding critical dialogue on the writing of historical fiction, providing a series of reflections on the process from the perspective of those souls intrepid enough to step onto what is, practically by definition, contested territory. The interviews in *Speaking in the Past Tense* address most of the central preoccupations of critics studying historical fiction in Canada over the last thirty years and, in that sense, provide a crucial supplement to our understanding of the place of history in the popular imagination.

Why so many writers in Canada have gravitated toward historical fiction at the turn of the twenty-first century is an interesting question. The

---

1 This consideration explains in part the absence of other writers who might have been in the collection, such as Joy Kogawa, Margaret Atwood and Daphne Marlatt. While I did write about their work in *Speculative Fictions*, all three have been the subject of a great deal of critical attention and of a good many interviews, as have, to a lesser degree, George Bowering, Susan Swan, and Jack Hodgins, three other authors addressed in *Speculative Fictions*. With the exception of Rudy Wiebe, whose work is so central to the genre, and Heather Robertson, whose trilogy has been virtually neglected, my concern here is with a cohort of novelists who have really brought Canadian history to the fore in the last two decades.

phenomenon is itself arguably the product of historical circumstances, such as the overthrow of a colonial mentality in which Canadian history was dismissed as negligible, even oxymoronic; an increasing desire to interrogate and challenge a narrowly defined national past and to venture beyond its boundaries; the influence of a wider questioning of the epistemological and ideological basis of history; an anxiety about distinguishing Canadian culture and identity from that of the United States in an era of increasing economic, cultural, and political integration; and an increasingly global, postnational culture that has perhaps cultivated (as a kind of compensation) a preoccupation with the nation's past. Finally, there is no discounting the fact that writers may gravitate to historical fiction for the simple reason that it is popular with readers.

The present vogue for historical fiction in Canada is by no means unprecedented. Historical novels and historical romances were extremely popular, for instance, in the second half of the nineteenth century. T.D. MacLulich observes that in the middle of the nineteenth century Canadian writers began "to inspect their own history for the marks of nationhood" and "to aid in the systematic creation of a collective mythology that would give Canadian history something of the dignity and significance associated with European history" (1988, 45). William Kirby's *The Golden Dog* (1877) and Sir Gilbert Parker's *The Seats of the Mighty* (1896) were extremely popular novels of their time, but also consciously served this nation-building purpose. In the second half of the twentieth century, however, that collective mythology, as Daniel Francis contends in *National Dreams: Myth, Memory, and Canadian History*, has experienced a crisis of confidence. If the "stories we tell about the past produce the images that we use to describe ourselves as a community," Francis argues, the inadequacies of the core myths of Canadian history have been thoroughly exposed, and English Canada needs a new set of narratives to reflect a much more diverse, and not necessarily unified, society (1997, 176). Contemporary historical novels, in contrast to their nineteenth-century predecessors, seem less inclined to participate in creating a collective mythology than to question traditional narratives of Canadian history and any notion of a collective, consensual experience of the past. Indeed, those icons (the Mounties, the railroad, the fur trader) and those iconic moments (the War of 1812, Confederation, and WWI) of Canadian history that Francis examines and deflates in *National Dreams* are likewise very much questioned in contemporary historical fiction. Wiebe in *The Temptations of Big Bear* and Wharton in *Icefields* examine the impact of the railroad on Native peoples, Robertson in *Lily: A Rhapsody in Red* (1986) provides a fictional portrayal of the RCMP's role in the "suppression of legitimate political dissent and freedom of speech" (Francis 1997, 50), and in *The Whirlpool* (1989) Urquhart spoofs the celebration of the War of 1812 as a watershed victory signalling the emergence of a nascent nationality.

As these examples suggest, one of the most distinctive features of contemporary Canadian historical fiction is its predominantly postcolonial sensibility. During roughly the same period in which historical fiction became a prominent literary genre in Canada, postcolonialism has become the pre-eminent critical framework within which to approach Canadian literature. As Laura Moss rightly observes, "searching for a postcolonial identity" has displaced searching for a national identity as a national preoccupation (2003, vii). The ascendancy of postcolonialism, of course, has been neither smooth nor uncomplicated. The definition of postcolonialism, "which can designate a subject matter, a period, or a methodology"(Brydon 1995, 13), continues to be hotly contested. Furthermore, the appropriateness of approaching a settler–invader culture such as Canada's *as postcolonial* has been a matter of ongoing debate. Nonetheless, what *is* indisputable is that criticism of Canadian literature of the last thirty years has been overwhelmingly informed by postcolonial theory. Three recent essay collections, Moss's *Is Canada Postcolonial? Unsettling Canadian Literature* (2003) and Cynthia Sugars's *Unhomely States: Theorizing English-Canadian Postcolonialism* (2004) and *Home-Work: Postcolonialism, Pedagogy, and Canadian Literature* (2004), have certainly consolidated the extensive and much-debated application of that body of theory to Canadian literature.

This critical preoccupation, of course, is in large part a response to the predominantly revisionist reappraisal of the legacy of Canada's colonial experience in Canadian literature, a spirit which is particularly evident in contemporary historical fiction. The historical novels of the past three decades have been preoccupied with such central postcolonial concerns as the politics of discovery and settlement, armed conflict and expropriation of territory, the imposition of European cultural and social standards, and racial and cultural hybridity. Wiebe's *The Temptations of Big Bear, The Scorched-Wood People* and, more recently, *A Discovery of Strangers* (1994) strive to deconstruct the Eurocentrism of traditional portraits of the colonization of Aboriginal peoples in the Canadian Northwest. Vanderhaeghe's *The Englishman's Boy* and *The Last Crossing* do much the same for "Whoop-Up Country" in the southwestern prairies in the late nineteenth century. In *Icefields*, Thomas Wharton includes the story of the displacement of Aboriginal people in his novel about the Columbia Icefield and the development of tourism in the Rocky Mountains.

Johnston's *The Colony of Unrequited Dreams* hilariously, but no less effectively, dramatizes the consequences of England's centuries-long exploitation and neglect of Newfoundland. In *River Thieves*, Crummey explores the complex politics between the colonial authorities, settlers, and the embattled Beothuk in early nineteenth-century Newfoundland. Finally, Boyden's *Three Day Road* chronicles the impact of the increasing circumscription of the lives of the Cree and Ojibway of northern Ontario by white society and the devastating impact of the residential school system.

The engagement with Canada's colonial past evident in these and other novels is extended in the conversations in *Speaking in the Past Tense*. Again and again these writers speak to the importance of recognizing the way in which Canadian history has traditionally been viewed through an Anglocentric prism and of the way in which colonial attitudes toward Native peoples, immigrants and the land itself have deeply shaped the dominant narratives of the nation's past. Urquhart, for instance, provides a searing indictment of the impact of colonialism on the landscape and on the self-perception of a colonial society. Sweatman describes Canada as a "squatocracy" (a term current in Australia for describing settler culture) and speaks of how being part of such a society, and being a non-Aboriginal writer in such a society, requires an accommodation with fraudulence, with a contestable claim to occupancy and ownership. Johnston talks of the unique colonial history of Newfoundland and the "perceived possession of, and after that the perceived loss of, nationhood" that distinguishes its history from that of the rest of Canada. As Francis argues, the second half of the twentieth century has been marked by an increasing distance from Canada's imperial heritage (see Francis 1987, 52–87), and that sensibility is very much reflected in *Speaking in the Past Tense*.

Also evident in these conversations, however, is a recognition of the colonial past as a more complex, nuanced, and double-edged legacy. Wharton describes his ambivalence about the Victorian scientists who pioneered exploration in the Rockies, recognizing that they were aesthetically sensitive and intellectually curious yet at the same time were an extension of the larger process of European colonialism in the New World. Vanderhaeghe speaks of the complexity of imperial designs for western Canada in the late nineteenth century, observing that the extension of British law and justice into the West was fuelled by "economic and political designs that were really only going to be of benefit to white Europeans" but also by benevolent moral intentions toward Native peoples that helped distinguish that process from the more violent confrontation on the American frontier. In this respect, these conversations contribute to a wider reassessment of the history of colonialism and a movement beyond a simplistically monolithic denunciation of its impact.

In part an extension of this largely postcolonial attitude toward the legacy of colonialism, an important aspect of these interviews is the writers' recognition of the significance of events that lie beyond the confines of the unifying national narratives typical of traditional political and military history. As Francis argues, one of the reasons that the dominant myths of Canadian history are under siege is that they are partial and exclusive: "Core myths are usually the property of the elites, who use them to reinforce the status quo and to further their claims to privilege" (1997, 12). Certainly, one of the dominant influences on Western historiography in the second half of the twentieth century has been social history, the concern with histories beyond the political and military history that has traditionally dominated the discipline. As Michael Bliss (unhappily) describes it, "there has been a massive shift in historians' substantive interests, away from political and constitutional history and towards the exploration of the experiences of people in relationships flowing from such non-national connections as region, ethnicity, class, family, and gender. The situations of interest to historians now tend toward the private and personal—states of mind, standards of living, conditions of health, family values, local hierarchies." In short, "political history has been out, social and personal history have been in" (1991–92, 6). That influence has certainly profoundly affected debates on historiography. In *Who Killed Canadian History?* J.L. Granatstein bemoans the atomizing effect of this shift to personal and social history and laments the erosion of the unifying traditional narratives of Canada's past (see Granatstein 1998, 56–57). As Linda Kealey et al. note, however, resistance to alternative histories such as women's history, labour history, and the history of Native peoples has tended to exaggerate the debilitating effects of social history in order to defend the status quo: "An understanding of ourselves as a 'nation' or indeed as many nations within one, will not come by propping up an older national history ... which is built on the suppression of women's, native and other voices. It might come, however, from a better understanding of our diverse experience and histories" (Kealey et al. 1992, 130).

This emphasis on the multiplicity of historical experience brings to mind one of the epigraphs to Michael Ondaatje's *In the Skin of a Lion*, John Berger's line, "Never again will a single story be told as though it were the only one." Citing Ondaatje's epigraph has become almost a cliché in discussions of historical fiction, but it is hard to find a phrase that captures so concisely the spirit that informs the work of most contemporary Canadian historical novelists.

While not dismissive of the importance of the "big picture" of history, these writers are nonetheless acutely conscious of its distorting effects and of the significance of what lies outside the frame. Vanderhaeghe talks of his interest "in the small event that may have had big consequences," as reflected in the central events of *The Englishman's Boy* and *The Last Crossing*, respectively the Cypress Hills Massacre—an infamous slaughter in 1873 of a band of Assiniboine by a mostly American party of wolfers—and the Battle of the Belly River, the last large-scale battle between the Blackfoot and Cree near present-day Lethbridge in 1870. These historical episodes, though marginal to the larger national historical narrative, if viewed from the perspective of what might have happened, take on a much greater significance, not just in the context of the history of the West but of the history of the whole country. These writers also emphasize the way in which so many aspects of Canadian history that do not fit these narratives have been suppressed or effaced. Clarke speaks of Canadians' self-congratulatory attitude toward questions of race and racism, repressing signs of racial conflict and prejudice in order to sustain a sense of moral superiority vis-à-vis our neighbours to the south. Boyden speaks to the neglect of Native peoples' contribution to Canada's participation in World War I and II, for which they volunteered in disproportionately high numbers. Wiebe has long acknowledged that part of the impetus behind the writing of *The Temptations of Big Bear* was his discovery that the history of the legendary Cree chief Big Bear, which had unfolded on the very ground on which Wiebe was raised, was excluded from the history he was taught in school (Wiebe 1981), a sentiment that is echoed throughout this collection. Both Robertson and Sweatman, for instance, remark on the way in which the history of the left—however much it might lend itself to comic and satiric treatment in their novels—has long been suppressed in this country.

While the increasingly postcolonial spirit of Canadian historical fiction is a recurring and significant theme, the central focus of *Speaking in the Past Tense* is unquestionably the complexity of the negotiation between the literary and the historical in literary representations of history. The collection provides much insight into the sources and historical models behind these writers' works, but more importantly these conversations explore the significant formal, aesthetic, and philosophical implications of reworking historical material in fiction. Nineteenth-century literary critic Goldwin Smith said of the historical romance that "the fiction is apt to spoil the fact and the fact the fiction," an observation that still resonates for most writers of historical fiction (Smith, in Daymond and Monkman 1981, 55). First of all, although novelists have more imaginative liberty in their approach to history and are less constrained by fidelity to the historical record, one of their principal concerns is nonetheless the way in which one is fenced in by "fact."[2] One of the most interesting aspects of these conversations is the light they throw on historical novelists' elaborate negotiations with the historical record and with particular historical sources—what records they deal with in their research, the challenges of interpreting those sources, and the biases and gaps in the historical record. Stenson, for instance, describes his use of the sole first-hand working-class perspective on the fur trade, William Gladstone's *Diary*, to revise a celebratory history of the Hudson's Bay Company that has been thoroughly reliant on the necessarily biased records of the company's officers. Clarke underscores the importance of oral testimony in understanding and evoking the history of minority communities whose experience has been largely excluded by, or problematically framed in, the historical record. Robertson speaks of how restricted access to records on the history of Igor Gouzenko, the Soviet embassy clerk whose defection was seen as a catalytic moment for the Cold War, prompted her to develop her version of the case in *Igor* as a parodic spy caper rather than as a historical novel. Both Stenson and Crummey describe how their novels (*The Trade* and *River Thieves*, respectively) took shape as a response to the gaps and tensions in the historical record. What distinguishes the historical novel as a genre is that it involves an extended dialogue with a variety of historical sources. The interviews collected here throw a good deal of light on the complex considerations and politics that that dialogue entails.

In the process, these conversations provide fascinating insights into the curious alchemy that is the transformation of historical material into the stuff of fiction. Unsurprisingly, though, opinions about that transformation vary widely from one writer to the next. Urquhart speaks of a repeated pattern in her fiction, in which historical figures begin as the epicentre of the work and then gradually move to the periphery as the writing progresses. Wharton talks of a boundary at which historical figures become so transformed that it becomes necessary to rename them and of how, as a writer working on his debut novel, he was cautious to transform those historical figures who became major characters in *Icefields*. Conversely, Crummey describes how he considered changing the names of the historical figures on whom his characters in *River Thieves* are based because he had "messed" with the historical record, but

---

2 In "On the Trail of Big Bear" (132–33), Wiebe observes that, "unless they are very carefully handled, facts are the invariable tyrants of story. They are as inhibiting as fences and railroad, whereas the storyteller would prefer, like Big Bear, 'to walk where his feet can walk.'" Interestingly, in the interview in this collection Wiebe substantially revises that stance.

felt it would be ultimately more dishonest to mask the story with which he was working. Sweatman confesses that she will "burn in hell" for capping her depiction of the bloody climax to the Winnipeg General Strike in *Fox* with an additional (and fictional) fatality. She describes writing about history as "a messy business" in which anxiety about "embezzling" the public property of history is balanced against the need to depart from the historical record in order to make characters one's own. As these conversations illustrate, writing a historical novel involves a complex and often precarious balance of aesthetic, epistemological, and ideological considerations.

Indeed, perhaps the most distinctive feature of contemporary historical fiction is its preoccupation with epistemological questions. Contemporary historical fiction, that is, often approaches historical sources not as the models for the pictures it paints of the past but as opportunities for probing the nature of historical consciousness and the nature of our experience of history, for exploring how we can know anything about the past and how we can convey that knowledge to others. As Kuester stresses, historical fiction involves a particular kind of parodic dialogue between different forms of discourse, a resituating of historical material within a fictional context that reconfigures its meaning: "Historical novels differ from other novelistic genres in their use of parodic strategies because the textual material they incorporate is often of non-fictional origin." Moreover, "this integration of 'real' elements into the fictional universe then leads to new metafictional, or rather metahistorical, questions about the quality of 'realism' in these novels" (1992, 148). Over the last few decades, there has been a sea change in attitudes toward historiography, and contemporary historical fiction has made a large contribution to the challenging of history as a kind of "master narrative." Naomi Jacobs sees the increasing presence of fiction engaging with history as "a fascinating symptom of the epistemological and aesthetic upheavals of our time," signalling "our questioning of the artificial boundaries between truth and lie, history and fiction, reality and imagination" (1990, xxi).

These boundaries are repeatedly probed in *Speaking in the Past Tense*. One argument that recurs in these interviews, for instance, is that the imaginative latitude afforded the writer of fiction can strengthen, rather than undermine, the epistemological validity of a representation of the past. Traditionally, the historical novelist's lack of empirical restrictions has been taken as sufficient grounds for drawing a fundamental epistemological distinction between, on the one hand, literary reconstructions of the past as a kind of imaginative (that is, fanciful) retrospection and, on the other hand, historical writing as a mimetic and truthful reproduction of the past. However, it can be argued that there are different ways to reflect the past and that steering closer to the (per-ceived) spirit of the past rather than the letter of the historical record, as his-torical fiction so often tries to do, may be at least as epistemologically valuable an approach to representing the past. Stenson, for example, argues for the validity of the central episode of his revisionist portrait of Hudson's Bay Com-pany Governor George Simpson in *The Trade*, the Governor's attempt to sex-ually coerce the Métis lover of one of his clerks. Though the incident itself is speculative, Stenson defends such a reading on the basis of Simpson's docu-mented sexual appetite, his proprietary attitude towards Aboriginal and Métis women in the company's employ, and the extreme likelihood that the attrac-tive woman would have caught Simpson's eye. Likewise, Crummey situates his version of the capture of the Beothuk Demasduit (Mary March) in 1819 against the documentary accounts of the incident that have prevailed, stand-ing behind the thesis (posited in fictional form in *River Thieves*) that not one but two Beothuk men were killed in the process and that the second, less defensible homicide was subsequently covered up, and pointing out the ten-sions and contradictions in the accounts upon which the prevailing interpre-tation has relied. What these examples suggest is not that historians are myopic slaves to the historical record—blind to its absences, tensions, and biases—but simply that the imaginative liberty provided to the writer of historical fiction can function as compensation for the empirical constraints by which histo-rians are more concerned to abide. As Stenson puts it, "Historians can't invent in the gaps, so they wind up just building the structure all full of holes."

A more profound consequence of the current reconfiguration of histori-ography, however, is that not only might historical fiction be much more informative and much closer epistemologically to historical writing than most historians would be inclined to concede, but also history might be much closer to fiction. In the wake of the work of Hayden White, Michel Foucault, Dominick LaCapra and other theorists, the distinction between history and fiction has increasingly been blurred, and the conception of history as a kind of mimesis of the past has been substantially questioned, if not quite staked through the heart. As Alun Munslow notes, drawing on White's work, the writing of history has much in common with the writing of literature in that it "is a figurative exercise in the sense of being a product of the literary imag-ination," with the difference being that "its relativism remains limited by the nature of the evidence" (1997, 75). Conversely, historical fiction, though more profoundly figurative and less empirically constrained, is nonetheless like-wise engaged in conveying, if not literal propositions about the past, then cer-tainly some form of understanding of it. As White especially has argued, all historians take imaginative liberties to some extent in transforming historical research into a narrative about the past, whether it's (to take some Canadian examples) the life of Louis Riel, the assault on Vimy Ridge, or the Winnipeg General Strike; otherwise their work would consist merely of an inventory of historical evidence. Any historical account requires a level of interpretation, imaginative synthesis, and narrative transformation of evidence, a process that is much closer to the writing of historical fiction than most historians would like to admit. As White puts it, "How else can any past, which by definition comprises events, processes, structures, and so forth, considered to be no longer perceivable, be represented in either consciousness or discourse except in an 'imaginary' way?" (1987, 457). To take an illustration from Canadian historical fiction, even though the historical record suggests that Métis military leader Gabriel Dumont's involvement in the first Riel Rebellion was limited to non-existent, Wiebe expands that role in *The Scorched-Wood People* to make Dumont's role as military figurehead of the Métis nation parallel Louis Riel's spiritual leadership of his people through both rebellions. Though historians might take issue with this aspect of the novel in literal terms, fewer I think would contest that vision of Dumont on figurative grounds—that he has this level of symbolic importance to the Métis cause.

To suggest that both history and fiction rely on similar interpretive, figurative, and narrative strategies, however, is not to reductively argue that all history and all historical fiction are somehow equally metaphoric and equally valid as accounts of the past. As Munslow argues, even though "historical understanding is as much the product of literary artifice as it is a knowable historical reality," historians are not free to cavalierly impose any sort of interpretation on the past: "No historian can work in ignorance of previous interpretations or emplotments of the archive" (1997, 176). Likewise, some works of historical fiction are undeniably more historically plausible and epistemologically closer to the writing of historians than others, and the differences between works of historical fiction are almost as interesting and instructive as the differences between historical fiction and historical writing. For instance, consider (especially in relation to Stenson's portrait of George Simpson or Wiebe's portrait of Gabriel Dumont) Robertson's depiction in her 1983 novel, *Willie*, of Willie's attempted rape of his fictional mistress, the heroine of Robertson's *The King Years* trilogy. This particular aspect of the portrait of William Lyon Mackenzie King was characterized at the time by at least one well-known Canadian historian as gratuitous sensationalizing but was defended by Robertson as an allegorical representation, an "imaginative recreation of 'that psychic and moral violence which the political system imposes on people'" (quoted in Cameron 1984, 2). Historians would certainly refrain from suggesting that King was capable of such a thing without substantial documentary evidence (though he certainly has been roughed up otherwise). Robertson's defence, however, points to the more figurative way in which historical fiction makes us experience history; her premise is that she is using a more concrete, particularized fictional encounter to convey a sense of the broader political dynamics of a particular historical era. Though this example reminds us that it's not always easy to separate figurative considerations from empirical ones (because it's hard not to wonder about the sexual volatility of the historical King as you read *Willie*), the larger point nonetheless remains: historical fiction comments on the past, but rarely with the same literal intent as typifies historical writing. Nonetheless, Robertson's portrayal of King is but a dramatic extreme of a fundamentally figurative impulse that historical fiction shares with historical discourse. Such an "insistence on the fictive element in all historical narratives," White concedes, "is certain to arouse the ire of historians who believe that they are doing something fundamentally different from the novelist, by virtue of the fact that they deal with 'real,' while the novelist deals with 'imagined,' events." However, both make sense of history "by endowing what originally appears to be problematical and mysterious with the aspect of a recognizable, because it is a familiar, form. It does not matter whether the world is conceived to be real or only imagined; the manner of making sense of it is the same" (1978, 98).

A number of the interviews in *Speaking in the Past Tense* touch on this speculative and interpretive dimension of writing about history. Vanderhaeghe, to some degree echoing Munslow's limitations on the freedom of historical interpretation, describes how his choice of historical material is governed by what "is more novelistically satisfying" but also by the desire "not to depart too far from what seems to be a plausible interpretation." Similarly, Wiebe speaks of the importance of sticking to the available biographical facts of historical personages because in a sense "a life is a sacred story, and if you are going to tell it you must respect it profoundly." Johnston, however, challenges the empiricist demand for authenticity in historical fiction, arguing that there is no ultimate arbiter of what constitutes an authentic or accurate historical portrait and that, consequently, historical fiction should be judged not in relation to the history it depicts but on its merits as fiction. As these comments suggest, historical fiction continues to occupy an uneasy position vis-à-vis the discipline of history, but in various ways the conversations in *Speaking in the Past Tense* not only map that position through these writers' reflections on their practice but also amount to a spirited defence of historical fiction as a vibrant and viable genre, rather than a compromised and dubious hybrid, as it is often seen to be.

Readers of historical fiction, of course, might beg to differ, and consequently, another topic of conversation in this collection is the reaction—both negative and positive—to the writers' treatment of history. Robertson, for instance, cites the indignant reaction of the historical community (or at least those historians committed to what she sees as the authorized Liberal version of Canadian history) to uncomplimentary revisionist portrayals of Mackenzie King (including *The King Years*) in the wake of the release of his remarkably frank and eccentric diaries in the 1970s. Johnston reflects on the storm of controversy that erupted upon the publication of *The Colony of Unrequited Dreams* a few years after the death of the figure at its centre, Joey Smallwood. Wharton describes locals' reaction to his changing of place names and other details of the Rocky Mountains in *Icefields* and how it made him self-conscious about tampering with the history of a place; in response, he provides a compelling parallel between that self-consciousness and the environmental ideal of limiting one's "footprint" on the natural environment. More encouragingly, he also talks about his sense of gratification at local readers' approval of having their place subjected to serious artistic transformation. Clarke not only ponders the wariness and unease in his own family at the prospect of a novel about his cousins' crime and execution but also describes how he was asked by the historical victim's family not to write about the story and, despite having explained his motivations, was subsequently accused of exploiting the murder for profit in writing *George & Rue*. As Clarke succinctly summarizes it, "the problem with historical fiction is that it forces a collision between real flesh-and-blood beings and events and the imaginary. Some readers cannot—*cannot*—separate the two." Being a writer is in many ways a precarious occupation, but writing fiction about history, as the experiences of these writers illustrate, invariably intensifies that element of risk.

Given writers' consciousness of the problems of writing about history, it is not surprising that this concern with the relationship between fiction and history on the part of both writers and readers has become increasingly reflected in historical fiction itself. A crucial feature of contemporary historical fiction is its self-consciousness and historiographical self-reflexivity, characteristics indicative of the influence of postmodern aesthetics and narrative techniques. Arguably, one of the most valuable aspects of contemporary historical fiction is that it helps us comprehend and appreciate the past because it is increasingly *about* the process of writing history. Timothy Findley's 1977 novel *The Wars* is a germinal example, because it positions readers in a way that compels them to consider and interpret the various sources through which the experiences of protagonist Robert Ross in the Great War are constructed: "You begin at the archives with photographs ... Boxes and boxes of snapshots and portraits; maps and letters; cablegrams and clippings from the papers. All you have to do is sign them out and carry them across the room. Spread over table tops, a whole age lies in fragments underneath the lamps. *The war to end all wars*" (Findley 1996, 3). Here historical fiction is as much the fictional experience of archival research as it is the fictional experience of the past. In this spirit, contemporary historical fiction is not only synthesizing historical material and conveying it in the form of narratives about the past but is also increasingly emphasizing that historical discourse is as much about process as it is about product. As Monika Fludernik argues, "postmodernist fiction has already been informed by the most recent developments in historiography," and contemporary historical fiction reflects "a reconceptualization of the historical novel and of historiography as much as ... a difference in fictional styles and techniques" (1994, 93). Writing about a select series of English-Canadian and Québécois novels in *New World Myth*, Marie Vautier points to a widespread shift in historical fiction in Canada, describing how these writers "make more blatant use, in their challenges to history and historiography, of the techniques that have come to be considered the markers of postmodernism in fiction: autoreferentiality, intertextuality, playful self-reflexivity, parody, irony, and multiple, often contradictory, retellings of the same event" (1998, 37).

Naomi Jacobs observes that historical novels "have always incorporated a great deal of verifiable or 'testifiable' information, based on research very similar to that of the historian; though rarely marking the boundaries between documented and invented materials, they have under realism felt bound to some degree of accuracy when representing historical events and figures" (1990, 71). While the writers interviewed in this collection largely adhere to that principle and are relatively conservative in their use of the postmodern techniques Vautier inventories, a number of the conversations here address the kind of self-reflexiveness about the writing of history that characterizes what Hutcheon has termed "historiographical metafiction." As Hutcheon argues in "History and/as Intertext," historiographic metafiction "does not deny that reality is or was; it just questions how we *know* that and how it is or was" (1987, 173). This sentiment is reflected here in the interview with Vanderhaeghe, who notes that one of the important messages of *The Englishman's Boy* is a caution against the seductive persuasiveness of fictional portrayals of historical events. Wharton, though skeptical of the label "postmodernist," speaks of a recurring, almost unconscious tendency in his work to reflect on the process of writing itself, including the writing of history. Johnston observes that history itself is an important subject of his work, and that throughout his fiction his characters are self-consciously trying to write their own history.

In the process, historical fiction emphasizes rather than suppresses the multiplicity of viewpoints and the interpretive and narrative strategies involved in constructing a plausible story about historical events, rather than unilaterally conveying an authoritative historical account to be passively consumed. Sweatman speaks of the influence of theorist Mikhail Bakhtin on her work and her attraction to a postmodern, polyphonic approach to history as the appropriate form for representing such a complex and divisive historical episode as the Winnipeg General Strike. In *Fox*, we see the conflict developing from the perspectives of upper-class women, strike leaders, business leaders, and beleaguered workers, and the novel, as Gabriele Helms points out, "becomes a forum, an argument, in which different contributions are placed side by side and are to be negotiated" and in which creating "cohesion or cause-and-effect relationships is left up to the readers" (2003, 130). In Wiebe's classic rendering of the last stand of the Plains Cree during the second Riel rebellion in *The Temptations of Big Bear*, segments are narrated by or through colonial officials, settlers, soldiers, and Big Bear. As Stenson argues, such perspectival multiplicity and polyphony helps to resist the tyranny of the singular, authoritative view of the past and to render it as an experience more approximate to an encounter with the archive—that is, with the multiple, varying, even conflicting perspectives in which the past in all its traces tends to be left to us. While the advantage of traditional historiography, as Dominick LaCapra puts it, is its "ability to join meticulous research with a form of critical rationality in the investigation of the past" (1985, 141), historical fiction such as *The Temptations of Big Bear* and *Fox*, as well as Stenson's *The Trade*, has in some ways more effectively evoked the complex experience of encountering history by combining multiple perspectives and self-conscious, metafictive strategies with the imaginative evocation of the social, political, economic, and emotional texture of a historical era. In short, as some of these interviews underline, self-conscious, polyphonic historical fiction makes us think more carefully about how the details of a historical account are selected, interpreted, and pieced together. Though less empirically scrupulous, historical fiction in this manner can provide an important counterpoint and/or supplement to traditional historiography's empirical rigour. More formally traditional but historically revisionist novels like Crummey's *River Thieves* reflect to a degree the prevalent postmodern skepticism about the notion of a singular, authoritative perspective on the past, but Wiebe, Stenson, and Sweatman formally inscribe in their texts that perspectival multiplicity and dialogue.

If contemporary historical fiction's adoption of postmodern narrative strategies has sharpened its ability to convey the complexity of our experience of history, however, its situation in a postmodern culture, in which both the novel and the past have become increasingly commodified, poses more of a problem. In his monumental work *Postmodernism*, Fredric Jameson argues that the sense of historicity in contemporary culture has become incredibly compressed and essentially commodified, characterized by "an omnipresent and indiscriminate appetite for dead styles and fashions; indeed, for all the styles and fashions of a dead past" (1991, 286). In a similar vein, in *Virtual Sovereignty: Nationalism, Culture and the Canadian Question*, Robert Wright links the "condition of collective amnesia in which Canadians (and others) increasingly seem to find themselves" not to neoconservative historians' *bêtes noires* of multicultural political correctness and "bureaucratic bungling" over the teaching of history but to the decreasing relevance of history to Canadians' lives (2004, 105). For Wright, the atrophying of historical consciousness is symptomatic of the neo-conservative, consumerist, globalized social order that has effectively eclipsed the state-oriented nationalism of the 1960s and '70s. This consumer culture, part of a "globalized, postmodern world," effaces the importance of historical differences and a more historicized sense of the past, cultivating instead an appetite for history in a commodified form, provided by "televisual, entertainment-oriented mass media driven almost exclusively by advertising profits" (106). Wright argues that to counter this atrophying of historical consciousness, "there must be a renewed emphasis upon history, not as a sterile academic exercise, but as the organizing principle of Canadians' lived experience." He cautions, however, that "any such restoration will require a great deal of 'unlearning,' as we attempt to deconstruct and subvert the dominant discourses of our times and to affirm the tangible, life-affirming narratives to which Canadians have a right" (121). In an increasingly postnational, globalized consumer society, then, however much postmodern historiographical novels might help us to experience history as process rather than as product, they are nonetheless part of a consumer culture in which the novel is firmly situated as a product. One of the crucial questions to ask of historical fiction—especially given the hot commodity it has become—is whether it is part of the problem Wright describes, or perhaps part of the revitalization of history for which he calls.

Consequently, a significant concern with, and in, the contemporary novel is the politics of aestheticizing and commodifying the past. Wharton, for instance, describes his efforts to navigate between his desire to cultivate in his readers an experience of the wonder of the Rocky Mountains and his anxiety about the potential equivalence between that aesthetic experience and tourism as "a kind of resource extraction." Crummey articulates his concern that the current vogue for historical fiction has the effect of transforming the past into "material" to be exploited for profit and stresses the importance of interrogating his own motives for writing about the past. In a different vein, Sweatman argues that in a neo-conservative social climate, in which the established order has vested interests in the effacement of history, "ghosts are our allies"; historical memory and a sense of historicity are crucial elements in resisting a complacent and myopic preoccupation with the present, a dangerous form of amnesia fostered by consumer society's insatiable desire for novelty. Writers of historical fiction increasingly find themselves caught between the commodifying, dehistoricizing tendencies of postmodern consumer culture and the more positivist sense of historicity that characterizes the traditional historical novel from which most seek to depart; these interviews show that these writers are well aware of how delicate is the navigation between those impulses.

Reflecting the prevailing reconsideration of the discipline of history and the prevailing reconceptualizing of Canadian history, these are the principal concerns of *Speaking in the Past Tense*, just as they are the principal concerns of the contemporary historical novel. But the interviews are wide-ranging and explore a variety of subjects beyond these recurring preoccupations. Wiebe's observation about the genesis of *Big Bear*, for instance, points to another repeated theme in the interviews: the way in which the roots of history and historical fiction are so often local, submerged in the soil of one's immediate environs. Robertson tells of how a life-long interest in history began with an epiphany experienced as a young girl accompanying her father on an expedition to a graveyard by the Red River, where the gravestones of pioneers told stories that brought history to life. Stenson depicts himself as the literary equivalent of a historical geographer, devoted to understanding and depicting the various historical strata of his native province of Alberta, a designation Urquhart uses to describe her own preoccupation with the landscape of rural southern Ontario. Sweatman's sense of history and sensibility as a writer have been shaped by growing up in the affluent south end of Winnipeg, a city whose class divisions are reflected in the geographical divide between north and south. These dynamics she describes as being rooted in an interplay between real estate, commerce, and history that dates back beyond the Red River uprising in 1869. Boyden describes how *Three Day Road* emerged as a way of getting to know his father, a highly decorated medical officer who passed away when Boyden was very young, and also out of his family's long-standing friendship with the family of the legendary Ojibway sniper Francis Pegahmagabow. Crummey speaks of the formative influence of growing up in a once-prosperous but dying mining town in central Newfoundland, accounting for a sense of loss that permeates his fiction and poetry. Poststructuralist theory's emphasis on the documentary textuality of history aside, a sense of place—the tangible, tactile experience of the locale in which particular events transpired long ago—is, as Stenson observes, one of the historical novelist's most important primary materials.

Finally, some of the interviews touch on what is generally a standard part of historical novels (and admittedly a particular interest of mine), the acknowledgements. The acknowledgements in historical novels are significant in two respects. Most obviously, they provide an opportunity to give credit to the many sources that it is crucial to consult when writing about the past. Vanderhaeghe, for instance, pays homage to the local historians whose labour of love helps to preserve and provide the texture and detail necessary for fictional reconstructions of the past "when they make a really conscious attempt to preserve the record of particular places." Boyden concedes that his tribute to Native veterans of World War I, that "their bravery and skill do not go unnoticed," is, in the face of Canadians' ignorance of their contribution, ultimately a kind of wishful thinking. In contemporary historical fiction, with its often more subversive and less historicist regard for the historical record, however, acknowledgements have become in some ways an extension of the more playful and less reverent attitude toward the past in the novels themselves, a site on which to engage considerations about the relationship between fact and fiction, author and readers, and so on. Johnston, for instance, talks of how his acknowledgements in *The Navigator of New York* (2002) are at once a legal disclaimer, an allusion to Don DeLillo's *Libra*, and an ironic nod to the controversy over the mixing of fact and fiction in the depiction of Joey Smallwood in *The Colony of Unrequited Dreams*. He also speaks of his refusal to list the many sources for *Navigator*, in order to encourage readers to suspend their disbelief and to resist the temptation to read the book against the historical record. Wharton blurs the line even more, confessing to having fabricated some of the sources acknowledged in both *Icefields* and *Salamander* (2001) and thus extending the interplay between fact and fiction beyond the boundaries of the narratives themselves.

These concerns, and more, recur throughout the conversations in *Speaking in the Past Tense*. At the same time, however, the interviews address a wide range of concerns, literary and otherwise, specific to the individual writer being interviewed. The interview with Vanderhaeghe, for instance, explores the reflection of contemporary attitudes toward masculinity and heroism in *The Last Crossing* and the challenges of adapting *The Englishman's Boy* for film. Johnston anticipates the public spat in 2004 between Newfoundland premier Danny Williams and Prime Minister Paul Martin over control of offshore resources, stressing the impact of transfer payments on the Newfoundland economy and articulating Newfoundlanders' resentment of their subordinate place in Confederation. The principal switch-hitter of the group, Heather Robertson, who has written more popular history than historical fiction, talks about the different challenges and different approaches involved in each. For all their common concerns, these writers have their own particular preoccupations and experiences, and these interviews are of interest as much for what they don't have in common as for what they do.

By the time they reach the page, interviews, of course, are a kind of fiction themselves. This was the most liberating piece of advice I received as I was embarking on *Speaking in the Past Tense*, courtesy of my friend Jeanette Lynes, who had conducted many interviews in the compiling of her anthology *Words Out There: Atlantic Women Poets*. It subsequently struck me that in fact the process of putting together these interviews was analogous to the act of writing history as it has been theorized in the wake of what has been called "the linguistic turn" in contemporary critical theory. Rather than transparent, word-for-word, unmediated representations of an exchange of ideas, of questions and answers, these conversations are shaped a priori—as Hayden White argues of the process of writing history itself—by the concerns and interests and experience of the questioner, as well as reshaped, revised, and refined (in some respects, as White would say, even "narrativized") in the process of editing. Like historical accounts, in short, interviews are substantially over-determined and processed records of what has transpired. At the same time, though, in a larger sense, these conversations remain just that: conversations. However much the interviewer frames the agenda, interviews are fundamentally dialogues between the concerns and interests of the interviewer and those of the writer being interviewed; though my own interests and assumptions undeniably shape these discussions, the discussions also repeatedly veer off in unexpected directions. Furthermore, the dialogue extended to the process of revising and editing the interviews themselves, in which most of these writers played an active and crucial role. So if interviews are a kind of fiction, the interviews in *Speaking in the Past Tense*, one might say, are authorized fictions.

Works Cited

Archives and History. Ed. Eva-Marie Kroller et al. *Canadian Literature* 178 (2003).

Bliss, Michael. "Privatizing the Mind: The Sundering of Canadian History, the Sundering of Canada." *Journal of Canadian Studies* 26, no. 4 (1991–2): 5–17.

Brydon, Diana. "Introduction: Reading Postcoloniality, Reading Canada." *Testing the Limits: Postcolonial Theories and Canadian Literatures. Essays on Canadian Writing* 56 (1995): 1–19.

Cameron, Elspeth. "From Whitton to Willie." *Quill & Quire* (Jan. 1984), 27.

Duffy, Dennis. *Sounding the Iceberg: An Essay on Canadian Historical Novels*. Toronto: ECW Press, 1986.

Findley, Timothy. *The Wars*. 1996. Toronto: Penguin Canada. (Orig. pub. 1977.)

Fludernik, Monika. "History and Metafiction: Experientiality, Causality, and Myth." In *Historiographic Metafiction in Modern American and Canadian Literature*, ed. Bernd Engler and Kurt Müller, 81–101. Paderborn: Ferdinand Schöningh, 1994.

Francis, Daniel. *National Dreams: Myth, Memory, and Canadian History*. Vancouver: Arsenal Pulp, 1997.

Granatstein, J.L. *Who Killed Canadian History?* Toronto: Harper, 1998.

Helms, Gabriele. *Challenging Canada: Dialogism and Narrative Techniques in Canadian Novels*. Montreal: McGill-Queen's University Press, 2003.

Hutcheon, Linda. *The Canadian Postmodern: A Study of Contemporary English-Canadian Fiction*. Toronto: Oxford University Press, 1988.

———. "History and/as Intertext." In *Future Indicative: Literary Theory and Canadian Literature*, ed. John Moss, 169–84. Ottawa: University of Ottawa Press, 1987.

Jacobs, Naomi. *The Character of Truth: Historical Figures in Contemporary Fiction*. Carbondale, IL: Southern Illinois University Press, 1990.

Jameson, Fredric. *Postmodernism, or, The Cultural Logic of Late Capitalism*. Durham, NC: Duke University Press, 1991.

Jones, Manina. *That Art of Difference: "Documentary-Collage" and English-Canadian Writing*. Toronto: University of Toronto Press, 1993.

Kealey, Linda, Ruth Pierson, Joan Sangster, and Veronica Strong-Boag. "Teaching Canadian History in the 1990s: Whose 'National' History Are We Lamenting?" *Journal of Canadian Studies* 27, no. 2 (1992): 129–31.

Kuester, Martin. *Framing Truths: Parodic Structures in Contemporary English-Canadian Historical Novels*. Toronto: University of Toronto Press, 1992.

LaCapra, Dominick. *History and Criticism*. Ithaca: Cornell University Press, 1985.

MacLulich, T.D. *Between Europe and America: The Canadian Tradition in Fiction*. Toronto: ECW Press, 1988.

Moss, Laura. "Is Canada Postcolonial? Unsettling Canadian Literature." In *Is Canada Postcolonial? Unsettling Canadian Literature*, ed. Moss, v–viii. Waterloo: Wilfrid Laurier University Press, 2003.

Munslow, Alun. *Deconstructing History*. London: Routledge, 1997.

Ondaatje, Michael. *In the Skin of a Lion*. 1997. Toronto: Vintage. (Orig. pub. 1987.)

Past Matters/Choses du Passe: History in Canadian Fiction. Ed. Jennifer Andrews, Robert Viau, and Herb Wyile. *Studies in Canadian Literature* 27, no. 1 (2002).

Smith, Goldwin. "The Lamps of Fiction." In *Canadian Novelists and the Novel*, ed. Douglas Daymond, and Leslie Monkman, 53–8. Ottawa: Borealis Press, 1981. (Orig. pub. 1871.)

Sugars, Cynthia, ed. *Home-Work: Postcolonialism, Pedagogy, and Canadian Literature.* Ottawa: University of Ottawa Press, 2004.

———, ed. *Unhomely States: Theorizing English-Canadian Postcolonialism.* Peterborough, ON: Broadview, 2004.

Vautier, Marie. *New World Myth: Postmodernism and Postcolonialism in Canadian Fiction.* Montreal: McGill-Queen's University Press, 1998.

White, Hayden. *The Content of the Form: Narrative Discourse and Historical Representation.* Baltimore: Johns Hopkins University Press, 1987.

———. *Tropics of Discourse: Essays in Cultural Criticism.* Baltimore: Johns Hopkins University Press, 1978.

Wiebe, Rudy. "On the Trail of Big Bear." In *A Voice in the Land*, ed. W.J. Keith, 132–41. Edmonton, AB: NeWest, 1981.

Wright, Robert. *Virtual Sovereignty: Nationalism, Culture and the Canadian Question.* Toronto: Canadian Scholars' Press International, 2004.

Wyile, Herb. *Speculative Fictions: Contemporary Canadian Novelists and the Writing of History.* Montreal: McGill-Queen's University Press, 2002.

Making History
Guy Vanderhaeghe

Guy Vanderhaeghe was born and raised in Esterhazy, Saskatchewan. A history major, Vanderhaeghe received a BA and an MA from the University of Saskatchewan and has worked as a teacher, researcher, and archivist. He began publishing stories in the late 1970s and won the Governor General's Award in 1982 for his collection of short stories *Man Descending*. After publishing another collection, *The Trouble with Heroes* (1983), and the novels *My Present Age* (1984) and *Homesick* (1989), in 1996 Vanderhaeghe garnered international attention and nominations for the Dublin IMPAC Award and the Giller Prize for *The Englishman's Boy*. A sweeping historical novel depicting the notorious Cypress Hills massacre in the Canadian west in the late nineteenth century and a megalomaniacal Hollywood film director's attempts to bring the episode to the screen in the 1920s, the novel won Vanderhaeghe another Governor General's Award. In 2002, he published *The Last Crossing*, a historical novel set in the same era, focusing on the role of famed Blackfoot scout Jerry Potts in the settlement of the Canadian West. I talked to Guy Vanderhaeghe in Saskatoon in July of 2003.

HW You have a master's degree in history, and you used to be a history teacher, and now, at least for the last few years, you've been a historical novelist. So, do you think of yourself as, in some respects, continuing your career as a history teacher by other means?

GV Probably not. One of the things that kept me away from writing historical fiction was that I was afraid that my so-called academic training would be too constricting when it came to writing fiction. I slowly worked my way into it, first with a play, which was set in the North Battleford mental asylum during the flu epidemic. I had stumbled across some material when I was working in the archive, and there were enough gaps and it was open-ended enough that I thought that I could use that as historical material. When I'm writing fiction, I don't attempt to teach or instruct, or any of those sorts of things. What's always first and foremost in my mind is that a novel is an aesthetic experience, but because I always had an intense interest in history, writing about the past or circling historical questions interests me and fascinates me.

HW Many years ago, before you started writing historical novels, you wrote an article, "Literature and the Teaching of History," essentially about the value of literature in teaching people about the past. One of the key points in that article was that literature is perhaps more capable than history of conveying the texture of the past. How do you feel about that now that you've put that to the test in writing your novels?

GV In that article, I said that it was more important to actually use texts from the time that you were studying, so that, for instance, if you were dealing with the plague in London, then it actually made more sense to read Daniel Defoe than it did to read a historical novelist on the period. I do believe that one of the things that literature does, because it's often interested in interior life, sensations, all of those kinds of things, is give people a sense of the texture of life. The historical novel, if it's well researched and well considered, I think, can help in doing that, which is paradoxical, at least in my own mind, because I think the historical novel is always about contemporary issues in disguise. At the same time, if you read journals, diaries, or novels written in the past, it's possible to create the illusion of how people may have spoken, what they ate, how they dressed, and to a certain extent how they thought, what their world view was. Now that I contradict myself, despite all of that, the historical novel is always written by someone whose experience is contemporary, and so it's impossible to fully inhabit people of the past, or even to understand their issues the way they understood them. So I think there is always a tension in the historical novel. Historians do attempt to make that imaginative leap also, but since most historical texts are constructed more or less on an analytical basis involving large abstract forces, they tend to be more explanatory (I know that's changing, the way history is being written now, so I'm making a gross and sweeping generalization here). So, in many ways they're analytical, abstract and often explanatory in terms of their texture or feel. There are historians like Simon Schama, or any number of them, in whose work you have many of the same elements that you do with the historical novel, but literature, at least most novels (and again this is a generalization), is dealing with characters, personalities, and individual, specific events.

HW I think that there is a greater consciousness of how concerns of the present shape the way that we construct history, and that many historians are moving away from that historical paradigm of striving to represent the past in its own terms. So there's definitely a parallel with the way that you described the historical novel in that article, because there you distinguish it from more fraudulent historical novels that basically take contemporary people and dress them up in period costume and put them in action. It sounded to me like you were essentially trying to develop a stance that's somewhere between a slavish historicity and a conspicuous sense of anachronism.

GV I think that's true. Even though as a writer I may be obsessed with contemporary questions—and clearly I'm conditioned by them in terms of my thinking, my social attitudes, etc.—if those are too blatantly, and I would argue unartfully, pressed into the historical novel, as an aesthetic experience it fails.

HW It creates a sense of discord or dissonance.

GV Yes, discord, an uneasiness on the part of anyone who has even a modicum of historical sense when they're reading that kind of novel. It creates resistance towards actually inhabiting the story as the story. So I do think that it's important that you attempt to create the illusion that people spoke in this fashion, that they thought in this fashion, that they ate these foods, that they wore these clothes, and that element of texture—again I know this is a generalization—is not present in most histories. Many readers look at the historical novel as being a genuine historical experience. As readers they feel that they are inhabiting that time, that place, and that they are getting a sense of how individual lives were lived in a personal fashion. To me that is an element of historical consciousness, but it's not an element that I think many historians exploit, or can exploit, because the historical mind tends to be analytic, it tends to be explanatory. Now there are obviously exceptions. The mind of a novelist is, I think, involved with textures, psychological reactions, all of those kinds of things. So, in many ways, I think the historical novel eschews the kinds of approaches that history has taken for a long time.

HW Trying to map the broad sweep and causality of events.

GV I don't think that many historical novels do that, and when they do do that, they are often making arguments that go against the general historical interpretation of an event. So if you have someone like Gore Vidal writing about Lincoln, in some sense he's debunking Lincoln or debunking the public perception of Lincoln.

HW It amounts almost to the development of a kind of thesis about history in the form of fiction.

GV I think so, but—to go back to Vidal—I think that it's part of a political ideology in Vidal's mind about the bastardization of republican ideals in the United States. He's very interested in contemporary questions, like how did we arrive where we've arrived, but in doing that he's engaging in a kind of historical revisionism about why America is the way it is. So I mean everything's a question of degree and niceties and shadings. You'll find some historical novelists with whom the political agenda is quite prominent in the novels, and there are other historical novelists who, though they may have definite ideas about historical developments, and about how we arrived where we are, are still mostly intent on telling the story or focusing on character development in the novel, or doing any number of things. I think that the motive in writing a historical novel is almost as wide-ranging as it is in writing any novel.

HW Even though those contemporary concerns are necessarily going to be there, are going to be projected onto that past setting, part of the art of the historical novelist is making them seem that they belong in the texture of the time. Just to take a couple of examples, there is a preoccupation with Hollywood in *The Englishman's Boy* and a preoccupation with masculinity especially in *The Last Crossing* and also in *The Englishman's Boy*. Those are two very current concerns, but there's no obvious sense in those novels of that dissonance. But what about postmodern novels that are very upfront about that anachronism and, right from the very outset, are not out to sustain that sense of historicity? What if that dissonance is obviously intended, say, to make people think of history in different ways, particularly to make people conscious of that projection of current concerns onto how we represent the past? Susan Swan, for instance, in *The Biggest Modern Woman of the World* is definitely not out to create this convincing historicist illusion. She makes her heroine quite evidently a twentieth-century feminist, for one thing.

GV I have no problem with that. That's part of the construction of the novel, to make the reader aware that they're reading a postmodern novel and that the novel revolves around these issues, as opposed to a bodice-ripper or a less sophisticated novel, in which you get some of the same sort of effect, but it's not intentional, and you're saying to yourself, "this is naive, this is gauche, this is poorly crafted." But that's not an argument that applies to a novel in which the conscious purpose is to put that in the forefront. I remember years and years ago, given my age, everybody was reading John Barth's *The Sotweed Factor*. Now, it was very clear that this was almost a historical burlesque or parody, and that it was concerned with stylistic issues and all that kind of thing. I've got no argument about that. If someone were to read Susan's novel and be dim enough to think that it was a historical novel in the sense of the conventional historical novel and to say that she had done a bad job—I mean, that would be ridiculous. I have no problem with that in any sense because it's inhabiting a sphere of the historical novel in which all of those elements and issues are foregrounded. I think that kind of novel, in some ways, comes closer to inhabiting the idea of the novel of ideas than perhaps the more conventional historical fiction that I write. I would hope to say that there are ideas in the historical fiction that I'm writing, but it's less apparent.

HW The Western has obviously had a great influence on all of your fiction, even on *My Present Age*, in which the protagonist, Ed, lives by this parodic code of cowboy integrity, embodied by Sam Waters, the hero of Ed's failed novel, but it's also obviously a central influence on your two historical novels.

GV I think that there are two things operating here. It is partly my age. When I was growing up in the fifties, the Western was a staple of television and the movies, so it's influential in that sense. Secondly, I think that for many men who were very young boys in the fifties, the Western provided a kind of chivalric code, which gets embedded in your mind, and it's something that you argue with. First of all, the historical record suggests that, as far as we can ascertain it, there wasn't a good deal of chivalry among the men who inhabited the West. The gunfights were not the sort of gunfights that were portrayed on *Gunsmoke* or in movies or anything else, and the gunmen tended to be cowardly, so that it really wasn't so much a duel as an attempt to get the upper hand and kill someone. But the simplest answer is that there is this residue of the Western which was everywhere when I was growing up. You can even think of Davy Crockett on TV as a sort of Western, or that Davy Crockett was a precursor to the guys in the white hats, only he wore a coonskin cap. So that's probably the biggest reason.

But the Western, at least in North America, is also an incredibly potent cultural icon for both those who dismiss it and those who were in love with it. The Western is in many ways a point of disagreement and argument, even politically. I mean, how do you react to John Wayne? There are people who loathe John Wayne the way they loathe Frank Sinatra, and there are people who admire the screen projection of John Wayne, just as there are people who admire Frank Sinatra—

HW But not the off-screen persona.

GV Yes. Really what you're talking about is the public persona when you're talking about Wayne. You may not agree with his politics, but when you come right down to it, he was not that political; but his political opinions also got projected onto the screen image, so by the late 1960s and early '70s, when ten-year-old boys who had admired John Wayne were now eighteen or nineteen, twenty and twenty-one, you had to react to him, you know? You had to, in a sense, almost dismiss those movies that you had loved as a child.

HW There's something Oedipal in all this.

GV Yes. It's like the anxiety of influence or something. You have to kill John Wayne. So, for North American culture, I think the Western is central. It's something that is going to continually be argued about, maybe not in terms of a logical, constructed argument, but it's going to be argued about in film and books and, likely, academia, forever.

HW In both of your historical novels, as you're writing about the Canadian West, the American Western is this parallel narrative that you have to work with, or through, or against, but part of the problem is that, in terms of the setting of both novels, those terms "Canadian" and "American" are really blurred.

GV Well, yes, because there was a border there, but it didn't exist in any real way in anyone's mind. There's the old story that you could pay your taxes in Fort Benton in either Canadian or American currency. Nationality was a very loose conception. People went back and forth across the border. I'm sure that Jerry Potts, who was born in Montana, would have been bewildered by the idea of a declaration of allegiance. He was born in the United States and died in Canada, but the border didn't exist for him. He passed back and forth. The border really didn't exist for whiskey traders until the North West Mounted Police showed up to enforce the border. It didn't really exist for the Native people in any real sense. They had an idea of the Medicine Line, but that was just a convenience, because they knew that if you crossed the Medicine Line, the U.S.

Cavalry couldn't follow you there. Sitting Bull, for instance—I don't know if it was political expediency or just that no one was very sure—often claimed he was born in Canada. So it's all very fluid, and, culturally, it's very mixed. There were large numbers of Métis in Montana and North Dakota. Riel crossed the border, for political reasons, but nonetheless he spent plenty of time in the States as well as in Canada, showed an affinity for American republican ideas, etc. So everything was very fuzzy and very malleable in that region.

HW The history that you focus on in *The Last Crossing* and *The Englishman's Boy*—I'm thinking of Jerry Potts, and the battle between the Cree and the Blackfoot Confederacy at the Belly River, and the Cypress Hills Massacre—is relatively unknown. Is there a sense in which our history in this country is a kind of palimpsest, that is, a story that is written over another history?

GV I think that's always true, and everything's conditioned by perspective. It seems to me that things like the Battle of Belly River and the Cypress Hills Massacre are going to carry more weight in western Canada, because in some ways they were critical moments for our development. They were also critical moments for the national development, but, because so often history is written from the centre, they're neglected. You know, the "what if?" question in history is unanswerable, but if you say, "What if the Cypress Hills Massacre hadn't occurred? How long would the arrival of the North West Mounted Police in western Canada have been delayed? If it had been delayed, what differences would that have made to the development of western Canada?" With the Battle of Belly River, you can say to yourself, "If the Cree hadn't decided to attack the Blackfoot at that moment, what might have been the consequences of the Riel rebellion of 1885?" The Blackfoot always had, as far as I can tell, an enormous grievance about that attack, because they were decimated by smallpox and it was an attempt by the Cree basically to wipe them out. So in 1885, when emissaries were being sent to the Blackfoot to rise with the Cree, even though the Blackfoot were unhappy about many things, they had the memory of the Battle of Belly River. They had a sense of grievance about what had happened. On the other hand—and who knows how much influence Potts had—Potts, acting in some sense as a government agent, probably was able to dissuade them more easily than if this event hadn't occurred. Now I also understand that, if I'm doing these "what ifs," maybe the Riel rebellion would never have occurred in 1885 if the whole chain of cause and effect, which you can never be definite about and never say that anything is inevitable, is changed.

HW Because if you change one thing, it will reverberate in other directions.

GV It's like chaos theory. You know, if a butterfly flaps its wings ... But on the other hand, it seems to me that with these little-known events that in many ways have been effaced or else thought not crucial, not critical, or not even in any sense important, there are two things. The less known an event, the greater leeway you have as a novelist, because you don't have to struggle with something that's more or less set in stone. To write a novel about John A. Macdonald ... I'm not saying it couldn't be done, but no matter how vague Canadians' notions are about John A. Macdonald, they are a hell of a lot more solid than they are of Jerry Potts. So it's easier for me as historical novelist to write about those kinds of figures than well-known figures. On the other hand, I'm interested in the small event that may have had big consequences.

HW At the end of his narrative in *The Englishman's Boy*, Harry Vincent essentially makes the point that you're making now, reflecting about the Cypress Hills Massacre that the "characters of those wolfers, Canadian and American, cast longer shadows than I had any inkling of," suggesting that individuals can make their mark on history. What impact do you see the Cypress Hills Massacre having had that makes it more deserving than a footnote in the history books, as Harry puts it?

GV For one thing, the uproar and furor about the Cypress Hills Massacre actually prodded the government to fund the police. The idea of the police had been on the books for some years, but they hadn't gotten around to it. The police were essential for the orderly settlement of the West. Without them, things may have been very different. You know, politics follows trade. There were American whiskey traders, rogue traders, in southern Alberta and southern Saskatchewan; at Fort Whoop-Up a variation of the American flag was being flown; there were many Irish Fenian sympathizers in Fort Benton. With all of these things, it's possible to imagine that the Americans may have laid some sort of claim to a part of the West basically by occupation. So that's a possibility.

HW Sort of making the doctrine of Manifest Destiny a reality on the ground.

GV Yes. I mean, I'm not arguing that that would have happened, but there is that possibility. The second thing is that, although the Canadian government's reaction to the massacre of Natives was in many ways political propaganda— the idea that they were American cutthroats, bandits, desperadoes, all the rest of it—it was different at least in degree (I'm getting into fraught political territory here) to what it was in the United States. The argument was being made that, actually, Natives had to be protected and that the police would be a force for the suppression of this kind of thing. So, in a sense, that moment is actually the beginning of a certain policy towards Natives. Whether you want to call it paternalistic, a subversion of a way of life by Europeans, whatever, the attitude is still somewhat different, and so that moment seems to me critical in terms of just getting a police force on the ground and making a Canadian presence felt and seen in the West.

HW Part of the background, too, is the National Policy and the plan to settle the West.

GV Well, certainly in Ontario, the idea was that you would be moving settlers and that you would be occupying this area. But the Canada West movement at that point was really only interested in Manitoba. That was going to be the Promised Land. But farther west, I mean, you have Palliser's reports saying that basically the area that the police are moving into is uninhabitable. What I'm saying, ultimately, is that, like anything else, it's very complex. There is the assumption that this is part of the British Empire, there has been an agreement about where the boundary is, there has been an agreement about who is sovereign in this land, so we have to make our presence felt. There is the hope that at some point this fledgling nation will be a nation from sea to sea, because they're negotiating with British Columbia, Macdonald has been promising a national railway, all those sorts of things. The idea is that this is going to be a significant part of Canada. At that moment in time, it's really worthless, and Canada is not really going to be able to occupy this successfully, fruitfully, economically for some time to come, but there is also the knowledge that you have had the first Riel rebellion in Manitoba, and there's the hope that such a thing will not occur again. To prevent this, a certain kind of protection has to be offered Natives, relationships have to be established between them and the police, they have to be assured that the occupation of these lands by Europeans is in fact going to be done in a different way than it was in the States. Now that's partly just a matter of resources. You know, you've got three hundred police, and you have trouble funding three hundred police. There's a Canadian militia but no real army, whereas the United States has hundreds of thousands of soldiers who are basically unoccupied after the American Civil War. So the Indian wars in the United States can be prosecuted by a military force, where they really can't be in Canada. Plus the whole relationship between the Hudson's Bay Company and the Natives has been different than the relationship with the settlers in the U.S. It's all a question of degree. The Canadian designs are imperial; they are going to occupy and use these lands for their own good and in their own interest, and part of their interest is not to have another

Riel rebellion or the kind of wars that Americans are conducting with Natives
south of the border.

HW Which is in part making a virtue of necessity.

GV Yes. I mean, all of these things are couched often in moralistic terms.
Now, I don't believe that it's either/or. I don't believe that the moralistic phrases
that are spouted in parliament are a conscious veil for political machinations
and empire. The two things go hand in hand: the belief that British law and
justice and the British genius for ruling other people is actually good for
Natives and that this civilizing mission is an honourable, ethical, moral issue.
It's not simply a subterfuge. But closely linked to that are economic and political designs that are really only going to be of benefit to white Europeans.

HW I'd like to go back to that issue of writing about something like the
Cypress Hills Massacre because you have more leeway, because there is less fixed
opinion and less of a historical record to have to contend with. That concern
brings up the epistemological anxiety at the heart of the historical novel, about
the distinction between what's fact and what's fiction. It seems to me that that
anxiety gets multiplied or complicated in novels like *The Englishman's Boy*,
which are not just writing about history like the Cypress Hills Massacre but
also drawing attention to problems of how to represent the past. We have, for
instance, the tension between what is presumably Shorty McAdoo's version of
the massacre and Damon Ira Chance's translation of it into the film *Besieged*.
Even though we don't see the film, so to speak, we sort of know what his narrative is and what his politics are. So, first of all, are we supposed to take
Shorty's version as authentic or more authentic?

GV My argument is that, while recognizing the subjectivity of any reportage
of any event, what we do know is that Shorty has experienced this, he's been
there. He may not remember the details, there is no objective certainty about
his interpretation, but he has been present, he was there. Chance, on the other
hand, is being given a text, Shorty's text, and what he is saying is that there is
a higher purpose which will allow for any amending and changing of "the
facts," because there's a higher purpose to be served here, and the purpose
that is to be served is the right ideological projection. So he is consciously, in
one sense, going against evidence. It's the only evidence he has. If he'd had
evidence from five or six different people, it would change—to what degree I
don't know, because there's only one character in the novel. But what he is
saying is, "I, as a moulder of public opinion—I, as an ideologue—know that
artistic representations serve an ideological purpose, a higher purpose." Now,

Shorty's not conscious of any of this. I mean, he has opinions about what should have been done, what was right, what was wrong, and all the rest of it, but he does have the experience. So, as with anybody, the old business applies about having three identities: the person someone else thinks you are, the person you think you are, and the person you really are. Well, we can't really arrive at the person you really are, but everything has to do with viewpoint. When you're dealing with history, it seems to me that you have to recognize that it's going to be a subjective enterprise, but it relies on something that we call evidence and interpretation, which at least you can argue about. You have a starting point for a dialogue and a discussion. If one historian, say, writes about John A. Macdonald and arrives at one viewpoint on his policy, and someone else has a different viewpoint on his policy, there are citations, etc. I know the record's not complete, never can be complete, but if one historian invents something—if he consciously claims that there's a letter in the archives that says this or that—and is caught out, then he's discredited. So, while I recognize that history is a subjective enterprise, as is the historical novel and all the rest of it, ultimately it is not and cannot be a whole-cloth invention. I mean, if you step into a realm of total subjectivity, how can you really criticize *Mein Kampf*?

HW I see what you mean, but I want to put that last question to you again in another way. If Chance's representation of history is depicted as manipulatively ideological—in the sense that he's taking Shorty's story and he's spinning it to suit his idea of the narrative of the American frontiersman—and as a novelist you want to position Shorty's version as somehow more compelling, does that put pressure on you to represent that incident in a way that squares with the historical record? Is there therefore that kind of onus on you as a novelist?

GV I would argue that there is a limited onus on me.

HW Another consideration is that the historical record about that massacre is contested. There are competing or conflicting versions.

GV There are several versions, with, I would argue, not a complete certainty in any account about what actually happened. Now, on the other hand, I mean as a novelist, I will pick and choose the account that for me is more novelistically satisfying. So, for instance, if they say that Little Soldier's head was paraded around on a pole, and other people say it was somebody else, or it never happened or whatever, but there's some sort of account, well right at that point I'm not capable nor do I want to sift with a toothbrush through all the evidence and say "okay, whatever," but I try not to depart too far from what seems to be a plausible interpretation. On the other hand, I've often said that *The Englishman's Boy* is not only a warning about the movies, but it's also a warning about the historical novel, that embedded in that is the notion that the more emotionally and psychologically convincing any artistic representation, the more it's possible that it drives out, by its persuasiveness, to a certain degree, any deeper investigation by the reader. Take a movie like Oliver Stone's *JFK*; many people who saw that movie would probably find it enormously persuasive, which doesn't mean that it's true. Probably, people would be more inclined to read *The Englishman's Boy* than say Philip Goldring's article on the Cypress Hills Massacre. What I always argue is that I am not contesting, for anything I write, the greater truth, veracity, or anything else. Also, in many ways, you can't be responsible for the unsophisticated reader or viewer, so that if someone watches a really violent movie and goes out and shoots someone, the responsibility is not on the movie, I would argue; it's on the individual. Indeed, I would hope that maybe the historical novels I've written would actually lead to people reading more about the events I portrayed, actually taking an interest in reading the history.

HW Let me jump in there with this quote from Chance: "Facts are of the utmost importance. If I can convince the audience the details are impeccably correct, who will dispute the interpretation? The truth of the small things leads to confidence in the truth of the large things." In that quote I see the fundamental appeal of the historical novel, which is making history more engaging and accessible, coming up against the problem of the manipulation of history that you dramatize especially through Chance. How do we square those things, or how do we find a happy medium?

GV Again, it's a question of perception. That, in fact, is part of the warning that I was talking about that's written into the novel: that appearances—the sheen or gloss of something—don't necessarily testify to the worth of it. On the other hand (and I hope I'm not sounding wriggly and weaselling here), I have always said that I'm writing novels. In many question-and-answer periods, newspaper interviews, and so on, I've always said that the work has to be judged as a novel, has to be judged on those terms. On the other hand, I feel a certain responsibility to hew fairly closely to what apparently occurred, and it seems to me that there are sometimes steps in historical fiction that are akin to Chance's steps.

HW A really good example is the role of the girl who is raped at the end of the massacre in *The Englishman's Boy*. In some accounts there were four

women, or there were two, but certainly making it just one has a kind of political and aesthetic resonance, as you've been describing, and that seems to me
a very compelling example of putting to the test that difference between the
spirit of the interpretation and sticking correctly to the details. It's obviously
a decision that has been made for effect, but it's an effect that you feel is much
more politically defensible and compelling than the kind of change that Chance
wants to make, which is an utter inversion of the spirit of the historical massacre as it is represented in Shorty's version.

GV Well, sure, and that's primarily an aesthetic question, but you can also
get into the hair-splitting thing. Four or two, which is correct? As a novelist,
which do you do, four or two? If you choose four, you make it more horrific.
If you choose two, how did they know that there were two women raped?
That's rhetorical, but that's the position you fall into. There's also the question
of the reliability of oral accounts. For instance, one Assiniboine chief claimed
that everyone had been drugged with whiskey laced with gunpowder and that
this made everyone fall asleep, and basically they were murdered in their beds.
So you say, "Is this plausible?" I would say likely not. There's obviously what
I would call a psychological necessity to portray the events in that light perhaps, you know, because they were defeated. "How could we be defeated? We
could only be defeated if there was a particularly nefarious trick played."

HW It's a kind of mechanism of self-justification, of rationalization.

GV It may be, but I'm only postulating. On the other hand, how much can
the whites' accounts of what occurred be trusted? So, ultimately, I'm saying that
in terms of plausibility it's very difficult, in what I would call a hard historical sense, to determine detail very closely.

HW Through the portrait of Chance you portray film as a medium conducive to a kind of authoritarian stamping of impressions and print as being
more conducive to reflection and dialogue: "Images take root in your mind,
hot and bright like an image on a photoplate. Once they etch themselves there,
they can't be obliterated, can't be scratched out. They burn themselves in the
mind, because there's no arguing with pictures. You simply accept or reject
them. A book invites arguments, invites reconsideration, invites thought."
Here, Chance is restating a point that you made in an interview with Alan
Twigg, quite a while before *The Englishman's Boy* was written. Is it fair to take
it that you would uphold that distinction?

GV [*sigh*] Yes, I do. I mean, I love film, and in many ways I think I'm writing my own reaction to it, which I also believe is generally the reaction to

film. There are a few people, critics, etc., who do subject film to that kind of critical analysis, reflection, argument, all the rest of it, whether it's film studies or anything else. But I think, certainly, at least in the past, for anyone who went to a movie, this was not a possibility. You walked away, and you carried that impression in your mind, because you didn't have a projector in your house, you didn't have film in your house. On the other hand, a book can be read and reread many times. I remember reading Nietzsche when I was nineteen and rereading Nietzsche when I was thirty, and my reaction was very, very different from my initial reaction. It's the same thing with novels or a book of non-fiction; you can sort of stop, turn a page back and say, "Did I get this right?" I think it's easier to carry on an argument with an author in your head as you read than it is to carry on an argument with a film. I mean, you're looking at a film and you may say "that's shit," you know, or "that's stupid," or "I wouldn't have shot the scene that way," or all of those kinds of things, but it seems to me that, in many ways, people are less aware of what they're viewing than what they're reading, and less likely to argue with it. Which doesn't mean to say that it can't be argued with or that there isn't a fair proportion of people who do have a kind of critical engagement with what they're watching.

HW Yes. There are a lot of hairs that could be split around that question, but I take it that—to make a sweeping relative distinction—you would argue that reading is just a much more active and dialogic process and watching a film is much more passive.

GV The interesting thing too, about film, is that, if you look at totalitarian regimes, they do care about books, but less so, because books are less influential for the general population than film. Many totalitarian regimes put the greatest emphasis on controlling film. You have Hitler and Leni Riefenstahl, and you have Eisenstein in the Soviet Union, and any number of attempts by the government to fashion people's reactions to events, issues, and all the rest of it. Now, I'm not saying that they forget about books and newspapers, but they know, or at least they knew in the 1920s and '30s, that film had more influence than books, because more people attended movies. Even in the United States, where there was less concern about the censorship of books, even though books underwent things like … you know, you couldn't buy *Ulysses* or whatever, governments and the movie industry itself were very intent on making sure that there was a kind of code that was embedded in the films and that they were not in some sense politically and socially offensive, because they didn't want the government stepping in and regulating it. In the States there were a lot of municipal and state film boards, so that your film might pass in New York, but it wouldn't pass in Boston or Newark or Los Angeles, or whatever, so Hollywood came up with a code that would set a groundwork that would say "We're not going to do this, we're not going to do that," all the rest of it, and sort of took censorship out of governments' hands.

HW Given all that, what do you make of the ascendancy of the visual media in our time, then?

GV Well, I think it works in exactly the same way, whether it's television, advertising, to a certain extent the Internet. All of these things clearly want to exert enormous persuasive power on the population. If it's advertising, it wants you to buy something. Television largely is an advertising medium, and so is the Internet now, which doesn't mean that they don't have possibilities for good. Clearly, the written word and the book are becoming increasingly less and less important. The thing that prevents visual culture from being deeper than it is, is that it's so closely linked to commerce. (Now, I know commerce has an influence in the book business and all over the place, but that too is a kind of form of censorship.) In the late 1940s and '50s everybody talked about television as being a great educative medium. With the proliferation of channels, there are nature programs, science programs, cooking programs, gardening, all that sort of stuff which you could argue is educative in some sense, but I think that people in the forties and fifties were actually talking about educative in the sense of making a democratic population more informed—

HW More civically responsible.

GV ... more civically responsible, and that hasn't happened. It's the same thing with the Internet. People can argue about the Internet in terms of politics and all the rest of it, but it's basically a commercial tool.

HW As I mentioned before, your portrait of the way in which history gets represented in Hollywood obviously raises very current concerns about transforming history into a kind of commodity with little or no relation to the material past or the historical record, such as they are. Your portrait of Chance and of the distortions of Hollywood's representation of history dramatizes the ways in which history can become an eminently manipulable sign, with nothing behind it. When the material past is so destabilized, and history is turned increasingly into a commodity, what strategies are there for resisting it being used in these authoritarian, even Orwellian, ways?

GV That's a huge question and a huge problem. It seems to me that a kind of historical sense is being destabilized from a number of quarters. One of them is the change from teaching history as a subject to something called Social Studies, which tends to be issues-related, discussion-based, and so on. I mean, every year newspapers run "fact-based questions" around Canada Day and— I can't remember what it was, because this was reported to me, and I'm not sure that I saw it in the paper—only 35 per cent of people under the age of thirty-five, when they were asked about what D-Day was, and they were given four choices, could actually get it correctly. So, despite all the old arguments that went on about how history was just memorizing dates and battles and all the rest of it, I think you have to have a foundational knowledge of some sort to even begin to talk about history and what history means and how it's interpreted. To even recognize the subjectivity of history, you have to have a certain amount of information. On the other hand, while I recognize many of the virtues of postmodernist approaches to literature and history—and I don't want to make too much about that—I think those approaches also destabilize history. It's increasingly seen as having no relation to contemporary culture, I mean in the sense that memory of the past keeps getting shorter and shorter, and so it seems to become less and less of consequence. If young people don't know a little bit of history, they're actually more likely to fall prey to totalitarian emotions, or government manipulation or—

HW Or believing that history is just a two-minute Heritage Moment clip or some other kind of commodified reflection of the past.

GV The other thing too is that, while one of the necessary corrections in the writing of history is the resuscitation of events, peoples, classes, races who were thought to be marginal or of no importance, all these corrections can lead to the sense that all history is kind of singular, individual, and related in one sense to one issue.

HW So there's a kind of atomizing of history?

GV Yes. For instance, though it's absolutely necessary that gay history be resurrected, that should not be the only issue for a gay man in terms of historical thinking, and I think that there's developing a tendency to really think and look micro and forget macro.

HW There's an increasingly refined segmentation of historical experience that in some ways diminishes our sense of history as a larger fabric of interwoven relationships and developments.

GV Yes, and it may even do something to diminish our sense of community or being related to people who are different than we are. One of the things I think that history can do is actually establish connections. I know the dangers of that also, and I know the danger of the master narrative, but I also feel the danger of the atomization of history, so that it seems like nothing is connected to anything else.

HW You have written the screenplay for the film of *The Englishman's Boy*. How did you cope with the shift in medium, from writing a novel to writing for the screen, and was there a certain irony in working in a medium about which the novelistic version of *The Englishman's Boy* creates quite a bit of skepticism?

GV I was perfectly aware of how ironic what I was doing was. But because I had a very temporary sense of power, and because I try to earn my living as a writer, and I am not so pure as to not take money from a film company, I wanted to write the screenplay, because I thought that I would be able to exert, or at least attempt to exert, more control than if it was handed over to somebody else. I also knew that you can't get a 330-some page novel into a ninety-page screenplay, and—going back to something we were talking about earlier—that the screenplay really had to approach what I thought was the spirit of the book rather than some sort of literal translation into another medium.

HW This is definitely an instance of life imitating art.

GV Yes, exactly. So that was my concern. I knew that I'd have to lose scenes, that some of the scenes would have to be invented, that some characters might have to go, and other characters might have to be invented, but what I was intent on was in some way trying to keep the screenplay as close as I possibly could to what I thought the book was about. The other thing of course is that obviously, as the book says, the picture is more important than the word in a film, and so a lot of the film was thinking visually.

HW Did you find yourself wrestling with that demon of film stamping impressions on people?

GV Well, yes, but part of the recognition in the novel about the difference between film and books is that the film does something other than books, that film is a visual medium, it's not really a thinking medium—and I know there are all sorts of film people who'll rip their hair out at that suggestion. It's really about, as Chance says, burning the thing into the mind, and so it is about pictures. Now what you're burning into the mind, in many ways, is your view of the world, so, in writing the screenplay, I was trying to burn my view into the film, even though the director has far more control about that than the writer does. But I was trying to write pictures that I thought would be in some ways emblematic of the book or able to convey what I took to be the meaning of the book.

HW Is there any space there for inviting thought?

GV The thoughtful parts of the film, as they can be, are in the dialogue. For instance, I just saw a movie called *True Believer*, about a Jewish skinhead, again supposedly based on a true story, and the film was very much a dialogue and an argument about how he had arrived at this position. So there are opportunities in which you can have exchanges in the film that are about ideas. It's sort of like sitting and watching a panel discussion, just never as extended, but there are opportunities for people to make points.

HW You dedicate *The Last Crossing* to local historians, essentially in appreciation for their doing the hard day-to-day work of keeping the flame of history alive. Can you elaborate a little bit on what's behind that gesture of appreciation? Can you give the extended version of the dedication?

GV We were talking about texture and these people supply a lot of texture, when they collect photographs, old artifacts, all those kinds of things, and when they make a really conscious attempt to preserve the record of particular places. For instance, when I went to Lethbridge, there were all sorts of little bits and pieces of things that I hadn't known about, that people who were involved in the Fort Whoop-Up Society could give me. I had never heard of the Sutherland brothers before, or the story of them being blond Cree, and so on. That would have been erased if people hadn't done interviews or collected all sorts of bits of material. Secondly, my brother-in-law was an amateur archaeologist. I think he had a grade eleven education. He was obsessed with finding Chesterfield House; he had an enormous collection of arrowheads, antique guns, all the rest of it. So partly it's homage to him.

HW And of course you used to work as an archivist and a researcher as well.

GV Yes, but I'm thinking of the quirky local historian even more than the archivist, because most archives are—at least in the past and probably to a certain extent still—official repositories. Local historians, they're often a very quirky bunch, and passionate—in many ways, far more passionate than professional historians, because for professional historians that's your profession, that's what you do; it's like being a mechanic or something else.

HW I can hear more hair being torn out in the background.

GV With the local historian, this is what they do in their spare time, because they love it so much. I just came back from doing a reading at Stratford, and a guy showed up at the reading and he said to me, "I loved the dedication to *The Last Crossing* so much I want to give you the history I wrote of a church in Stratford." The history is about 350 pages. Now, no professional historian in his right mind would devote years and years and years to writing the history of one church—you know, maybe St. Paul's in London, but not some small church in Stratford, Ontario.

HW But out of that quirkiness comes that incredible repository of local, specific detail.

GV Yes.

HW There are multiple heroes, one might say, in *The Last Crossing*, but obviously Jerry Potts sticks out for his subtle subversion, his forbearance, his unsung accomplishments. You talked a little bit about Potts's role in the history of the West, but perhaps you could elaborate a little bit more. For instance, how much are you behind Thomas Harkness's conclusion at the end of the novel, that he was unwittingly a tool in the destruction of the world he loved?

GV I would probably adhere to that—that Potts, by his actions, did destroy the world that he loved—but, on the other hand, he's not absolutely central to that destruction. I'm not saying that if Jerry Potts hadn't existed his world wouldn't have been destroyed; I'm just pointing out the irony of him being placed in that position and of his effectiveness at helping to do that. I first got interested in Potts when I was about eleven years old, and the *Star Weekly* magazine, which used to come with the local newspaper, had a little article on Jerry Potts in it. At that point Jerry Potts was supposed to be Canada's answer to John Wesley Hardin and Jesse James and so on—in other words, Canada's killer, someone who could rival in his exploits any of the heroes of the American West. Now, at ten years old, I found this very appealing, and so Potts always stuck in the back of my mind as a fascinating figure but also a central figure. As a novelist, though, I was always suspicious of his portrayal. I mean, all the famous stories about, you know, the moustache trimming …

HW This was the running gag he had with his friend George Star, where they would trim each other's moustaches by shooting the ends off.

GV Right. All of those kind of things I didn't put in the novel. One of the reasons I didn't do that is that it's almost a parody of the Western, so that's a novelistic choice. But secondly, I always had the suspicion that the taciturn Potts must have had more going on in his head than anyone ever guessed or

FIGURE 1. Jerry Potts, with rifle. Glenbow Museum NA-1237-1.

allowed for. Now that's just a novelistic hunch, right, because there's no record of what he was thinking.

HW Because of that, your decision to explore Potts's interior life strikes me as one of the big challenges of the novel, particularly developing his struggle with his dual heritage. It's another instance of writing into the gaps in history, I suppose, but how did you feel about taking that on?

GV Well, I wouldn't have written it that way if I didn't think I was right, you know? [*laughs*] I mean, it's my suspicion that Potts may have been like that. Now, I don't think anybody knows or can know what went on in his head. People may argue with my interpretation, but I believe it to be convincing, otherwise I wouldn't have written it that way. That's the best that I can do; when I try and imagine his world, that's its configuration in my head.

HW His estrangement from his Crow wife, Mary, fuels his internal conflict between his two heritages and fuels his sense of grievance at going in some ways unrecognized, unappreciated, even abused in white society. It is recorded that Potts's wife left him and went back to her people, so it seems a reasonable extrapolation from there that at the foundation of that estrangement was a kind of cultural conflict.

GV One of the things that I tried to do with Potts is in fact suggest how complex and difficult all accommodations are. Let me offer an anecdote here: some time ago I was talking to a young woman who had grown up in Germany; her father was English and her mother was German. The father lived in Germany with the mother, never really learned how to speak German, was never happy in Germany, and the accommodation was that the family moved to neutral ground, which was Canada. So how people arrive at compromises, and how they work their way through them, is really fraught with peril. Accommodations within the Native world were likewise complex and often difficult. The Crow and Blackfoot were hereditary traditional enemies, yet Potts married a Crow woman. We're not sure how this happened or why it happened. We know that Potts was celebrated as being the victor over the Crow any number of times. So what does a woman think, whose husband is a killer of her people? What is Potts's reaction to what I would imagine would be her own dividedness about this? How does that dividedness—you know, his Kanai blood, his Scottish blood—play out in him? Where did he feel most comfortable? Well, the supposition is, likely with the Kanai rather than with the whites. Yet he worked for the whites most of his life, in one way or the other, as a scout with the North West Mounted Police, as a guide for whites in the West,

FIGURE 2. Jerry Potts, interpreter with the North West Mounted Police and First Nations people, possibly at Maple Creek, Saskatchewan. Glenbow Museum NA-3811-2b.

for trading companies. So here's a man who as far as we can tell did not inhabit a culture the way let's say that the Métis did. Not that there weren't divisions there, but you know there are Métis communities and all the rest of it. So, in some ways, Potts seems more individual, probably more lonely, more separate, and in more difficulty in terms of working out what I would guess was his own destiny and his own identity.

HW In *The Englishman's Boy*, the anarchic frontier conditions of "Whoop-Up Country" are positioned in counterpoint to a culture that is outwardly moralistic but inwardly decadent, Hollywood of the Roaring Twenties. In *The Last Crossing* you do something similar with Victorian England. Again you have a culture that presents this facade of moral uprightness and propriety, and, as we see through the Gaunt brothers, there are all kinds of internal dissension and corruption and immoral behaviour. So what is it about this combination of cultures that appeals to you, and is there also a point there about Canadian history always intersecting with other histories?

GV Well, I think certainly the intersection with other histories, and our accommodations with those other histories, of both Britain and the United States has always been kind of a balancing act for English Canada. In *The Englishman's Boy*, Harry Vincent says that half the country wanted to be British and the other half wanted to be American. So it's a kind of psychological problem in English Canadians about a cultural allegiance of some kind or a way of behaving. But speaking in a more general sense, I am fascinated by what society or institutions profess and how they often act in ways that deny the profession. There is obviously as large a discrepancy there as we find in any individual. A nation always has an official version of its history, for instance, the one that is taught in public schools. Underneath the acceptable history there is invariably another interpretation that often contradicts or subverts it. For a novelist, that tension between interpretations is interesting. I also feel that history is a narrative about intersections among peoples, cultures, economic forces, etc. It's what brings about change and modifications of the status quo—some good, some bad, depending on the perspective. But if history is anything for me, it's the story of how intersections and collisions work themselves out in surprising and startling ways. Just to draw on present conceptions, once the official story of Canada focused largely on the French–English duality, the knotty problems of differing religion, language, culture, race. In time, that broadened to include a recognition of the impact of immigrants—usually of European stock. Gradually, the official history of the country began to emphasize multiracial, multicultural notions, because that was a growing reality. Now, I think we are dealing with the question of how First Nations fit into the national mosaic. Our present condition would, I think, have been unimaginable for any of the Fathers of Confederation. A country with mosques, Sikh temples, a country that permits women to vote, or is considering legalizing gay marriage—what would Sir John A. have thought of that? The chain of circumstances and events that brought us to this moment was unforeseeable, just as the future is.

HW There's a definite preoccupation in your work with masculinity—the whole idea of "man descending" that permeates not just that short-story collection but also a novel like *My Present Age* and the story collection *The Trouble With Heroes* as well. But it also permeates your forays into history, and I'm wondering whether the temporal distance that writing a historical novel involves refracts that view of masculinity, shapes it in a different way.

GV Because conceptions of masculinity are conditioned by societal norms, religion, upbringing, all of those kinds of things, they have to be put in a context of plausibility, in terms of how men probably behaved. But secondly, I think, at least in my work, there is a kind of dialogue between older, more conventional notions of masculinity and newer, more contemporary ideas of what it means to be male. There is a kind of dialogue that goes back and forth between how we are supposed to think and act as males now, as opposed to how males a hundred years ago were supposed to think and act.

HW The relationship between Custis Straw and Lucy Stoveall is a good example of that, because on the one hand you have that romance convention in which, in both *The Englishman's Boy* and *The Last Crossing*, the narrative pivots on the victimization of a young girl and on a male character's upholding of her cause, or coming to her defence, or avenging her death. On the other hand, in both cases your exploration of masculinity seems to go beyond the polarized gender roles that that romance convention typically involves.

GV Yes. The other thing is that Lucy Stoveall doesn't want to be protected by Straw; in fact, she doesn't want to take anything from him. She holds him at arm's length. Of course, she does fall into that sort of thing that, when she's captured, he kills her persecutor, but, very much like the Englishman's boy, he feels he had no choice, that he's in circumstances in which there's no way out except to kill him. So, in that sense, he's a flawed protector in every way except his doggedness in pursuing her. When I was on the book tour—this is a strange thing I found—many women who might be described as sophisticated, urban types would confidentially say, sort of flippantly and ironically, "I want to marry Custis Straw," or "Where do you find men like Custis Straw nowadays?" You know, there's an element of humour there, but there was also something confessional about that. I think the thing about Straw is not so much his effectiveness as a protector (even though at one point in the novel he's very effective) but his devotion and fidelity to Lucy and the selflessness of his love.

HW There is also—picking up on that distinction you made between an older form of masculinity and those expectations of how men are supposed to behave now—that distinction that gets brought up in your story "Things as They Are: Man on Horseback," in *The Trouble with Heroes*, between moral courage and physical courage. The main character, Joseph, is thinking about his academic colleagues' sense of moral courage and their adopting the right moral positions, and he reflects that in some ways it's meaningless, or not as meaningful, unless there is physical courage to go with it.

GV Well, I think he said something slightly different from that. He says that it's impossible to have moral courage, or often impossible to have moral courage, without physical courage, that one can be morally correct but not necessarily morally courageous, if you don't have the courage to follow through. He says, for instance, that it wasn't Heidegger who tried to kill Hitler, it was the army. Now, I'm not making a blanket celebration of physical courage, but in my own mind I know that there's a kind of courage that is simply moral— I shouldn't even say simply moral—but that's moral, in which you run no sort of risk except opprobrium. This is not to say that those aren't risks, but it would be very difficult to be in Hitler's Germany and stand up and attack his policies without also having physical courage. In more civil societies, you can be morally courageous and run the risk of being despised, making enemies who may harm your career, and all the rest of it, but in my mind, as admirable as that is, it still falls short of risking your life to support a position.

HW Especially in *The Last Crossing*, but also in *The Englishman's Boy*, that exploration of masculinity is bound up with an abiding concern with honour and reputation. What does honour mean in this world, in "Whoop-Up Country," and what does it mean to you that it seems to be such a preoccupation?

GV Honour, in my mind, is closely identified with a moral sense. So in some ways it's chivalric—this may sound very trite, but, for instance, that the strong should protect the weak is honourable. To make hard choices and to do the thing that you don't wish to do is honourable. To be able to conduct yourself with dignity in the most undignified circumstances is honourable. I had a friend who said that they truly fell in love with Custis Straw after he had shit himself—

HW And gets wiped down in the bath house.

GV He gets wiped down in the bath house, and then he knows that everybody's talking about him, and ridiculing him, and laughing at him, and he can walk down that street. So, in my mind honour is not necessarily identified with physical courage, completely or separately or anything else. Honour means to conduct yourself as best you can in a world that is provisional, in which all of us are beset by our own moments of weakness. It's doing what you mightn't necessarily want to do. Now, that implies some kind of metaphysical support for all of this, but that's the closest that I can come. Of course, no one would use the word "honour" any more, in contemporary society. It's fallen completely into abeyance. Of the words that are applied to men now, in many circles, the most laudatory is "sensitive," or "nurturing," or "a good father," and on and on. I don't think I've heard anyone in contemporary society, in my circle, use the word "honour."

HW Going back to that retrospective projection of contemporary concerns, why then does honour figure so prominently in the novel?

GV In terms of how I think I've defined it, honour is not a bad concept. I've always been a believer in stoicism, and part of my conception of honour has to do with stoicism. It's not whining and bitching and pissing and moaning. If you're faced with something that, in some sense, you can't really do anything about, you have to resign yourself to it, and those things that you feel you have some kind of influence upon, you should as best you can act on them. Now, it seems to me that—here's a gross, gross generalization—a lot of young men don't have a very stable notion about how they should behave, which is different than ideas of honour and dignity and all the rest of it. In a sense, it seems to me, they live life ironically, in that everything is treated, at least publicly, very lightly, that irony has become the attitude, rather than what might have been over-earnestness in the past.

HW Sort of a coping mechanism for—

GV Not exactly knowing how to behave.

HW ... for dealing with the eclipse of those traditional scripts for masculine behaviour.

GV Yes, exactly. Now, there has been a hell of a lot in men's reconfiguring themselves that's all to the good. For instance, eschewing violence for violence's sake as a stepping stone to prove that you're masculine, fighting, what I think was at one time a generalized contempt for women, and the saint–whore view of women. All of those things have made, dare I say it, men better. On the other hand, because males have undergone so much (probably justified) criticism, I think that they haven't fully integrated older conceptions of masculinity with newer conceptions of masculinity. I think that there are certain older conceptions of masculinity that are valuable and would do very well to be integrated with newer ideas about what it means to be male.

HW In a way we're perhaps within a dialectical process of adjusting conceptions of masculinity.

GV Yes.

HW In one of Chance's various speeches on the nature of history, you have him say that "every man is the servant of historical forces—that no man can deny the spirit of his age, any more than a fish can renounce the water for the land. But the fishes which know the currents, the pools, and the eddies of the stream they inhabit, these are the fishes who increase their chances of survival." Now, Harry casts a lot of doubt on Chance's views of history, and there is a kind of inscribed skepticism in his narrative about those views, but what about this one? Is this a view that you would uphold? You mentioned earlier, in response to another question, that not all of what Chance has to say is automatically coercive or manipulative.

GV Sometimes I put opinions that I subscribe to into minds that I may have an aversion to. I would say, roughly, that that's one of my interpretations of history. I do subscribe to Chance's position that of course we're all—I've used this word over and over again—creatures of context. On the other hand, there's the notion of personal acts, personal decisions, and the ability to make moral choices, ethical choices, and different ways of thinking. So I grant what Chance is saying, and I would also agree with Chance that the more historically aware you are, the better chance you have of navigating the large issues, but again with no guarantee. To be historically aware in some ways helps people react and people in power react in a more predictable and sometimes reasonable way. We are creatures of our own time but not completely creatures of our own time.

HW It doesn't mean that we should succumb to those forces or give into those forces or sacrifice our sense of agency.

GV Yes, or that we can't do something to in fact modify those forces. I mean, there are some forces that are so large that human beings are likely to feel absolutely powerless. On the other hand, I guess I've always been a bit of an existentialist, in that I believe that existence precedes essence. We're in the process of making ourselves, and in making ourselves as individuals we're also making history.

Walking Where His Feet Can Walk
Rudy Wiebe

The son of Mennonite immigrants who escaped from Russia in the late 1920s, Rudy Wiebe grew up in a small Mennonite community near Fairholme in northern Saskatchewan. Wiebe studied at the University of Alberta, from which he received an MA, and at the University of Tübingen in Germany. After teaching at Goshen College in Indiana for four years in the mid-1960s, Wiebe returned to Canada in 1967 to join the Department of English at the University of Alberta, where he taught creative writing for over two decades and has been professor emeritus since 1992. Wiebe's first novel, *Peace Shall Destroy Many* (1962), caused a great deal of controversy in Mennonite circles for its frank and critical portrait of a Mennonite community and its debating of the Mennonite ideal of pacifism. Wiebe's work represents a sustained engagement with Mennonite culture and history, reflected in novels such as *The Blue Mountains of China* (1970) and *Sweeter Than All the World* (2001). He is perhaps best known for his novels about the history of the Northwest, the Governor General's Award–winning *The Temptations of Big Bear* (1973), which focuses on the trials of Big Bear, the last of the Plains Cree chiefs to sign treaty in the late nineteenth century, and *The Scorched-Wood People* (1977), which chronicles the fate of the Métis nation over the course of the two Métis uprisings led by Louis Riel in 1869 and 1885. Wiebe has also had a long-standing interest in the North, dating back to his early novel *First and Vital Candle* (1966) and evident in *The Mad Trapper* (1980), a novel about the shooting of the man known as Albert Johnson, his historical novel about the 1819 Franklin expedition, *A Discovery of Strangers* (1994) (which also won the Governor General's Award), and in his non-fiction, such as *Playing Dead: A Contemplation Concerning the Arctic* (1989). Wiebe's latest book is *Of This Earth: A Mennonite Boyhood in the Boreal Forest* (2006). We talked in Edmonton in August of 2004.

HW You have described how your beginnings were essentially those of the pioneer. You were born into a family trying to scrape together a living on a bush farm in a small Mennonite community in northern Saskatchewan, after fleeing from Russia in the 1920s. Do you think having that experience of the immigrant pioneer—as opposed to, say, being raised in an urban environment—shaped your sense of history?

RW It certainly did. I have often thought about what you are given when you are born. You are given things that you have nothing to say about: the place you were born, the parents you were born to, their status in the world. I sometimes think about what would have happened, say, if my parents hadn't gotten out of Russia in that last desperate attempt in 1929. There was a time when I thought that it would have been very lucky for me as a writer if they had stayed in Russia, if they had survived and I had survived. I was born in 1934, roughly between Alexander Solzhenitsyn and Jozef Brodsky. Think of what they have done and what kind of world audience they have. When Solzhenitsyn's book *One Day in the Life of Ivan Denisovich* came out, it was a world-wide sensation because of the subject (of course he's not just a one-book writer). But I was born in western Canada, as part of a small immigrant group out in the bush. I mean, who in the world cares about this? So I sometimes thought it would have been much easier for me, as a writer, if I had been born somewhere else, not in the city, say, but if I had been born in Russia instead of here and stayed there. But we have what we are given and we can't do anything about it. I ended up writing about western Canadian history, even though no one really cared about it in the way in which I tried to explore it, getting past the usual stereotypes—farmers being dried out in the dustbowl of the thirties, and so on.

HW In all of your fiction there is a preoccupation with the past, and it seems to be a braid of two strands: the history that your family brought with them, so to speak, that of the Mennonite diaspora, a scattered people whose tortured history (literally and metaphorically) you chronicle in *The Blue Mountains of China* and more recently in *Sweeter Than All the World;* and the history that you found, that of the North and the Northwest, particularly the history of the displacement of the Aboriginal people, chronicled in *The Temptations of Big Bear, The Scorched-Wood People* and *A Discovery of Strangers.* To start with the first strand, what kind of influence did your being part of that Mennonite diaspora have on how you view history and how you view the history of this country?

RW If you're Mennonite you are very, very conscious of history, because your history is basically one of flight or movement. If not literally flight from, say, the inquisitional kinds of persecutions that happened in Holland in the sixteenth century, then the flight of always having to find new places when, after being offered refuge and shelter for a time, suddenly for some reason (and often it was the fall of a despot of some kind, a king or a czar) you find yourself in a social crisis. Those rulers are seen as your patrons and if you received concessions, as Mennonites often did—in terms of not having to perform military service, or your own schools—and you have your own community, then often when the social system that gave you those dispensations is destroyed for one reason or another (war or revolution or whatever), as has happened to Mennonites several times, then you have to leave. So history becomes very important to you. You have a kind of history in the blood of leaving home, of being chased out of home, of escaping from home. None of my relatives, on both sides of my family, got to Canada. Of my father's ten siblings, he was the only one to get out of Russia. There are descendants in Germany now, whom I met, but none of his brothers and sisters. Then you end up in Canada in the 1920s and '30s, where suddenly the difficulty is to make a living, but it's nothing like persecution; there is no persecution, even though during the 150 years Mennonites have been in Canada there was some, which caused migrations to Paraguay and Mexico in the 1920s, but there has been no persecution since then.

So you have that in your past. At the same time, you are living in a place your parents know nothing about. They don't tell you stories about this place, because they have no more history in this place than you have. So place becomes a very important thing, especially in a country like Canada, which is so diverse in so many ways, where so many places are offered to you. As you grow up in the kind of stony, glacier-formed land that I was in, in central

Saskatchewan, which is north of the easily habitable part, you become very aware of that place because you're just a kid and this is your world, this is your place.

HW You have reflected elsewhere that your parents were essentially part of the last generation of homesteaders in this country. That would give you, I think, a different perspective on history than if your parents had immigrated, say, to urban Winnipeg right away.

RW As many Mennonites did. That's right. Well, for one thing, you're the first people there to pursue agriculture. You're making the jump from a hunting and gathering society to the agricultural society that makes our contemporary world possible, because agriculture allows you to store food. Hunters and gatherers can't store food, basically; they've always needed a whole terrain. But you suddenly try to adapt this landscape to farming and then you discover how tough it is, though it can be done. At the same time you have living beside you the descendants of the hunters and gatherers, who are still there. So again, this underlines the past, but in this place now. Thus you have a kind of marvellous double whammy.

It is an extremely interesting place to be born in, but readers don't necessarily care about it. The world isn't desperately waiting for one more book about homesteading. But, for a writer, it is a marvellous place in which to be born because at first you're in a world where the horse is the fastest way you can get around. Then suddenly you have the internal combustion engine and, lo and behold, before you are middle-aged you're part of this electronic world that we are submerged in now, where everything is instant. I grew up for the first twelve years of my life without being connected to electricity, without any kind of running water unless I ran for it myself, or any hot water unless it was heated with the wood stove. This is a great advantage in terms of your novelistic experience. At the time, you don't even know about it because you're just a kid. You are just growing up; this is the world. You have this very strong sense then of a past that is gone and a present that is facing you right now, and in that sense it is good for a novelist.

HW There is perhaps also, in a Mennonite community, a desire to preserve a culture that in some ways makes you less attentive to the culture or to the history that is there.

RW Well, for one thing you don't know very much about it. You live in a community basically of Russian Mennonite immigrants who, with a couple of exceptions from the United States, have all just recently come from Russia. They all have suffered the same kinds of trauma, and they all have the same kind of Mennonite village experiences, and suddenly they are in a world that is not like that at all.

HW Let's talk about the other strand in that braid, which is your interest in the history of the North and the Northwest. Your interest in Canadian history has in many ways taken the form of a preoccupation with a series of particular figures—Louis Riel and Gabriel Dumont, Big Bear, the Cree chief Maskepetoon or Broken Arm, and Albert Johnson—most of whom are mentioned already in *Peace Shall Destroy Many*, your first novel, and all of whom crop up repeatedly in your fiction and non-fiction. Do you have any thoughts about that pattern?

RW Big Bear shows up in *Peace Shall Destroy Many* as the great-grandfather of one of the minor characters in the novel, which is ironic. As you know, many years later I actually met his great-great-granddaughter, Yvonne Johnson. Things happen in your life which are serendipitous, or marvellous, or just plain mysterious, or you could call them coincidences, though I don't believe much in coincidence. When you start working, you're thinking about a particular place and particular people, and very quickly people and events begin to connect.

As far as relations between the Mennonites and Native people are concerned, if one human being encounters another, often race doesn't matter so much; it's how we interconnect. Herman in *Peace Shall Destroy Many* encounters a human being who's willing to accept him as he is, even though his Mennonite community does not, so he marries her, and she is a Native person, which happens all the time, especially with Native people. They're not so discriminatory, generally speaking. Mennonites are very discriminatory, very classist, especially Russian Mennonites, who felt themselves very superior to Russian or Ukrainian peasants, so when they came here they tried to re-establish that old world as closely as possible in many ways. But, being born here, I carry nothing of that Mennonite colony village concept with me. I can't live in a Mennonite village. I just saw for the first time a month and a half ago the village where my father was born, which it took me seventy years to get to. I couldn't live in such a tight place; I can't even pretend that I want to. And I can't pretend through creative literature the way some Mennonites did, that if you are going to write a literature in Canada, you should do it in German and create a German literature for Mennonite people in Canada. There was a very fine writer named Arnold Dyck, who came from Russia and tried to do that and of course got completely discouraged about it, because nobody would read it. It's not my world anyway. I would have never tried it.

So the other strand of history that I found so exciting and interesting was about the place and the people who had been in my place, the only place I'll ever be born, and what had happened there before we came there and tried to make a farm out of this stony land. That's what intrigued me, because wherever there are people, there's a story. Then I discovered Big Bear, the main chief implicated in the Riel Rebellion, because his warriors supposedly killed all those people in Frog Lake, nine or ten people including two priests. Anyway, I discovered that Big Bear, whose band had killed these ten unarmed people, was born within twenty miles from where I was born. Then something clicked. I saw that this was an intriguing history that had taken place here, which basically nobody knew anything about.

HW It had been essentially suppressed or grown over, you might say.

RW Forgotten. Big Bear is simply seen as a rebel who is condemned and who died of the effects of his imprisonment. Then the theory developed that the Indian people would die out anyway and what we had to do was destroy their culture, take the children away from their parents, because the parents would keep teaching the Native culture, and train the children to be good little Canadian workers. We didn't credit them with any brains, but they could be workers in factories or on farms. So white Canadians felt that the Native people would just die out, and it was absolutely a policy of the Canadian government that we must assist them to become Canadians who were indistinguishable from everybody else. And of course you know all that sad history, the residential schools and endless prejudice against them. Of course they didn't die out and their culture was not destroyed either, although it came within a whisker of being destroyed.

HW In your essay "On the Trail of Big Bear" (I know that's going back quite a way) you describe how the impetus for the writing of *The Temptations of Big Bear* came out of a sense of outrage at how you lived on the very terrain on which Big Bear's story unfolded, and yet your public school had erased that history, had said nothing of it. How much do you think that attitude towards Canadian history, and particularly the history of Aboriginal peoples in this country, has changed since then?

RW I think there has been a substantial proliferation of information about Native people, and they've done it themselves, basically, through the organization of the Indian Federation of Canada, which began in the 1930s and then especially gained momentum after the veterans came back from the Second World War, where you know the Native people, out of all proportion to their

FIGURE 3. Mistahi Maskula (Big Bear, ca. 1825–1888). Library and Archives Canada C-001873.

population, were contributing to the military effort in very substantial ways. Then came the rise of the Black movement in the United States, and then of course the Native people in all of North America followed suit, with the great march on Washington in 1971, which Canadians took part in too. It's also due to the increase in Native writers. There are many stories that, say, European-origin Canadians don't need to tell now because there are superb writers like Tomson Highway or Richard Van Camp from the North, people who can tell those stories of contemporary Native life. The other thing of course is that you can see the Native person is not just the classic image of the poor or the drunk person staggering down the street. There are many Native people who are very successful in many ways in Canadian society. In that sense, you don't have to show just one element, which is sadly still there in a terrible way. Things are being done in Canada that are important and that are getting attention in the world. For instance, the news of the creation of Nunavut has made it around the entire world. If you go to China or you go to Europe, of course, people ask you about Nunavut: "What does this mean?" So it's not the way it was, say, in the 1960s, and it's certainly not the way it was when I went to school in the forties and the fifties, when Native people were basically ignored, as far as mainstream Canada was concerned.

The other horrible thing that has happened, of course, is the whole problem of the residential schools, and that has raised the whole issue of our handling of Native people. That's interesting too, because that did not become a public, important issue until after the sexual scandals of other schools, like Mount Cashel in Newfoundland, which was only in the 1980s. Sadly, those kinds of horror stories bring it to everyone's attention, and finally something is going to get done about it. Indeed, we've reached the point where I'd say that maybe in the twenty-first century one of the biggest social questions that we face is justice for Native people. Part of that is the trauma of the residential schools, which largely came to the attention of Canadians because of Mount Cashel.

HW Because the trauma of whites had been dramatized first, essentially.

RW Yes. And then Native people said, "You know, that happened to us a lot longer ago and for a lot longer."

HW And furthermore, as part of a systematic and government-approved policy of assimilation.

RW Assimilation and destruction of a culture, of which this was only one part.

HW What about attitudes towards the history of the West? In various articles and interviews you have pointed to the radically different sense of identity, of story, of history in western Canada. I'm thinking of the title of an article you wrote many years ago—"In the West, Sir John A. is a Bastard and Riel a Saint. Ever Ask Why?"—dramatizing that difference in perspective, particularly about history. Do you see that dynamic as having changed much in the last twenty-five years or so?

RW It's hard to tell when you look at the political map of Canada [*laughs*]. There was a time when the two solitudes, Quebec and Ontario, was the story of Canada. Sadly, there's still too much of that in politics, but nevertheless I think in terms of storytelling, in terms of our understanding of the West, the West is finally out from under the colonial yoke of the East. If Ontario and Quebec were a colony of England, then the Prairie provinces were a colony of eastern Canada, and they were always seen as that: you went out west to make money and to ship the money back, but you really lived in Ontario. There are perfectly obvious reasons why that historically developed to be the case. But I think Alberta in its own way has now become too powerful for anybody to do that to.

HW You have had a long-standing fascination with the North as well, evident early on in *First and Vital Candle* and more substantially later on in *A Discovery of Strangers* and in your musings on the North in your essay collection *Playing Dead*. Is the idea of history and of the past different for the North than it is for, say, the Prairies or the Northwest?

RW The interesting thing about Arctic Canada, of course, is that the history there is closer to us than it is on, say, the Prairies. The encounter there happened later and Europeans have never wanted that territory for anything in particular. You can't farm up there, so the only thing you can do up there is mining or drilling for oil. Furs aren't worth anything now. The white men have never really wanted very much in the North, so the Native people have been able to maintain their traditions much longer than Natives to the south. Of course, they were just as devastated by the encounter and particularly devastated by the diseases that white men brought there, just by casually passing through. You can destroy an entire people by smallpox or whooping cough or something minor (well, we might think it's minor). So things are closer there. The other thing about that is that there is more space there. You walk out of any tiny little village there—and they're all tiny—and it's as if no human being has ever bothered this place. This place is the way it was since Creation, or human existence, anyway. You get a tremendous sense of the unimportance of human beings up there, which is very good for you.

HW So the sense of place in some ways gives you a different sense of time.

RW Yes, and of yourself and your own significance. The most positive experience I've had of that was my stay on Ellesmere Island. I went up to the far north end of Ellesmere Island, about eighty-one degrees north, in 1999, with the Geological Survey of Canada. I spent three weeks there in the mountains with a geological team. I was a helper, carrying rocks for one of the geologists. It was a marvellous experience—a big geological camp that you had to fly in to, and there were thirteen or fourteen people there, including a helicopter pilot and a helicopter mechanic. In the morning the helicopter would fly us to the top of the mountain, and the geologist and I would spend all day walking down the mountain, he taking geological samples and me carrying them, and in the evening they'd pick us up and bring us back to camp. It was absolutely a perfect way to live there. You were walking on terrain that I'm sure no human being had ever walked on before and would ever walk on again. And you were in this world of mountains. Ellesmere at that point is just mountains, and across the strait—it's the place where Ellesmere and Greenland come closest together, so it's only about thirty kilometres—there you see Greenland. You see this flat Greenland and here you are in this world of mountains, covered with ice, and you're walking down over the bare rocks and ice. It was one of the most marvellous experiences I've ever had, that experience of a place where there are no people at all.

But they did once live there. They lived there before the Little Ice Age that came over Canada. The world has gone through various ice ages over time. The Little Ice Age was somewhere around 1100 to about 1750 or so when the whole culture that was living there died out because it was too cold. Today you can still see the rings of stone on the beaches where that earlier culture lived. They lived in tents, with whalebone for ribs to hold up their tents, and they lived basically on whales and sea animals. They lived on the shores, and you could still see the stones of their tepee rings and their three-stone hearths on the shores of the Kennedy Strait, between Greenland and Ellesmere. It's wonderful. At the same time, there are muskoxen grazing there, and I spent one whole day with the muskoxen, taking pictures and watching them. So you get that sense of original wilderness, that sense of a world that human beings have basically tried to destroy for their entire life. Human beings are always trying to make worlds they can control, but when you live in the Arctic, it's a world you can't control. You suddenly feel yourself powerfully attracted to that, by what we call wilderness, the wild, out of which we grow ourselves, and which doesn't care about us one way or another. If we don't protect ourselves, the mosquitoes will eat us up in summer or we'll freeze to death in winter. The "wild" world will not care, and we can't control it.

HW It just implacably resists that effort to control.

RW It just is what it is and it doesn't pretend to be anything else, and the human being hasn't affected it one way or another. It's so wonderful to go into a world like that, and there are so many places in Canada where you can still do that, where you still feel that sense of some kind of pre-human world that human beings have neither messed up nor had anything to do with. It's just itself.

HW In many respects, traditionally, history is a kind of commemoration of achievement: Wolfe defeated Montcalm on the Plains of Abraham, George Simpson transformed the Hudson's Bay Company into a grand commercial empire, Cornelius Van Horne engineered the building of the transcontinental railway, all that sort of thing. But your fiction—like so much contemporary historical fiction—seems to be more about bearing witness to and resisting the erasure of the history of minority cultures. I'm thinking about your anger over the effacing of Aboriginal history on your home ground, the territory you grew up in as you've just been describing, or Adam Wiebe's desire to burn the names of all his Mennonite predecessors into wood in *Sweeter Than All the World*. Do you think that's a conscious impulse when you look to the past, to resist erasure, to bear witness to those cultures?

RW I speak as someone who, as far as I know, has this ancestry going back for four or five hundred years, and it's just what I've been given. The story of the Mennonite people has always been that we're a small people. We don't amount to much. We're not a large part of any population. We've never been great warriors, and we've never been great rulers. We're the kind of people who get, as you say, no record in history. There have been actually more than you think and one of my delights was my discovery of my ancestor Adam Wybe, who I discovered in *The History of Danzig* published in 1683–87. There's just a little note on him and his famous cable car. I like that story, because it's not about someone conquering anything, or destroying something, or leading an army somewhere. It's about a man who invented a machine to protect people exactly from those kinds of hordes, and this is what was so delightful about him.

HW Then there is the irony, of course, in *Sweeter Than All the World*, that this man who does so much to defend the city of Danzig is not even allowed to live within its walls.

RW They never make him a citizen, but eventually they allow him to live inside, build some houses beside one of the gates of the city walls. He ends up moving out of the city, and he and his sons build dykes and they make more land arable by flood control, and they build villages there. This is why a character like this would be intriguing. He's not going to be famous for killing more people than anybody else in his generation. He did something to protect some helpless people. These are the kinds of people that I am obviously attracted to, having always had a sense in my own family that we're very minor. We don't amount to anything. There is something in the attitude of our people, people who for generations have been basically living on the margins of things and not particularly successful at anything. When *Peace Shall Destroy Many* erupted into a big controversy in the Mennonite church, my father just laughed, whereas my mother was very saddened. They couldn't read the book because of course they couldn't read English, so they just had to stick with what I told them. But my father was incredibly intrigued and felt so good about it, that a son of his could create such a ruckus among all these big men and get all this attention all over Canada. He thought it was great. He never thought it would happen. It's just the kind of attitude he had about himself and about his son. But in Canada anything is possible. It's this sense of the small person struggling with the large obstacle. Every fiction writer knows that the smaller people struggling with large problems are more interesting generally speaking than the big shots.

HW In a way, that is a real bridge between your writing about Mennonites and your writing about the Cree and the Métis.

RW They are both seemingly unimportant in terms of anything that's happening on the larger scale of Canada. Then when you start writing about them you discover that people don't care. A lot of my fiction is structured out of, you might say, discrete pieces, and they concern very small people, unimportant people in the history of the world. But they are human beings, and they are just as important as every other person, even though they aren't Gustavus Adolphus leading armies across Europe and destroying half of Europe during the Thirty Years' War. What intrigues most fiction writers are the small people. I mean, it's the confessions of Nat Turner that interested William Styron, right? Nat Turner is a nondescript slave who gets into the history books somehow and writes a short diary, but it's John Brown, the white guy, who is talked about in the history of emancipation in the United States. So because of my own history, because of where I grew up in Canada, it's the small person, the unimportant person, who intrigues me—but the small person somehow at a cusp of history, at a point where the pressures of history suddenly become obvious.

HW The tectonic plates are rubbing up against each other.

RW That's the way Big Bear is, I think, and clearly the original Adam Wybe, the sixteenth- to seventeenth-century Adam Wybe, is like that.

HW I think it's fair to say that *The Temptations of Big Bear* and Timothy Findley's *The Wars*, which were published a few years apart in the 1970s (both winning Governor General's Awards), marked something of a watershed in historical fiction in this country. Both novels took a somewhat revisionist attitude toward two national preoccupations—Native people in the case of *The Temptations of Big Bear* and the Great War in Findley's novel—but, more importantly, took a dramatically different approach to writing fiction about history, by bringing to the fore the way in which history is written and stressing the multiplicity of perspectives involved in the relaying of the past. What would you say was the state of historical fiction at the time of the writing of *The Temptations of Big Bear*, and what do you think led to this aesthetic shift?

RW I had always been intrigued by Big Bear since I first read about him in William Cameron's *Blood Red the Sun* in the 1950s, and that's why he shows up in *Peace Shall Destroy Many*. *Blood Red the Sun* is basically a description of William Cameron's encounter with Big Bear during the Frog Lake incident in 1885, and I was thinking about him when I came back from working in the United States in 1967. There was a tremendous euphoria over the centennial in 1967, and that's when I thought I should do something about this character. There was a general valorization of Canadian history at the centennial: we existed this long, there is this kind of a country, we have a history and it's uniquely ours. It's not the United States at all. The fact that we haven't had a civil war so that we can glorify ourselves and have military parades makes it more problematic but in some sense makes us a more developed (and later we're a postmodern) country. Instead of shooting each other, we talk, and we talk and we talk and we talk and we talk, and it's wonderful how much better talk is than guns and war, going around killing people. So there was a wonderful euphoria then around Canada in general, and of course that spilled over to the kinds of stories we tell about ourselves. Expo '67 in Montreal, which we went to, was a glorious thing, too. We'd never seen anything like it in Canada. So there is that, that we came back just at the right time in the summer of '67.

HW What about the shift in how those stories were told, in the movement away from that kind of omniscient narrative perspective on the past, presenting history as cut out of whole cloth? Instead, both you and Findley were in a way presenting history as a much more fragmented picture, were really encouraging readers to be conscious of how we experience the past, whether it's through archival traces such as transcribed conversations, photographs, records, or whether it's by forcing readers to look at the past through the prism of very contrasting and conflicting perspectives, those of a Cree chief on the one hand and all these government officials and military officers on the other.

RW That was part of what was happening in the sixties. My family lived for four years in the United States, during the time of the biggest revolution in Black consciousness and all the freedom marches. Then there was the rise of the whole opposition to the Vietnam War. At the same time the women's movement grew, and the prevailing idea was that everybody had a valid story to tell. I remember going to a conference at a Mennonite college in Kansas, and one of the professors was making a big thing about the way Mennonites used to cook, and I had never in my life thought about the validity of a woman's work and cooking as something particular to make an art display out of, but there it was. So there was this kind of valorization, if you want to call it that, of ordinary people's work and how that contributed to the kind of world we live in. It's not Mackenzie King or Roosevelt or Eisenhower who is important in the war. It's just the ordinary foot soldier, right? This is part of what happened in the sixties, the development of that sense that everybody has a valid story.

HW So it's a fracturing of the idea of the authoritative version, in other words.

RW Yes, the fracturing of the Carlyle idea of history, that history is the biography of great men. It's not. History is the biography of all kinds of little people, what we call little people, who are just as great, and perhaps greater, than the great men that we know about. Generally we know about them because they have been great killers, right? This is the way we come to our history. Why do we know about Alexander the Great? Because until his time he was the greatest killer the world had ever seen, or Genghis Khan or people like that. But no, there are other people. Big Bear is great not because he killed anybody—that's the whole point—but because he tried to stop it, and of course he couldn't.

HW And he was blamed for it nevertheless.

RW Yes, he was blamed for it anyway because he was supposed to be the authority figure, and if he was the authority figure he was supposed to be able to order his warriors around. Well, if anybody knows anything about the social structure of prairie Native people, to expect a chief to order anybody around, like a general, is ludicrous. It won't work.

So this was part of what was happening then and I think Tiff [Findley] must have already been thinking of it as he was working on *The Wars*. Of course it's not the kind of novel that I could ever have written, because it was not a part of my family experience in the First World War, which was different. My father was a conscientious objector in the First World War in Russia, and he had a very different experience than a young man in the trenches of France. The other thing about fiction is that you want to write about that distinctive, unique experience that intrigues you. I've learned in a long life of trying to write fiction that you always go with the things that interest you; whether they're odd or popular it doesn't matter, go with it.

HW Going back to that idea of fracturing the authoritative version, in both cases—*The Temptations of Big Bear* and *The Wars*—you can see the impulse to find a different kind of narrative language to do that, because it requires the story to be told in a different way, and again it's a different approach that foregrounds history as a much more complex experience.

RW Yes, I would agree with that. When history first became a discipline, the Germans formulated it as the effort to find out *so wie es eigentlich war,* "the way it actually was." That phrase *so wie es eigentlich war* sticks in my memory from somewhere.

HW It's from the nineteenth-century German historian Leopold von Ranke.

RW They actually thought that if you could make a complete scientific discipline out of this then you could tell it as it actually was. Of course they didn't realize—which is the first thing the novelist has to understand—that your point of view is all-important. Who is looking at the way it really was? I always use the Kennedy assassination as the perfect horrifying example. How many thousands of people saw it, literally saw it happening, on television or on that Zagruder film, and then they have the chief justice of the United States and the biggest committee that you could imagine investigating it, and they wrote a big thick report on it, and they still don't know "the way it actually was." They still don't know how or why it happened.

HW Another example you've used is from an incident during the Riel Rebellions, in which the eyewitnesses couldn't even agree on the day on which something happened.

RW History as we know it always happens in the past, and the past is always more and more elusive, so historians end up depending on, say, written documents, or archaeologists go back to whatever imprints are accidentally left in the rocks somewhere, which they accidentally find. So the idea of knowing exactly what happened is, of course, ludicrous, as we perfectly well know from our own experience of the present moment. The strength of fiction is that you tell a story from particular points of view, and if you choose a kind of postmodern way of doing it you can tell it from a number of points of view, not to confuse people, but to show people how complex things really were. For most of us contemporary novelists, I think the most intriguing things are when we're trying to stimulate people to think about the story, as well as to tell the story.

Another thing about writing historical fiction is that, rather than the idea that you read a story for the good story and then you're done with it, you want the reader to participate. So when you're reading a novel, you are experiencing something yourself, and you're not just sitting in front of the screen watching it happen. That's the romance. Romances are perfectly legitimate in their own way, but that's not the kind of novel I want to write. I want to write a story where a reader is puzzled. Am I supposed to like this guy? There is no necessary reason why you should like him, even the protagonist of the novel. Some people said that about the contemporary Adam Wiebe in *Sweeter Than All the World*. He's kind of an asshole isn't he? It takes him a long time to figure some things out in his life, and drastic things happen to him before he can actually figure them out or realize what he is really doing, and even in the end he hasn't really figured things out yet. But that's an interesting kind of person to write a novel about, because the reader is involved in trying to decide. I feel the same way about the historians who tell you "this is the way Big Bear was, this is the way Edgar Dewdney was, this is the way Alexander Morris was when he negotiated the treaties" and all this kind of stuff. No. Life is more intriguing than that.

HW In some ways there is a violence to that kind of finality as well, a somewhat coercive attempt to just close the lid on the past, whereas the past is ever being reappraised and revised.

What do you think about how the genre of historical fiction has developed in Canada since the publication of *The Temptations of Big Bear* and *The Wars*? Historical fiction by the end of the century has become one of the principal and most popular literary genres in this country. Any sense of why this might have happened?

RW One of the things I have always said is, Why make up extravagant science fiction worlds? Our world is so interesting, if you only get into it. It's far more intriguing. History gives us the best stories we have, if we just learn about them, if we just figure them out or notice them. We don't have to make these people up. The stories exist already. And I think Canadians are really discovering that our history, though it isn't the cowboy history of the American West or something like that, in its own ways is as intriguing, and a book like Fred

Stenson's *The Trade* of course proves it. Our history is full of marvellous people; it's just that we know little or nothing about them. And the historians skip over the most interesting ones and they stick with the Family Compact or something. The worst mark I ever got in university was in Canadian history. I couldn't stand it as it was taught at the University of Alberta at that time. But it is full of marvellous things and people.

HW So we've reached this level of familiarity with that history and a level of confidence in the validity of that history?

RW When China validates Norman Bethune, we recognize that we have a true hero in our midst, right, but he was there before China validated him. You get other people like that in Canadian history. It's just that we never had the confidence to write their stories, and I think that contemporary novelists do have the confidence.

HW It seems that the validity of that history now is almost taken for granted, not something that one enters into with a sense of apology almost, or the classic inferiority complex.

RW When *Big Bear* was first published in October 1973, there were people who said to me "Why do you bother writing about a man like this?" It's true. They did. "Why do you bother? You've got all these skills, why do you write about a minor Indian character?" That was still there in '73, and I think there are still certain ways of thinking like that. Now of course they'd say, "Well, how dare you write about an Indian?"

HW And that is my next question [*laughs*]. You've written about the absolute necessity, when writing about the history of this country, of linking the present to Aboriginal peoples and their past, "to somehow, in a small way, show that what we are now has some connection to a past which was here before any of us whites." Your own work reflects a sustained effort to do just that—from *The Temptations of Big Bear* to *A Discovery of Strangers*. At times, though, that effort has led to controversy, especially in terms of the whole issue of appropriation of voice and of stories. You were certainly in the thick of those debates during the 1990s, both because of your criticism of W.P. Kinsella's fiction but also because of skepticism about your own writing about the history of Native peoples—that question, as you put it, "How dare you write about that?" What's your thinking now on the issue of whites or non-Natives writing novels and stories about Native people? Another way to ask this question, maybe more provocatively, is, if you hadn't written it yet, would you write *The Temptations of Big Bear* now, or would you maybe go about it in a different way?

RW Where do I start with that one? No, of course I couldn't write *Big Bear* now because it has already been done. Novelists must in a sense anticipate and (I am not trying to brag here or anything) think further ahead about what's really interesting in terms of human experience. Historians and critics can only come afterwards in a certain way. I didn't know I was writing historiographic metafiction when I was writing parts of *Big Bear* or, say, "Where Is the Voice Coming From?" The term hadn't been invented. The scholar reads the fiction and makes up the general theory about it.

HW The practice precedes the theory.

RW That's exactly right. There are at least two issues about writing *Big Bear*. One is that I've never written any contemporary Native stories, because I think there are many superb Native writers who can write the contemporary stories, who can write from their own personal experience, the kind of things that I write about my Mennonite background. I have never written a contemporary Native fiction story the way W.P. Kinsella tried. I've always worked in the past and I've always asked the question, "Do you know what your ancestors did 150 years ago? Do you know what they were doing in 1832?" As new writers find out, you couldn't just sort of intuit this, you have to do a damn lot of research to find out, which I do. I take it very seriously. The other thing is that I've never actually been accused of appropriation of voice by any Native writers or any Native people. In fact, when they did the production of *The Temptations of Big Bear* as a television show (it was done by a Native/white co-op, one company from Saskatchewan, one from Quebec, and the director was Cree and all the actors were Cree that needed to be Cree and all the whites were whites), every time I came on the set the actors, the Cree actors especially, would come to me and thank me for writing this story, because they had such a great time trying to re-enact the story of this great man. That appropriation of voice debate was an interesting discussion, and it was important to have it, but I never really particularly suffered from it or thought that I had done something reprehensible, because I have an absolute idea that human beings are human beings. I don't own the Mennonite voice, any more than Maria Campbell owns the Métis voice, or Tomson Highway owns the Cree voice. We bring our past with us, but the voices that we have are our own; they are not *the* voices of a people.

HW You have to be careful what kinds of imaginative fences you wish for, because you might find yourself in a very small pasture. That was an idea that came up again and again in those debates, figured in various kinds of images, including that of a kind of imaginative apartheid.

RW Tomson Highway, who is a friend of mine, is not fond of it. He asks, can only Native actors act in his plays? This kind of thing has basically destroyed his writing ability, in some sense. He has great difficulties with this. Why should that be? It plays both ways. Suddenly, Tomson told me, he could write nothing but Native stories and only Native people could act them. It goes both ways, and it's not healthy at all.

HW It strikes me, though, that there are some complex questions of power involved in those debates that are in a real tension with the ideal of imaginative freedom, and that those concerns would be less intense if there was a more level playing field for all writers. But there is also the interesting issue of the historicity of those debates. As you said about the writing of *The Temptations of Big Bear*, the response then, perhaps the mainstream response, might have been, "Why do you want to write about these Native people?" I think that is a reflection of the cultural climate at the time, in some ways just as the question "How dare you write about a particular culture? You are not a member of that cultural community" was a reflection of the cultural climate of the 1990s, when those concerns were much more highly publicized and much more part of mainstream cultural debate.

RW There's a third point at issue, which is that I have never told these stories in isolation. I've never gone back to say where the film *Atanarjuat* goes back to, where there's no white person around. These novels have always involved Europeans and encounters, often first encounters like *A Discovery of Strangers*, or encounters like the land takeover in *Big Bear*. So I have never written just Native people's stories; instead, I have written about the encounter and the clash between them and the Europeans that are moving in and doing things that inevitably bring them in conflict. The stories that I've told historically have been those moments of first encounter, of conflict, that really bring out the pressure points, and also the kinds of personalities and the kinds of societies that these are. So you have Alexander Morris coming in, and when Morris says something, that's it, because he speaks with the voice of the Queen. Big Bear doesn't speak that way. This is where the interesting stories happen, when two societies like this come together. Historically, I've never tried to tell only one kind of story. I've always tried to tell that particular story, which I myself experienced in a very small way when my family tried to make a farm out of land that was basically hunting and gathering land. You can say that in a certain way, my family had a first encounter too. It wasn't so much with people; it was mostly with a really stubborn and recalcitrant, almost unalterable, land. When I go there and look at it now, it astonishes me, because there is no farmland there at all; it's become a community pasture. People gave up on it. So these are the ways I would deal with "How dare you write these stories?" The fourth issue, of course, is that it happened in my place. That may be even the most important one. It happened here, where I was born. This is my place. When I go sixty miles from where I was born, to North Battleford, and I see the site where these eight Native men were hanged as a result of the rebellion, and I see where their grave was, by the bank of the Battle River, well, that's my country. It's just as much as if I were a Jewish person living in Brooklyn writing about a Jewish person in Brooklyn. I'm writing about Canadian society in North Battleford, Saskatchewan. That's what I am writing about.

HW Also, in some ways, if you don't, you're back to square one, that those stories are suppressed.

RW Yes. They have no validity, because in certain ways they aren't important now until you tell them. Then gradually these stories get into the world. But if you don't tell the stories, there's no validity to them, because they disappear in forgetting.

HW You yourself, though, have recognized some limits to that imaginative freedom in the sense that you have talked about there being a kind of proprietary claim in Native cultures, to a degree—particular people, particular families, owning stories. That's a claim that you have talked about respecting. You've heard these stories and have been asked not to share them because they are private stories. So, in that sense, it's slightly more complex.

RW That's another issue, of personal stories that you own. In the Native tradition that very much has to do with sacred songs and sacred stories that are given to you alone and that you use perhaps in your prayers and in your spiritual communions with things and pass on to other generations. I see that validity too in the kind of story that you live. For example, I can't say Herb Wyile did this and this and this and make up all kinds of stories about you. I mean, I'd get hauled before the law; I could get sued for libel. I feel this way very strongly too about the past, that you can't simply make up stories about people in the past. If you talk about Big Bear, you have to stick to the story of Big Bear that you know. Now if there's no evidence, then you can extrapolate from that the kind of person he is, but you must respect his story for the facts that you have, and follow those facts wherever they lead you, and if he hated white men or didn't like priests or killed someone, that's the story—he did it. You don't whitewash someone, or you don't make up things, unless the history gives you nothing; then you extrapolate from the personality as you know it.

You have to be honest to the person that you know. In that sense, a life is a sacred story, and if you are going to tell it you must respect it profoundly. I did that with Keskarrah in *A Discovery of Strangers*, and with Greenstockings, the main character. There are only a few details recorded of them, but you must respect those limits, and you can go on from there by discovering the history around them and the way of the world they lived in, and then make some shrewd (or not so shrewd) judgments about what they might have done.

HW How do you square that with the idea of history, as you described it earlier, being in some ways a fabric of multiple and very often conflicting or contradictory perspectives?

RW Well, the other thing is that you don't pretend that you are telling the only story that could be told about, say, Greenstockings. I've told one; I wish someone would tell another story, perhaps her entire life, or what you can gather from the Franklin journals and the Back journals, which are, at the moment, the only historical references that we have to her existence. I would be intrigued and would be the first person to read it. This is only my version of the story in that sense, using the few facts that we have. Greenstockings is a good example, because we only know three or four things about her. When I went up north to where the Yellowknives used to live and talked to the people—I did readings from *A Discovery of Strangers*—some of the young people started saying, "You know, there might be some stories in such and such a place," and I wanted them to follow up, but they never got back in touch with me. But there may be some stories about her existing still. She died in May of 1840, so you only need about, say, three really old people passing the story on, and a really old person now might still know her, some think. If I had known the story like that, for example, maybe my Greenstockings would have been quite a different person. So I never pretend that I am the only person that can write the story. Write it again, tell it again.

HW *Big Bear* and *The Scorched-Wood People*—and, to some degree, *My Lovely Enemy* also—stress the way in which the history of the West is the history of the triumph of the written word, through the coercion and manipulation of the treaties, for instance, but also through the hegemony of written accounts of the past, which have been accorded almost absolute authority over the tribal memory of the oral cultures of Aboriginal peoples. In so much of your writing you're talking about the power of the word. What do you see as the power of the word—both oral and written—and what role has it played in the history of the Northwest?

RW Well, the written word, according to theorists now, is the result of farming. People started writing, first in Babylonia, just to keep records of their grain. So writing is in a kind of strange way the result of farming. That's one thing. The second thing is that I participate in this world in an interesting way, because my first language was Low German, which was not written. It was strictly a spoken language within the community of Russian Mennonites, and it developed out of the language that they brought with them when they left Prussia. So I come by an oral language genuinely, and it's completely different from the English. Then I went to school and I started to read and write, so I've got the benefits, in a sense, of both of these worlds. And it's quite clear that the written language triumphs, and it has triumphed in North America. In a sense, a symbol of that is the treaty, which has to be translated orally for the chiefs to understand it, and they touch the feather. They don't even make their X, you know; they just touch the feather. I got that wrong in *Big Bear*. They just touch the feather, and the white man makes the X. My historical fiction is full of all kinds of little mistakes like that. I only discovered that after *Big Bear* came out. So in an odd kind of way I understand that oral world, because I never spoke anything else except that language to my parents all their lives. Yet at the same time I live in the world of the written word, so I understand the enormous power of that. The thing that taught me that the quickest and the sharpest was the publication of my first novel, which created such a powerful reaction among some people in the Mennonite church that if I had ever doubted the power of the written word I couldn't have doubted it after that [*laughs*]. So in a kind of retrograde way I experienced the power of the oral and the written word from the very time I was born, and I grew up in both of those traditions.

HW In an interview with Eli Mandel many years ago now, you observed that, "unless they are very carefully handled, facts are the invariable tyrants of story. They are as inhibiting as fences and railroad, whereas the storyteller would prefer, like Big Bear, 'to walk where his feet can walk,'" which is a wonderful image, especially thinking about these issues. Has your experience writing historical fiction over the twenty years since then changed your opinion at all?

RW Actually, I think now that I would say that facts are the jumping-off places for story. They inhibit you in the sense that I was talking about before. I mean, I can't make up Big Bear's life story because there are certain things we know about him and that's it. One of the arguments that I got into with Bill Kinsella was that he was using the names of actual people, and then just making up funny stories about them. I believe that is immoral, so in that sense, you are inhibited by facts. But you are held in by many things. I mean, you're held in by the limits of your imagination. There are certain things you try to imagine that you can't. Sometimes you get this kind of inchoate feeling that there's something beyond this that you're not getting at. You can't even put words on it, you know. It's just a sense that you have, and if you're lucky, and maybe if you don't think about it for a while, someday it will resolve itself. I haven't got the kind of imagination, say, Douglas Glover has, thinking about what he does with his novel *Elle*. Maybe I don't even want to have it; I don't know. So you're hemmed in by these things. But I think facts can give you the jumping-off places. So I would probably argue in the opposite direction to what I said in that interview [*laughs*].

HW A good example to put it to the test would be the way that in *The Scorched-Wood People* you give Gabriel Dumont a much greater role in the Red River Rebellion than seems to have been the case historically. That might be an example of where facts become inhibiting to the direction in which you want to take the story.

RW George Woodcock, I think, took me to task about that, but in fact there is a little bit of evidence that Gabriel might have been at Fort Garry at that time. He could have been there. Probably not, but he could have been, and that's enough [*laughs*].

HW A lot of contemporary writing about history stresses the reconstruction of history as a textual experience. In some models of history you get the sense that we never get beyond a kind of textual hall of mirrors and that we have to be aware that what we are dealing with are not scraps of the actual past but textual reflections or traces of it. The experience of history, in other words, is not only indirect but primarily discursive. What impact does it have, though, when, aside from all the secondary reading and all the archival research that you've done for your books, you actually have the opportunity, as you have had, to talk to people involved in the history you write about? For instance, you met Duncan MacLean, who was one of the hostages taken by Big Bear's band, and Lazarus Sittichinli, one of the Dene men who was involved in the hunt for the man called Albert Johnson. What difference does that make?

RW I was very fortunate to meet these very old men, both of them in their nineties, who had actually literally taken part in these historical events that I tried to tell stories about. I was particularly lucky with Duncan MacLean, because he died very shortly after that, although Duncan MacLean in factual terms didn't help me at all. His memory was so far gone it wasn't really

FIGURE 4. Gabriel Dumont. Glenbow Museum PA-2218-1.

helpful, especially about that event. But there's just something about physically seeing a person who you know, some time about ninety years ago, experienced this.

Meeting Lazarus Sittichinli was actually a more profoundly moving experience, because he told me something that I didn't know about that story, that nobody ever told me before and that nobody had ever recorded anywhere before, so far as I know. Lazarus told me that story, which he must have told a lot of people, and actually I revised the ending of *The Mad Trapper* in the light of what he told me. He told me about that strange moment on the Eagle River, after they had shot Johnson and approached the body in the snow. He was one of the men who came from a different direction, approaching the body, waiting—because if he leaps up they're all going to shoot him again—and of course he's dead. The man is lying face down in the snow, and then Lazarus stoops down and he picks him up out of the snow and turns him face up, and nobody's ever seen this man before. Lazarus was the man who bent down and picked him up, and he says his body didn't weigh more than a big dog. This old man ... you know, it was a marvelous moment. He died a year or so afterwards, too. But he told me something that I'd never heard before, and then I was sorry that I didn't meet him before, because that really would have permeated the whole text in a kind of a way it didn't before. I was sorry in one sense, but this is one of the wonders that happen when you try to tell stories about actual events. The other person that was important in terms of *The Mad Trapper* was the airplane mechanic who flew up with Wop May, Jack Bowen, a very old man living in St. Albert, Alberta, when I talked to him. He told me some things too.

Those are wonderful moments, and it gives you this sense that you didn't just make it up out of your own head, but you are truly telling a human story, that human beings have experienced even before you told it, which gives it a marvelous dimension. It's rooted in a human experience. That's why place is so important. Story is rooted in place. Things happen in places. They don't happen just generally anywhere. They happen here in this office. They happen by the river bank. They happen on the ice of the Eagle River. They happen in the Great Sand Hills. And I go there and look at these places. So even more important in some sense than history, or at least as much as history, is place, the place where it happens, because human beings are not birds. We don't fly around. We walk on the earth and have places where we live. We have to have places on earth, and they remain after we are gone. Like stories.

Confessions of a Historical Geographer
Jane Urquhart

Rooted in rural southern Ontario, but reaching out to embrace the landscapes of west Ireland, France, and Yorkshire, Jane Urquhart's work explores themes of memory, cultural and familial heritage, and artistic and romantic obsession. Urquhart was born in 1949 in Little Long Lac in northern Ontario and spent the latter part of her childhood and adolescence in Toronto. She has been writer-in-residence at several Canadian universities, including the University of Ottawa, Memorial University, and the University of Toronto. Her first novel, *The Whirlpool* (1989), earned her the Prix du Meilleur Livre Étranger in France in 1992. She followed this with *Changing Heaven* (1990) and *Away* (1993), a novel about Irish immigrants coming to Upper Canada in the mid-nineteenth century, which was nominated for the IMPAC Dublin Literary Award and won the Ontario government's Trillium Prize. *The Underpainter* (1997), a retrospective of the life of repressed artist Austin Fraser, won the Governor General's Award for fiction. *The Stone Carvers* (2001), a novel about the building of the war memorial at Vimy Ridge, earned her a Giller Prize nomination and another Governor General's Award nomination. Her most recent novel is *A Map of Glass* (2005). Urquhart has also published three volumes of poetry and a collection of short fiction, *Storm Glass* (1987). I talked with Jane Urquhart in Stratford in July of 2002.

HW Your fiction seems to exhibit a preoccupation with the past. How important is the past to your fiction?

JU The past is important to my life and therefore, I suppose, important to my fiction. I come from a multi-generational family that pays a lot of attention to generations that have preceded them. Long stories are told concerning people who have been dead for years, mementos are kept. There's a story associated with many of the things in my mother's house. My mother now is ninety-one years old, and you can point to an object and she can tell you who it belonged to and she can tell you a story about it. For instance, she still has her aunt's trousseau in the attic—embroidered pillow-slips and table cloths and the like. This is because my mother's grandmother took the sleigh, one very cold January night, to a farm where her very young and newly married daughter was dying of pneumonia and also giving birth. She brought back the daughter (my mother's aunt), who was dead, brought home the baby, brought home the trousseau trunk, and left her daughter's husband alone on his farm.

I think there are probably interesting stories associated with the past in anyone's family, and many interesting stories associated with the present as well. But the past seems to me to be more multidimensional, partly because it involves a narrator and a narrative, whereas the present is something you're experiencing. The past is a story being told, and as such it takes on a different tone and a different shade.

HW I'm thinking about the fact that all your novels are set in the past. Is that something you've ever reflected on?

JU Well, not really. My first novel, *The Whirlpool*, was not something I consciously believed was a novel. I had been writing poetry, and I had been writing a little bit of short fiction, very short stories in sequence that had to do with my husband's family's past. I convinced myself that I wasn't writing a novel, because it left me quite free to explore my husband's family's past without having to engage in the sort of self-censorship that comes into play when one is writing for publication. I thought, "Oh well, this doesn't matter because no one will publish it, and so I can just do whatever I want." Part of what led me into his past was the discovery of a little book that his grandmother kept, a book in which the various bodies that were taken out of the Niagara River were described, and the book itself, a little notebook, was such a powerful object, I knew I had to write something about it. That was when I began to do research about Niagara Falls and its history.

HW That's where the character of Maud, the owner of the funeral home in *The Whirlpool*, emerges.

JU Yes. The interesting thing was that I had never known Tony's grandmother on whom the character of Maud is based. She was dead before I met Tony, and I had only heard stories about her. She was very important to him, and she fascinated me, because she ran a funeral business, a very complicated and difficult business, by herself, after her husband's death. So the character of Maud is very definitely based on what I heard, and the rest, as always, I imagined.

HW So you write about the past because the past is where the interesting stories are.

JU You know, I wonder whether that's true. I don't think that the past is necessarily where all the interesting stories are; I think there are plenty of interesting stories in the present. But I remember once Alice Munro said something to me that I found intriguing: she said we write about the past because we can see it whole. We may not see it accurately, but we know what transpired, how events unfolded, whereas in the present you're in the middle of it, you're experiencing it; there's no sense of completion, there's no sense of—

HW Distance.

JU Yes.

HW The classical historical novel tends to revolve around a publicly shared past—pivotal events or important historical figures—but your own fiction tends to go a little farther afield. For instance, in *The Whirlpool* you address the war of 1812; *Away* reaches a climax with the assassination of Thomas D'Arcy McGee; and your last two novels, *The Underpainter* and *The Stone Carvers*, are preoccupied to a great degree with Canadians' role in World War I. Despite all that, you seem less concerned with revisiting these events in fiction than in marking the terrain around them.

JU I think that's very true. I think that the large events provide me with a kind of anchor. I might float away altogether were it not for that anchor, which is not to say that I'm not interested in the historical events in their own right, because of course I am. It's fascinating to look back on what happens when I write a novel, because I often believe at the outset that I am writing about a pivotal historical character. For instance, *Away* was really meant to be a book about D'Arcy McGee, and in the final analysis we only see him once for a few fleeting moments just before his death. I had completed a large amount of research about D'Arcy McGee, just massive amounts of stuff. I honestly believed when I entered that book that he would be a major figure. That was also true in *The Underpainter* of Rockwell Kent, the American artist, who lived for a time in Newfoundland. I started that book with Rockwell Kent in mind as the central figure, after I had seen his house in Brigus in 1992 when I was writer-in-residence in Newfoundland, and yet, he became peripheral as well. It's almost as if I need a historic figure to act as a hook to draw me into the texture of the time, and then gradually the person in question will withdraw to the outskirts of the story.

HW Any sense of why that happens?

JU I think partly because they don't become fully rounded in my mind as a character, perhaps because they are so easy to research, and maybe that means that I'm given so many facts that the imagination is not as free as it might be with a non-historical character to flesh out the details of the personality. I'm really not sure. There was one character in *The Whirlpool* who was based very loosely on the Confederation poet Archibald Lampman, again someone about whom I did a lot of research and a lot of reading, and although he remains a central figure in the book he became transformed to such an extent that I knew I couldn't use the name Archibald Lampman any more. He had become someone else. Also, I've never been a public figure, I've never been a historical figure myself, and it's important to be able to imagine within yourself the various characters that you're writing about—especially main characters.

HW Obviously you do a lot of research for your fiction, and it plays a substantial part in the germination of your novels; I think that's particularly the case with *The Stone Carvers*. I wonder if you could talk in general about that process of research. How is it different from the kind of research that historians do?

JU Well, obviously I can't comment about the kind of research that historians do, because I'm not a historian, but I think it's different in that the writer of fiction doesn't have to be utterly accurate. If he or she can get away with extrapolation or exaggeration, then he or she can do almost anything with the facts. But you have to be able to intuit when to use facts and when to rely on imagination, because you don't want to push your reader too far. I'm the kind of person who doesn't take notes when I'm doing research. I just pour it into myself, and then try to work with what stays, what surfaces. I usually go back and fact-check later—an obvious necessity for a book like *The Stone Carvers* and, to a certain extent, *Away*. But the facts are points of embarkation for me rather than a final destination, and I suppose that for a historian the facts have to be the destination and not the road taken. I have also discovered that once I've entered the research it seems to come to me as much as I go to it. Things seem to fall into my path, and it almost makes me think that hidden forces are at work.

HW There are moments of fortuitous discovery.

JU Exactly, exactly. Now, of course, unconsciously you're looking for these discoveries, and so no wonder they fall into your path, but it really is marvelous what will come your way once you start to enter a particular territory and pay close, close attention to it.

HW Can you think of a good example?

JU I was thinking in particular of something that happened to me that was related to research. I had to choose a spot for the family to settle in *Away*, and I chose a location on the Fifth Concession in Elzivir Township along the Black River near Queensborough, Madoc, the Moira River, and Lake Moira. I was fairly specific in my description of the place, though I believed that the landscape I was describing was a product of my imagination, because in our family we know the area where our Irish ancestors settled, but we don't know the exact spot. After the book was published, I met a woman at Harbourfront, who said to me, "How did you know where my family settled? Why were you writing about my family?" Her name was Lynn, not Quinn, and it turned out that the Lynns had married into the Quinn family in the mid-nineteenth century. So we were related. Her family had settled at the spot I had described. Also, a cousin of mine appeared a few years ago with a packet of letters that she had discovered at a garage sale. At the time I was working on *The Underpainter* and trying to develop the character of a nurse in the First World War. The packet of letters my cousin had discovered was from such a nurse to a young man in Cobourg, Ontario. It was as if the character had walked up to me, rather than the other way around.

HW And said, "Let me in."

JU Yes, "Let me in and tell my story."

HW That's wonderful—not to mention convenient.

In *Changing Heaven*, the main character, Ann, says of losing her connection to the countryside, "In Canada much of the past has been thrown away. No one cares. No one records it. It was very hard for me, losing the past like that." Also, David MacDougal in *The Whirlpool* says, "This country buries its history so fast people with memories are considered insane." Are they speaking for you there?

JU A little bit, I guess. They're speaking for themselves, of course, but I was brought up in a country where Canadian history was not taught, or at least it wasn't taught to me. We learned a little bit about the explorers, but really even that was from the point of view of the Mother Country—a description, in other words, of how Britain seized and maintained its North American property. Our own past, as Canadians, was not taken into any kind of serious consideration. In the same way that our literature wasn't being studied when I was in school, our history wasn't being studied. We were very much a colony when I was in public school, and so the past as I knew it survived in a physical sort of way. It existed in barns and rail fences and Ontario Gothic farm houses, old wood stoves, and various other phenomena, all of which I'd had complete access to on my uncles' farms, and at my grandmother's house in the village of Castleton. I have seen much of that disappear. Well, it hasn't completely disappeared, of course, but I have seen it disappearing from various places in Ontario. I remember Matt Cohen saying once that rural Ontario exists only in our imagination; it isn't really there at all. You can actually drive from Toronto to Stratford without seeing any more than one or two startling examples of nineteenth-century architecture. My childhood connection to history manifested itself in the architecture I knew, fence and concession lines I became familiar with, and the stories that my family liked to tell about the past.

HW So it was a very personal education, as opposed to a public one.

JU Exactly. There was no public education to speak of. When we studied the First World War, the Second World War, we studied it from the point of view of the British Empire, not from the point of view of what happened to Canada.

HW Now, you're interested in the past, and you're obviously somebody who's interested in "thinking Canadian," to use David McDougal's phrase. So, given all that, I'm intrigued that a character like David in *The Whirlpool*, who is a nationalist historian preoccupied with the war of 1812, is such a basket case. He has a kinky Laura Secord fetish, he obsesses over the size of General Brock's hat, and is so paranoid about the Americans that when his wife disappears he thinks that she might have been abducted by some jealous American historian. What's up with him?

JU Well, I had a great deal of fun with that character. I'm fascinated by characters who are eccentric and obsessed. I have a tendency to be obsessed myself, so I suppose I relate to them to a certain extent, but I've seen men—especially scholars of various types—become so completely fixated on their narrow little patch of turf. David MacDougal was an exaggerated example of that type, and I had a lot of fun with him. I became quite fond of him eventually, but he was really quite an odd case. I do believe in "thinking Canadian"—by that I mean I'm proud of my country and I feel privileged to live here, very grateful that I do—but I don't think that it's as easy as David McDougal thought it was, to pin down exactly what Canadian is. I don't think it's necessarily the fact of winning the War of 1812 or not winning it, or winning the Battle of Lundy's Lane. I don't think you can focus on one aspect of the past and mythologize it to that extent. The other thing of course that amused and entertained me (and put me off, I must say) is that he was a military historian. But it's true of history generally that it is war-dominated, military; it's quite frightening in a way to think that one has to learn about the past battle by battle.

HW I just finished reading Pierre Berton's *Vimy*, and his relishing of gory details sometimes I find a bit bizarre.

JU Perhaps the business of who won what is a masculine approach (and when I say masculine I mean the masculine side of the human personality—the animus-driven side). I would say that there are two things that seem to drive the official telling of history: one of them is territory and the other one is war, and they're usually connected.

HW David is also obsessed with defending a Canadian interpretation of the War of 1812, that not only was it a defeat for the Americans but it represented a kind of nationalist coming of age, a moment of almost tribal identification. How ironic were you being?

JU Totally [*laughs*]. I've run into people who will quote patriotically passages of dialogue from David McDougal, and I always think, "Oh my God, don't take that seriously!" No, I was being very ironic with him. You mentioned the kind of history that is presented to us by someone like Pierre Berton, and I'm very grateful to him for his research and for the time he spent and for all of the work that he's done; in fact, I think I've acknowledged him in a couple of my books. But there's more to history than the battles. Also I'm made nervous by this business of Canada having to have a moment of definition, and it seems that it's either when we won the Battle of Lundy's Lane or it's the Battle of Vimy Ridge—

HW Or Confederation, for that matter. It's interesting that your novels are picking up on those distinct moments.

JU But those moments do make me very, very nervous, because I don't think nationhood can be that easily defined. Those moments are usually tragedies of one kind or another; Confederation I hope wasn't a tragedy (I'm starting to wonder now), but certainly huge battles are a series of tragedies. One of the things I discovered through my characters, by writing, in the oblique way that I did, about the battle of Vimy Ridge, was that the participants often had no idea what was going on. They didn't know that they were participating in a great victory that would, supposedly, define Canada; in fact they didn't even know who won until a few days later. The battle itself would have seemed like utter chaos.

HW I found it really intriguing that at the end of *Vimy*, after again and again framing it as a very defining moment for Canadian identity, Berton asks the question "Was it worth it?" and says no. I was really taken aback.

JU Well, I don't think it was worth it. The horror of that war was not worth it.

HW No, but I certainly had been led to think that he might say, in one way or another, that it was worth it.

JU Yes, I do remember that Berton stated that at the end of the end of the book. No, it wasn't worth it, and I don't believe it defined us in any particular way.

HW I would be tempted to say that not so much the battle but the war defined us by scything away a huge part of a generation.

JU Yes, that's right. It was a terrible tragedy, massive. The whole country must have been in mourning by the time it was over, and at a time when nobody talked about sorrow, so it would have been a terrible, silent mourning. No, the whole First World War wasn't worth it. It wasn't worth it at all.

HW You've mentioned elsewhere that your ancestors are famine Irish and came to "the country north of Belleville" in the mid-1800s. To what degree is the history of the O'Malley family in *Away* based on the experience of your ancestors?

JU Well, very superficially, in the sense that my ancestors, as far as I know, came into Port Hope and then went northeast, to the country north of Belleville. They came from Northern Ireland; we know that. The name was Quinn, so we have to assume they were Catholic. But we also know that the entire family survived the voyage, and that was quite unusual, so maybe they weren't Catholic; maybe they'd "gone Proddy," as they say in Ireland, and therefore had a little money. A lot of the book was very loosely based on my family, but I think the accurate aspect of the narrative would be what I perceive to be—again I use the word *obsession*—an ongoing obsession on the part of my family with Irish

politics. It amazed me that all these years later, my uncles could still be as fero-
ciously involved—and by that I mean just interested, engaged—with the politics of Ireland as they were. These were people who'd never laid eyes on the
island in question. So part of what drew me into that novel was trying to
understand that kind of mindset, and then trying to understand it in terms of
how it can breed violence. Though certainly my uncles were very far away
from any official participation in the political situations in Ireland, there are
other North Americans who aren't. There are a lot of people in the States, for
instance, who are still actively involved in the politics of that country despite
the fact that their families have not lived in Ireland—

HW For generations and generations. You tie that obsession, and that cultural
and political retention through the generations, to immigration and to the
adaptation to a new land. In that sense, the novel really seems to underline the
importance of immigration in Canadian history as a whole.

JU Yes, another hook that drew me into that novel was the fact that increasingly many of my close friends were people who were first-generation immigrants, and I was fascinated by their experiences, and for the first time began
to wonder what it was like for my family when they were first-generation
immigrants. Also, I was interested, to a certain extent, in what happens when
certain political issues are brought to another geography, the tribal rivalries
and, in some cases, wars that are brought into another geography. I was also
very disturbed by hearing (fortunately from nobody I'm close to) opinions
stated about new Canadians—"Oh, yes, well they bring all their troubles with
them and then we have to deal with them"—and I realized that of course this
has been going on forever.

HW This has always been a part of Canadian immigration, yes.

JU It's always been a part of any immigration. Of course people are going to
bring their troubles, whatever they may be, with them when they migrate to
a different territory, because while it is possible to leave an actual, physical
geography behind, it is almost impossible to leave a mental space behind. It
would be asking too much of human character to do that. You would have to
be put through an amnesia clinic, if there is such a thing. So that was all part
of what was absorbing me at that time and led me into the research for *Away*.
I discovered that what I had intuited was absolutely true; there were ferocious
tribal wars taking place in nineteenth-century Canada that seemed to me to
have been all but forgotten. I'm thinking here about the conflict between the
Orangemen and the Irish Catholics in the nineteenth century. In fact, the

openly anti-Catholic Orange Lodge was in power in Ontario until the 1950s. You couldn't even run for public office, for example, unless you were a member of the Orange Lodge; you would not have been allowed into the club. So there it all was. Now, thank goodness, that has all dissipated in recent years, but up until about 1953 in Ontario we were, in some ways, dealing with the same issues as Northern Ireland faces right now.

HW It's still, in a lot of ways, such recent history and yet so remote at the same time.

JU Because we don't look back, we don't reflect, and we don't pay enough attention. Had we paid attention we would have known that, whatever the problems were, whatever the problems are now, they're actually nothing compared to what they were in the nineteenth century. Really, quite astonishing things were going on: farmers with pitchforks stabbing young men to death who were participating in St. Patrick's Day parades, and barn burnings, and real racial hatred.

HW *Away* strikes me as a fascinating combination of history and mythology. How do you see the relation between those two, not just in the novel but in general terms? Are history and mythology different?

JU I think they purport to be different but are essentially dangerously alike. Someone has to choose what point of view official history is going to take. That leads to questions of power, and whose story is being told, and all of those things that have been under discussion in recent years. There's another way in which history and mythology are alike, and that is the tale-telling aspect of history; it's very similar to that of mythology. I have spent a lot of time in recent years in the southwest of Ireland, and really it's a wonderful place to be because, in a more benign way (though even in this benign way it can lead to trouble, I should add as a corollary), history and mythology are just completely interwoven. For instance, the bay that's just down from my house is supposed to be the bay where Brith, Noah's youngest daughter, disembarked with eighty other women and three men. It is said, by the way, that all three men died of an excess of women. I don't know whether or not the people of the region believe this story in the literal sense, but this is one of the ways the people of the Iveragh Peninsula explain how their ancestors arrived in Ireland thousands of years ago. This is clearly mythological, not just because of the unlikeliness of the tale, but because we have no way of proving whether or not it's true, even though we strongly suspect that it isn't. And yet if you pick up a history of Ireland, you'll find that story in it. All the place names have stories of that nature associated with them. You go over to Ballagh Oisin Pass and, if you are with an Irishman, he will tell you that Oisin, when he came back from Tir nan Og, went to the top of this mountain to look for his hunting companions. Because he'd been gone for three thousand years, however, he encountered St. Patrick instead, who had just arrived, because it was, by now, the sixth century. They had a great argument about Christianity in the face of the "old ways." The early Irish monks, when they were making their manuscripts, recorded the original mythology along with the so-called factual events.

HW What about in Canada? Do you think that there's mythologizing in what Canadian historians do—somebody like Berton, for instance?

JU Yes, I do, I do. I think that in Canada there's a great hunger for mythology, and one of the things that sometimes worries me about my own popularity is that it may have something to do with this hunger. I think that Canadians may want and need mythology in an exaggerated way simply because they haven't had it, and I would feel very nervous if I thought that anyone felt that I was some kind of an authority on Canadian history, because I'm not, at all. But I believe that we are as focused as we are on those watershed events, like the Battle of Vimy Ridge, like Confederation, because there isn't much else.

HW Your portrait of D'Arcy McGee in *Away* is fairly distant and indirect. We see him through the eyes of other characters such as Brian O'Malley and Eileen, and the Shaunessey brothers, characters who for the most part are hostile to his conciliatory politics in the run-up to Confederation. We find out that Aidan Lanighan has been working as McGee's spy, but we don't really get a sense of what he thinks of McGee until the very end. Why the distance, why is he such a refracted character?

JU I expected that he was going to be the central character in the book, but somehow he didn't come into focus for me, partly because I gave myself too many facts, and therefore I didn't have enough leeway for fiction. It would have been a case of his character being in control of me rather than the other way around, because of the constraints of the factual situation. However, I did develop a few theories. One was that he was, like many politicians, power-hungry enough that he really did turn coat, in a sense; he really did turn away from what had been his life's focus, which was to bring freedom and independence and equality to Ireland, and he did this simply so that he would have a seat at the Confederation table. I also believe that he was used by our noble first prime minister, Sir John A., to get the Irish vote, and then pretty

FIGURE 5. Thomas D'Arcy McGee. Library and Archives Canada c-016749.

much dismissed afterwards. He wasn't appointed to the first cabinet, which is kind of shocking under the circumstances.

HW There was a lot of demographic jockeying about who was going to be in and what interests they represented, and so on.

JU Exactly, exactly, and so I think that he would have been a very bitter man by the end of it all, because I'm sure that jockeying couldn't have escaped his attention. As a matter of fact, I seem to remember that he had been on record as saying he was bitterly disappointed by not being included in the first cabinet.

HW Macdonald I think had promised that he would be—

JU And reneged on the promise. Of course it's not surprising, because again we have these two guys, the member of the Orange Lodge and the Irish Catholic, side by side—it would seem likely that, in the end, one of them would betray the other. I've always wanted to write a play about that wild winter campaign tour they took, both of them drunk as skunks, going from backwoods town hall to backwoods town hall under the same buffalo rug, with several cases of Scotch in the back of the sleigh. And they say Canadian history is boring! I guess in the final analysis I didn't like McGee as much as I might have, though I still admired his skill as an orator. I think the speech I quoted in *Away* is one of the great speeches. Its sentiment would still be relevant today. He was interested in the various aspects of Canada. He felt that education was important, that the arts were important. He was interested in a multicultural country, where all the various groups were given equal rights. I thought it was fascinating that he was presenting multicultural issues in 1868.

HW But it all comes across as fairly muted in the novel.

JU By the time I got to D'Arcy McGee, I was very involved with the other characters, particularly Eileen, and interested in the fact that her vision was becoming distorted, that she was starting to look at things through the lens of politics, and as a result she was misinterpreting what was happening around her. From the point of view of the novelist, that's more interesting than the facts that surround D'Arcy McGee. However, who knows who murdered him? That's another issue.

HW [*laughs*] We won't go there. We'll never come back. I'll ask you about the Sedgewick brothers instead. I was wondering whether they were modelled on anybody, because they're such great characters.

JU They are. They're modelled on Aubrey DeVere and his brother. Aubrey DeVere was a British landlord who took up the Catholic faith. And he was a poet, a very bad poet. There were a lot of bad poets in *Away*, actually; D'Arcy McGee was a terrible poet, Brian O'Malley was a bad poet, and Aubrey DeVere was another really bad poet. But his heart was in the right place. He sailed with his tenants when they immigrated to Canada, and then came back and presented to Parliament the terrible facts about conditions on the vessels later known as "coffin ships." He was a great sympathizer with the cause of Irish independence, as was his brother. The two of them "went Papist themselves and forsook the old cause and gave us our freedom, religion and laws." But knowing about the DeVeres was really just a way of approaching the mostly imaginary characters of the Sedgewicks. One of the amazing things about writing *Away* was that, when I began it, I knew little more than my uncles. I'd visited Ireland a couple of times, I'd gone to the North, I'd seen it physically, but I really didn't know its history or geography in the kind of depth that I now know it. I couldn't have written that book now. I know too much. Those particular landlords would probably not have existed in Northern Ireland. They might have existed in Southern Ireland. The worst landlords of course weren't in Ireland at all. They owned the land but they were absentee; they stayed in Britain.

HW An important part of *Away* is the quarrying of limestone that's going on, in the frame story, as Esther rehearses the history of her family. It seems to me that you're drawing an association between that kind of industrial activity and an erosion of history. Is that a fair theory?

JU Oh, absolutely. And of course that's one that's based in current fact, because the place where I spend my summers, which has been a very big part of my family and my family's history, is gradually being eaten up by a multinational cement company that has created a quarry probably bigger than the Grand Canyon by now. Every year when I go there another few farms and fields and apple orchards have disappeared into a gigantic hole in the ground, which is kind of astonishing, because the extracted limestone is being used to build cities, so it's not only, to my mind, a metaphor in terms of disappearing history; it's also a metaphor in terms of—

HW The urban eating the rural.

JU Yes. The change in focus of the majority of the population from the rural to the urban experience, which is precisely what happened in my own family. Only a couple of my uncles remained farmers; for instance, the youngest brother was able to go to university, become educated, become a professional. And, of course, in my generation, nobody has a farm.

HW Beginning with Timothy Findley's *The Wars*, there has been quite a bit of fiction published in the last few decades about World War I, including your last two novels, *The Underpainter* and *The Stone Carvers*. Any speculation on why that is?

JU I do believe *that* is a pivotal event, not in a good way necessarily, but certainly in a way that can't be argued. The world changed forever with the First World War. It really was the end of innocence, in the sense that we moved into mechanized warfare, we moved into mass destruction in ways that no one had ever imagined. When I look at the history of the Western world, I really think the true industrial revolution began then, in the sense that suddenly it was possible to use machines in this way, in this horrible mass killing. I think that's part of the reason why people focus on World War I to the extent that they do. Hiroshima to me is just an extension of the First World War. It isn't the moment when man suddenly decided that he was going to use a weapon of mass destruction; he was just using the best one he had. And by that time people, although they were not prepared for that scale of destruction, had seen quite a lot of mass violence around them in recent years. As a matter of fact it's kind of astonishing how little time there was between the First and Second World War. I'm sure five hundred years from now people will look back and see it all as one great continuum of carnage. So, yes, I see the First World War as a huge trauma, in a sense. Also, it was interesting to me again from the point of view of immigration; essentially it was a reverse migration, because the very people who had come over a couple of generations before, to escape, in many cases, wars of their own—whether it be some kind of political war, like the Irish famine, or a territorial war, like the Highland clearances, or whether it be an actual war, in the case of the people who lived in the northern parts of France or the southern parts of Germany—those very people were sending their children's children back into the European fray, on the same turf.

HW In some cases against their own families.

JU Oh, sure. There are lots of German names on the Vimy memorial.

HW Talking about *The Stone Carvers* you've said that World War I was the birth of modernism and that that might explain why it still haunts us.

JU Now, that's not my idea, really; I learned this as a result of reading a wonderful book, *Rites of Spring*, by Modris Eksteins. What he points out is that Stravinsky's *Rite of Spring* anticipated the First World War—that's when art started to fragment. And I believe it's true, I believe it's true. I don't think it was going to be possible to look at the world in the same way after the First World War (the Western world we're talking about again; you should always make that point, because there is more to the world than us). It changed collective perception, in other words.

HW What about George's comment in *The Underpainter*, to Austin Fraser, about there being only one world of art now, after the war, that is?

JU I believe, or at least George believed and I believed through him, that the First World War killed off artistic skill in some sense. People who were actively engaged in trades that had been in their families for thousands of years were killed, and somehow the line was broken, the chain of inheritance was broken. The father who would have taught the son how to apply the gold leaf to a painted ceiling was killed in the First World War. So that's really what George was referring to, because he was the kind of person who was dedicated to the decorative arts, essentially, which is a very ordinary way of putting it. It's interesting that, when we think decorative arts, we think, "Oh, that's a lesser form of activity." But it was hugely important in Europe—well, over here too, in the times leading up to the First World War and during the preceding thousand years. It affected landscape as well, in that I believe that war was the beginning of the end of the small farm.

HW In *The Underpainter* the war is described as a kind of vandalism, a wanton destruction of centuries of European civilization. Can you expand on that a little bit?

JU Yes. Obviously, first and foremost one has to think about the people and the animals, but after that comes the patrimony, in a sense (which is a word that I don't necessarily like to use, but that's the best I can come up with), and that is what one generation leaves for another generation; wonderful works of art for the next generation to enjoy, or fabulous public buildings that are works of art in themselves, or gorgeous cathedrals, powerful frescoes—just gone, along with the patina that time has given to them.

HW What role do nationalism and colonialism play in all that vandalism? I'm thinking of the scene in *The Underpainter* in which Augusta first meets Maggie at Étaples, in the fog. Maggie asks Augusta—as a form of sonic location, I guess—to sing "The Marseillaise" to help her navigate her way. They end up having this very critical exchange about national anthems, and Maggie says of England at the end of it, "Such a small place for so much trouble."

JU The vandalism doesn't always take place as a result of war, although usually it's preceded by some kind of war or territorial takeover. I think colonialism was a huge act of vandalism; there's just no question about it. When one learns about what this country was like before it was clear-cut *the first time*, one has to admit that the original timber industry was immensely destructive. And, interestingly, Britain began by clear-cutting Ireland. Ireland never looked the way we imagine Ireland looks. It was not originally a patchwork quilt of green fields. It was in fact known as Derry, and "derry" means "oak" in Irish, and it was an entirely forested—hardwood forested—island. The first thing that the British did when they got there was clear-cut it, because they had already clear-cut England. A moor is not a natural phenomenon; it's a reaction to clear-cutting. So all these marvelous moors that Heathcliff inhabited, that one thinks of as great open natural spaces, would have been forests at one point, before they were clear-cut. Colonialism is absolutely part of the vandalism. Whether you walk in and plant the flag down and then starve everybody to death and give them diseases to take over the territory, or whether you go in there and fight and kill and gain property that way, it is about territorial takeover—a takeover that is usually followed by a kind of rape of the landscape. That seems to be pretty much the way that things go.

HW How about the First World War as the start of the death throes of nationalism? The national allegiance that was a kind of innocence was really shattered in the First World War.

JU It was. I think it was, however, retrievable for the Second World War, which was a much more moral war, of course, but even so. I don't know if you've read Simon Schama's *Landscape and Memory*, but there's a wonderful section in that book describing how landscape was used to convince soldiers to fight. A poster depicting idealized, rolling English countryside, for instance, would suggest to soldiers that "this is what you're fighting for"—and what they were fighting for was some kind of bucolic, pastoral, farm-studded, healthy-looking, wonderful landscape that was supposed to be England, the "green and pleasant land." In fact, I believe that that particular image was used with colonial soldiers as well, which is amusing in a way, because they wouldn't know England, and also with the urban poor who were soldiers, and most of them were Londoners, Cockneys, who also had no real experience of the landscape of the English countryside. Yet somehow the image of that in the mind was what would spur them on.

HW I noticed that *The Stone Carvers* is dedicated to Sandra Gwyn, who wrote about Étaples as well, in her book *Tapestry of War*. Did her work on the war have any bearing on your own? Is there any connection there?

JU There are a couple of connections with Sandra. First of all, she was a friend. She became a friend after she read *The Whirlpool* and not only really liked it but also did her best to make sure that other people read it as well. She also generously provided a quote for the back of the book. I hadn't met her at that point, but I was delighted that she had provided the quote because I had read and loved her previous book about nineteenth-century Ottawa, *The Private Capital*. I think, looking back, what attracted me to Sandra's work was, again, the focus on the personal rather than the public. She always followed a couple of people through the labyrinth of historical events. This made the historical not only more accessible but also so much more moving. Sandra, of course, was a marvelously gifted writer with a sizable intellect. I have a tendency to want to daydream most of the time, so I greatly admired her ability to be both imaginative and scholarly at the same time. We took different routes in our methods of writing, but I really loved her work very much, and later, when I came to know her, I enjoyed her company and admired her as a person. Her death was a great loss.

HW Reading *The Underpainter* and *The Stone Carvers*, with the emphasis on the Great War, I'm beginning to think that the unofficial motto of your fiction is "Lest we forget." This also seems to be the obsession of Walter Allward, the architect of the Vimy memorial in *The Stone Carvers*. Any thoughts about that as a—well, "mission" sounds like a strong word—an important principle in your fiction?

JU The word "forget" is important to me, but I'm more interested in how people forget or why people forget, or for that matter why they remember or how they remember, than whether or not we should or shouldn't. Perhaps as an individual I may have opinions about that, but when I sit down to write a novel preconceived motive is not part of the experience. It's an exploration rather than any kind of mission, as you say.

HW I'm wondering how important it is to you personally.

JU Personally I would hope that we wouldn't forget, and that applies not just to the wars but to many things. But, on the other hand, I would hate to see us spend all our time trying to remember and not paying attention to the way that things are now. I would like to see a balance.

HW I find Allward to be a fairly ambivalent character in *The Stone Carvers*. In some ways, he's portrayed very sympathetically, especially through his approval of Klara Becker's carving her lover Eamon's face and name in the monument. He comes across as very avuncular, in a way. Yet elsewhere, the whole complicated and hierarchical production of the building of the monument comes across as almost a repetition of the war, with Allward as the general.

JU [*simultaneously*] The general. I hadn't thought of that, but that's true.

HW Furthermore, here is this guy spending all kinds of government money, at the height of the Depression. Could you talk a little bit about those divisions in Allward's personality?

FIGURE 6.
Walter Seymour Allward. Library
and Archives Canada PA-103158.

JU Allward, again, was supposed to be the main character. I never learn anything from one novel to the next, so it's always the same surprise. He was my entry into that novel, because the monument had really, solidly, caught my attention while I was doing research for *The Underpainter*. I went to Étaples, and then of course after that I went to Vimy, and for the first time I agreed to go down into the tunnels. My husband had been down in the tunnels lots of times. I didn't like it down there at all because I was always terrified that we were never going to get out again. There are various levels of tunnels, and they branch off in various directions, but as tourists you're only taken down a particular loop, down into Grange Tunnel. I wanted to know what motivated this man to build such an extraordinary monument, because it really is quite a staggering work of art and the best war memorial in Europe; there's no question in my mind about that. It's a very powerful, powerful work of art. And then there is the size! I knew that, particularly in that war-torn landscape, the erection of the monument would have been a near impossibility. I was intrigued by the personality of the man who would want to try to do it.

HW Because he would have to have been one determined son of a bitch.

FIGURE 7. The War Memorial at Vimy Ridge. Reproduced with the permission of Veterans Affairs Canada, 2006.

JU *And he was*. Again, it was something I intuited in the beginning and later verified with research, at Queen's University Archive. Reading the official correspondence between him and the various levels of government was quite an experience; it was like reading a novel itself. It was very, very interesting research; really fabulous.

HW Plenty of intrigue, in other words.

JU Yes, because, as I read, the difficulty of erecting the monument became more and more clear. It was necessary for Allward to spend much more money than he was allotted, for instance, and the government couldn't make him stop, make him come home. It was very contentious, and there was even a suggestion that he might have had a breakdown at some point. There were letters suggesting that he take time off. What really happened at Vimy when that memorial was being built was unbelievable.

HW So he's a manifestation of your obsession with obsession.

JU Yes, he was really the final end of it. He was a greatly obsessed man, and the memorial stands there as a kind of tribute to his obsession, because it worked. I think in order to accomplish something like that you almost have to be obsessed.

HW His approval of Klara's deviation from his plans softens that egomaniacal side, and I'm wondering why that was important to you.

FIGURE 8.
The Spirit of Sacrifice, Vimy War Memorial.
Reproduced with the permission of Veterans
Affairs Canada, 2006.

JU It was important to me partly in the making of his character, because I don't believe that any human being is one way or another; that was part of it. But also I was playing with gender a bit at that point (obviously) and the interaction between masculine and feminine within the psyche of an artist and how that affects the making of the art. I think that likely it has something to do with intimacy and distance and public and private. He was making a very public memorial where everything was an allegory, and it seemed important to me that this one sculptural group—at least—include a portrait among the allegorical figures. In fact, looking at the actual monument, I began to feel that the dying young man in the sculptural group entitled *The Spirit of Sacrifice* might very well have been a portrait. But for the purposes of the novel, I wanted to make that part of the monument more intimate.

HW And you wanted to make him able to appreciate that particularity—

JU Able to accept that, and to let that into the building of that monument, because I don't think it would have worked without it.

HW The novel's other visionary, Father Gstir, like Allward, is obsessed with the construction of a monument, the hilltop church in Shoneval. That part of the novel is to a degree based on historical sources. Can you elaborate on that historical background?

JU I can. As matter of fact you could visit, while you're here in southwestern Ontario, a place called Formosa, home of the Formosa Spring Brewery. The church in question is in Formosa. I had thought, "I'll call it Shoneval. No one's going to know where it is; and then I can move the architecture around and add and subtract significant landmarks and no one will care." I got an e-mail the day after the book was reviewed in *The Globe and Mail* from the great-granddaughter of the man upon whom Joseph Becker was based—in other words, the man who carved the altars in the church in Formosa—even though I hadn't called it Formosa. So it was recognized immediately.

That part of the narrative came from a little historical pamphlet about Formosa, in which there was a translated letter from Father Gstir's predecessor to the Ludwig missions in Bavaria. I have a friend who's German, so I asked him about the date and the Ludwig missions and he told me that, indeed, as I had hoped, these missions would have been under the patronage of "Mad" Ludwig himself. I knew then how the narrative of that part of the book was likely to unfold. I felt I was off to the races! Once you think about those wonderfully impractical castles in Germany, and, again, a man completely driven to make impossible things, you can't help but see the connection with Allward. And it makes sense that Ludwig would have funded a church in what was then the middle of the wilderness in Canada. He probably loved the idea.

HW Especially if the appeals were framed in spectacular, fantastic detail.

JU Yes, well, all of that, I have to say, came directly from my imagination.

HW In all of your novels there is a very intimate association, an interplay, between history and the landscape. It's dramatically and dangerously evident in *The Stone Carvers*, with all the unexploded munitions in the terrain around the monument, but, beyond that, that interplay recurs in various ways throughout your work.

JU I've always been very drawn to landscape, and particularly landscape where some evidence of human activity is left behind. Pure wilderness really doesn't interest me that much, because there are no traces left by human beings. The agricultural landscape, where you can see evidence of the past, interests me more. I probably should have been a historical geographer. A historical geographer once told me that I should have been a historical geographer [*laughs*]. I didn't even know what a historical geographer was at that time, but I've since learned that essentially it's a person who pays attention to marks made by previous human activity on the landscape. I suppose in Canada a historical geographer would be someone who's paying attention to those cairn-like piles of stones in the middle of a field that were left there a hundred years ago by farmers, or pays attention to First Nations petroglyphs, things of that nature. I do believe that there's a kind of presence in landscape, perhaps because of the Irish influence in my background as well as in my present life. There is a little road near where I stay in Ireland. It is only two miles long, and yet there are ten to twenty, or maybe even twenty-five, places on the road, places that are named though there is no architecture near them, and that I find fascinating. That seems to echo the way I feel about landscape. For instance, there's a place called Coshcummeragh, which means beside the Cummeragh, the little river that runs through the valley. There is another place called Cappanagrown, which means the highest point of land in the area, and there's no sign of architecture there either [*laughs*]. It's almost as if every boulder has a particular and very ancient name, and often there's an associated story—

HW Reflecting the human significance of the landscape.

JU I'm sure that "beside the Cummeragh" was important for catching trout or "the highest point of land" was important in order to be able to see what was coming or to take a look and see where your flocks were, or whatever. Landscape I think is terribly important.

HW It's a kind of embedded, physicalized memory. Would that be a good description?

JU Yes, exactly. That would be a good description. And I think that it's hard to let it go. I believe that it's one of the things that people mourn almost as much as they mourn the loss of a person who's close to them. They may even mourn for a longer time. I know that people who have lost their towns or their villages are just heartbroken, because it will not be possible to introduce this "known" world to their children or their children's children; again, the chain of inheritance is broken. A lot of immigrants will say that they don't really think they belong to a place until they've buried someone there. By the same token, of course, it's tremendously painful to leave behind a place where all kinds of people, whether they be your ancestors or contemporaries to whom you are close, are buried.

HW I was just thinking about how people who have passed away most often live on in others, whether their children or other relatives, and it's much harder to say that about landscape.

JU Unless that landscape is in Ireland, which is one of the world's sacred homelands. Unfortunately, what happens is that those sacred homelands become imaginary, eventually, fantasized. They become idealized, locked in an idea of the past. I think of Israel on the one hand and Ireland on the other. They are both sacred homelands, but they're also almost imaginary homelands. They're a state of mind almost. That was part of what I was trying to explore in *Away*.

HW Well, I think you *are* a historical geographer, but you get to be a novelist at the same time. It's probably a pretty good deal [*laughs*].

JU Yes, it's not bad!

HW While I'm somewhat uncomfortable with the term "regionalism," it seems to me that your fiction, and its preoccupation with history, has a fairly defined geographical hub to it, so that it's still very tempting to see it as regional. Do you have any thoughts about that?

JU The truth is that my fiction will likely continue to be Ontario-based because Ontario is the landscape that I know best, the landscape that provides me with some sense of reality. Writing is, for me, a very filmic experience; I need to be able to see the world my characters are moving through, and my visual memory bank is stocked with images of rural Ontario. So in that sense you could, I suppose, call it regional.

HW One might say that the entry into history is somehow always local, or at least often local.

JU It is with me, yes. I think that's very true. For instance, I would be unlikely to have connected to the extent that I did with the landscape in most of my narratives if I hadn't lived in rural Ontario for a long period of time. I wouldn't have known the tributary system of, say, the Nith River if I hadn't done a lot of driving over the concession roads of Wellesley Township in Waterloo County. The physical knowledge of Northumberland County is generational; it was handed down to me and has always been part of my experience, but it took a long time for me to understand how interested I had become in the atmosphere of southwestern Ontario. I had to live here for over a decade.

HW A recurrent theme of your fiction seems to be the challenges of women fighting for a place in history. There's Eileen's desire to fight alongside Aidan in the republican cause in *Away*, there's the inventory of Augusta Moffatt's limited options in *The Underpainter*—she could be wife, schoolteacher, nurse— and you focus on Augusta and Maggie's experiences in the war more than George's. Finally, there's Klara's disguising herself to journey to France to work as a sculptor on the memorial at Vimy in *The Stone Carvers*. Do you feel a need to redress a kind of gender imbalance in representations of the past, essentially to put women back into history?

JU Women have always had a history, of course, but I believe that they should be put into the official history. But I don't think that I'm the person to do it. I think that I am as intent as I am upon giving the female point of view because I am a woman; it's that simple. I'm fascinated by men as well, however, which may have something to do with the masculine side of my own personality.

HW In both *Away* and *The Stone Carvers*, there's an emphasis on history as an oral heritage. For instance you have, in *Away*, Esther as the equivalent of a Celtic bard retaining her family's history, and then in *The Stone Carvers* you have Klara explicitly retelling the story, essentially retailing it for the nuns. What's behind that concern with orality?

JU That brings us back to what we were talking about at the beginning, the fact that, in Canada, until recently, that was the way history has been passed from generation to generation, because we didn't have (and maybe this is a good thing) an official history, per se. But we did have our family histories, and those are told histories rather than written histories in most cases. Small stories with large implications. It brings to mind the poem "Epic" by the Irish poet Patrick Kavanagh. In it he describes a territorial dispute between two Irish farmers, and then hears Homer's ghost whispering in his ear, "I made the *Iliad* from such a local row."

An Afterlife Endlessly Revised
Wayne Johnston

Wayne Johnston was born in 1958 and grew up in Goulds, just outside St. John's, Newfoundland. He went to Catholic schools and had a peripatetic childhood, moving from neighbourhood to neighbourhood around St. John's. He received a BA from Memorial University and worked as a court reporter for the *St. John's Daily News* from 1979 to 1981. He then moved to Ottawa and embarked on his career as a writer, subsequently receiving an MA in creative writing from the University of New Brunswick. Since 1989 he has lived in Toronto. His first novel, *The Story of Bobby O'Malley* (1985), won the W.H. Smith/Books in Canada First Novel Award, and he followed that debut with *The Time of Their Lives* (1987), *The Divine Ryans* (1990), and *Human Amusements* (1994). Johnston's historical novel about Newfoundland premier Joey Smallwood, *The Colony of Unrequited Dreams* (1998), was shortlisted for the Giller Prize and won the Leacock Award for Humor. His memoir *Baltimore's Mansion* was published in 1999. His novel *The Navigator of New York* (2002) centres on the rivalry between polar explorers Frederick Cook and Robert Peary. His latest novel is *The Custodian of Paradise* (2006). I spoke by telephone to Wayne Johnston in Toronto in December of 2003.

HW Prior to publishing *The Colony of Unrequited Dreams*, you had written a series of mostly comic novels, *The Story of Bobby O'Malley*, *The Time of Their Lives*, *The Divine Ryans*, and *Human Amusements*, exploring the unique unhappiness of a series of families, to paraphrase Tolstoy. With the three books that you have published since then, starting with *Colony*, you have been consistently preoccupied with the past as well as the family. Did anything in particular trigger that shift?

WJ *Human Amusements* is where the shift really took place. That book is about a family, but it is also about the invention of television, and it's about a real-life historical figure named Philo Farnsworth, who invented television in America in the 1920s and hasn't really been given credit for it, except in America. That was really my first foray into historical fiction. I mean, that book is not about Farnsworth's life, in the sense of taking his point of view, but it is about people who write about him, who actually make up a TV program about him, which becomes a cult classic, and all kinds of mayhem ensues because of it. That was really the first point of that departure, I suppose. I had just moved to Toronto, and for various reasons I didn't really want to immediately set another book in Newfoundland. I forget how I discovered Farnsworth, but that is where it began. I also took another real-life program named *Romper Room*—

HW I remember it well.

WJ —and changed the name of it to *Rumpus Room*, so really I was starting to play around with history then. It was closer to contemporary history than the history I would eventually write about, but I think the ideas were starting then. I had also been asked to write a piece for a literary book about hockey called *The Original Six*. What I was asked to do was write a fictional account of the riots at the Montreal Forum in the 1950s, from the point of view of an imaginary character who was in contact with real characters like Rocket Richard and Clarence Campbell and people like that. That made me go further along the road and made me start thinking in those terms. I was surprised to find the variations that I rang, not so much on the historical events but on the context in which they occurred, quite intriguing, because I was doing this hockey thing as a favour, and thought it would be just kind of a nuisance actually, but I became quite interested in it. Out of *Human Amusements* and that piece the impulse to write a historical novel grew, but not a historical novel set a thousand years ago. I wanted to write about contemporary Newfoundland, and as soon as I made that decision I knew it had to be about Smallwood.

FIGURE 9. Joseph Smallwood. Library and Archives Canada PA-128080.

HW You didn't exactly ease yourself into things by picking to write about such a controversial and polarizing figure as Joey Smallwood. What would you say were your principal concerns when you came to that prospect of writing about Smallwood?

WJ Well, they were manifold. I wasn't living in Newfoundland; I was living in Toronto, so in the case of this particular book I had that in my favour, because certainly I've always found it difficult to write in Newfoundland—in fact, impossible—but to write *The Colony of Unrequited Dreams* there would have been completely impossible. So I didn't have to face the sense that I was carrying a secret, because I would certainly never have told anyone, if I was living in Newfoundland, that I was writing a book about Smallwood. I didn't tell anyone anyway, but it would have been a very censorious atmosphere to be writing the book in. So I dodged that particular problem. By the time I started writing the book, it was 1994, I think, and by then Smallwood had been dead only three years, and it wasn't so much that I anticipated that any kind of fictionalization would be misunderstood by people—that they wouldn't get the distinction between fiction and history—but that they would simply not want someone so recently deceased to be written about. Unfortunately, I wound up getting both problems. The distinction between fiction and non-fiction, the use of history in novels, was believed in many corners not to have been done before, which flabbergasted me. It seemed to be only in Canada that that notion was current. I mean elsewhere people knew that from before Shakespeare this kind of thing was done. They also had contemporary examples like E.L. Doctorow's *Ragtime*, or Don DeLillo's *Libra*, or any number of books that had used the basic premise of mixing fiction and history that I was using, and, by doing that, writing about history. It never occurred to me that some people would have the misconception that this was in any way new, and I think that that was the cause of most of the initial controversy—which hasn't all died down, but a lot of it has. I think a lot of the people who first had a problem with it hadn't really read the book and had only heard about the book, but some purist historians have problems with such books as well, which is fine with me as long as they understand that I am writing in a tried-and-true tradition and not doing what no one else had done before.

HW In his review of *The Colony of Unrequited Dreams* in *The Globe and Mail*, Rex Murphy criticized your Smallwood as being a "pasteboard substitute"—in other words, a pale imitation of the real thing. You responded in a subsequent piece that Murphy and others missed the point that the novel's goal "is not factual accuracy but narrative and fictional plausibility." That distinction essentially frees you to go beyond the historical Joey Smallwood's experiences in order to provide a more comprehensive vision of Newfoundland's history, to cover more ground. A good example of such expansion is, say, having your Smallwood witness the 1914 *SS Newfoundland* sealing disaster. When you make a decision to go beyond the historical record, as in that instance, what do you think you gain and what do you lose?

WJ That particular instance is in a way based on historical fact. There was a young journalist the same age as Smallwood is depicted as being in the book on the *SS Newfoundland*, and he went on to eventually write a book about the sealing hunt called *The Greatest Hunt in the World*. So, first, the idea that someone could do this was covered already because someone had; one of the objections to Smallwood being on that vessel was that no captain would have allowed a reporter on a sealing vessel—well, in fact it happened all the time. Second, the real Smallwood did go on another voyage, getting on board a ship in disguise.

HW This was on the hunt for bootleggers?

WJ Yes, on a Canadian destroyer that blew the smithereens out of an iceberg. So, since fictional plausibility, as I said in that article in *The Globe and Mail*, is what I am shooting for, I had no problem putting Smallwood on that ship. Now I only did that rarely; in fact, I don't think I ever did it again in the book. I did it in that case because basically the dramatic structure of the book called for something that large to intervene in Smallwood's life. The interesting thing is that Smallwood wrote about the sealing disaster and reacted to the sealing disaster exactly the way he does in the book. It was an important event in his life and it did affect his political thinking. It did incline him down the road towards socialism, and he often referred back to it as the first thing that made him begin down that road.

HW In some ways, then, it is sticking to the spirit of the past if not the letter.

WJ It is definitely sticking to the spirit of the past, so I had no trouble with it. Again, for the people who did, I always just point out examples of what other writers have done. If you read Don DeLillo's *Underworld*, in the first roughly eighty pages of that book, which are all about the fans watching a baseball game, there are at least half a dozen people who actually historically existed who are depicted in those scenes doing things that they never did, and I don't think anyone made a peep about it in the States. It is not because people there are more tolerant; it is because there is a tradition of this kind of writing, so that the premise is understood from the start. You know, Michael Ondaatje had the same problem with *The English Patient*. I think the problem comes when you write about recently deceased people or people who are still alive, but again the problem seems to be that, in as much as a controversy rages, it only seems to rage in Canada. In *Underworld*, J. Edgar Hoover dresses up in women's clothing, and I don't remember a letter to the editor of *The New York Times* from Hoover's family protesting those scenes.

HW The other side of the concern about adding things to the historical record is, of course, what aspects of a historical figure's life are left out, especially if those aspects are seen to be significant. I realize that readers' fixation on these absences, if we can call them that, is probably a source of some frustration for writers, but on the other hand in some ways it is an understandable impulse. It would have been pretty conspicuous if, say, confederation had played no part in *The Colony of Unrequited Dreams*. In this respect, what strikes me about the novel is that there is no reference to Joey Smallwood's intervention in the bitter 1959 loggers' strike, which seems to have been a defining moment in his career. Some, like Richard Gwyn, for instance, see it as Smallwood turning his back on his populist past very dramatically. Now I speculated that perhaps it was just too inflammatory a part of the historical Smallwood's story, but would it be fair to say simply that it just didn't have a part in the novel's narrative and allegorical design?

WJ I think that's basically it. When something is left out like that, I'm not making a claim, even within the novel, that it didn't happen. You can't be all-inclusive, and I would make an argument, and I definitely think it's true, that

Smallwood was long, long, long severed from his socialist and populist past by 1959. The IWA strike was definitely a very big mistake on his part. People died. It probably marked a point in union history, not necessarily confined to Smallwood, and became a kind of rallying cry for unions across the country. But my Smallwood is that corrupt by the time he is twenty-five, and I think the real Smallwood was too. There are other things that I leave out; I mean, I don't mention William Coaker in *The Colony of Unrequited Dreams*. Coaker founded the Fisherman's Protective Union.

HW He was Smallwood's idol in a lot of ways.

WJ He was Smallwood's idol and eventually absconded with most of the funds of the Fisherman's Protective Union and moved to the West Indies. I just saw no reason to put it in. It is exactly the same kind of decision novelists make when they're writing so-called pure fiction; something occurs to them that a character, in a certain context, must be doing during part of his day, and the writer says, "Well, it is not germane to the story, so I won't put it in." Say, the character is in good shape but you never show him going to the gym. Those are just fictional narrative choices.

HW I guess my inner historian is saying that the Smallwood in *The Colony of Unrequited Dreams* seems to be at his most conciliatory, at least as far as Fielding goes, because that is around the time that they bridge their differences, when the historical Smallwood is perhaps being his least conciliatory.

WJ Well, but one of the things that I keep pointing out to people is that the book is not about politics. In fact I think by 1959 he and Fielding have parted ways; Fielding has gone to New York by then. Confederation has come, Smallwood is premier, but how Smallwood acts with Fielding and how he acted as a politician, even in my book, are two different things. Fielding never let up on Smallwood in her columns. She always depicted him politically in the same light. So again, this Smallwood that doesn't seem to match the real Smallwood is not supposed to. That is not the point.

HW Like so many contemporary Canadian historical novels, *The Colony of Unrequited Dreams* emphasizes the deleterious effects of England's colonial control. However, there is perhaps a big difference in historical experience here between Newfoundland and the rest of the country—that Newfoundland can be seen as doubly colonized, or as having been passed from one colonial master to another, namely Canada. So a historical novel about Newfoundland does not necessarily sit easily in the same company as other Canadian historical novels. Do you have any thoughts on that?

WJ I think there is a nugget of truth in it. The main difference between New-foundland and the rest of Canada—and I don't know how many Newfound-landers of, say, the current generation, people between twenty and thirty, understand this—is that there was a time, a very recent time, when New-foundland was more or less a country; it lapsed from nationhood to you could say colony or province in the past fifty or so years. That definitely puts us in a different category. People say, "Well, look at Saskatchewan and look at the West," but no one lived there before about 1900 except for the indigenous peo-ple, and these were just territories, so that comparison doesn't hold. New-foundland had a four- or five-hundred-year history before these events took place. It had a very well-defined culture and character, and that is what I am writing about partly in *The Colony of Unrequited Dreams* (and in *Baltimore's Mansion* actually, from a different perspective), either the loss or perceived loss of those things or the fear that some time in the future those things will be lost.

I would actually say that Newfoundland was triply colonized, because I would add the Americans to the mix as well. Probably the most significant reason for confederation was the presence in Newfoundland during the ref-erendum of American servicemen, because they were much richer than Cana-dian servicemen and they showed Newfoundlanders what the outside world was like. For a while, joining the U.S. was a very serious possibility in the ref-erendum, and Smallwood and Harold Horwood and others, who were sim-ply better at using the media, managed to discredit it, but for a time it looked very likely that Newfoundland would join the U.S. Aside from that, in terms of colonization, Newfoundland, like the rest of Canada, is a colony of the U.S., a cultural, social, political, and geo-military colony of the U.S., so all those things are there as well. But yes, to get back to your original question, I think there is a unique context, historically speaking, for Newfoundland, and I think it all comes down to the perceived possession of, and after that the perceived loss of, nationhood.

HW Both *Colony* and *Baltimore's Mansion* have an extremely elegiac quality to them, with their references to an alternative "ghost history" of Newfound-land and so on. They're permeated by a sense of loss but also a sense that that loss was inevitable, that independence was a luxury that Newfoundland couldn't afford, as your Smallwood suggests. Would that be an accurate char-acterization of the tone of those books?

WJ They are definitely elegiac, kind of valetudinarian in some ways. "Ghost history"—and I do use the phrase "ghost history" not only in *The Colony of*

Unrequited Dreams but in other books that aren't historical novels—has always been a theme in my work, the question of what is versus what might have been, and how the road of what might have been does still go on, at least people are aware of it all the time, so they have this parallel existence between their reality and their hopes and their dreams. That is the way that people are in general, so that is a theme in all of my books, not just in the historical novels. But in Newfoundland there is—and in many ways I think it is a healthy thing—an infatuation and maybe, if an obsession could be healthy, an obsession with what might have been, not so much because things were lost, or not so much because nationhood was lost, as because of how it was lost. If the referendum had gone just a few votes the other way, there would have been a different result, but when I say "how it was lost"—and this has been hammered into me not only by my father but by a lot of other people—it would be a mistake to think that the people who voted for confederation did so gleefully. The people who voted against it, and my father makes this argument in *Baltimore's Mansion*, really were the only ones who knew what they were voting for, who had something emotional and heartfelt that they were voting for, and they knew that there would be a really high price to pay for it. The people who voted for confederation, many of them, I have no doubt (and I have spoken with them), did so very reluctantly and did so with an enormous burden of guilt on their shoulders. They believed in their own hearts that they were acting as traitors, that they were bargaining self-reliance and self-definition, for material, if not wealth, at least security. What made the decision especially difficult was that what they were going to be getting in return wasn't all that much. The social services that Canada would provide, although they wouldn't be that much, would be secure; they would always be there. My guess is that in 1948, something like seventy-five to eighty-five per cent of the population, from an emotional point of view, wanted an independent Newfoundland. If that is true, and again I think it is, there is an enormous legacy of guilt and regret that goes beyond just the usual crying in your beer over what might have been, because it is something you have done yourself. No one put a gun to our heads, and today when we have Royal Commissions about Newfoundland's place within confederation and when people go about wearing their "Free Newfoundland" T-shirts, as they do, and the pink, white, and green flies all over the city, as it does, there is something really interesting about it to me, other than the nostalgia of it. It seems to be fuelled more by guilt than by anything else, and that is not the case with places like Scotland, where independence was something that people fought for, that people died for. A shot was never fired literally or figuratively in defence of Newfoundland's nationhood. I think that is the legacy of guilt, and that's what distinguishes Newfoundland from the other parts of Canada.

HW Those books make me think of Benedict Anderson's concept of nation as an imagined community, that in those books you're revisiting what has been posited as an intensely divided community and finding ways of reinvesting it with a sense of cohesion, with a sense of shared loss, as opposed to one side being to blame and being blamed by the other.

WJ There was, under the surface, a tremendous battle going on during the referendum. To an outsider it would look like side A against side B, partly because of the sheer viciousness of the debate, in many cases. But it has always been my belief that that kind of demagoguery and those kinds of divisions within families were an over-compensation for something else. When things get that out of hand, something is happening psychologically that is not apparent in newspaper stories or in radio debate, and I think that happened in Newfoundland. People talk about post-9/11 America suffering from a kind of post-traumatic stress syndrome collectively, and I think that's true actually; it's certainly true for the city of New York. The energy and the animus of those Newfoundlanders who were campaigning for confederation matched the other side, in fact probably overmatched it, and one of the reasons, I think, is that they were overcompensating for the guilt that they felt and that they tried to suppress. Now, this is not something that is easy from a purely historical point of view to prove; it is an impression, and historical fiction as I understand it, or as I practice it, records an impression of history. It is impressionistic writing in exactly the way that some painting is impressionistic painting. No one objects when an impressionistic painting of a tree doesn't look like a tree, but as soon as something in history doesn't look exactly like it is supposed to have looked, then there is an objection.

HW Central to the history of your own family in *Baltimore's Mansion* is the nature of the rift between your father, Arthur, and his father, Charlie. The book suggests that, contrary to appearances and contrary to your family's support of independence, Charlie secretly voted for confederation. That decision, though, is represented quite obliquely in the book, presumably because your own knowledge of the truth is oblique. But it also suggests to me that the usual challenges of writing about the past, as you have been describing them, are intensified when that past is one's familial past. The past is that much more emotionally charged. Do you have any thoughts about that?

WJ I think inevitably that is true, but there is a way of controlling it, and it is called revision. You go over and you go over and you go over a piece of writing in which your first impulse was to take sides, until it becomes refined, until it becomes something better and something very different. You can read *Baltimore's Mansion* on many different levels. There is the personal drama of the characters involved and the sense of loss that my father felt because he was away at university when his father died, and away at university when Newfoundland the country ceased to be, and the parallel that he does in fact draw between those two things. In fact, if you want to take a kind of allegorical view of the book, my father and grandfather could easily be pre- and post-Confederation Newfoundland, with the interesting inversion that it is my father who represents the past, while it is my grandfather who represents the future or the more recent past. Yes, you are writing about some things that you actually witnessed yourself, things that you have a personal stake in, and so you do get wrought up in it. One of the things that I do is what I call method writing, which is use the actual emotion of an event in your life to write about an event in a novel that is completely different in nature but that needs that intensity. Well, in *Baltimore's Mansion* I didn't have to do that, because the actual events had that emotional intensity. People who like *Baltimore's Mansion* the best of all the books are responding mostly to the intensity of emotion in the book. I think—and it is not just because they are coming to the book with the knowledge that it is a memoir instead of a novel and so they feel it more powerfully—that I tapped into a vein of emotion in that book that is probably impossible to tap into in fiction.

HW At least a couple of scenes in *Baltimore's Mansion* are recognizable as experiences that either Smallwood or Fielding has in *The Colony of Unrequited Dreams*. I'm thinking of the scene of you arriving to find your family packing up and getting ready to move to another house, the scene of your father using a map to convey the size of Newfoundland, and the scene of your leaving Newfoundland for the first time by ferry. Was that a conscious intertextual strategy on your part to foreground that historical fiction like all fiction is to an extent autobiographical and to underscore Smallwood as an invention rather than a replica?

WJ The scene of coming home and finding a truck in the yard and all the furniture piled on top and never again seeing the inside of a house that you left that morning, you know, that happened to me. I mentioned it in *Baltimore's Mansion*, I mentioned it in *The Colony of Unrequited Dreams*, and in fact I mentioned it in *The Story of Bobby O'Malley*. It stuck with me personally. It wasn't that I had a great attraction to that particular house; it was just the sense of rootlessness that washed over me that particular time. My real family had moved by then many times, but never in those circumstances. Thematically the scene works well too; that is, it connects with themes that run through all my books. When it came to writing *The Colony of Unrequited Dreams* one of the things I noticed, and hadn't had any notion of before, was how many similarities there were between me and Smallwood. The reason I didn't know was that so little had been written about Smallwood's early days, and so much focus had been put on his record as a politician. I was far more interested in what he did between his infancy and, say, the night of the referendum than what he did afterwards. Essentially I had to write *The Colony of Unrequited Dreams* because no one else had. Richard Gwyn's book *Smallwood: The Unlikely Revolutionary* disposes of the first fifty years of Smallwood's life in about thirty-eight pages, and it seemed to me that if you wanted to write a book that was really about Smallwood, in a century where psychologists and psychiatrists tell us that character is formed early, then it was much more interesting to write about his early years. So I started thinking about it, started researching it, and I found that Smallwood's family, like my family, were forever moving from house to house. They didn't have enough money, and so sometimes they couldn't make the rent, or in other cases houses they were living in were sold essentially out from under them, or they could no longer keep up the repairs in a house, whatever. They were constantly moving. They went all around the city, until finally they wound up in what was considered the most awful and shameful part of the city, called the Brow. That's pretty much what we did as well. In the small town of Goulds, believe it or not, there were many neighbourhoods, and some of them were seen as good, and some of them were seen as bad, and we wound up in sort of the ultimate bad one. Smallwood's going to Bishop Feild, which on the one hand opened up a new world to him but on the other hand closed it as well, was very similar to my own experience of going to high school in St. John's after having spent nine years going to elementary school in Goulds. A whole new world was opened up to me. I was finally with students who didn't think it was sissy to get a good mark in something and get a good grade.

HW What kind of character mark did you get?

WJ [*laughs*]. Well, we didn't do character marks then, but I think I would have done okay. On the other hand, at the school where I went in St. John's there was a city elite based on an intergenerational elite going back hundreds of years that I hadn't known was there and that it took me decades to understand. I didn't understand it when I was at Brother Rice. I remember the brothers deferring to certain students as though they were grown-ups, and I didn't understand why, and the reason was the families that they came from. Small-wood sees this as well; he sees the other side of a good education, if you come from a "bad" background.

There were all sorts of other parallels as well between Smallwood and me. Smallwood was determined to succeed at anything. I wanted to succeed as a writer, but I was aware of being driven by an ambition that was fuelled by the failures of other people, some of them close relatives, but also fuelled in general by a view that maybe I either shared or protested against, a general view, a self-view, of Newfoundlanders having failed. I remember when I was about twenty-six or twenty-seven reading a short story of someone visiting a reset-tled community in Newfoundland, something I had done in the past basically for the quaintness of it, but this writer (and I forget who it was, not a well-known writer) said that failure and defeat were everywhere. I had never thought of it like that before. The determination to be an exception to that failure and defeat was something that Smallwood and I had in common as well.

We were both newspaper journalists, started out very young as newspaper journalists, and made our way on our own up through the ranks; it just happened to be different ranks.

HW On that note, I remember you telling a story at a reading in Edmonton about being a court reporter and having a strip torn off you by Smallwood, who gave you some advice about how to go about your craft.

WJ Yes, it was one of those classic Smallwood moments. He wasn't premier at that time. He had been out of power for quite a while, about a decade by then, and the Come-by-Chance oil refinery was in receivership. It was one of many megaprojects of Smallwood's that crashed and burned, and this was taking place in the Court of Appeal in Newfoundland. Because I thought it would be of interest to readers, I mentioned that Smallwood and the Ameri-can industrialist who had sold to Smallwood the idea of the Come-by-Chance oil refinery, a guy named John Shaheen, were sitting together in the audience at the back of the courtroom, and he objected to my making mention of that. I made no editorial comment about it; I simply noted their presence in the courtroom. Anyway, the next day he was all over me about how I didn't know how to report, how he had been a reporter in the great cities of the world and he had never seen such drivel in his life, that kind of thing. You know, I was nineteen years old.

HW It is hard not to see *The Colony of Unrequited Dreams*, and particularly Fielding, as you getting the last word on that matter.

WJ I suppose in a way, but as I say—

HW That's not what it's all about.

WJ It's not. Revision, whether it's on paper or in your mind, gets rid of those things. You can fantasize all you like, when you are writing a novel. You can send Smallwood flying off Signal Hill on a toboggan. You can work all of that out of your system, and then write in the book something more even handed, which I think I did.

HW I want to go back to that sense of nostalgia that you feel is prevalent in Newfoundland at the moment. In *Baltimore's Mansion*, you make mention of a kind of generational amnesia, that the intensity of feeling over the confederation vote has gradually evaporated, and now, I think as you put it, no one under forty can remember Major Cashin, the point man for the pro-independence forces. What does it mean for Newfoundland that that intensity has ebbed and that its source is for the most part forgotten, or at least by the younger generations?

WJ It has and hasn't been forgotten. The actual accurate knowledge of the referendum is something that young people in Newfoundland today don't have. But it is interesting to see them with their "Free Newfoundland" T-shirts. When I was over there in the summer, these T-shirts were all the rage. When you first looked at the T-shirt, it looked like an army on the front, but when you looked closer you saw that it was in fact a kind of army of musicians. They were holding musical instruments and not weapons, and I think the message was that we are not politically free, but we can be culturally free, or we are not politically self-defining, but we can be culturally self-defining. That idea, at least in the young artistic community in Newfoundland, is very prevalent still. Now, your average person, who is not especially interested in either culture or history, is not really all that aware of Newfoundland's historical context, in fact is not even really aware of a Canadian context. That's why I wanted to add the Americans as the third colonizer, because if you drive through the city of St. John's, it is pretty much, in a way, like any city in North America. You see this massive influence of American culture. I am not saying it is good or bad; I am just saying that it's there. So I think those old feelings and the vitriol of the debate are there; they get stirred up from time to time. In 1999, the fiftieth anniversary of confederation, there was a re-enactment of the confederation debate, and I had been resisting reading from *Colony* in Newfoundland because of the controversy. Finally I agreed to read at this particular conference—kind of foolishly agreed, as I realized, because I read after the re-enactment of the referendum debate. It was natural that the people who re-enacted these debates, both of whom were actually around in 1948, got all worked up, but the interesting thing was that the young people in the audience got all worked up as well, and chose sides. The whole sense that this was just a re-enactment was lost, and people in the audience were shouting arguments and telling the people who were just actors in many cases to sit down and shut up.

HW Going back to that idea of the imagined community, I was tempted to say that perhaps what has happened is that a politically divided community has gradually given way to a more unified cultural community, but that probably would be simplifying things.

WJ I think it would be very much simplifying things, because what is true of everywhere in the world is true of Newfoundland, and that is that literature and art are generally unknown commodities. In Newfoundland there are people who read *The Colony of Unrequited Dreams*, but I would suspect most people haven't heard of it, just the same way that most people haven't heard of some well-known book in the States. It's the same with painting and music, unless it is popular music. I don't think there is that kind of unity.

I can tell you one thing that does unify most Newfoundlanders at the moment—and you don't need knowledge of pre-confederation history for this—and that is a sense that Newfoundland has been hard done by within confederation. The economic situation in Newfoundland has been terrible for a long time, and it is assumed by outsiders that it is terrible because of a lack of resources or a lack of good bargaining and planning. What is not understood is that Newfoundland's resources, were they under the control of Newfoundland, would wipe out Newfoundland's debt ten times over, and that one of the reasons the debt is so large, aside from Smallwood's two decades of mismanagement, is that the Canadian economic system is set up in a way that there is a built-in disincentive for "have-not" provinces to develop, and that disincentive has to do with transfer payments. In the early stages of Newfoundland's confederation with Canada, the federal government put a lot of money into Newfoundland, into building infrastructure, things that had never been there, and into health—into all kinds of things—but these were not gifts. These were loans, and they have to be paid back, and the way they are paid back is that if Newfoundland—as they are doing now, for instance, with the oil—develops a resource, it has to put most of the profits from that resource against the debt that it owes the federal government. So the billions of dollars that are being made on Hibernia are not going into the coffers of Newfoundland. Some of it is going to Mobil and Shell, but most of it is going back into the federal system, and, unless the rate of development changes, that will be the case for hundreds of years. So there is this disincentive. Governments get into power and they look at the possibility of industrialization, and then, as former Newfoundland premier Brian Tobin did, they say, "Well, even if we do this, we are not going to make any money from it; we are not even going to get any jobs from it."

HW It perpetuates a cycle of lack of investment and lack of incentive to invest.

WJ And a sense of grievance, which is what I am much more interested in, the sense that we are bereft of our birthright and that we always will be. That is the animating myth of Newfoundlanders. I cast it in *Baltimore's Mansion* and I think in *The Colony of Unrequited Dreams* in terms of Arthurian legend— the idea that the true king is always in exile while some pretender holds the throne. That is the animating myth of Newfoundlanders, and by myth I don't mean something that is untrue; I mean a story or a version of events that is held onto and cherished—

HW That is culturally foundational.

WJ It is culturally foundational and sustaining, because it is something that brings people together and holds people together. Whether it is true or not is not really the point. The point is that it is there.

HW At the end of *Baltimore's Mansion* you talk about having to write about Newfoundland as an exile, and it seems to me that it is the fate of Atlantic writers more than most other Canadian writers to go down the road to write, to practice their craft. One thing that means is that, when it comes to writing about history, it would seem that the sense of distance and time necessary to write about the past is overlaid with a necessary sense of distance and space. Do you have any thoughts on that?

WJ I think that the necessity of artists, writers in particular, to, as you say, go down the road is not as strong as it used to be. The phrase implies that writers do it not because, as in my case, they just can't write in the place they are from. It implies that they are going to a big city because they need to make contacts, or they need to make more money, or they need to raise their profile or whatever. That was never a reason for me to leave, and more and more writers are not having to do that—and I think that the reasons are technological. A lot of Newfoundland writers stay in Newfoundland now. In fact, Newfoundland is one of the few places where artists have tended to stay, again because of that so recent sense of nationhood. For a person to go from Saskatchewan to Manitoba is simply to go from one province of this country to another; for a person to go from Newfoundland to anywhere else in the world is to leave a country, not literally, but in every other sense. In my case, I went away for an education, went to the University of New Brunswick to do an MA; my thesis there was *The Story of Bobby O'Malley*, and the book was published and did well. So I decided to go back to Newfoundland, because I had never tried to write in Newfoundland before and I saw no reason not to go back. So I went back, and I spent three years there getting pretty much nothing done, and not because I was wasting my time. I couldn't get any writing done in Newfoundland, no matter how hard I tried. That was in 1986 when I went back, and so I left again in '89 and went to Toronto. The choice of Toronto was just a fluke, because it happened to be where my wife got a job. We knew we wanted to leave Newfoundland, but we didn't really have our minds made up where to go. She applied for jobs in various places and happened to get one in Toronto, and so we wound up in Toronto. Thus it hasn't been a planned career on my part; I am interested in my development as a writer more than my development as a commodity. When I was living in Toronto—when I'd been away for long enough, going on ten years—the spatial and temporal remove from Newfoundland, especially the spatial remove, finally allowed me to see things from a new perspective, and also removed an inhibition that I think a lot of Newfoundland writers feel about writing about Newfoundland in a certain way. When you're there, there are certain things that are *verboten*, things you don't mention. You don't portray a downtrodden Newfoundland or an embittered Newfoundlander or things like that, no matter how many of them there might be around. Thus that spatial remove is really important.

I share the view expressed in an essay by the British-Japanese writer Kazuo Ishiguro that homesickness is not a nostalgia or a yearning for a place but a nostalgia or a yearning for a time, not a historical time but a personal one. He believes, and I believe, that the foundation of homesickness is a yearning for childhood, a yearning for the one time in your life when you felt protected, at home, when your knowledge of elsewhere was sufficiently small that you didn't yearn after other things, so you had a sense of rootedness and belonging and safety. I think *Baltimore's Mansion* and *The Colony of Unrequited Dreams* are full of characters who mistake the one thing for the other, who mistake a yearning for either a real or an idealized childhood for a desire to actually return to a physical or geographical home.

HW One of the most interesting parts of historical novels, to my mind anyway, is the acknowledgements. I am just reading Douglas Glover's *Elle*, and he has this long list of sources, and then he says something like "beyond that I've felt free to mangle the facts as I see fit." But the acknowledgements themselves often point to the particular challenges of writing about history. When you insert, as you do in the author's note to your most recent novel, *The Navigator of New York*, a comment like, "While it draws from the historical record, its purpose is not to answer historical questions or settle historical controversies," it's a concession that people are not going to be easily satisfied by the usual disclaimer, "this is a work of fiction." What are you trying to forestall there, if you don't mind my using one of Robert Peary's favourite words?

WJ I am familiar with Doug Glover's book, and I was familiar with Doug's work before. You can be fairly certain that irony is playing a large part in some disclaimers these days, and it certainly does in that pseudo-disclaimer of Doug Glover's. He was aware of the controversy surrounding *The Colony of Unrequited Dreams*, and what he essentially is saying is "I'm not only going to change things, I am going to celebrate the fact that I'm doing it and I am going to have fun doing it. I don't give a hoot who thinks what." Now that is something you can get away with better when your character has been dead for four hundred years than it is when your character has been dead for a decade, but still, that was the intent. An interesting thing that I have never told anybody about the disclaimer to *The Navigator of New York* (I thought somebody might notice but they haven't yet) is that the original edition of Don DeLillo's *Libra* contained a disclaimer that was more or less exactly the disclaimer that occurs in *The Navigator of New York*. DeLillo didn't want to put it in, but his publishers and lawyers said, "Stick it in there just in case," and so he did. In subsequent editions he took it out, and so I put it in, in *Navigator*, so that it can work on two levels. It can be taken as it seems, as a way of trying to avoid the controversy that I wound up in with *The Colony of Unrequited Dreams*, or it can be, for those who are knowledgeable about it, an invocation of this disclaimer of DeLillo that he simply removed from subsequent editions of the book, because he thought that a disclaimer was a kind of apology for what he had done. So my intent was ironic. Now, one of the things I have discovered from forty-five years of living in Canada is that the ability to appreciate or even detect irony is not something for which Canadians are famous.

HW In *The Colony of Unrequited Dreams*, you included some acknowledgement of the sources that you relied on for that book, but there is no similar acknowledgement in *The Navigator of New York*. Why the difference?

WJ Basically the difference is that (not for my own sake, but for the readers' sake) I didn't want readers running to the library and getting all the books that I had gotten to write the book and start making comparisons between what I had said in the book and what was said in those books. That subverts the point of a historical novel. It explodes the suspension of disbelief that a reader needs while reading a book, and so I just didn't put it in. There would have been many, many, many more books, too, and that was part of it, but I just did not want people doing that.

HW And anybody who is interested in doing it is just going to have to work harder, right?

WJ If they want to, but unless they are historians, or unless they're exploration buffs or something like that, my advice to them would be just don't do it. If you find something that is different, all I am going to say is "so what?" and if you find something that's the same, all I am going to say is "so what?" and you will spoil the point of the book on whatever level you are reading it. So I just didn't put in any sources at all. I hate to invoke him again, but if you look at Don DeLillo's *Libra*, there are no sources quoted, not the Warren Commission, not books written about the event, nothing. Nor are there any sources quoted in *Ragtime*. I think those writers avoided doing so for the same reason that I did.

HW Yet at the same time, Frederic Jameson talks about the historical novel as being a kind of dialogue between the fiction and readers' knowledge of that history, and it seems to me that, in the way that you just described it, the second part of that equation is sort of left out. Would that be accurate?

WJ No, I don't think so. I think everyone, in most cases, has a measure of knowledge of the material on which a historical novel is founded. Newfoundlanders might be expected to know more about Smallwood than, say, people from British Columbia. Canadians would be expected to know more than Americans, etc., etc. Everyone brings to the book a different amount of knowledge that was acquired either by accident or not for the purpose of reading the book. That is the kind of knowledge that I want people to read the book with, because my intent in writing the book is to create a kind of myth. If at every point you go running to the history books to find out things you would never have found out otherwise, it is an unnatural and non-organic way of absorbing knowledge, unless you are a specialist in the field or something. One of the things I wrote in *The Globe and Mail* piece was that if historical accuracy of the kind Rex Murphy is talking about is to be expected of novelists, then who is going to be the arbiter of what accuracy is?

HW That struck me as a very telling point. Let me ask you this question, which I think presents the issue in a slightly different light. You argue in responding to Rex Murphy that portraits of historical figures in historical fiction are not assertions of historical truths, as essentially you have just been say-ing, but can they be seen implicitly as imaginative theses about these histor-ical figures? *Navigator*, for instance, would amount to an indictment of Robert Peary and a relative acquittal of Frederick Cook. Would that be a fair way to read the book?

WJ No, I don't think so, not because events in the book don't seem to point that way; they might. But, aside from the most fundamental interest of any nov-elist—no matter what kind of novelist—which is character, my interest in *The Navigator of New York* was the difference between the perception of these char-acters and, not so much their real lives, as their plausible real lives, the differ-ence between a public and a private persona. That is the case with both Cook and Peary. In terms of personality, I certainly find Cook more appealing, as did everyone who met both Cook and Peary; everyone found Cook more appeal-ing, and no one really found Peary appealing. In modern parlance, he didn't present well. He had a tendency to tick people off; it was in his nature just to be that way. But in terms of what they do, I am not sure who comes off bet-ter in the book, and I am really not all that concerned with it. The pro-Peary and pro-Cook factions, though, still exist today, and they are quite virulent. The Cook people have claimed my book as being a vindication of Cook, and the Peary people have condemned it as yet another indictment of Peary. I think that happens simply because that is who Peary and Cook were as peo-ple, but I am not trying to vindicate Cook historically or condemn Peary his-torically. I am using history, but again I would go back to what I said a long time ago, that a historical novel is a kind of work of impressionism.

The characters are emblematic of larger themes as well, especially in *The Navigator of New York*. Cook and Peary are very much men of their time, and that is one of the reasons that so much of the book takes place in New York. Essentially, the modern world was created in New York around the time that I am writing about in *The Navigator of New York*. They were part of it, they were victims of it, they were caught up in it in by forces that were larger than them, and they did things that you would expect from people in such a predica-ment. But I am definitely not trying to incline anybody to an opinion of the historical Cook or Peary. I am aware of the inevitability of people coming away from the book with an impression, but I would just remind them that that is all it is.

HW As you have certainly experienced in writing about Smallwood, there is a certain proprietorial behaviour that comes into play in people's reactions to the representation of particular historical figures and historical episodes. Do

FIGURE 10. Robert Peary in the Arctic. U.S. National Oceanic and Atmospheric Administration—People Collection b3552.

you feel that that proprietorial dimension is intensified when you are dealing with what might be seen as other countries' histories, in this case writing about two notorious American explorers? Is there a sense, in other words, that history as a heritage is a kind of preserve, a sort of national park of the past, and that only certain activities are permitted there?

WJ I have encountered that sense, but only in the reverse, only on behalf of Canadians who resent Americans who write about Canada. You know, when

Annie Proulx wrote *The Shipping News*, there was a lot of talk about the value of the book in literary terms, but there was much more talk about whether or not someone should do this. Should an American, as the phrase was being passed around, parachute into Newfoundland, write about it, and then get airlifted out, and my answer is, "Well, why not?" There are no rules until you see the results, and if the result is a good book, then to heck with the rules. I had no one complain about me writing about Peary and Cook from the point of view of a Canadian writing about Americans. A book about Virginia Woolf written by an American won the Pulitzer Prize, and nobody in England complained about the writing of that. I think that in Canada we are a little insecure because, for one thing, there is the obvious American monolith that is always there and whose effect on our own culture we are always worried about, but the other thing is that we haven't yet written our own fictional history—in fact, in many cases we haven't yet written our own history—and so there is an unnecessary worry that Americans who write about Canada will prevent us from doing so.

There is a writer named Harold Norman, an American who lives in Washington, and every one of his books is set in some part of Canada. He set one in Newfoundland, one in Nova Scotia, one in Manitoba, one in Quebec, and has another one coming out in Nova Scotia soon. He doesn't have a home in Canada; he has no people or relatives here. He calls it his spiritual homeland. When his book *The Bird Artist* was published, there was a review in a Toronto newspaper simply dismissing it because it was a book by an American about, in this case, Witless Bay, a town just outside of St. John's. He took all sorts of liberties with geography, etc., etc., but I would go back to the piece I wrote for *The Globe and Mail*, and the question I asked there is how much knowledge is enough to bring to a book? If an Icelander did for some past president of Iceland what I did for Smallwood in *The Colony of Unrequited Dreams*, and Icelanders objected to it, but Newfoundlanders not knowing anything about Iceland thought it was a great book, then who is right? I mean, how much history do you have to acquire before you are qualified to read a historical novel? The problem with Rex Murphy when it came to writing the review (and I don't think there was any malice in that review at all, though I think it was completely wrong and misguided) was that he knew too much about the subject and couldn't put it aside for the purposes of the review. I think that, as a reviewer, you have to either put it aside, or say you can't and then not review the book. But the question of how much history you need is an unanswerable one. I mean, if we take the kind of argument that people like Rex make, then no one should write about anyone else. Even in a work that is not historical fiction, but that is just called fiction, I should never write about anyone else, because I am not a weatherman, or I am not a woman. In fiction you are always writing about something that you are not; that is the basic premise of it, and historical fiction is just the logical extension of that.

HW Now, I know that, with this next question, basically I've been a bad boy and gone and done the kind of research you were discouraging, but one of the effects of historical fiction, of course, is that it interests readers in history and very often does have the effect of sending them off to find out more about the history, in this case about the Peary/Cook controversy and the enmity between them.

At the end of *My Attainment of the Pole*, Frederick Cook's 1913 account of his polar expedition, with much seeming reluctance, he launches into a sustained counterattack against Peary, and he lays out a series of actions reflecting very badly on Peary, most of which are contained in the narrative of *Navigator*. At the end of these charges he hints darkly at a further, more incriminating secret: "Yet all, indeed, has not been told. Although Mr. Peary did not scruple to lie about me, I still hesitate to tell the full truth about him.

In the white, frozen North a tragedy was enacted which would bring tears to the hearts of all who possess human tenderness and kindness. This has never been written. To write it would still further reveal the ruthlessness, the selfishness, the cruelty of the man who tried to ruin me. Yet here I prefer the charity of silence, where, indeed, charity is not at all merited."

There are some pretty dark hints there, and I am wondering if you found out anything more about this in your research for the novel, or is this one of those aporias or gaps that provide for writers a seductive opening onto history?

WJ I am familiar with the piece that you read, and I balanced it with a lot of other writing. You should read some of the things that Peary said about Cook, and some of the innuendo. You know, innuendo is one of the easiest things in the world. One of the things Cook was famous for was, "I could tell you an awful story, but I won't," that kind of thing. Yes, I was aware while writing the book of this hint at a dark incident, but if you read about Peary, these hints are everywhere. There were always people disappearing on Peary's expeditions. There were always disagreements between Peary and medical officers, because the medical officer, in spite of not having a military ranking, was actually the second-in-command in terms of power, and so Peary was always concerned with what the medical officer would do. That particular passage, I am willing to acknowledge, did stir my imagination, but again keep in mind

FIGURE 11. Frederick Cook. Courtesy of the Ohio State University
Archives Frederick A. Cook Society Collection RG 56.17, image 34_2a.

that this is not a guess at what Cook was talking about; it was simply a jumping-off point for my imagination. It got me wondering about what were the
possibilities that Cook could be talking about, and what was plausible. One of
the reasons that Cook never spells out those things—aside from not having
enough proof and therefore putting himself open to libel—is that it is sometimes better to hint darkly at things than to spell them out. They seem more
sinister and subversive—

HW And it also makes you appear more virtuous for withholding them.

WJ Sure.

HW The image near the beginning of *Baltimore's Mansion* of the iceberg in
the shape of the Virgin Mary seems to me to be a crucial metaphor, not just
for that memoir, but for almost all of your writing, which is governed by the
sense of there being so much more beneath the surface. In all your novels,

your protagonists seem to be wading against the tide of social opinion and trying to see beyond a social facade, and that facade has been constructed to con-
form to social conventions. I am thinking about things like the O'Malleys'
marital *détente* in *The Story of Bobby O'Malley*, and the Ryans' suppression of
Draper Doyle's father's homosexuality in *The Divine Ryans*. The pressure of
social conventions and the pain of having to preserve false appearances are just
as central in your historical novels as well. I am wondering if you have any
thoughts on the impact that these pressures have on historical developments
and historical achievements.

WJ I don't know if that iceberg is a cliché, but the cliché view of the iceberg
is of the thing that is nine-tenths unseen, which is in fact the name of a book
by a Newfoundlander named Ken Harvey. That metaphor is a little heavy-
handed for me. There is no question that all my books are about the difference between what appears to be the case and what is the case, what is public
and what is secret, and how the secret subverts the public persona. The
metaphor of the iceberg fits very well with that, but I used the Virgin Berg in
Baltimore's Mansion for completely other reasons, and I think I am not going
to tell you what they are. There is a whole vein of the book that no one has written about, or acknowledged in reviews or in conversations, and I think I am
just going to leave it for a while.

HW You can hint darkly too [*laughs*].

WJ I can hint darkly too. The leitmotif of ice is there in *Colony* and *Navigator* as well, but in *Baltimore's Mansion* ice is kind of domesticated; it becomes
something different than it is in the other two books. It becomes not an overwhelming part of the landscape, but something else, something religious,
overtly in the sense that the piece of ice is shaped like the Virgin Mary, but less
overtly (and this is about as far as I will go) when you look at a scene like
Charlie, in the final moments of his life, taking the buckets of frozen water to
the forge and drinking from them and being in the act of drinking ice water
when he dies, or my father and his father cutting ice when my father almost
dies, when they were led back home by a horse. That is how ice is being used,
more than in what I feel is the more obvious way of it as a metaphor of things
that exist but are unseen.

HW I wasn't so much trying to penetrate the mystery of the Virgin Berg as
to get at the impact of social conventions and conforming to social expectations on history itself. Often we think of the makers of history as being these
idiosyncratic and independent mavericks, but in a lot of ways what comes

through, especially in *Navigator*, is the way in which so much of history is shaped, and perhaps negatively, by social conventions and social expectations.

WJ All of my work has that as one of the themes, not necessarily their impact on something as broad as history, but on people's personal lives—the weight of trying to live a free life under the burden of social conventions and under the burden of the past and under the burden of history as well. But yes, usually the first thing that knocks historical figures, especially explorers or people who are considered heroes, off the pedestal, is the ways, often the petty ways, in which they are forced to deal with people in order to make their expeditions possible and in order to keep intact their persona as heroes. Peary, and perhaps to a lesser extent Cook (because there is no recorded instance of this having happened with Cook, to my knowledge anyway), had something like half a dozen children with what were then called Eskimos. This was kind of an open secret in New York among the people who were backing him, but it was a secret, *period*, to most other people. These are the kinds of things that were socially disapproved of, not fathering a child that you didn't take care of, but fathering a child with somebody racially different. So characters like Peary and Cook expended a great deal of psychic energy and moral energy trying to live up to the personas that they needed, or believed they needed, to create to accomplish what they wanted to accomplish. That runs through other of my books as well. I mean, Smallwood does the same thing at an enormous cost to him, at the cost of Sheilagh Fielding to him, because Fielding is someone that Smallwood knows the man he wants to become cannot be with. She will be disapproved of, she will be a loose cannon, he won't know what she will do. Thus, in spite of the fact that he loves her, he chooses to go in a different direction, and that is the great tragedy of his life. I am talking now about my Smallwood, not the historical Smallwood, although, interestingly enough, there is a real-life parallel. But yes, those kinds of social conventions are things that historical figures, just like anyone, have to deal with, but it is especially a problem with historical figures because they are generally famous people, and the famous have to keep up appearances, and they have to make a lot of compromises to do that.

HW The fates of the main characters of both your historical novels—I am thinking of Smallwood, Cook, and Peary—suggest that striving to make history is at best an ambivalent objective. Ambition is depicted as a distorting, even corrupting force, more a destructive force than a creative one. Smallwood's ambition, for instance, is the source of his romantic and social alienation, and Peary's ambition is fuelled by a megalomaniacal, misanthropic fear of his own obsolescence and erasure by time. What do you think, in general terms, of the desire to make history?

WJ I have always thought that, especially in terms of politicians, but in terms of anyone who does turn out to be famous, it is usually a fatal thing to try to see yourself in historical terms while you are, so to speak, in midstream. What you said of Peary is true of Smallwood; there is a kind of fear that you will go unrecorded by history, and therefore it will be as though you never lived. One of the things that I don't make overt in *The Colony of Unrequited Dreams* and *The Navigator of New York*, because these things didn't play a large part in the lives of the characters, is that this craving for immortality, the immortality of being recorded by history, is something that is especially pronounced in modern times because of the decline in religious belief. If you no longer believe that an eternity of either hellfire or bliss awaits you, but as a child you were led to believe that it did, then you will be tempted to replace that immortality with something else. That is what Smallwood does, and that is what Peary does, and in fact that is what Cook does as well, although Cook tries to do it both ways: he tries to be recorded by history and he wants to have a son, and children are a form of immortality as well.

HW So in some ways the history books become the afterlife.

WJ Yes, history books do become a kind of afterlife that is endlessly revised. History, as you know, is not a fixed thing; it is not synonymous with the past. The question of what happened is not the same as why did it happen. Even what happened, the notion of what happened, frequently changes; archaeologists find new things. But history changes mostly because of the developments of new ideologies and therefore new interpretations of history. People who are thought of as heroes become thought of as villains. Feminism changed the whole view of human history, as Marxism did as well. Freud's views changed the whole view of human history. So it is ever-evolving and forever being revised. One thing that I would like to add as a kind of coda to the whole thing is that in my historical novels, history is always one of the main subjects, not the events of history but the making of history and the writing of history. In *The Colony of Unrequited Dreams* there is a historian, Judge Prowse; there is also Sheilagh Fielding, who is a historian. But the characters themselves are historians because they are trying to, with their lives, write history. It is a built-in part of human nature to experience life in retrospect, and that is what these people are trying to do, and they are trying to influence how other people view their lives. Smallwood's great encyclopedia of Newfoundland (and I don't use "great" ironically), which was invaluable in the writing of *The Colony of*

Unrequited Dreams, is also intended to commemorate Smallwood. One of the interesting things about it is to go through it and look at what is left out, and one of the things that is left out completely is Smallwood's father. Smallwood's father is almost left out completely of the autobiography *I Chose Canada*. So Smallwood himself at the end of his life became a historian and was writing what was essentially, in *The Book of Newfoundland* and in *I Chose Canada*, a work of fiction.

HW One of the great small histories of the world.

WJ Yes, one of the great small histories of the world, but, as I say, he was not calling it fiction, he was calling it history. And the question of what you call something, the question of what expectations a reader brings to a book, is very important as well. I think you have to be honest when you stick that label on the book, you know "memoir," "autobiography," "novel," whatever, and I think people would do well to look at a book and see what it claims to be.

"We Have to Recover Their Bodies"
George Elliott Clarke

Poet, dramatist, anthologist, academic, and (most recently) novelist, Nova Scotia native George Elliott Clarke is a veritable Renaissance man on the Canadian literary scene. Of African-American and Mikma'q heritage, Clarke has roots in Nova Scotia going back to the early nineteenth century on his mother's side and to the late nineteenth century on his father's side. Born in Windsor Plains in 1960, Clarke was raised in Halifax. He did his bachelor's degree in English at the University of Waterloo, his MA at Dalhousie University, and completed his doctorate at Queen's University. He taught at Duke University in North Carolina from 1993 to 1999 before moving to the University of Toronto, where he is the E.J. Pratt Chair of Canadian Literature. Clarke's writing reflects his sustained engagement with the history and culture of African-Canadians in the Maritimes, whose place in and contribution to Canadian society has been sorely neglected. His promotion of the community that he has dubbed "Africadia" is also evident in his editing of the two-volume *Fire on the Water: An Anthology of Black Nova Scotian Writing* (1991) and in most of the essays collected in *Odysseys Home: Mapping African-Canadian Literature* (2002). Clarke has published five volumes of poetry, including his debut collection, *Saltwater*

Spirituals and Deeper Blues (1983), and the highly acclaimed *Whylah Falls* (1990), a lyrical portrait of a fictional Black community in Nova Scotia during the Depression. His play *Beatrice Chancy* (1999) relocates the story of Beatrice Cenci to the era of slavery in Nova Scotia in the early nineteenth century. In 2005, Clarke published his first novel, *George & Rue*, based on the hangings of two of his cousins, George and Rufus Hamilton, for the brutal killing of a white Fredericton taxi driver in January of 1949. The murder was also the subject of *Execution Poems*, which won the Governor General's Award for Poetry in 2001. I spoke to George Elliott Clarke in Wolfville on June 27, 2005.

HW You have written extensively about giving voice to the imagined community of what you call Africadia, and one element of this objective is that your poetry, going right back to your debut collection, *Saltwater Spirituals and Deeper Blues*, has a strong historical bent to it. Can you talk about the importance of the past in your writing?

GEC Well, I think we can't understand where we are until we know where we've been. I know that's such a simple, straightforward, even clichéd notion, but I do think that we have to locate ourselves in time, to look at what's happened before, what we hope might happen in the future, what we hope won't happen in the future, and that means having some kind of knowledge of history. One has to know one's particular cultural history, familial history, but also general social history, national history and world history—all of the above. I think it's good to have a handle on as much of that as you possibly can, basically so that people cannot trick you as easily in the future, or in the present. Just to give a quick example from contemporary arguments going on over health care: what's crucial for people to remember is that our health care system—as malfunctioning as it may be—was created after a struggle that took decades and people sweating blood and tears to make it come about, because they were tired of seeing others lose their homes and their savings because of unfortunate illness or disease. And if we lose sight of the roots of the health care system, then it's easier to say, "We don't really know why we have one anyway, so it's no problem if we change to a private system." That's why I believe it's important to know the history of a society, where we've been, where we hope to go, so that we can avoid mistakes or not repeat mistakes.

HW How about the history of Africadia specifically?

GEC The history of Africadia, what I call Africadia, particularly Black Nova Scotia, African Nova Scotia, is a history that's crucial partly because of the fact that it's so poorly known, so unrecognized, so disparaged, and partly because it's a matter of pride and just self-preservation. To give an example: there's a very well-meaning academic book published back in 1973 called *Forgotten Canadians: The Blacks of Nova Scotia*, by Frances Henry, a Trinidadian-born anthropologist who now teaches at York University. In reading it, if one is Black Nova Scotian, one is slapped across the face over and over and over again by her findings, which are basically that we don't have any culture, we're so completely devoid of anything that it's a miracle that we still exist. I'm exaggerating a little bit, but only a little bit. She may have felt that she was doing us a service by raising the alarm about how desperately, poorly off these poor forgotten Canadians, these Black Nova Scotians, were. Maybe she felt that by communicating this message to the world there would be more assistance, but for me and many others of my generation, growing up and reaching adolescence and coming across books like hers, it basically told us we were worth nothing, had done nothing, were confused about our identity, and didn't know what it meant to be Black. Most outrageously, she claimed that we didn't even have a musical tradition. How could anybody say that Black Nova Scotians didn't have any music? This book, a major academic text published in Toronto, just seemed to be full of (I'm going to use strong language here) a pack of lies, which may not have been her intent, but that's how it was received. And that's just one example; I can talk about Robin Winks's *The Blacks in Canada*.

HW I was just going to bring him up, because you have reacted, particularly in your review of it (which is reprinted in *Odysseys Home*), to a tone of disparagement in what is considered a fairly significant history.

GEC Absolutely. Again, when I first read it, I thought that maybe he had a point, but when I reread it as an adult I thought he had really gotten things mixed up. It's not to say that people can't be critical of Black Nova Scotian history; of course they can. There is a lot of stuff that harmed our ancestors, a lot of stuff that people got wrong or did wrong, sure. But it's one thing to be critical; it's another thing to say, "Well, you're a complete failure as a people." I just don't accept that definition of Africadian, Black Nova Scotian, African Nova Scotian history. I don't think it was a complete fiasco. I think people struggled against overwhelming obstacles and sometimes, maybe frequently, didn't succeed, and it's not surprising that they didn't. On the other hand, did they create a culture? I think they did. I think it was actually a grand, heroic thing that they created the churches that still exist, up and down the Annapolis Valley and around Nova Scotia, basically on their own. There was even a different architecture, and although outsiders may easily have spurned it, or said, "This is ridiculous or stupid or cheap or just derivative," the fact is that people created this stuff out of their own heads, with their own resources, and I find that an incredible feat. With the whole of this society telling them, in the mid-nineteenth century, "You're not worth anything; you're no better than slaves; you don't deserve anything but to be our servants and clean up after us, and nurse our children and put us to bed at night—"

HW Or giving them the most meagre resources and expecting them to thrive, as with the Black Loyalists—

GEC That's right, the poorest land, and all that was done deliberately. Despite all the oppression and persecution that people faced, they still created their own church, the African Baptist United Association, *ex nihilo*, and staffed it and ran it, for now well over a hundred years. Again, you might walk into the churches themselves and say, "Hey, there are only ten pews in this church. There's only one stained-glass window. It's a relatively small structure," but (and maybe this is like looking for silver linings in many clouds) to me it was a statement of people's faith that they wanted to maintain some sense of separate identity, Black identity, in Nova Scotia.

HW Even though *Whylah Falls* is set in the Depression, the central episode of the collection, the death of Othello Clemence, is based on the death of a Black man in Weymouth Falls just a few years before *Whylah Falls* was published in 1990, Graham Cromwell, who was shot by a white man who was subsequently acquitted by an all-white jury. What impact did that incident have on the shape of *Whylah Falls*?

GEC Well, huge, and to explain it I have to go back a bit further. When I was eighteen or nineteen, in the late 1970s, I was involved in a very loose-knit group of young people (we ultimately called ourselves the Central Planning Committee, given our Marxist inclinations) and we wanted to organize a Black youth organization. We were actually given money from the federal government, the now-defunct Black United Front of Nova Scotia, and the Human Rights Commission of Nova Scotia, to go around the province and marshal Black youth together. What that disparate group really accomplished (because we never succeeded in founding a real organization) was to hold three conferences in Halifax. In order to organize those conferences, a smaller group of us would go around the province, to Sydney and down to Yarmouth, wherever there was a Black community, to see if the Black youth would be interested in coming down to Halifax to take part in one of our conferences, and we would maintain contact with these communities. For me it was the first real time to be in other Black communities, outside of the North End of Halifax, where I grew up—which was a very mixed, working-class, immigrant community—and my mother's community, Three Mile Plains, the entranceway to the Annapolis Valley, which I visited a lot and really loved as a kid; my grandparents' place just outside Windsor was my home as much as my home in Halifax. But working with the CPC was my first time to really get out around the province and see all these little communities, and I decided that I really liked Weymouth Falls. It sits on a hillside above the Sissiboo River. The church—Mount Beulah Baptist Church—sits on the top of the hill, and it's just a very striking geography. There was one particular family I ended up gravitating around, full of lovely daughters, and very handsome guys too, and they were very down-to-earth but fun to be around.

So I knew the shooting victim, Graham Jarvis, because of that association with Weymouth Falls. I had gone away to university in 1979, and I came back in 1985, to be a social worker in the Annapolis Valley, for the Black United Front. No sooner do I take up the job than I realize that Graham Jarvis has been killed, and that as far as the Black community is concerned, it was murder. It was partly my job to try to organize some kind of campaign around it, and we organized an appeal of the acquittal. Of course, we were unsuccessful in that; all we managed to do in the end was simply to have a meeting between the Attorney General of Nova Scotia—

HW This was Ron Giffin?

GEC Ron Giffin, and Mrs. Cromwell. That's not a whole lot to show for a three-hundred-name petition and many months of letters and newspaper coverage. On the other hand, here is the guy in charge of the Nova Scotia justice system sitting down with a Black woman, probably for the first time in his life, who is not a maid or something of that sort and having to explain to her how the system did or didn't work, in terms of handling the death of her son. We even succeeded in getting transcripts made up of the trial, because the Crown was resisting having transcripts done up. The other thing that happened was that the very first meeting of the judicial council, which examines the misdeeds or potential misdeeds of judges, took place around our case, because a *Toronto Star* reporter reported that the judge who handled the bail hearing of the accused in the matter had made prejudicial statements.

HW The judge had supposedly said something like, "You know what Blacks are like when they get drunk," right?

GEC This really blew up everything, and they had to call a meeting of the judicial council to decide who they were going to believe, the judge or the reporter. Of course they believed the judge [*laughs*]. That was back in '85 and '86, and that was a huge emotional and psychological commitment on the part of everybody who was involved. I put together a group called the Weymouth Falls Justice Committee, and that meant that I was in Weymouth Falls, as I like to say, for a year of weekends. Though I still was very much an outsider, I became somewhat more part of the community life and for the first time really got to see the folkways of rural (mainly Black) people, and it was eye-opening. Here I was, I had a newly minted (as of 1984) honours bachelor of arts in English, from the University of Waterloo, where I studied basically all British literature, with a nod to the U.S. and a nod to Canada and virtually no Black writing but filled up with Milton, who I'd fallen in love with, bizarrely; I just loved *Paradise Lost*. Then, about a week before I was supposed to come back to Nova Scotia, I was sitting in a donut shop in Kitchener, early in the morning, and all of a sudden I started thinking about Weymouth Falls, and this poem started to come to my mind. I sat down and wrote it, and it became a poem in *Whylah Falls* called "How Exile Melts to One Hundred Roses."

HW An epiphany in a donut shop [*laughs*]. This *is* Canadian literature.

GEC As I was thinking about going back, that was the poem. Of course I didn't know at that point, in May 1985, that I was going to write anything like *Whylah Falls*. I was sitting in this donut shop and this poem happened, in that hour of the morning when you're not really awake, and I realized that, for probably one of the first times in my short career as a poet, I'd written something that was truly, genuinely out of my own experience and memory. Then, as fate would have it, I ended up back in Weymouth Falls, and during that year I was there I started thinking about doing a second book. I put together this manuscript that was a mishmash of things, and I was calling it *The Book of Liberty*. At the same time, I was writing these pieces based on my experiences around Weymouth Falls and other Black communities up and down the Annapolis Valley, from Three Mile Plains basically down to Yarmouth, although most of it was about Weymouth Falls and the people I was meeting there and the things they would say and the stories they'd have to tell. Living with the Cromwell family there was a (now unfortunately deceased) older woman who used to sit there all day just talking, and I would often be the only one sitting there with her, and she would go on to talk about the bad old days or the good old days. So I would write down some of the things that she had to say, and some of the stories were so vivid. A lot of the stuff that she told me never ended up in *Whylah Falls*, but the things that she recollected just created the whole texture of the community and the people and the times. I started to write these pieces based on the things I was hearing, based on stories that people were telling me, and the life going on around me in this community. For this manuscript I was calling *The Book of Liberty* I had about a hundred pages of material—poems, pieces of prose—but there was this other section, which I was calling "Weymouth Falls," which was suddenly a hundred poems. Then a good friend of mine, Paul Zemokhol, reading over the material, said to me—and it was so simple—"You have two books here" [*laughs*]. "You have this book, which you don't even know what it is, and you have this other book, which is pretty much intact, and if I were you, I would be working with this other book." That was in 1988, and so the next two years were spent figuring out what the plot was and adding some characters and some dialogue and fashioning this other part of *The Book of Liberty* which of course eventually ended up becoming *Whylah Falls*.

HW One of the myths about Canada that you come back to again and again is the prevalent and mistaken impression that there was no slavery in Canada, or, if there was, it wasn't bad like in the United States. Now that's obviously something that your play *Beatrice Chancy* is challenging. What do you think that that impression is symptomatic of? Why do Canadians comfortably have that belief?

GEC I think it's part of our complex regarding the United States. We position ourselves as being on the side of God and the angels and the United States being on the side of the devil and the demons. I mean, that's a cliché, but that's how it is. From here, slavery and the question of race and racism are viewed as being American issues and American problems. The other side of the coin is that we don't have these problems, we never did, and we don't have them now.

HW So it's almost a national (and nationalist) state of denial.

GEC It is. It's constant. It's in everything. To give you an example: I think they've done about three Heritage Minutes segments dealing with aspects of Black Canadian history, but really it's not Black Canadians who are the subjects. It's good white Canadians. Look at the Underground Railroad. Yes it's true, thirty to forty thousand African-Americans sought refuge in the Canadas, mainly Upper Canada (Ontario), and when the Civil War ended, most of them went back. That was partly because they wanted to try to reunify families split up by slavery, but the other part of it was that they weren't welcome in Upper Canada. They got the message and they left. They were segregated in Upper Canada as they were segregated in the South. But we don't remember that.

We just say, "Well, we're the land that welcomed the fugitive slaves." Yes, but those fugitive slaves and their allies had to really fight to get the protection of the British Crown and to be able to settle in Upper Canada and all the rest of it. We only tell ourselves the part of the story that makes us look good vis-à-vis the United States, and everything else has got to be covered up and denied, so we can never be shown to be virtually the same as our American friends and allies.

HW Both *Execution Poems* and your novel *George & Rue* are based on the story of your cousins, George and Rufus Hamilton, who were hanged for murder in Fredericton in 1949. You didn't find out about the history of your cousins until about ten years ago, when your mother mentioned it in passing. What was your reaction when you heard the story and how difficult was it to decide to write about them?

GEC Well, I have to say that I was astonished when I heard this information, but then I never had any qualms about writing about it. Never. That may suggest I have absolutely no moral qualms, I don't know, but I just felt that I had to write about it. As soon as I found out just a little bit of the story, I went out to find more information, which I got from some relatives, and then, that first weekend in late May 1994, I started writing stuff for what I knew was going to be a novel. I needed something big, something that was going to be able to contain everything I wanted to say, because I felt that *George & Rue* would be my way, rightly or wrongly, of talking, without sentimentality, about race relations in the Maritimes in the 1930s and 1940s, basically the same era in which my parents were born and grew up (my father was born in 1935, my mother in 1939).

HW A very unsentimental era, the thirties and forties.

GEC *Very* unsentimental. But the problem, at least for me—and this is partly a problem of Canadian historiography and Canadian fiction in general—is that our fiction and our history are often sentimental, about race in particular. Terrence Craig has written a book, *Racial Attitudes in English-Canadian Fiction*, which is a great window on the whole thing, but I think it would be terrific to look at how Black characters, Aboriginal characters, Jewish characters, Chinese characters, Asian characters have actually been depicted in Canadian fiction. I think it would be eye-opening. Now a lot of those depictions wouldn't necessarily be racist or negative, but rather very treacly and sentimental, basically saying, "Well, it's too bad that so-and-so suffered this or that, but that's just the way it goes, and aren't they nice people?" and also that sense that, "Well, they may have it bad here but it's worse in the United States, and so we're willing to shed a tear but only one and move on." In *George & Rue* I'm not trying to make anybody feel sorry for Black Nova Scotians, or Mikma'q people, or Blacks who are also part Mikma'q (as they were, and as I am). It's not a question of making anybody feel bad. It is a question of recognizing what things were really like, so that we don't kid ourselves and don't have false impressions about that history or about the way the society was.

HW Your great-aunt, as you mention at the end of the novel, was the famous opera singer, Portia White. Did anybody ask you why you didn't write about her instead? That's a way of asking, in effect, about the vexed issue of how, in a racially conflicted and charged social atmosphere, the telling of stories about a minority community is almost inevitably linked to the public image of that community. Did you worry about the potential charge that telling such a story would merely reinforce stereotypical notions of Black violence?

GEC Our friend Shakespeare comes to my rescue [*laughs*]. I'm being a little facetious, but not really. The way that I can start to answer that question is to look at *Titus Andronicus*. I first read it in my early twenties, and when I went back and reread it in the later 1990s, I was struck by his treatment of Aaron, who is a Moor, and often drawn as being Black, and the language around him is very racialized. Aaron is a villain. He's a nasty piece of work, and he's out there arranging robberies, rapes, framing people, murders. He doesn't care. Now in some ways he's a caricature and an over-the-top villain, but Shakespeare gives him enough complexity that I began to see him as an alienated minority. He's a visible minority at the centre of imperial Rome, basically a vassal of the Queen of the Goths (although soon she will be his vassal, because she will become his lover). The point is that this guy is completely alienated, and he has no compunction about arranging all these vile deeds and laughing about it. He is making the emperor, Saturninus, a cuckold. He's making the whole empire dance to his tune. He is a slave, but he has the whole Roman Empire, because of his work in the boudoirs and behind the throne, following his policy. Everybody in that play is basically enthralled by the devious machinations of the guy who is the slave. Now, I'm sorry to sound so excited about this, but this is a play that is at least partly a study of what it means to be an alienated, disaffected minority who therefore feels that he or she is not bound to respect any of the rules of that society but is prepared to bend them to suit his or her own needs. He's a free-agent destroyer, because it is the only way for him to get power and respect.

Another, more distantly phantasmal, intertext is William Styron's *The Confessions of Nat Turner*, which my father brought home when I was a kid.

HW This is a historical novel about a slave revolt in the United States.

GEC That's right. The cover image of that novel haunted me as a child because it was a drawing of a Black angel with a sword, and he was definitely getting some vengeance. For me as a seven- or eight-year-old, this image was frightening. Then eventually I got to read the novel, and found out how messed up Styron was in his view of Nat Turner and the rebellion. So I do in my own, secret heart consider *George & Rue* [*laughs*] my own particular answer to Bill Styron.

HW In a way, you could see *George & Rue* as a slow-release slave revolt.

GEC [*laughs*]. That's a good way—yes, indeed—of putting it. A slow-motion, long time-release slave revolt. Yes.

HW What I'm wondering is whether anybody—your relatives, people in the Black community—essentially asked, "What do you want to tell that story for?"

GEC I can understand that we still live in a society where we're judged by our heritage, colour, what have you, and that anything that makes one of us look bad makes all of us look bad, especially if you're a minority. A cloud is imposed on everybody when one person does something wrong, even though these are individuals who have to take responsibility for individual actions, or non-actions, for that matter. But I also like to believe that the society's a democracy and that I have a right as an artist to follow my inklings wherever they may lead. For me, what was important about writing this book was to explore the reality of being two young men of colour in a time when there were no opportunities for them. I don't make excuses for what they did, because they could have decided to shine shoes, sure, and sell newspapers, and maybe, if they're lucky, get a job on the railway. They could have done those things, and they decided they weren't going to, or that they couldn't. I don't believe there's never any possibility to escape a life of crime—of course there always is—but the point is that they didn't see any other way, and they were, in a sense, right to believe this, because society didn't say to them, "You can be a lawyer, you can be a teacher, you can be a doctor." It said to them, "You can shine our shoes and make up our beds." They replied, "Well, no thanks," and I wanted to explore that reality. I'm all in favour of African Heritage month, Black History Month, celebrating our heritage, but sometimes—and this may sound perverse—the celebration obscures the reality of people who struggled and didn't make it, people who struggled and got *crushed*. Their history is also our heritage. Their history is also part of our community. So I really wanted to look at what happens to, in this case, two guys who didn't figure out the simple truth that crime does not pay, who didn't figure out that, unfortunately, you have to work harder than others and make do with less pay than others, but just that's the way it goes. You don't go and hit somebody over the head with a hammer because life is unfair to you. They didn't understand that. They didn't see that simple truth, and I wanted to see that for myself and try to understand the psychology of someone who says, like Rufus, "I'm going to hit somebody over the head with a hammer, so I can get my clothes out of the cleaners." That's cold-blooded and it's nasty and it's immoral and it's wrong and it's stupid—all of the above—but it's also a not unreasonable response when you don't believe that there is any other way to get your clothes out of the cleaners. I wanted to try to understand that, and again I made this effort to not think about race relations in the 1930s and 1940s from some kind of Pollyannaish perspective—"Oh well, times were tough but we made do and we worked hard and we got ahead." No, not everybody was able to do that; not everybody wanted to do that. I wanted to understand that Aaron-the-Moor attitude, because I thought it's a kick-ass attitude. It's a sort of projection, because I could never be Rufus, nor would I want to be Rufus. On the other hand, I needed to understand how guys from my community ended up like Rufus, maybe not committing murder but ending up in jail.

When I was involved in that youth movement I made a trip to Springhill Penitentiary.

HW This was when you were working with the Central Planning Committee.

GEC Yes. I walked into this bullpit amphitheatre where I was asked to address all these guys I went to grade school with. Even if you could say that a minority of them were there because of wrongful convictions or because they didn't have good legal representation, the majority were there probably because they did make bad decisions. I addressed them on the standpoint of race, saying that as Black people we have to do better and not be in jail. But here I am, I'm nineteen, I don't have a real job, I haven't gone to university. I'm a kid off the same streets as them, except that I haven't yet (and thank God I have not yet) made those kinds of choices that would land me in the place that they were. That made a big impression on me. Why are these guys here? There are plenty of answers to that question, but still it was troubling, because they were from the same community as I was from, North End Halifax, guys I used to be scared of in school, because they would beat you up, and here they were. So I started asking myself why it was that I and my two brothers did

FIGURE 12 (left). Rufus Hamilton. Library and Archives Canada C-147475.
FIGURE 13 (right). George Hamilton. Library and Archives Canada 0131147.

not end up that way. Of course a lot of it has to do with the lessons our parents taught us and so on, but also there was an ability on our part to handle social disappointment without having to resort to violence, or crime, theft, robbery, in order to get what we thought was "rightfully ours." These guys didn't have those kinds of constraints.

So, in writing *George & Rue*, I wanted to think about what it is not to have those kinds of constraints, particularly with Rufus, because I think George is a character who would be very happy to be at home with his family, raising some cows and sheep, tending the apples, and picking the berries. Incidentally, one of the ironies of this case that has always struck me is that, according to George's own testimony, when he went AWOL from the army in Quebec, he joined the merchant marine (though no one's been able to prove that). The merchant marine guys didn't get recognized as being participants in the war, and therefore didn't get benefits and access to veterans' pensions, until two years ago, fifty-eight years after the war ended. Now I often wonder, "Damn, if all of them could have been recognized in '45 and gotten those veterans' benefits, it's very unlikely that George would have ended up in a situation where he was thinking, 'I have to go steal money to get my wife and newborn child out of the hospital or to buy firewood or buy something to drink.'" He would have had that pension benefit coming in at least every month, anyway, which would have provided some stability for him and his little family, but that didn't happen for fifty-eight years after the war.

Rufus, though, wants more. He wants a GQ life, and he doesn't have the wherewithal to have that legally, so he's going to have it any other way he can. Those were the kinds of issues I wanted to explore in looking at George and Rue—how these guys get to be the way they are.

HW One of the distinctive things about *George & Rue* as a historical novel is that while this is a historical event—a documented part of the public historical record—it is also, first and foremost, family history. It's not uncommon for the historical novel to be grounded in family history (Timothy Findley's *The Wars* is a good example), but the fact that this is family history is obviously very charged in this case, as suggested by your discussion of genealogy in the "Verdict" section of the novel, in which you describe the book as "a tryst with biography." How did your family react to the news that you were going to write about this history, and what has the reaction been in the family to the novel now that it's out?

GEC The simplest thing and the best thing to say is that everyone was completely helpful to me in giving me information to write this book. I already had *Execution Poems* out, so people already had a sense of where I was going. But there was a huge difference between *Execution Poems* and *George & Rue*. *Execution Poems* was more an act of fantasy, even though it was based on fact. The dialogues I give the guys in *Execution Poems* are poetic, very imaginary, and some of the things I had them do, like breaking into the Palace Restaurant in the poem "Spree" and messin' up a guy and a woman, are all made up. So, even though *Execution Poems* was out there and it was linked to the real-life events, no one was really worried. This goes to show the place of poetry in society and the place of fiction, because with the novel, suddenly everyone was far more nervous, because the novel is somehow taken as being more real. In some ways it actually is more real, because it uses more documents, it reflects more on the actual events and actual characters, and so forth. I do carry over some of the characters from the book of poetry into the novel, like the character of India, but for the most part the novel is far more real. I like to think of the two of them as being a stereo treatment of the story. First you have the snapshot of poetry, and then you have the film version of fiction. It just seems more real, just as documentary film seems more real than a collection of snapshots. So I think anxiety over the novel was greater in the family, though I was not particularly aware of that, or maybe I didn't allow myself to become too aware of that, because, again, everybody was very forthcoming with information. But I think, even though it's fifty-six years ago that all these events happened, that there is still a segment of the family (maybe all the family but me) that feels, "Let bygones be bygones. These guys are dead and gone. It's an embarrassment. It's humiliating for the family for us to be talking about these guys." My own (maybe selfish) standpoint as an artist is, "Look, these guys are also our flesh and blood. My writing about them is not to say what great guys they were, nor is it to excuse what they did. But it is to say we have to understand, for the family but also for the society, exactly the kinds of conditions that they faced. This is not about our family; it's about the society, and it's a society that existed back then and may still exist in certain ways today."

I think about all the "brothers" shooting each other in Toronto—and this is not to get into so-called "Black-on-Black" crime—and in my own simplistic understanding of that kind of violence, a lot of it has to do with a loss of bearings and a loss of perspective and a loss of understanding of who you are. You need to remember, "Holy smokes, my ancestors survived the inhumanity of slavery. It was meant to work people to death, for crying out loud, and yet they survived." So you don't get a job over there, or you're not wearing clothes that are as nice as somebody else's, or you didn't get that bank loan because of the "racist" bank officer. So bloody what? Not to say that you shouldn't protest or push for change—of course you have to do all that—but does that justify gunning down somebody for some crack? You have to say to yourself, "What am I doing, attacking my own brothers and sisters, mothers and fathers, for stuff that's going to injure myself and others, to benefit exactly whom?" The book is not about how screwed up our clan is. No. The book is about how people did screwy things because of a history of very screwed-up interpretations of what their place in society should be. That is the emphasis.

HW It strikes me—especially after talking to a series of writers who have been writing about history—that it takes a lot of courage to do it, but that's even more the case when you are writing about somebody who is part of your family.

GEC I have to be honest and say I don't know what the family thinks. I don't know. One of my cousins said to me just a couple of days ago, "I read your book. I think it's really good." I'm not saying that just to puff up the book here, but that meant a lot to me coming from a younger guy, a first cousin of mine who, when he was a teenager, was grabbed by Halifax police when they saw him standing at a bus stop with a boombox, and they took him into custody, claiming it was stolen. It wasn't; it was his. This is not to say that all those encounters are always wrong and that the police are automatically racist (although I suspect that might be true of most of them most of the time), and it's not to say that while he was reading my book he was flashing back to that moment for himself. But as a young Black man growing up in Halifax, he had his own experiences with law enforcement or with the feeling of outsiderness in the society that I'm going to presume he could recognize in the lives of characters like Rufus, if not George. So it was really good for me to hear that and at least to guess that he liked the book for reasons of that sort. My brother read it, and his only comment on the book was, "I read your novel." Period. He ended up writing something about it, so that was nice, but while he didn't say anything negative about it, he also didn't say anything suggesting he was glorying in the reading. It's interesting because it also suggests that it's far more difficult for us to suspend our disbelief and just simply accept the novel as a novel, and that's because I think we do have a lot invested in history.

Maybe what we have invested in history is its chronicling of pain, its documenting of pain, which, despite all the successes and triumphs of an individual, a family, a people, can never be fully erased. History is a record of injustices and injuries that can never be repaired. How can any number of payments for residential school abuses, or the theft of Aboriginal land, actually compensate the victims? For instance, all of the City of Vancouver is open to land claim initiatives, but even if Aboriginal people win, can they recover the original, pristine "Vancouver," their undisrupted folkways, or should they even want to? But the problem goes deeper. Even if someone were to argue that the historical George and Rufus Hamilton can be excused for committing robbery, because they were in need—and murder, because they were hitting back at a truly racist, white-supremacist society—how do their crimes actually ameliorate their dreadful circumstances? And what about their victim, the real-life Norman Phillip Burgoyne (whose name is altered in the novel)? Even if he had been an out-and-out Ku Kluxer (and he was absolutely the opposite), how would his murder have resolved slavery, segregation, and the relegation of Black people in the Maritimes to a bottom-of-the barrel and back-of-the-classroom economic status? But the actual victim, Mr Burgoyne, was a pretty nice guy, charitable, and he had four young children who, as a result of the actions of my late cousins, were left to grow up poor and fatherless.

HW That must have been one of the most difficult aspects of deciding to write about this history.

GEC He was surely a victim of the Hamiltons as much as the Hamiltons were victims of their circumstances—including racism. Yet, history—even fictional history—demands facing unlovely, ugly truths, such as the probability that, somewhere along the line, Burgoyne was an innocent beneficiary of the invasion of North America by his ancestors and the creation of vast wealth—wealth that drove the Renaissance and created Modernity—sapped from South American gold mines and the blood of Aboriginal and African slaves. Still, in writing this story, I had to be sensitive to the clear, immediate fact that an innocent man was struck down in his prime by two guys acting on animal instincts—to fill their guts and clothe their backs using somebody else's means. But, again, the irony here is that that was what slavery was all about too—filling guts, clothing backs, all based on violence or the real threat thereof to a class of slaves.

Still, in reference to Mr Burgoyne, there was no way I could be insensitive to his real situation as an innocent victim, especially since his elder daughter wrote to me back in the summer of 2000 to ask, on behalf of herself, her siblings, and her mother, that I *not* write this story. They were worried, she said, that my aim was to profit from a tragedy that had wrecked their family life. I responded that my aim was certainly not financial gain, but that, given that my late cousins' crimes harmed *two* families—hers and mine—I had to try to understand why they did what they did, that I had to reclaim their bodies for us (meaning my family). Mr Burgoyne's daughter wrote back that she and her family still disagreed with my desire to write about this story, but that they essentially understood my motivation. Now, I should say, that was the understanding that pertained to *Execution Poems*. I heard nothing from Mr Burgoyne's survivors when that book appeared, and nothing from them when it received the Governor General's Award. However, when *George & Rue* appeared, Mr Burgoyne's daughter wrote letters to the Fredericton *Daily Gleaner* and even did an interview with CBC Radio, blasting me for "exploiting" her family's pain in the hopes of making a million dollars. Permitted to reply to this charge, I affirmed the right of artists to address historical—and even contemporary—events, explained my own familial interest in the story, and reiterated, again and again, that the book was not a biography of her father, but a *novel*, and that while it may earn me some dough, that was not the purpose in writing it, but to explore a matter well inside the public domain, and one now relatively remote in time. Even so, it was strange to do interviews and to have to address the crime and punishment of 1949 as if they had just happened. I had to keep saying, "You know, this incident happened fifty-six years ago! And my story is *fictional!*" But again, what the Burgoyne family "reception" of *George & Rue* (as opposed to their strict silence on *Execution Poems*) demonstrates, is the very different weight people give to the novel (not just art, but "real"—and "merchandise") as opposed to a poetry collection (art, artificial, and non-commercial). The problem with historical fiction is that it forces a collision between real flesh-and-blood beings and events and the imaginary. Some readers cannot—*cannot*—separate the two.

HW It's an occupational hazard with the genre, it seems.

GEC To come back to something I was trying to say earlier (not to sound sanctimonious or high and mighty, because that's not really the point), my interest in the story of the Hamiltons was to say that we have to recover their bodies. They belong to us. They are our skeletons in the closet, but they are ours. If most folks choose to rattle the cages of their ancestors, there is bound to be at least one skeleton coming out. In other words, I don't think our family is worse than anybody else's. The point of writing the story was to throw a light on the society, on what it was like before there were attempts at amelioration through Civil Rights legislation and fair-employment legislation and multiculturalism and all those things that have made life somewhat better for minorities and others in Canada. What was it like before anybody thought of saying, "we really have to change the way those people are treated"? Remember, this was the era of the residential schools, this was the era of attempted forced assimilation of Aboriginal people in general, this was the era in which the Doukhobor children got taken away from their families and placed in internment camps in B.C.

HW The same with Japanese-Canadians.

GEC You're right. This was an era in which groups of people could be policed and coerced into pseudo-slavery, which is what happened to Japanese-Canadians. If you read Joy Kogawa's *Obasan*, you know that some Japanese-Canadians were forced into sugar-beet farming in Alberta, as part of their punishment for simply being Japanese and living on the west coast of Canada and prospering in the fisheries. So I really wanted to look at that and try to remember what that era was like. I found the way my father and my mother had to grow up very interesting, so I wanted to try, in a strange way, to bear witness and also honour that history, that reality, when you were supposed to know what your place was and stay in it and not transgress, because if you do, the full weight of social sanction and the law will come down on you, so you had better make sure that you accept your place and not be too uppity.

HW One of the challenges of working in a history that has been marginalized, excluded, ignored, is that there isn't the wealth of public, archived sources that one can draw on when, say, writing about "white Canada." What does that mean for somebody who wants to write about the history of African-Canadians?

GEC It means you have to go and look at unconventional sources, and particularly it means you have to be more interested in dealing with oral records, folklore, orature (to use that word). No one has written the history of Black Nova Scotia between 1925 and 1949, or of Black New Brunswick for that matter, but luckily there are plenty of people still living who have memories that are, I think, pretty good, who can give you a perspective on what it was like. I had a chance to talk to a lot of people, and no one was shy about sharing information about the era, what life was like in Fredericton or Saint John or Halifax. Of course, it was a lot like it is now, in that there were scandals, and people had passions, and people behaved badly, but they behaved badly and had their passions in a particular context, which the oral testimony was able to flesh out. Of course, from a strictly academic standpoint, you can't trust a lot of that. For instance, one of the stories I heard from somebody who now lives in Kentville was that, when she was a girl, her father took her to the barn when George and Rufus were hanged, and she was nine at the time. Now I talked to a police officer who was there and he said, "No police officers brought their children with them to the hanging." So who do I believe? I believe the woman, because she has a clear memory of having been there; who knows, maybe, from a police officer's point of view, this could be an object lesson about how to not make mistakes in life. So you have these conflicts, but nevertheless there's still this richness of atmosphere and texture that you get from those oral accounts. I was really lucky. When I went down to Fredericton to do research in 2000, and I was on CBC Radio, people wrote me letters, because of course in Fredericton the story is still very much remembered. People wrote me out of the blue, sent me poems, sent me clippings, gave me names of other people to talk to and phone numbers. I had a treasure trove of materials that was basically this oral testimony from people.

HW You did have access, though, to the transcripts of the trial.

GEC Yes, that oral testimony was supplemented by 1300 pages of trial transcripts. I don't really have that much dialogue in the novel, but a lot of the dialogue is based on what I read in the transcripts: the way the detectives would speak, or the way lawyers would speak, or the guys themselves. For instance, one of the prosecutors asked George, "Is it all right to hit a man with a hammer as you would kill a fly?" and George's answer was very simple but yet elegant: "Both a man and a fly want to live." Holy smokes! This guy's got a grade-three education and he's dancing circles around this prosecutor, at least in terms of philosophy. It was a great response, and there were many of that nature in the transcripts. I also read through issues of the Fredericton

Daily Gleaner from the moment the crime was discovered and first announced in the papers, right up to the executions, a full seven months' worth, and that was the greatest education about '49, about exactly what was going on, what people were thinking. The advertising was brilliant.

HW How about the line about McAdam's Funeral Home, "First Choice in Last Respects"? Is that out of the paper or is that George Elliott Clarke?

GEC That's McAdam's Funeral Home. That was their slogan. I'm sorry; I want to take credit for it, but I can't.

HW Manina Jones has pointed out a whole strain of Canadian literature that she describes as "documentary collage," in which documents or ostensible documents are being essentially reworked into the fabric of a fictional narrative and being recontextualized. In *George & Rue*, too, there is that intertextual effect, the integration of documents such as the trial transcript you've already mentioned, the medical report on George Hamilton, the brothers' letters to the Governor General, newspaper reports on the trial and on the hangings. How did you use documents, and how did you feel about using them?

GEC It's all material. In every sense of the word, I mean it. I just felt that I had to enter the universe of 1925, 1932, 1949, and this was the way to do it. I had to understand the context in which these guys lived out their lives, and that meant understanding those documents. Everything is completely interconnected anyway, in life, everything is, and it was interesting to try to find these little threads of connection amongst individuals and peoples and places, even if the people who were being connected didn't realize it, and to think through everything. Plenty of stuff I never used in the novel, but it was nonetheless a window on the era.

HW But I also get a sense in reading the novel that you are reworking the language of those documents, resituating it in a different context and in a lot of ways contesting or parodying its authority.

GEC It was fascinating to see pages and pages of telegrams back and forth between Fredericton and Ottawa, the day before the hangings, confirming that they were going to take place. They're just flimsy little pieces of paper, but yet they are literally carrying life or death. I never particularly used the telegrams in the novel, but it was fascinating to see the machinery of capital punishment at work. As you pointed out, there were other texts that I did decide to use, like newspaper accounts, which were fascinating, because they were definitely riddled with race, and I can say racism too, although the reporters may not have seen it that way. They would have just seen it as putting forward information that was absolutely germane, such as that these were two Negroes who had done this. They may not have understood that that kind of racial identification was going to inflame actual racists in the community, to the extent that ten thousand people showed up in the streets of Fredericton to try to witness some aspect of the hanging—to hear something, to see something—in the wee hours of the morning. They had to get a hundred RCMP officers in to surround the jail, to keep back the mob. I talked to people who were out that night. One guy, who in fact was Black (and I loved his answer), said he was in the air force flying around bombing people in Germany, so being out there with a mob of ten thousand people in the streets of Fredericton didn't bother him. On the other hand, there was a Black woman who said that she was so frightened for the safety of her children that she locked them up in the house and turned off all the lights, and said, "We have to sit tight and be quiet and hope that this will happen and blow over." Two different people, both Black, two radically different attitudes towards the throng in the street.

HW That scene is a good example of the recontextualizing that I'm talking about, because I'm sure the newspaper accounts didn't suggest that a kind of orgasmic spasm passed through the crowd at the moment of the executions, as you do in *George & Rue* [*laughs*].

GEC Well, I'm guessing that that's partly what's going on. It was sort of like a moment of crisis and release, because, according to the witnesses I have spoken to, there was all this music and singing and noise prior to the actual moment, but as soon as people heard the trap fall open (and they could hear that) there was silence—perfect, complete silence.

HW Probably the biggest hazard in writing about the Hamiltons is avoiding the appearance that you are defending or exonerating them. Yet both *Execution Poems* and *George & Rue* certainly work, if not to excuse the crime, then to provide a broader context for the crime, and you have talked already about how that was a big part of the impetus to write the book. In "The Killing," the poem which describes the murder in *Execution Poems*, you stage this exchange between George and Rue:

Rue: Here's how I justify my error:
        The blow that slew Silver came from two centuries back.
        It took that much time and agony to turn a white man's whip
        Into a black man's hammer.

George: No, we needed money,
      so you hit the So-and-So,
      only much too hard.

Who's right?

GEC [*laughs*] Well (and this is not to take an easy way out) I think they're both right. I have to say for the record that my dad, who has just turned seventy, still drives a taxi. He's been driving a taxi for the last twenty years since he retired from the railway. He takes precautions, and he's been very safe, and nothing serious has happened to him, and of course I pray for his safety continuously. So I understand the horror and the revulsion that the murder of a taxi driver specifically creates. A murder of anyone is awful, but a taxi driver and persons like taxi drivers, like convenience store workers, are public servants. Yes, you pay a fare to a taxi driver if you're taken from one place to another, but it is first and foremost a service that is essential in a lot of cases. So I understand why people were so revolted by this crime committed by the Hamiltons in 1949. Of course things were just made worse by the fact that they were Black/Mikma'q (although they would have been seen just simply as coloured guys back then, and that was bad enough). The fact that the money was spent on "wine, women and song" (to use the old cliché) also did not stand them in good stead. George tried to make it a little better for himself by saying, "Well, I used the money to take care of my newborn baby," but still it was "blood money," even though one could make a strong legal argument for excusing George, presuming that it could be proven beyond a reasonable doubt that he was not involved in the actual slaying (if you buy his argument, which is suggested by one piece of circumstantial evidence, that he was not in the car). But they were two young men who had been in and out of prison already, both had criminal records, hadn't worked to do much for themselves, constantly seemed to be on the wrong side of the law. Rufus had just gotten out of Dorchester Penitentiary, George was put on trial for arson but acquitted. These guys were ne'er-do-wells and troublemakers. Rufus certainly had a capacity for violence; he'd already been in Dorchester for striking a gentleman in the head and grabbing his wallet. George, on the other hand, was somebody who would do theft and burglaries—not violent crime, but nevertheless invading people's property. So, from the standpoint of the law-abiding, white, propertied gentlemen of Fredericton, these guys were better off out of the way.

    This is not to mention the fact that their victim was completely the opposite—never mind the fact that he happened to be white. The really important point was that the actual victim had four children; he was an entrepreneur; he was a veteran, and that counted for something; he was a householder, which also counted for something; and, according to all the reports I've ever come across, he was a very nice guy who was very happy to ferry anyone around. And he was only five feet tall. George and Rufus were more like 5'9", 5'10", so they towered over him, literally, so even if it had turned into a fight, and even if he had been aware that they were going to attack him, he still would have had a big fight on his hands. But it was completely unfair; the guy was struck in the back of his head. It was a cowardly attack. So I'm giving you all my very good understanding of why people were rightly revolted and why they howled for blood. At the same time, I'm more than aware of the fact that their race was not overlooked. If it had been two white guys, people would have been calling for their heads too, but the fact they were Black made it that much worse and made it that much more certain that they would be convicted and hanged.

HW You underscore that by mentioning the very similar murder committed not long afterwards by two white men in Montreal, whose execution was commuted.

GEC When I first heard about that crime I thought that here was basically the same crime, in fact, worse, if you want to take into account the number of times the taxi driver in Montreal was struck and the fact that the proceeds from that crime were used to support yet another crime, a bank robbery, for crying out loud. Now it has to be said, there was great extenuating circumstance for those two guys in Montreal; that is, they both were young. They were seventeen and nineteen when they committed these crimes, and it's probable that the Crown or the Governor General in council said, "These guys are just teenagers; they have a chance to get their lives back on track. We'll let them think they're going to hang up to ninety minutes before they go to the gallows and then we'll commute it," which is actually what happened. Ninety minutes before they were going to be hanged, they received the commutation, so basically they were shown the shadow of the gallows to put them on the straight and narrow for the rest of their lives. Nevertheless, even though you can make that argument, teens were still being hanged at that point in 1950. Look at the Stephen Truscott case; he was put on death row at age fourteen. So the fact that they were teens may have played a role in it, but it didn't necessarily have to have been the case. George and Rue were only in their early twenties, and if they too had been shown the shadow of the gallows, that also might have had a salutary effect on them. The difference was (and this is the point of bringing up the other trial) they were Black. There could be no mercy extended to them. I grant that the crime was revolting and I understand that they deserved the sentence they were given, but, on the other hand, racism was not absent from the decision-making that went into the trials and everything else. As a matter of fact, I got a letter from the grandson of the actual trial judge, who wrote to me to say, "Look, my grandfather was not prejudiced against coloured people, because his daughter married a guy from the West Indies." I wrote him back to say, "That's fantastic, and I'm sure you're right, but if you read the trial transcripts you'll see that your late grandfather unfortunately made racist statements during the trial."

HW In that verdict on the murders in the novel itself, the trial judge, Justice Chaud, delivers a self-congratulatory speech exonerating not George of the crime of murder but Canadians of the crime of racism. Given that the transcripts of the trial were one of your key sources, to what degree is that speech based on the historical verdict?

GEC Very much so [*laughs*]. People would say, rightfully, "Look, in our minds we didn't sense that there was anything prejudicial going on. Justice was being done. It was unfortunate that these guys did what they did, but everything was fine in terms of the justice system." In fact, what the grandson of the judge wrote to me was, "Look, my grandfather was haunted, basically until his dying day, by what he had to do," pointing out that the judge, in a sense, had a guilty conscience about the verdicts that he had to bring down. But the grandson also explained that if his grandfather hadn't sentenced them to be hanged, they would have been lynched. Now that's too dramatic. I really don't think they could have been lynched, but I do think there would have been a hell of a lot of public unrest. The actual George and Rufus have a sister (who still lives, and I've spoken with her), and she was there every single day of the trial and described it as a lynch-mob mentality. And it would be surprising if it were not that, frankly. The grandson's testimony would seem to square with what she reported to me.

At the actual sentencing, though, something very interesting happened involving the judge. It was in the newspaper coverage of the sentencing, but it's not in the transcripts and I didn't see it anywhere else, because it was independent of the Hamilton trials. There was a Mikma'q man who had (excuse the expression) blown away a guy with a shotgun. He was also convicted of first-degree murder and was being sentenced in the very same session; all three guys were in the courtroom at the same time, before the same judge. They've all been convicted of first-degree murder, and they're all men of colour. The Mikma'q guy comes up first, and the judge says, basically, "You've messed up, but I'm going to give you a three-year sentence and send you home to your family, give you time to sober up and get your life back together." First-degree murder, and the judge says [*snaps fingers*], "You go home after three years in the big house." The Crown appealed and lost the appeal. This was unbelievable; a first-degree murder conviction, and a guy goes to jail for three years? So he's taken off to jail. Now it's George and Rufus, and the judge says, "You guys messed up and you're gonna hang, on this given day." I mean, he didn't give the other guy twenty years or even ten years; he gave him three years. Oddly, that was the judge wrestling with his conscience, knowing that these two guys were definitely going to hang. He wasn't hanging three. He was going to hang two, yes, but not three.

HW Still, that seems like a remarkably stark inconsistency.

GEC Yes, the Crown saw it as being odd [*laughs*]. I really do think, though, that that was his way of salving his own conscience about this matter. And there were people who were extremely upset, especially about George. Rufus's very record showed that he was the archetypal hardened criminal, and his two years in Dorchester obviously didn't make him better. I do believe (and the novel follows this line of thinking) that he struck the blows. I can't say for sure if George was there or not, but I tend to believe him when he says, "Look, I had planned to hit somebody, but when I saw Silver, I decided no, and I told my brother that." It's possible that George is lying through his teeth through his entire testimony, but it's fascinating that all of the points on which you could test whether he was telling the truth were corroborated by independent analyses or investigations, but on the one point that could exonerate him— at least of actual murder—there was no evidence that he was telling the truth and wasn't in the car. But I tend to believe that Rufus did it, because Rufus had already carried off an assault and robbery involving hitting someone over the head in a Fredericton alleyway, and he went to Dorchester for that for two years, and when he came out he was meaner and hungrier than ever. Within three weeks of being released from Dorchester, he had, I believe, committed a murder and robbery and was back in custody, now to his dying day.

HW Especially in the novel, you give Rufus a certain subversive quality. At times, he very deftly takes white authority to task, and he's certainly not bowing down before it during the trial. Was that characterization based on your sense of him from reading the transcripts? He comes across almost as a poet *manqué*.

GEC Yes, he does, although in the actual trial transcripts he created this entire fantasy world. He basically says, "Look, my brother gave me some money. We rode around in somebody's car, and I got drunk. I took a bath. I went to see a girl I like. I didn't murder anybody." That was his testimony. "I don't know why people were saying I murdered someone. I had nothing to do with it. Yeah, I got drunk. That's not a crime. Somebody gave me some money; I'm not going to say no." So his testimony was just a different world that had nothing to do with a murder or taking somebody's car. So it was George's testimony that hanged both of them, even though George felt that his testimony was basically about what his brother did, as I pointed out in the novel. In section 69 of the Criminal Code back then (and it didn't change, by the way, until 1992), if more than one person went out to commit one crime, and a larger crime resulted, even if everybody but one of those people wasn't involved in the actual crime, they were all collectively responsible. The Crown took the view that if you were all going out to do one crime, you were prepared to do another one. It was like this domino theory of crime [*laughs*].

HW Historical fiction by writers of non-European heritage (wholly or partly, I should add) is relatively scarce in Canada. There's Michael Ondaatje's work (*The English Patient, In the Skin of a Lion*) there's *Obasan*, Sky Lee's *Disappearing Moon Café*, and more recently *George & Rue* and Joseph Boyden's *Three Day Road*. That's not an exhaustive list, but ultimately the work of such writers is still a small part of what is a burgeoning corpus of work in Canadian literature. Do you have any thoughts on why this might be, and do you think that is something that's changing now?

GEC As you know—powerfully, wonderfully, richly—a lot of our literature is created by immigrants, whose first focus quite rightly is on childhood or familial memories connected to back home, wherever back home was or is, and so if they're going to write about Canada, it will be about what it's like to be a Torontonian, what it's like to be in contemporary Montreal or Vancouver, as opposed to going back historically and saying, "Well, it was like this or it was like that." I really think that the reason why Sky Lee and Joy Kogawa and Joseph Boyden and myself (if I can put myself in that group) are writing historical novels anchored in Canada is that we are of a generation that is secure enough finally, after umpteen years of inhabiting this space called Canada, to be able to write about our cultural Canadian past.

It's a way, too, of laying claim to that territory. I mean, I would love to be able to write about Cuba or Trinidad or Mozambique or South Africa, which is not to say I can't; if I do enough research I can probably go and write about those places and maybe do a half-decent job. On the other hand, *I got a story to tell*, or at least I had a story to tell, that was about right here, about places just down the highway, places I grew up in and used to drive by a lot. For me, the exciting thing was, "Hey, this is my territory," in the sense that I could write about this place because I knew it. I didn't really know 1949 or 1935 very well, but I could certainly read some books and get a better sense of what those eras were like. I knew that if I was going to write a novel I was going to have to write something that dealt with being here, and besides, it's a fascinating, rich, interesting, complex, atrocious, and beautiful history, all in one, just like everybody else's history. But I don't have access to everyone else's history. I have access to this little piece of terra firma, so I knew that's what I would have to work with.

HW So it has to do with being grounded in a particular sense of place?

GEC Yes, and then there's Halifax. You know, I've now lived most of my life away from Nova Scotia. I spent twenty-one years in Nova Scotia, and I've spent twenty-four years outside, now, and it gives me distance, definitely, and a little perspective, the perspective of being middle-aged and all the rest of it. I look back now on Halifax, among other places, and I can see what a fascinatingly rich and strange and bizarre place it is, and always was, and probably always will be. Now, as a writer, I have the freedom to be able to describe that. The Halifax I find interesting is the Halifax of the brothels, the Halifax of the class divisions, the Halifax of the understated racial conflicts, which burst out into actual riots every ten years or so, which is fascinating, because it puts Halifax in the same league as some American cities. It's an odd thing for a Canadian city to actually have race riots, and Halifax has had them. I look back on it now and I can see what a complex place that is and how difficult it is to write about it, as someone who can now call himself a novelist. I find it a very daunting place to try to write about, because parts of it are so intensely different and seething with these clashing cultures and histories and so on.

HW I don't think the Chamber of Commerce is going to be adopting that description in its promotional literature any time soon.

GEC [*laughs*]. I remember going to school in Halifax and there would be guys laying out on the sidewalk, practically just around the corner from my house, blood gushing from their foreheads. They were too drunk and fell down and cut their heads open on the sidewalk, and the police were not coming to pick them up and take them to the drunk tank. They were just laying there till they slept it off.

HW Just part of the municipal fauna.

GEC Yes, exactly. This is all a way of saying what a tremendous place this is. There was an African-American guy, who's passed away now; I never knew him, but I remember seeing him on the streets. He always hung out on Spring Garden Road and would always say hello, always with a nice big smile, and he was clearly eccentric, because he would wear winter clothes all year round. On the hottest day of the summer he'd have on a big overcoat, scarves all over the place, big hat and gloves. But—and I think he partly made his living doing this—this guy was an awesome pianist. He'd walk off Spring Garden Road into one of the piano stores, and he'd sit there and he would play the piano to get people to come in and hang out and maybe buy a piano. And he was awesome! He probably had stepped off a ship and decided "I ain't going back there," and just walked around Halifax like this, and nobody bothered him. There was also a cross-dresser who you'd see on Spring Garden Road, and what would be odd was that he wasn't a complete cross-dresser. It was just shoes and sometimes stockings, nylons. You'd see this guy, and he was clearly a guy, dressed in a grey business suit, conservative, with a shirt and tie, but he'd be walking oddly, and you'd look down and you'd notice that he was wearing bright red pumps. And again nobody made a big deal about it. Halifax is this amazingly complex place where you can have people who are eccentric, who basically go about their business without a whole lot of undue social interference. In other places they might be hounded, but not Halifax. I think that has to do with the weird power of it being a port, like Amsterdam, like "Paree," like London, like New York, or New Orleans. Ports almost always have more openness than a godforsaken Prairie town, where the Bible-thumpers are saying, "You better not wear your red pumps" [*laughs*].

At any rate, I finally decided, at middle age, that I needed to continue to try to write about this space, because it's what I know best and I do think that there's some terrific history attached to it. I haven't done anything with this story, but there's a minister of the African Baptist Association, who apparently, back in the 1880s, tried to fly to heaven, with wings made of sheepskin, and crashed into a burdock patch. This was in Weymouth Falls, and he's one of the great ministers, F.R. Langford. This is an epic guy.

HW You have written about him already in *Whylah Falls*.

GEC Yes, and I'd heard these stories about him, including one I heard from the elderly lady that I used to sit down and talk with in Weymouth Falls. She knew F.R. Langford when she was a girl, and he apparently was a very tough parent, and he made his daughters build a stone wall around their house with their bare hands. I don't know if it was punishment or what, but it's like, "You all get out there and build me a stone wall around this house with your bare hands." So one of the daughters rebelled and ran away and joined the circus, going to the U.S. I never put that in *Whylah Falls* or anyplace else, but it goes to show that, like anywhere, people do odd things or interesting things here too. I realize that there are more and more of these kinds of characters that I need to engage and think about. In *George & Rue* there's a scene where Asa is murdered, and his shoes are left on the wharf. Well, that came from a story my uncle told me about a guy (he wasn't a minister, he was a deacon) who was beaten to a pulp and thrown into Halifax Harbour in the 1950s, but his shoes remained immaculate on the dock [*laughs*].

HW A recurring feature of your creative work (including *George & Rue*) that really fortifies its historical orientation is the use of archival photographs. What's behind that particular preoccupation, and what role do you see those photographs playing in your texts?

GEC I think it's in some ways a sign of being a frustrated artist, just as I am a frustrated musician. I also have this idea that any book should be this complete production, and for me visuals and particularly photographs are a way of presenting a greater sense of fullness to the text, as opposed to it just being all these words. I wanted to have some other textual matter that would give the eye something different to look at, provide some different information, and just to help conjure up a milieu. In *Saltwater Spirituals and Deeper Blues* I had a bunch of photographs, but they weren't organized. The publisher, Lesley Choyce, said to me, "You should have some photographs in the book," so we went to the Black United Front and the Black Cultural Centre, and we just grabbed whatever we could, and he took a few photographs himself, and we threw them together, in three sections. So suddenly we had the poems, and we had photographs, and that's just the way the book worked. But I thought, next time the photographs are going to be arranged in a way that makes some kind of narrative sense, so I chose the photographs for *Whylah Falls* very deliberately and then decided I would keep trying to do that, because I wanted to add a greater sense of what I was talking about—the characters, the landscape, and just certain images that struck me as being interesting. In *Whylah Falls*, I wanted to present photographs of Black women that were not stereotypes in terms of roles: here's a maid, here's somebody who's a nurse, or somebody who's pushing the baby carriage. I really didn't want that, but those were the photographs that the public archives had. Luckily, I helped them discover a group of photographs that had been given to them, and they were of these women picnicking. As soon as I saw them I said, "These are definitely going

in the book." I had to change the whole time period of the book around to suit
the photographs, so that's what I did. I needed to have these images of these
women just being themselves. It was just an answer to a prayer that they turned
up.

HW This connects to our earlier discussion about the historical record,
because it shows how the historical record is exclusive or selectively inclusive,
in the sense that, as you said, there tend to be only certain kinds of photographs available, images which tend to reinforce certain stereotypes and reinforce social inequalities, and in some ways make you as a writer have to deal
with images in a different way. It's partly (as you're suggesting) about wanting to provide texture, but also in some ways about engaging in a kind of subversive dialogue with a public record that is flawed. Two images that come to
mind are the picture of the murder victim in *Whylah Falls*, which is not Graham Cromwell, and the pictures that you used of a hanging victim in *Execution Poems*, which of course is not Rufus and George Hamilton. You're having
some fun there, but I think you're also making a comment, too.

GEC It's funny, because when *Execution Poems* came out, one of my uncles
(in fact, one of the ones who gave me a lot of information about George and
Rufus) didn't read the photo credits very well and looked at the book and
said, "Is that George and Rufus?" I said, "No, I would never put their actual
hanging photo in the book." I have at least that much respect for the dead, at
least for the family's dead, not to expose them in such a way. On the other
hand, this photograph of José Ama I do find fascinating and troubling, because
it was taken by a Canadian photographer during a rebellion in 1932 by Aboriginal miners against a company in El Salvador, in which the army just mowed
them down. The photographs of the two dead Aboriginal people in *Whylah
Falls*, who are supposed to look like the fictional character Othello Clemence,
are from the same incident, as is a photograph of a row of dead bodies in *Lush
Dreams, Blue Exile*, taken by the same photographer, Victor F. Brodeur, who
was with the Canadian Armed Forces in El Salvador. I think what I was trying to do was to suggest the reality without actually having to give the reality.
So no, I'm not going to show Graham Jarvis, his thigh blasted apart with a shotgun. I am going to show two Aboriginal people from El Salvador who've been
massacred by the Salvadoran army, because these photographs are removed
enough in time and, in a sense, culture for me that I can say, "Here's another
horror, but we'll use this horror to suggest the horror I'm writing about," but
it's another, independent horror. You are invited to go and find out more
about this.

HW That dialogue between image and text, though, is getting very ontologically complex and interesting, even more than it already is in traditional historiography, in which there is a written narrative developing and often images are used to reinforce that narrative, but it's a different medium.

GEC It's a counter-narrative. It's propaganda. What I mean is that the photographic image—or an illustration, if well chosen—accentuates the mute polemic (or polemics) within a text. It's a counter-narrative in the sense that it's a different narrative, an alternative narrative: to "read" the photographs in *Whylah Falls* or in *Beatrice Chancy* or in *George & Rue* is to "read" the book in shorthand. With *Whylah Falls*, the photos indicate themes of travel, work, crime and punishment, redemption, and love. *Beatrice Chancy*'s images are more abstract, but still indicate a theme of the black body under stress. The photos in *George & Rue* may represent rural poverty, calamity, marginalization of people of colour, and death. (But I may be reading them too literally!) But these images are propaganda in the sense that they direct the audience to enter more fully into, participate more fully in, and accept more readily, the "world" of the text—and its polemical constitution.

HW In the "After Words" to *George & Rue* you "accept total guilt for all errors and faults herein—as well as for my usage of Blackened English. These capital crimes are my own." You make a similar observation in the acknowledgements to *Execution Poems*. Now, I appreciate the ironic edge to these observations, but doesn't that seem a little flippant?

GEC Yes, it is a little flippant.

First I'd like to address the question of language in the novel, which I realized I had to do in a very direct way. There are pieces in *Whylah Falls* written in so-called dialect, where I try to do a voice that's closer to Black English, but for the most part it's in Standard English. But I couldn't write the novel in Standard English. I wrote a first draft of it that was completely disastrous, because I tried to write it in Standard English, and it was cold, artificial, a super-self-absorbed series of intellectual games. I wasn't really digging down into the material, into the reality of the lives of these guys. It was completely artificial, so Iris Tupholme at Harper Collins said, "Please go and do this again" [*laughs*]. It took me two years to go and do it again, but when I finally got to do it again, I said to myself that I had to write this novel in the language that seems most natural to me, and that is an English that is partly from the 'hood (to use the slang) where I grew up, North End Halifax, the way we spoke in the school grounds and so on, but also reflecting the other part of my linguistic heritage, which has to do with my mother, who was a teacher, and my father, who's a very polished speaker of English and whose diction and enunciation and vocabulary are greater than mine and greater than those of most people I know. That's my inheritance—the streets, the home, school is in there too of course—and somehow I had to blend them together into what I call Blackened English. So, it's true to my own linguistic heritage, but also true to the way I think a lot of us tend to speak—Black Nova Scotians, that is, or Africadians (to use my highfalutin' term). So that's why I wanted to put that in the acknowledgements.

A book that I've taught a few times now called *Correggidora*, by an African-American woman writer, Gayl Jones, which came out in 1975 and is still in print, was also very informative and transformative for me. It is the story of a Black woman blues singer in Chicago in the 1930s, who is actually the third generation in her family out of slavery in Brazil. So it's about how she has to deal with her life in 1930s Chicago with the ghosts of Brazilian slavery hovering around her, literally and also in the abstract, and how messed up she is as a result. I think it's a particularly important novel for Black writers who are trying to find a register in English that can work for them to express their particular tone or style in English. It shows how you can take this English language and use it to express, in her case, a blues tone and blues sensibility. You feel like you're sitting in a blues nightclub in Chicago when you're reading her book. It seems completely real and natural, and that's the kind of thing I was aiming for.

But you're also asking me if it is kind of risky to end the novel with this disclaimer.

HW Yes, are you concerned about seeming flippant about the whole history by referring to any shortcomings of the novel as "capital crimes"?

GEC No. Again, it's kind of a defensive manoeuvre, recognizing that this is pretty serious stuff, as anybody knows by the time they've reached the end of the novel. It is based on real events, and so real people have been hurt in very serious ways, and that's not a laughing matter. On the other hand, it is fifty-six years later. I am from a different generation. I have had the benefit, or maybe the problem, of having read many similar books (*True Crime*, that is, or crime fiction) and so I do come at it from a certain distance that allows me to seem flippant or to be joking. But I did deliberately try to embed the whole story with comic moments, or moments that would make you sort of chuckle. You're saying, "Oh my God, that's horrible," but you're laughing at the same time, saying, "You're not going to put him in the trunk of his own car?" I felt it was the only way for me to ever talk about the story. If I'd written it with the feeling of "My God, it's so horrible, so grotesque" and you have to feel sorry and you have to cry, "Oh, my God, he's not going to hit her again," it would be dreadful. I mean, I would find it dreadful. How on earth could I read a book like that? Instead, this is a book where the narrator is letting you know from time to time that it's fine if you find this a little bit bizarre or funny or absurd, or that these guys were completely stupid to be doing it; it's fine, because they were. But at the same time you also have to stand back and say, "Oh my God, George Hamilton had children, and yet he's wrapped up in this stupid crime and he's going to die. Oh my God."

HW He had children, but he also had to buy his wife out of the hospital, too.

GEC That's right, so it's absurd all the way around, while at the same time they still have to take responsibility for what they did. But you could also see that they're not thinking straight, they're not doing things in any kind of proper frame of mind, beginning with the idea to pick up a hammer and go hit somebody. I mean, I haven't written a comedy, and I don't expect people to be going through it with belly laughs, but I was trying to write about this dark, heavy subject with a light hand, to say, "Yes, you can find this funny, you can laugh," because nothing we do now can bring these guys back, bring their victim back. We can't change the decisions of 1949. It's over and done with. But we can look at it and understand it better, and now we can also afford to laugh at things that were funny. It is funny. When I first heard about the story, I thought, "This sounds like the Coen brothers' movie *Fargo*." I mean, you drive around the south of New Brunswick, on bad roads, two-lane highways, in winter— snow and ice on the road—with a stolen car, two Black guys, one man wearing the dead man's taxi cap and jacket. That would be recognized [*laughs*]. You know, it just doesn't make sense. It's pitiful—I have to use that old word— that they're going to do this, but they could have gotten away with it too, at the same time, by saying, "Silver gave us his car." There's nobody who can say that he didn't. "He gave us a car, and he told us to drive it over here, and we did, and we left it." What got them hanged was George saying, "Here's where you find all the physical evidence, and here's the narrative that ties all the physical evidence together. The reason Silver's Rolex watch is in my stove is because we were trying to burn it" [*laughs*].

HW This confession in turn was motivated by his belief that he had not hit this man, and that therefore he was not guilty of the crime. So it is this thoroughly ambivalent narrative which, on the one hand, is hilarious but on the other hand is tragic, and there's a miscarriage of justice and … that's history.

GEC That's history.

Ghosts Are Our Allies
Margaret Sweatman

Margaret Sweatman was born and raised in the south end of Winnipeg. She received her BA in English and History from the University of Winnipeg and did her MA at Simon Fraser University. Her first novel, *Fox* (1991), a panoramic portrait of the 1919 Winnipeg General Strike, won the McNally Robinson Book of the Year Award. In 1996 she published *Sam and Angie*, an intense portrait of a downwardly spiralling relationship. Her most recent novel, *When Alice Lay Down with Peter* (2001), traces a family of Scottish immigrants through five generations, from the first Riel uprising to the late twentieth century. The novel won a number of awards, including another McNally Robinson Book of the Year Award and the Rogers Writers' Trust Fiction Prize. Sweatman currently divides her time between Winnipeg and Waterloo. I talked to her in Winnipeg in April of 2003.

HW Two of your three novels, *Fox* and *When Alice Lay Down with Peter*, reflect Winnipeg's central role in the history of the left and of labour in Canada. The city is the site of perhaps two of the three most substantial challenges to established authority in Canadian history—the Riel uprisings and the General Strike are obviously associated with Winnipeg, while the 1837 rebellions happened in Ontario and Quebec. What is it about the city? Is it something in the air?

MS Yes, and in our immigration patterns. The city has been split ever since, say 1885, the Sifton real estate boom, when minister of the interior Clifford Sifton began to choose particular immigrants, mostly Eastern European immigrants, for their feisty ignorance—big muscles, not too many urban people, not too many educated people, really good farm stock, peasants. But they brought with them all kinds of sophisticated political and religious dissent.

HW So exactly the opposite of what Sifton was trying to engineer?

MS He tried really hard to engineer a stupendous level of ignorance in the lower class, and it didn't work. Instead, it created the conditions for labour agitation and organization that ultimately led to the 1919 general strike, whose effects were still being felt when I was growing up in the fifties and sixties. Even then, everyone would know which side of the strike you or your family had been on. I knew that my grandfather was a prosecutor; he was a lawyer, and so I felt invalid, like there was no way that as a WASP I could truly understand enough about the world to write well. I was always aware that you were from the north end or the south end.

HW Because the geographical divide between north and south Winnipeg is also a class divide.

MS Very much a class divide—class and race and ethnicity. It was a huge cultural divide. It's changed since then, somewhat, but there is a stratified class culture in Winnipeg.

HW Both of your novels, of course, stress those class divisions. Do you think that class is something of a repressed consideration in Canadian literature—and in Canadian history for that matter?

MS Well not always, but it certainly can be. Upper Canada still dominates the publishing industry. There are some great books about class, but I think, generally, if you're going to be really successful, you just want to suppress money, make it not a character in your story. I still am troubled by books that ignore money.

HW There's an implicit assumption—this was documented, for instance, in John Porter's book *The Vertical Mosaic* in 1965—that Canada is somehow a classless society. That assumption seems to be mirrored in Canadian literature as well, where those issues are quite invisible a lot of the time, though they're certainly becoming more visible.

MS I just read Margaret Atwood's novel *Oryx and Crake*, a satire. She's very much writing about the powerful and the powerless. A writer like that is much more aware of where money is from; it is actually a potent character in the story. I hate to think of a replication in Canadian literature of the idea of Canadian culture as classless. I find it very offensive.

HW I found it interesting that in *Fox*, though you cover a broad social spectrum, from the government, members of the elite, and their families to anonymous workers, strikers, and their families, you approach the Winnipeg General Strike, which is probably the key moment in the history of labour in Canada, by focusing primarily but not exclusively on two upper-class characters, the cousins Eleanor and Mary, both of whom live a life of conspicuous luxury—Eleanor with resistance and Mary very self-indulgently. What was behind that narrative choice?

MS At that time in my life I felt that I was coming from a very privileged class. I never had any money myself because I was always trying to write. But I was aware that I was from a privileged class. I did play golf at the St. Charles Country Club as a little girl. My parents too are kind of outsiders; that is their class, but yet they're quite solitary. And I think I grew into being aware that there was a lot of old green money—that is, the money of the so-called establishment, gained through trading futures at the Grain Exchange—and into being an outsider in that strange society. I set my first sketches in the 1970s and '80s. I wanted to write about the privileged class. I found the excess hilarious.

HW This is in *Private Property*?

MS Yes. Then I was studying Bakhtin's "Discourse in the Novel," and finding the form for a novel, his model of the forum or the matrix as a marketplace of discourse and discord—a paratactic, discontinuous, fragmented structure comprised of different voices. The strike was the perfect structure for me. So then I shifted my characters into this forum, this marketplace argument, this sort of civic argument, and then began the research. I was really frightened of trying to represent a historical moment, so I did a lot of research. Before this, I had never thought I would ever write a historical novel. I came at it from Bakhtin, because this notion of the marketplace freed me from a linear narrative. His notion of a matrix as the structure of the novel was perfect for me, because I found linearity and the Aristotelian structure too frightening to start with. Geographically and structurally it was the perfect model for me, freeing me from all this terror of plot, so I could have an intersection of voices.

HW It's also about mirroring the experience of history as a kind of polyphonic experience.

MS Exactly, and about avoiding a linear narrative that is teleological, and where there has to be a judgment of right and wrong. Instead you can have a mess. I wanted the mess, and interference, and qualifications, and contradictions as a proper representation of something so important and salient in Canadian history as the Winnipeg General Strike.

HW One of the key decisions in writing a historical novel is about which characters to leave intact, so to speak, and which to sort of change or invent. *Fox* is populated by a lot of the historical strike leaders, like William Ivens, Bobby Russell, John Queen, and Fred Dixon, and there are other historical figures like Major General Ketchen and Winnipeg mayor Charles Grey. The central characters, though, are fictional, and yet it seems that there are resemblances to figures who were involved in the strike. MacDougal, it seems, is modelled on Ivens, and is there maybe a little J.S. Woodsworth thrown in there for good measure?

MS Even a little bit of Bobby Russell, there [*laughs*].

HW Another character, Sir Rodney Trotter, the pork magnate, is modelled on Sir Joseph Flavelle, the meat-packing magnate who headed the Imperial Munitions Board during the First World War. Can you talk about the kinds of choices that you make as you're approaching your characters?

MS I want to be free enough to inhabit characters, and if they are real historical figures I feel I can't do that. It's impossible. It's boring too because you can't put on a pair of shoes without finding out who really owned those shoes, you know. I mean, the writing process is awful.

HW Why not just go ahead and put on whatever shoes you want? Like some more carnivalesque historical novelists do, like Thomas Pynchon, for instance, or Robert Coover, who wrote this wonderful historical novel about Nixon and the execution of the Rosenbergs, *The Public Burning*. It takes plenty of liberty with the historical record and is not interested in sustaining a sense of historicity.

MS You want to be able to make stuff up. I needed MacDougal to be a compendium. I had a lot of trouble with him. I felt so honoured by reading, say, Fred Dixon; he's such an extraordinarily beautiful human being. Bobby Russell and Ivens frightened me. I knew Ivens wouldn't like me because I was a south-end girl. So I had to try and find characters that wouldn't hate me per-

FIGURE 14. Winnipeg General Strike leaders at Stony Mountain Penitentiary, ca. 1920. Provincial Archives of Manitoba, Winnipeg Strike 35 (N12322).

sonally and that I could approximate, and so I made MacDougal. But even with MacDougal, I always kept to exterior shots; I don't think there are any interior monologues, or if there are, they're superficial, soliloquys. And I never got into him sexually. I couldn't find his sexuality, I couldn't sleep with him, you know? It's vulgar, but I just … Eventually, I had to turn him into a play. I wrote a play of *Fox* and then I *had* to sleep with him, I had to hear him laugh, I had to know. Even then I think I never did quite find him. I felt so honoured by the historical figures that it was difficult to represent them in the figure of MacDougal. It just felt invasive moving in too close, and in ways that you have to, you know, when you're really knowing a fictional character.

HW Still on the subject of characterization—the point man for the Citizens' Committee in *Fox* is the real estate shaker and mover, Drinkwater. The figure who played a comparable role in the strike was Winnipeg lawyer and politician A.J. Andrews. Were there some echoes in the book of him?

MS No. I studied Andrews and I put Andrews in *When Alice Lay Down with Peter*; he did play a role in Blondie's story. There's a Drinkwater in every book I write. He's the quintessential south-end boy in Winnipeg. He fascinates me.

He populates, from what I can see, the south end of Winnipeg. Drinkwaters are running the Great West Life, they're running the University of Winnipeg, they're the Friends of the Winnipeg Symphony Orchestra. I knew them growing up, a particular type of male character that I'm actually fond of satirizing. They've got lots of money, you know, they've all got clothes and BMW's. They seem to be broken men; money actually somehow emasculates them, really disempowers them. Andrews certainly played a role in the book, but from what I know of him, he was a much more firm and really quite an honourable guy in his own way. He loanèd money to the character who became Blondie McCormack in my most recent book, at no interest, and she was a Ukrainian married to a Métis. He had his bigotry, but he was really a much more fleshed out and strong guy, I think. He would be really quite interesting to write about. I don't think I really ever have. I've put him in whole and then left him alone.

HW But in some ways he's representative of a larger social force that you see replicated generation after generation in Winnipeg.

MS Perhaps while I was researching *Fox* I thought of Andrews; I maybe didn't respect him then as much as I've come to respect him as I read more about him. He did some really ugly things—deporting the strike leaders without any cause—and his bigotry was pretty ugly, and he was terrified of the Russian Revolution. So I thought "well, he's an idiot." But as you watch him through the years, he's actually quite a nuanced man. I wouldn't want to treat him lightly. But I probably treated him quite lightly in *Fox*.

HW What about Mary and Eleanor? Are they based on any historical figures?

MS No, not really. Eleanor, when she first came to me, physically was based on a neighbour friend of mine in St. Norbert who guest-starred as herself, a beautiful woman, an artist, and I gave her Virginia Woolf's nose and eyes, sort of imperious. I think I gave her something from myself, too, not physically at all, but someone who's terminal south end and anxious as hell about it. So I think she was probably kind of a parody of myself, certain aspects of myself. Mary, I just gave her the proper sort of Drinkwatery, addictive, timid, alcoholic well-being. She's pathetically blinded by money. Her highly gendered, highly sexual way of looking at the world will actually imprison her, and she'll just end up being a lush, though she'll have a low handicap on the golf course. She's also representative of some people I've seen.

HW As far as I can tell from the history of the strike, there were two men killed, and if my reading is right, you add another death, that of Stevie, the young boy who appears periodically throughout the novel to run messages for the strikers. Can you talk a little bit about the decision to invent that character and add his death, because that's a pretty conspicuous departure.

MS Yes, and I'm gonna burn in hell. I really worried about it, but I needed him, and it was just sort of a cynical departure. I mean, not so cynical in the sense that I didn't really, really worry about it and feel uneasy about it. I'm doing it again with the book that I'm writing now. It's always kind of creepy when you do depart and steal and lie when you're working with the public domain. So I am an embezzler, you know, in public property, the history. But I needed someone of my own to die, imaginatively, in order to gain access to the tragical qualities of the strike. You need to get rid of the historicity for a while and really begin to just own your characters; you need to depart from the historical record in order to create them on your own, so that you can be alone with them. And history does suffer as a result. After this book I don't think I'm going to work with history for a while, just so I can really rethink some of these things. It's a messy business.

HW How is that kind of imagination different from the kind of imaginative investment in narrative that any historian is going to have to make to paint, say, that picture of the strike? To put all those fragments and voices that make up whatever we're left with from history in a narrative pattern obviously involves a certain amount of narrativizing and imaginative speculation. But at the same time, your concern about embezzlement indicates that you feel that there is a kind of divide between historical discourse and fictional representations of history. Do you have a sense of where that divide is?

MS I don't, and I worry about it a lot. With the book I'm writing right now, I need three years to pass, and it's completely ruining my tension, the narrative drive. I'm working as fast as I can with the linear narrative drive, but I have these three years in history that I have to get rid of, you know? So far with these drafts I've retained the three years in the narrative, but the one editor so far who's read it said, "Can you get rid of these three years?" I hate it, I hate this problem. That's why I don't want to work with history after this. I suppose then you're stuck with drawing a portrait of your father or something. Either way you're kind of doomed. Every kind of writing has its problems, but I hate the feeling of violating what has become accepted as public knowledge and not being true to fact. Also, you get the letters from readers. For instance, I apparently had the Golden Boy on top of the Manitoba legislature too early in *Fox*. With *Alice*, I had some woman tell me that somebody did return to the country later, I've forgotten what it was; I think, "Well, who cares?" It would seem like somebody had combed through it looking for an error and found one, I guess, and I'm still thinking she may be wrong. I have been trying to be fairly accurate, in that the inventions don't hurt anybody.

HW So, ultimately, using the defence that it's just fiction isn't good enough, because fiction does have a kind of rhetorical and moral and political weight that puts on you as a writer some sense of responsibility to the past. It isn't necessarily a matter of being able to achieve some kind of authenticity in representation but trying as hard as possible to be fair in spirit to the past as you see it.

MS Yes. How you diagnose or name that spirit is a whole other question, whether you're going to write straight historical fiction, which I don't want to do, or if you are working with various forms of postmodernism, or a refracted take on history, a recontextualization of it—then that spirit, the place you're trying to honour in history, is of a different ilk. You've got quite a different sensibility, but, even if you're writing postmodern historiography, you still try to determine where the line is drawn in the sand.

HW Reinhold Kramer has a really interesting argument about *Fox* that you just echoed there, which is that you're trying to navigate between a traditional sense of historicity—that is, using fiction as a mirror image of the past, of the historical time—and a more radically postmodernist version in which there's really little fidelity to that sense of historicity, and you can flout those codes of historical representation and be wildly inventive and wildly anachronistic and non-linear and polyphonic, and so on. His argument is that *Fox*, in some of its narrative strategies, is obviously much more postmodern than the traditional historical novel, and yet there is, as you've just been articulating it, still that desire to be …

MS Responsible.

HW I guess, responsibly historicist to a degree.

MS Yes—to have contemporary techniques but without anachronisms. Beryl Bainbridge—whose writing I admire—often delves in on a real diagonal on historical language and discourse; that is, she takes a phenomenological approach, in which she captures the precarious immediacy of the present while writing about the past. She always says, too, that she just can't stand anachronisms in a historical piece. Yet you are always trying to preserve your own style to communicate with a contemporary audience while you're trying to represent historical discourse and a historical setting. I always felt I had to put on white gloves and do my hair before I started to write *Fox*, you know, to move right in and try to keep it true to the period. And yet it's hard … in the earlier drafts of *Fox*, for instance, I was using some of the beautiful, millennial socialist rhetoric, but it was too thick. It was as if we only eat our Swiss cheese sliced fine now; it was unbearable to the contemporary palate. So I dimmed it down. I still felt I was keeping the spirit of the rhetoric, but it was sliced thinly. I actually had to make it more porous, use shorter phrases, for example, shorten their speeches literally and take out a little bit of the beautiful literacy that existed then. I actually had to water it down a little bit in order for a contemporary reader to be able to get through it. So again, it's a matter of what you are diagnosing as the spirit that you are going to preserve and honour. And I felt that edited language was still okay; it doesn't feel wrong. I'm working with seventeenth-century rhetoric now and I'm doing the same thing, because at the end of the day I'd like people to read the novel. They could just go and read some seventeenth-century stuff now for themselves, but to read seventeenth-century language in the twenty-first century is a really interesting—and different—game.

HW *Fox* is what I would call very synchronic in approach; that is, you're looking at a wide horizontal spectrum of society at a particular and quite definitive moment in that society's history, 1919 in wide-angle lens. In contrast, *When Alice Lay Down with Peter* looks at that same society, Winnipeg, over the course of a century, at different stages in its history, from before the first Riel uprising almost up to the present. It's quite a radical difference.

MS As I mentioned earlier, with *Fox* I was going for the Bakhtinian marketplace as a structural model. I found it freed me into a type of writing that really interested me then, which was impressionistic and oral: different voicings and from various characters, so I could go right into those characters and inhabit them and then let them speak. But I was also avoiding plot, because I was frightened of it. So with my next novel, *Sam and Angie*, I began to work with plot. I translated *Fox* into a play for Prairie Theatre Exchange, which again forced me to start to learn about linear narrative, and I'm still interested in learning that. How does one scene compel itself? How do you make the next scene necessary and inevitable? I find narrative structure really interesting. So *Fox* was a way to avoid something that really frightened me, and it happened to work. I don't know if I'll ever go back to the marketplace model I used in that novel; I'm still interested in linear structure right now. I just find that interesting—what is it that makes people want to turn a page?

HW Those considerations of linearity and narrative compulsion obviously have an interesting connection to history as well: what makes one thing lead into another? That linear narrative is a much-debated approach to history, because it reflects a desire to make it into a story that hangs together in a way that raises concerns about how the past is interpreted and transformed into narrative. That desire to make a mirror of those events in story form, some argue, necessarily distorts them as a representation of the past.

MS Yes. But I still think that, even though you're working with a linear form, you always see it as a form of counterpoint. So in each utterance you hope that you are deploying issues of sexuality and gender, economics, hunger, the physicality of a situation, the weather, what people want to get out of it, status exchange, and all within one syntactical structure. So in a way, in *Alice*, I'm taking what *Fox* was, a matrix, but moving it into a sentence and still keeping some of the same stratified interests. I'm trying to deploy them all within one character, and at the same time keep moving forward.

HW It's a tall order.

MS It is. It's a different way of thinking. With *Fox* it was really fun, because when I sat down to write I'd think, "Okay, what's the weather, who's the character, what's she wearing, how's she feel, okay, any dreams," set down an utterance and then get the hell out of there for the day. "Phew, maybe I'll call this a book." But in *Alice* I was consciously trying to work sex and politics, clothing, appetite, and the next scene all into one sentence, and each sentence had to proceed like that.

HW One big difference there, I guess, would be that *Alice* is not polyphonic in the way that *Fox* is. That is, you have Blondie as the narrator, and we're seeing things through her perspective, as opposed to the multitude of perspectives that we get in *Fox*. How does that affect the representation of the past?

MS There's still a certain degree of polyphony in the narrative styles, there. I made the scene of Helen's marriage to Richard more omniscient. I backed Blondie away; she was still the focalizer, and whenever she needed to become loud, she would break out and speak. But I did let her become omniscient sometimes and changed her language. The sentences got longer, and she became more Art Nouveau, a boulevard novel style for a while, just to get her out of there, because I thought the readers would get so sick of her. She kind of narrated that book to me. At one point during the editing, Diane Martin at Knopf was putting in all these semicolons and I was saying, "Blondie doesn't talk with semicolons," and she said, "No one's going to read this as an oral novel." I said, "I wrote it as an oral novel." I thought Blondie narrated it. But I wasn't trying always to find Blondie's tongue or her voice. It was still very writerly.

HW I was also thinking about the fact that she is "dead as a stick," as you put it, and that obviously projects the narration onto a very different ontological level that makes all kinds of things possible.

MS To have her being able to know her whole life, for instance. Yet it also got rid of the problem of anachronism, so she could mention the absence of telephone wires, or she could refer to the Gulag. I loved that. It opened up the twentieth century. That was fun. It gives you a lot more latitude—

HW And gets you, in some ways, out of those problems of historicity that you talked about in conjunction with *Fox*.
     When Alice Lay Down with Peter is in some ways a history of impossiblism, and that term of course is associated, as I understand it anyway, with early-twentieth-century socialism. But it seems applicable in the novel to a much wider range of egalitarian dreams. The novel seems to provide a chronicle not of Heritage Moments, but impossiblist moments, moments of anti-establishment idealism and disappointment. You have the dream of a Métis nation in the Riel uprisings, the 1837 rebellion that Alice stages with her pupils in a Winnipeg schoolroom, the On-to-Ottawa Trek of the unemployed during the Depression, and Canadians' participation in the Spanish Civil War.

MS Well, it is complicated and difficult, but the impossiblism is anarchy—the McCormacks are anarchists in the really classical tradition. Helen was modelled after Emma Goldman a little bit—her incredible discomfort and agony at being herself. I think a lot of women are anarchists, especially at certain times of the month, when there's a certain self-hatred and being alive is impossible. Also, I think, I keep circling an ideology without being able to enter it. I had to have them impossiblists because I couldn't go with my characters into a secure, left-wing ideology. I think I've always been anxious about left-wing politics, never really believing them. We always need a critical position from the left, but I'm always an outsider; I'm an outsider to all politics, a kind of homeless political person. The McCormacks also had to be more anarchist because the novel required a constant transformation. If they devoted themselves to any political form, then they'd solidify and the story couldn't move forward. I needed them to be constantly deconstructing, which anarchism always is. And they are always very painful transformations, constant revolution. So that constant transformation suited my narrative form, the odyssey; I had to keep things moving from one strange island to another. Also personally, I cannot commit to writing a really left-wing book. I just can't. My family wasn't all that rich; in fact, they weren't rich at all. I just somehow feel dyed-in-the-wool distrust for any sort of political belief. I sure hate the right wing. But I actually don't trust the left wing either, and so I needed my characters to reflect a certain kind of outsiderness to all political forms. For a while I struggled with whether Peter would really be able to join the CCF. But I found that the impossiblists helped me to keep him mobile, keep him restless and homeless, so the characters could keep moving forward.

HW There is a sort of distrust of rigidity that is being figured here, through those metaphors of transformation, of movement, and so on.

MS I kept Ovid and Fitzgerald's translation of *The Odyssey* on my desk while I was writing *Alice*. Whenever I could feel things settling, I'd read some chapters from them. The characters have got to dissolve, they've got to transform into the next person that they had to become. That became the motif. I wanted people always moving. That is a statement about history—that we are provisional, contingent, and if we stay solemn and still, of course we're dead. People are really created in time, and if they're going to survive, they're going to have to change. My grandmother, for instance—it's very beautiful—lived 104 years. But she's extinct, you know? She's not only dead; she's extinct. Her kind, her sensibilities, the way she would look at an occasion, what she would be able to say, even her vocabulary, is extinct. It's fascinating. The same goes for the ghosts in *Alice*. Just to keep people in your breath is the only way to keep them. Once you've expired, then they really are dead, and they can't exist anymore. It's fascinating.

HW The ghost of Thomas Scott, whose execution by Louis Riel's men obviously was an absolutely pivotal moment in the history of the West—of the country—is literally presiding over much of the next century in the novel. That seemed to me to be such an apt metaphor. Can you talk a little bit about that device and also about Alice's reflection a little bit later on that "what is right is also wrong"? It's a bit ambiguous, but it does seem to apply in part to that execution.

MS Because of change, being right is definitely wrong. By necessity it's wrong because being right implies a conclusion, which is absurd, because you're speaking about people who are in process.

HW So it's a resistance to political and moral absolutes that are historically transcendent?

MS That's where comedy and history dovetail; that's where history is comic. Because it's a series of transformations. The king is constantly falling off his horse. There's always upending, there are always overturns, status is constantly

FIGURE 15.
Thomas Scott. Glenbow
Museum NA-576-1.

being shifted. The gorgeous young people walking down the street, well, ha ha, they're going to be old one day. It's a funny thing. Time is also very funny; it's laughing at us. Change is innately comic because you're always being upended, you know? You can make these grand statements of summary and definition but they're essentially comic, they're essentially wrong. Death makes us funny.

I love ghost stories, too, and the ghosts are also there to point out that this is literature, this is a yarn. I think we all have ghosts, and if we let them go, if we stop speaking of them, obviously they're dead.

HW Yes. But Thomas Scott's ghost also seems to me to capture that very lovely line in the novel, "It takes more than mortality to make somebody dead." I think that's a beautiful encapsulation of a really important historical principle.

MS I think that if anything in this book truly could be perceived as being ... I don't know, "left-wing" isn't the right word for it ... but aimed at resisting totalitarian and right-wing states that do efface history, then that is. For example, the failure of the Americans to protect the museums in Iraq—that's no accident; the Americans really didn't give a damn about preserving that history. It's not in their interests. History is *now* for them. I find that the effacement of history is usually a fascist move, a move for power, and that memory and ghosts are kind of our left-wing guys, you know. They're our colleagues that are innately comic, because they're dead, for God's sake, they're drooling, they're all wrong, and we need them in order to remind ourselves that we're not there yet, that there is no "there." And their lack of perfection—I mean ghosts are really disgusting creatures—their imperfect quality, their unfinished quality, is necessary to us.

HW So in some ways, perhaps paradoxically, they're a resistance to the idea of the end of history?

MS Yes, exactly.

HW Scott's ghost is one of a number of what I would call magic realist elements in the novel. Quite a few Canadian novels set in the past likewise introduce elements of the fantastic or the mythological or the supernatural into otherwise historically real or credibly historicist settings. What do you think might be behind that trend? I'm thinking of Jane Urquhart's *Away*, for instance, and Thomas Wharton's *Icefields*, *The Invention of the World* by Jack Hodgins, and others too.

MS Those elements in *Away* permitted Urquhart to translate a dreamlike sensibility from one continent to another, so physically they got her there, you know? Hodgins and I used them to cover an enormous amount of time. So it was a way of galloping around, keeping characters in play. It's sort of bad theatre, too, if you come in and you drop the characters; it's that kind of impulse where you have to keep the characters in play, for your dramatic structure as well. It's a way of writing a much more comprehensive history. You can cover a lot more time if you have dead people [*laughs*].

HW It's interesting that the antagonists of both novels—I'm thinking of Drinkwater in *Fox* and Richard Anderson in *Alice*—are real estate developers. Especially in *Alice*, that transformation of land into property and real estate is absolutely central. I wonder if you could address how you see the role of land in the history of Winnipeg in particular, but more generally in the history of the west.

MS I keep going back to Irene Spry, a historian at the University of Toronto. She writes about history as real estate and land use as our key signifier for tracking historical change. I find that really, extraordinarily compelling and useful, central to my ideas of how to write history. Another place where I got that preoccupation with land was from studying with Robert Kroetsch, let's say "Stone Hammer Poem," for example. In that one very short poem he covers the whole issue, tells the whole story right there, in that astonishing master-piece. It's fascinating too the way the land is haunted by prior use. There's a terrible amnesia evoked by the Holiday Inns, and that is a political, totalitar-ian force—to knock stuff down and put up Disneyland.

HW There is the idea of palimpsest, too, the idea of just writing over top of something: commerce as a kind of superimposed narrative of power and of history.

MS Yes, exactly, and when you do find that you're in a culture where there is an interest in human beings over money, there usually is a stronger heritage and interest in architecture.

HW What about Winnipeg in particular? Because *Alice* is charting that process of effacement of the past and of prior occupation. Can you talk a little bit about those politics and *Alice* as a kind of narrative about that effacement?

MS In Winnipeg, maybe because we don't have many other natural resources, we do sort of farm our past; you know, we need something. In a bizarre way we're lucky that we started off wealthy, because the establishment has slowed down economic and cultural change, with the unintended result of a static economy that has slowed down the major forces of money moving in. I'm so glad we don't have oil, for example. They use the heritage still, for commer-cial purposes, for, I think, quite a delightful end. We can't afford to knock down all the buildings, and I think we're just not that powerful out here. So people put the new Red River College down in the Princess district and pre-served those buildings. They put the theatre department of the University of Winnipeg in the old Salvation Army building. It's partly financial, and it's partly a mix of finance and politics. We've had kind of zero–one per cent growth forever in this town, and so a lot of the buildings that we're still try-ing to preserve were put up in that one boom in 1885. So we're lucky. I like it. It's why I think a lot of us choose to live here. You get a certain kind of humanity.

HW *Alice* seems to link that idea of real estate also to the process of colonial-ism and wiping out Aboriginal history, a process happening quite palpably in terms of territorial relations and questions of land ownership and so on.

MS Yes. There's always an ambivalence. For instance, where we were living, on an oxbow in the Red River: now the land is wrecked, but we fought hard to keep it, fought a couple of floods there. We felt, "this is our home" and we nearly drowned trying to fix it, trying to keep the place, and yet it wasn't our home, not really. So there's this crazy double life that you have to live where you pretend to own. And anyone who is white in this culture is pretending to be indigenous, but you're not, you know. That's something that haunts *Alice*. The McCormacks are always aware. The mother-in-law, Marie, who is Métis, lives with them after she's dead. They just have to live with the fact that they're squatters, and it's a squatocracy, just like Australia, or any of these British colonies. I heard that term from an Australian. They talk about that a lot there. It's absolutely true. We don't own this place at all; we're just pretending to be. So the whole thing is a fraud, you know? The ugly, ugly land shift after 1869, 1870, the real fraud of the Métis children's land rights—that was an absolute swindle. That was a lie, and they stole that land, for the white people, the white Protestants.

HW What about the issue of writing in that culture? Is the literature of a squatocracy essentially fraudulent, or is there some kind of accommodation that can be made by self-consciously writing about that fraudulence?

MS Well, I guess that's what I've been trying to do with *Fox* and *Alice*. It's about the fraudulence. It's just there; there is no way to get around it. *Fox* was essentially a book of origins. Eleanor's self-consciousness, her sense of being a double agent crossing class boundaries, reflects my own fraudulence going to theatre classes with my communist, Jewish friends, when I was fifteen, fourteen years old. I felt like a complete fraud. Well, I thought, "I'm a writer; I better write about being a fraud."

HW Speaking of being frauds, three generations of McCormack women go into battle dressed as men. Alice participates in the execution of Thomas Scott, Blondie marches off to the Boer War, and Helen joins the Mackenzie-Papineau Battalion in the Spanish Civil War. Is that a comment on the role of women in history and on the dominance of political and military history in shaping our view of the past?

MS Yes, and the fact that, as Wollstonecraft pointed out, women are bred to be eavesdroppers. We're educated to gain our knowledge of the world and to participate as political people from the wings. So in *Fox*, they're always over-hearing, and they're never quite hearing right. That was actually my experience, too, even though I haven't been repressed in any way. Then in order to get the women in *Alice* to war and for them to participate in history they had to disguise themselves, you know? Otherwise they couldn't go out. It's that old Kroetschian thing about horse and house—you know, "Women are in the house, men are on the horse." So I had to get them to be men to get them out of the house and on the horse. It is also a comic device, obviously, and an act of compassion. I think it's comic partly because it is compassionate—that a woman would understand men in a more holistic way by actually becoming one. So Alice recommends to her daughter, really if you do want to love men you should be one. At least for a while.

HW There all sorts of comic riffs on their sense of masculinity and on gender confusion.

MS Yes.

HW My sense is that, historically, though there might have been a few women on the On-to-Ottawa Trek, those conflicts were almost exclusively masculine. The participation of the McCormack women in those conflicts ends up being somewhat ambivalent, not bloodthirsty and whole-hearted and satisfying. Alice is absolutely racked with guilt after Scott's execution. Blondie doesn't even make it into battle; she abandons her friend Clark and turns back as they approach the Modder River in South Africa. And Helen, during the riot in Regina, prevents her friend Ida from braining a policeman with a brick. There seems to be a tension, in other words, between underscoring women's agency by inserting them into those conflicts and portraying them as warriors, and the actual violence that tends to accompany that role.

MS It's a funny thing. The women have almost a terminal self-consciousness; it almost kills them. The fact that they're acting means that they are really vulnerable and in danger in those situations. If you're going to go into battle you can't be acting, and so they do have to fall back because they are frauds. In a way, too, I think the female culture is somehow terminal to them. They are killed by being women. Maybe it's something to do with the sense of being a fraud and being unable to completely enter history. You're always tying up your shoes, you're always putting on a bit of lipstick; there's a certain amount of narcissism that prevents you from completely entering history. Self-reflexivity causes them to hesitate and get killed, you know? So they have to leave; they end up failing.

HW But how does that relate to the rigidity that we talked about? In some ways that could be seen, even though it's fatal, as a healthy thing. Earlier on you were resisting that sense of rigidity as fatal, because history is fluid, ever-changing, the river that you step in which is never the same twice.

MS Oh, sure. I mean, I still really like these women. I don't think they're failures as human beings, these fictional characters, at all, but I just think that, at that moment, that's what they are experiencing, this sense of theatre that overrules their ability to act. Kurt Vonnegut, in his anti-war novels, always has people who are acting, and they always have this terrible self-consciousness about the absurdity of war. I think that when you are writing a critique of violent politics, you often point out that characters are acting. It's maybe a way of bifurcating human motivations and so on, making them more porous.

HW Yes. It does seem that there's a kind of skepticism about certainty, and violence requires certainty, at least in some respects. I mean, there is arbitrary violence and impulsive violence, but in terms of politics there's also quite consciously engineered and strategic violence, which the opposition in *Alice* doesn't have any problem with—whether it's the Canadian soldiers in 1869, the Citizens' Committee during the Winnipeg General Strike, or Franco's Falange. They're deadly serious and deadly certain.

MS That's right. Yes.

HW Another thing that jumped out at me about that pattern of the women going into battle is that, whereas Alice and Helen, and even Dianna, Helen's daughter, are all participating in anti-establishment struggles, Blondie doesn't really fit the pattern, in the sense that she's participating in the Boer War, which is basically the opposite; it's an imperialist venture. Is that difference a result of just having to roll with history, because that was what was going on at the time of Blondie's coming of age?

MS Well, partly it was the timing; she had to go to war around then. But it was also because these women choose irrelevance, and Blondie, by that time, was a student of irrelevance. She was consciously participating in a ridiculous venture, and she felt very badly. One reason she feels responsible for Clark's death is that she knew his participation in the war was ridiculous and then she pointed it out to him, pointed out that he was acting at a time when it made him vulnerable and it killed him. She was saying, "Are you nuts? This is ridiculous," and his response was, "Oh, then I am not real," and then he couldn't fight and he was killed. So I think she was just very interested in a sort of willful investigation of irrelevant behaviour—whatever is wrong at that time. She was also trying to seduce Eli, and she thought that if she went to war then he might sleep with her finally. One thing led to another, and she just found herself being pushed into setting off for war.

HW In quite a few contemporary historical novels, there's an interesting interplay between what we think of as history and what we think of as myth. In *When Alice Lay Down with Peter*, there's obviously a conscious evocation of the mythological Helen of Troy in the histories of the McCormack women. What was the intention behind giving the story this particular, mythical resonance? You talked earlier about *The Odyssey* and the importance of keeping things moving.

MS The myth—say, having Helen as the most beautiful woman in the world and clearly referring to Helen of Troy—gives you a broader scope, obviously, but I guess it's just more fluid. It's bigger and more open. You don't really think of it as myth when you are working with it. It's more like coloration, I suppose, and dynamics, in musical terms. When you're writing about quotidian events, a specific family like the McCormacks living in a specific place, then you need that amplitude that myth has, so that in your book you don't have something too monophonic. Myth softens the edges, and also it's an augmentation of reality, of history, with much more fluid edges. And I think it's a relief for the reader.

HW That idea, though, of mythic repetition is really interesting, because in a more historicist conception of history every age is essentially unique and not replicable because history moves forward. But with the kind of mythic structure that you have, which reminds me a lot of the mythic structure in *Away*, you have this repetition of events in the lives of these women—

MS Who are related to each other—

HW Which makes them essentially be the same woman.

MS Well, I think I do that kind of thing just for joy and as a way, too, of planning a linear narrative but with circular motifs, and to write motific patterns that help you as a novelist with certain game plans. A novel often is constructed out of constituted rules, and those are the constitutive rules of the game, so that repetition was a way of getting to the next platform. When is the next lightning bolt? And when is the next generation? Patterning can be a beautiful way of working both with a synchronic structure and a linear structure.

HW So it's an aesthetic and structural device. But it also introduces a different perspective on history and resists a much more empirical and rationalist sense of history. It's a resistance that seems to tie into the politics of the novel as well—resisting this very Protestant, Orange, commercial, and rational view of how the world should be.

MS Very much so. It also imposes a fallible humanism on things. When you look at the myths, they're so unreligious; you know, they're all rape and transformation and cruelty that isn't really observed. It's not honoured necessarily; there's no shocked pause in the narrative. All those things working in a historical narrative that purports to be covering 109 years of Manitoba history helped to fight against what would be a traditional conception of historical fiction. I don't want to write historical fiction, so these other elements are essential to counteract that. The myths are so rude and violent and transformative and essentially comic, because they don't ever permit the moment of tragedy before the next moment has to unfold. It's very beautiful.

HW Isn't it also escapist, though, in that sense?

MS Yes, it's escapist, certainly, but I don't think that's a pejorative. I think that escape is a very useful and exciting narrative device, and also a stylistic device. It's wonderful for the readers to be able to escape, like in René Clair films—where they would zoom out from their room and go off with that airplane and then suddenly be in Toronto? It's a beautiful way of moving the story, and it's a revelling thing too, because it resists the dominance of the protagonist, because you're then going to flow out to the next protagonist. Escape serves so many very beautiful functions in storytelling.

HW But it can also be an evasive action, avoiding a kind of political reckoning.

MS Sure, but sometimes a political reckoning wouldn't be really possible anyway. It might just be bad writing, and it's time to move on. I think escape is very, very exciting. I often teach it when I'm teaching creative writing. Where it becomes problematic is if you use it too much, and then your reader is dissatisfied, because the writer keeps introducing new characters, so she's always beginning; she always wants to start everything over at the beginning, because she can't stand the middle and therefore can't get to the end. In that way, structurally, it can be problematic.

HW Yes, I see what you mean. I'm thinking, though, about, say, the costume historical romance, which is just *Nurse Betty Goes to Hawaii* but set in the American Revolution or whenever. Isn't there a kind of unhealthy escapism in that, to a degree, at least in terms of the attitudes that it cultivates towards history? That it's just this empty form without the political and social substance of history.

MS Yes, but I still really like it. One of the problems is that you can end up writing too glibly, and I think people would accuse me of writing that way, but

I wanted to keep things moving and to be comprehensive. So I might have sacrificed what some people would maybe prefer to see, some sort of, I don't know, ultimate judgement or some sort of teleological form. I just didn't want to do that. People can read other books for that.

HW Helen's participation in the Spanish Civil War also seems to be a bit different from the other instances in the sense that it's accorded a greater level of seriousness. There's a kind of passion and rage and perhaps less ambivalence than is accorded to Blondie, or to Alice, or to Dianna, who has that fight with the Hungarian refugee who objects to her anti-American leftism. But when Helen goes off to the Spanish Civil War there seems to be more unalloyed anger in her resistance.

MS She has Emma Goldman's notion of female anarchy, where she's constantly destroying herself. Helen became kind of a desperado of luxury. She moves into things with a violence. She's a very tormented woman, partly because of her beauty. It did kind of displace her, and so she was made homeless by herself. She was always in a lot of psychological pain. She was an impossibilist more than anything else. You know, she was with Ida, who was a Communist, but they fought like crazy. She was an anarchist and it was a place for anarchists. She just needed to be killed; I think she found life intolerable. I stole this idea from the autobiography of Emma Goldman, *My Life*. Goldman was in court in the States, and the judge said, "Why do you have to live in the States? Why don't you leave the country? Go back to wherever it is you German Jew people go," and she said, "There's nowhere on earth I can go, and I can't bear to be in Heaven. I have nowhere to go." It really was so sad, and I think that was Helen. She at one point comes back with Bill and she's complaining, and Dianna hears her saying those words, or something like that. I think really she is almost committing suicide in a way.

HW She doesn't want to be governed, and there's nowhere that you can't be governed, essentially.

MS She can't be a mother, she can't be a partner, she can't truly love, she hates herself, she never owns herself. She is extraordinarily beautiful, and I've seen that with a few people.

HW There's a kind of dispossession of yourself which you figure in the novel, where her beauty is always standing in front of her, like this intrusive friend, as you put it.

MS Yes.

HW Helen joins the Mackenzie-Papineau Battalion, and ultimately she's executed by the Falange in Spain. The participation of Canadians in the Spanish Civil War strikes me as one of the larger lumps swept under the rug of official history in Canada. Why was it important to you to write that particular history into the novel? How did you get to that history?

MS Well, it starts in the beginning with Alice and Peter's being members of the Opposition in God's House of Lords. Whatever is wrong is what they have to do. That's why Blondie goes off to the Boer War, because it's totally inappropriate. With the Mac-Paps, it's the fact that they are premature anti-fascists. I love that notion, that they're ahead of history; in a historical novel it's hard to resist that. It was the beginning of this blossoming of idealism, and the unofficial heroes, you know, all of the people in *Alice*, have to be comic fools. And the Mac-Paps in a way are comic fools. If you read *Homage to Catalonia* you find that Orwell too felt that he had become a fool. He was made a fool by his own ideals. It's a very disturbing war for that reason. I think they were all comic fools, in a really honourable way. They went off to the war, and, as much as they were all fighting the Fascists, the communists were also trying to fight with the anarchists and the socialists, and then they'd kill each other. Their ideals preceded them; they then walked into the trap of their own rhetoric and got killed. Then they came back here, where there's the notion, of course, that they're invisible, just like the ghosts that haunt us, and the land use that has been effaced by real estate, too. That they ghost us and are unacknowledged is really, really fascinating.

HW We've talked about how *When Alice Lay Down with Peter* is about the pursuit of impossible dreams, and the collapse of impossible dreams, and the comic quality of that. But at the same time there's also a certain elegiac quality about it too. I'm thinking about Eli's "politics of regret," because the characters are always on the losing side. Is that a quality that you're trying to evoke? I know that in some ways the novel is paying homage to a piece of land—to your lost, flooded home on the oxbow in the Red River. But is the regret over the politics as well?

MS Absolutely. You know you have to carry around with you what you've lost, and the pain is quite profound. I find, as I get older, too, I carry around a lot of pain; it just accumulates. I also found that funny, because, by the back door, that's conservative politics too, obviously—to conserve. In this town, conservatives are like the Drinkwaters of 2003. They want to go to the Manitoba Club, they want things the old way. Most of the upper-class people here that are Tory Anglicans, that type of class, are conservative in the sense of conserving. So they have their own regrets too. It's double-edged, right? We all share it, that sense that the old ways are the best ways. I suppose, too, when you're writing about history, you fall into that.

So the novel is elegiac, and the impulse to write historical fiction is elegiac, but it's a kind of necrophilia too. It's ghoulish writing this type of fiction. You get off on these dead people.

History "from the Workingman's End of the Telescope"
Fred Stenson

Fred Stenson grew up on a farm in the foothills of the Rocky Mountains near Chief Mountain in southwestern Alberta. He has had a long career as a free-lance writer of film and video scripts and is a two-time winner of Alberta Motion Picture Industry awards for his documentary scripts. He has published a number of novels including *Lonesome Hero* (1974) and *Last One Home* (1988) and the short story collections *Working Without a Laugh Track* (1990) and *Teeth* (1994). He has also published *Thing Feigned or Imagined* (2002), a book on the craft of writing. In 2000 Stenson published his first historical novel, *The Trade*, a sweeping portrait of life in the Hudson's Bay Company during the reign of the company's dictatorial governor George Simpson. The novel was nominated for the Giller Prize and won a number of prizes including the inaugural Grant MacEwan Author's Award. His latest novel is *Lightning* (2003), set in Montana and southwestern Alberta during the open-ranch lease era in the late nineteenth century. I talked to Fred Stenson in Calgary in June of 2004.

HW You do a lot of non-fiction writing and journalism and writing for television, and part of that is a fairly long-standing interest in history. How far back does that interest in history go? What are the roots of it for you?

FS I started writing for film and video in 1976, when an opportunity came up for me to be a writer and a researcher for a small film company in Banff. What they were doing were historical films, using paintings and artifacts from the Devonian and Glenbow Foundations for visuals. At that point, I really had very little interest in history (beyond reading novels that involved history); it was an unawakened interest. They wanted to do a film on Native history first, and then Native religion, and I was just dropped into it and essentially told to become an expert and write a film. But going back before that is the influence of my family background. I was raised on a mixed farm in southwestern Alberta, south of Pincher Creek, about twenty minutes from Waterton. My family had been in that area quite a while; both my parents were born there, my father south of Fort MacLeod and my mother in the same place that I grew up, southeast of Pincher Creek. Because my family went back a couple of generations in that place, there was history in the sense of knowledge of the community. When my family gets together it is like this big genealogy lesson. It's funny that my sisters and I are doing this now, because it bored us to death as kids when my parents would sit there every meal and talk about who was related to whom and keep tracing families back, or somebody's name would pop up, or somebody would have seen somebody driving by on the road, and it would go from something that small to an entire investigation of their history, back to when they first came to the country.

HW So in some ways that interest in history is an extension of the general principle that we are destined to eventually become our parents.

FS In modern times, we tend not to stay in the same place, and we break the chain with our families' history, so there will be some subtle or not so subtle differences in how people are and what they know based on that. Almost in spite of myself, I grew up knowing quite a lot about the history of my area. It may not have been thorough, and it may not have all been accurate, and it certainly was not cross-referenced properly, but that is history in another sense. Let me give you an example of how that would work. When my father was fifteen, he was a cowboy on the Hatfield Ranch, right across Yarrow Creek from our farmhouse. That image of my father working on that ranch for a period of time as a teenager was something that was rooted in my head, and I would develop stories in my own mind out of that, and when I wrote *Lightning* it was certainly on my mind. I mention in the acknowledgments to *The*

Trade that James Riviere, who was a family friend and used to buy hay from us, was a grandson of William Gladstone, who is mentioned periodically in the novel. So that comes out of connections from my childhood.

HW You wrote a book for Parks Canada about Rocky Mountain House. Was the research for that book the impetus behind the writing of *The Trade*?

FS Very much so. I was working as a freelance writer on films and video scripts, and Parks Canada had a proposal competition for a book about Rocky Mountain House National Historic Park. I went after it and I got it. All the people who are in *The Trade* are found somewhere in that Rocky Mountain House book; it was basically all the material that was left on the cutting-room floor. I felt that the details that could not go into this small guidebook were the stuff of a good novel. Such a novel, though, was a complete divorce from anything I had attempted in fiction before. My entire corpus of historical fiction at that time was one short story about the origins of the Calgary Stampede. It also happened to coincide with a time when I was feeling that I had not plumbed myself very well as a fiction writer. I had locked into a certain path of writing, usually contemporary comedic works, and I had been telling myself, "If you are going to write more fiction you should just write a big book."

HW So that material presented itself to you at a kind of crossroads.

FS That's exactly right. It hit me at a time when I wanted to attempt something large and difficult. In this choice, I was influenced by a conversation with a friend of mine, playwright Gordon Pengilly, who talked about how perhaps the way to greatness or better art was to not do what was easiest for you but to write against the grain, to go against what you found most easy to do.

HW Before we start talking about *The Trade*, I want to talk a little bit about the fur trade in Canadian history. How do you see the role of that operation, of that economy? How important was the fur trade to the shape the country has taken?

FS The Hudson's Bay Company and the other massive trading companies of the eighteenth and nineteenth centuries had almost nothing to do with the countries that would eventually develop there. This was as true in Indonesia as it was in Canada. We have a strange history in this country in that, up to 1870, western Canada was basically just a commercial region through this one company that had the blessing of Britain. It was the form of government, and the only kind of law and order was whatever it chose to manifest. Then in

1870 it wanted to get out, and the nation of Canada wanted to get in, wanted to expand sea to sea. So it was a handy moment for the Hudson's Bay Company to get out of this large role and just continue as an ordinary company. In that sense, there is this division between the history of the rest of the country and the history of the West that may account in some ways for why the West and East don't see eye-to-eye. They have an entirely different pre-history. I always find the two Métis rebellions interesting, because there was a blind presumption that the people living in the West would not care who governed them and would blindly go along with whatever it was. But the Métis were smart enough to say "Wait, before we do that we'd like to investigate our rights and our nationality," and so on. The Métis reaction to the change in governance was important, because it showed that there was still a spark of the desire for freedom left after almost two centuries of being indentured servants.

HW The Métis community was really shaped by the commercial history of the trade.

FS It was. In *The Trade* I wrote a lot about the practically imprisoned nature of the workers in the fur trade. Yet when the yoke was removed, the Métis actually sprang up with a lot of energy. Obviously the Indians were entering a very dark age of starvation, but for some of the other people in the West there was a real liberation. They were the phoenix rising out of the ashes of two centuries of being indentured servants to the Company.

HW You talked earlier on about the material that was left on the cutting floor after you wrote the book on Rocky Mountain House for Parks Canada. At what point did you decide to make *The Trade* a story about Hudson's Bay clerk Edward Harriott's relationship with the company's governor, George Simpson? In your overview of Rocky Mountain House's history in that Parks Canada book, you talked a bit about Harriott's role in the company, but there is no sense of any kind of animosity between Harriott and Simpson. In the novel, however, they are involved in a series of politically and economically and sexually charged triangles. There is a labour triangle between Simpson and Harriott and Fort Edmonton's Chief Factor John Rowand; then there is a sexual triangle involving Simpson and Harriott and his wife Margaret; and then there is also a political triangle involving Simpson and Harriott and Jimmy Jock Bird (and John Rowand is part of that mix as well). Is there any kind of historical evidence for that antagonism between Harriott and Simpson, or is it closer to a credible historical speculation about what that relationship might have been like?

FS After immersing myself in the research for the Rocky Mountain House book, I sat down and very speedily wrote sixty pages, which are in the book as it exists today, almost intact. It is the part that begins the section called "The Missionary," which involves the arrival of Methodist missionary Robert Rundle and the contrasting reactions of Rowand and Harriott to his arrival. At the beginning I really liked what I had written and felt I had the voice and the language and the narrative stance that I wanted for the book, but I had no idea what it was part of. For quite a long time I kept trying to write with that as a beginning and finally I understood that it wasn't. Originally I thought John Rowand was going to be the antagonist in the book, but as he evolved as a character I started to see him a lot more sympathetically and to understand a kind of symbiotic big dog–little dog relationship between him and Harriott.

Then as I sculpted out the book I realized that I wanted it to be about the power relationship between the company and the workers and their families and the sexual politics that grew out of the economic power relationship between them. That increasingly led me to having Simpson as an antagonist and Margaret being a kind of commodity. That was the most basic triangle, which stands at the heart of the book. "Can there be love?" was the question that intrigued me. "What happens to love in a society where everything is assigned a value, everything is a commodity?" The way the Indian people relate to the company is almost entirely through the medium of trade, and everybody is more or less trained to that commodity relationship. So I established an oppressive structure, and then various people have a need to get outside that structure. I started from the principle that people do seek freedom, do seek love, but it is difficult with the company there, this oppressive, omnipotent force, because of the charter given to it by the English government. So people have to go to some fairly extreme measures. Harriott, for instance, is always seeking a way out. He begins quite happily. As a young fellow, he is a favorite and learns quickly. He gets along well with Natives, and his uncle is powerful in the company. Everything looks very, very good for him, but then he makes something of a cross-step. He gets going in a bad direction with the company, and the dark side of its power comes crashing down. He is no longer this youthful guy ascending; he is now at cross-purposes with the most powerful man in the company, somebody who represents the whole power of the company.

HW Is that cross-step in the novel mirroring what you see as there having been possibly a cross-step in the historical Harriott's career?

FIGURE 16.
John Rowand. Provincial
Archives of Manitoba,
John Rowand 1.

FS The things that are true are that Margaret was his first cousin; Peter Paul Pruden was his uncle, the factor in charge of Fort Carlton, where Harriott learned his place in the trade. Harriott and Margaret at some point did become lovers, and Peter Paul Pruden did not approve. They eventually did go off and live together at Fort Assiniboine, where she began to be subject to episodes of insanity. The other truth is that she was reputed to be the most beautiful woman in the Northwest.

HW Which makes it very likely that she would have caught George Simpson's eye.

FS Yes. Simpson seemed to prefer the Métis women in the trade for his mistresses. I am sure he probably went for the prettiest just as a matter of showing his authority, his ability to do whatever he wanted. There is no place in the record that I know of that suggests any relationship between them. I was just going with the idea that if she really was the most beautiful young woman in the Northwest, of course he would have been interested. The more of a tyrant he was, the more likely he would have needed to have her to prove the absolute nature of his power.

HW Ultimately, it does seem like a reasonable historical speculation, just based on trends of behaviour.

FS Sure. Harriott was a very promising guy in the trade. I mean, he was selected at quite a young age to be among the leaders of the Bow River expedition, and something shortly after that did seem to go very wrong for him, something that sent him in the direction of alcoholism. His chosen country wife was at times insane, and the way she dies in the novel is exactly the way it was in historical records.

HW She disappeared on the Athabasca Pass.

FS Yes, she left the camp in the middle of the night, left behind her baby of six weeks, and wandered off and was never seen again.

HW One thing that really resonated for me while I was reading the novel was the way in which the revisionist portrait of Simpson echoed the growing skepticism toward business leaders in our own time. Through the 1990s the CEO became practically a sanctified figure, but now with corporate leaders being indicted for fraud and various other shenanigans, the shine is starting to come off their reputation. Somewhat similarly, traditional scholarship about Simpson, if not quite hagiography, tended to downplay his callousness and his vindictiveness, because he was so good for the profit margin, because he was so good at economizing and basically revolutionized the way the company did business. In *The Trade*, though, you flip that emphasis around and highlight Simpson's utter lack of humanity in dealing with his lessers in the trade.

FS I did try to understand Simpson in terms of certain modern corporate practices. We have had a great many mergers and downsizings in corporate history in Canada, and quite often someone new is brought in to do the dirty work, someone with no particular human relationships, no personal debts, no personal loyalties. They bring somebody like that in to do the hacking and cutting, to get rid of the duplication. To me, the historical Simpson was always that. He leaped over all kinds of men of far greater experience when he was made the governor of the Northern Department. He always seemed to me that cold-hearted figure who is brought in to do the dirty work, who has the requisite inhumanity, almost, and the lack of personal connections in the situation. Because his department was the profit centre for the company, being the governor of it made him very powerful, and he became more powerful. For the longest time, Simpson was praised in a way that I found very similar to the way people have been praised since 1989. Corporations have become our gods, and their leaders have become the stars in that firmament. We read about

FIGURE 17.
Sir George Simpson, 1857.
Library and Archives
Canada c-023580.

them and are told about how they reduced indebtedness and increased profit
and increased company efficiency. That was very much how Simpson was
looked at for a very long time.

HW And what is effaced in those glowing reports is of course the human
costs of their productivity.

FS Yes, the pain and cost. So Simpson seemed a very modern figure to me, and
the way he has been perceived by history is like a record of how we have perceived corporations and corporate leaders, the economically powerful people
in our society, over time. Even Peter C. Newman, in his trilogy about the Hudson's Bay Company, did both when it came to Simpson. He worshipped Simpson's economic revamping of the company, his restoring of its profitability
after the fur war, and then he brought in the whole issue of his mistresses,
this other side of him. But to me, the total vision of Simpson was still one of
almost solemn reverence, and with his mistresses there was kind of a nudge,
nudge, wink, wink, which in a sense was worse because it was including all of
that as being his colourful side. So I just thought, "Enough." I had been studying the literature of the fur trade even before the Rocky Mountain House
book, and I had never liked Simpson. My instinct was that he was a terrible

abuser of his power and a vengeful man. I remember coming across the story about Colin Robertson back in 1979, and it contained that fact that Simpson had refused Robertson retirement on a full share, after Robertson had done decades and decades of service, preceding, during, and after the fur war. Robertson had had a stroke, and he really couldn't function, and Simpson said, "No, you haven't earned it yet; you have to go back," and he gave him a remote post to run. I thought to myself, "What had Robertson done to him?" And the only conclusion I could ever come to was that Robertson probably looked down on Simpson when he was first made a governor—because of Robertson's much longer and deeper experience with the company. So, I never did like Simpson, and I had no qualms about creating a fiction in which certain things are implied to have been done by him that may not have been done, because the opposite benefit of the doubt has been given to him over and over again for over a hundred years. In various ranks, he has always been given the positive benefit of the doubt, so I thought "Well, I'll bend it in a negative direction, and it can't be any more imbalanced." In a way, it helped me to examine the power politics, because I did believe that, in the absence of any real supervision, power drove many men insane. There was a lack of checks and balances on what people were doing, and it pushed them in a way that resulted in incredible cruelty visited on the workers. People will talk about how the Natives were mistreated in the West, but I am not sure that, in that era, that holds water. I think that the Natives, because of their trading position, were in a much better position than the company employees to resist the abuses of the company.

HW In your book on Rocky Mountain House you refer to one of your key sources for both that book and for *The Trade*, which is William Gladstone's diary, as providing a unique opportunity to see the fur trade from "the workingman's end of the telescope." The fur trade is a really good example of the way in which history is skewed by social class or social status, because most of the records were kept by the officers in the trade. Gladstone's diary is an example of the importance of oral history, because he was interviewed for a Pincher Creek newspaper and provided a kind of corrective or at least an alternative to an official history that is dominated by the elite. As Gladstone says in the novel, "What you call history looks upside down to me."

FS William Gladstone's memoir is one of the most important documents about western Canada in the nineteenth century, because it is the only working-class record of life in the Hudson's Bay Company in the era and place it addresses. He was the only literate man who actually left a document that was written by him.

FIGURE 18.
William Gladstone and granddaughter Nellie (later Mrs. H.A. Riviere, Pincher Creek, Alberta). Glenbow Museum NA-184-23.

HW I didn't realize it was unique as a historical document.

FS Matthew Cocking in the eighteenth century left a document as well, but in the nineteenth century, as far as I know, Gladstone is the only working-class author of a document. When I read it, it was like a Rosetta Stone experience, because all of a sudden I was seeing contradicted a great many things that stand like rocks in the historical record, particularly through Gladstone's view of people. For instance, he hated John Rowand, despised him more than any man he had ever met, had been personally struck by him and cursed by him.

HW He cheered when Rowand died.

FS He cheered when he died, and that is the truth. So that is how William Gladstone's document informed me as a writer who wanted to look at that history from the bottom up; he was very important in helping me take that stance.

I use him in a very different way in the book; that is, I create a correspondence between Gladstone and the newspaper editor that did not exist, though it could have existed, because William Gladstone did write his memoirs for the *Rocky Mountain Echo* in 1900. The document deals only with when he arrived in 1848 forward until about the early 1870s, so it really does not duplicate my story in any way; there is just a tiny overlap near the end. But I use him as a commentator on history, which is what he was, in a sense. He was a working-class commentator on that world, and he may have been the only one whose record has survived. So I tease that out further and let him speak at various times in the book, talking about how history gets made. My favourite line in the whole book is probably where I have him say that—

HW "If the history books are right and the people who told me are wrong, that makes history the only kind of water that gets cleaner—

FS —the further downstream you go." If there is a key sentence in the book, that is probably it. I think that there has been a progressive sanitization of what occurred, and nobody really bothers to go back up the stream to locate things. That was something that I thought I could accomplish with *The Trade*, to create something that had not existed before.

HW Gladstone also gets a cameo in your last novel, *Lightning*. He is working at the same homestead with your main character, Doc Windham. What is it about Gladstone that makes you want to use him in your fiction?

FS Gladstone is an incredible figure in the history of western Canada, because he was here for a very long time. He actually lived through three economies, and I can think of almost no one who did that who left a record. He started as a working-class guy in the fur trade, and then he built mission churches for the Methodists; then he got the gold rush fever and headed down to Montana. He built various buildings around Fort Benton and lived in Fort Benton for a while. This was the beginning of a five-year period of scary chaos in southwestern Alberta history, when whiskey traders, equipped and funded out of Fort Benton, moved in to the southern prairie area of what became Alberta and traded with the Indians. The first and biggest whisky fort in that period was Fort Whoop-Up at the junction of the St. Mary's and Oldman Rivers, which William Gladstone built. His next and maybe last bonanza as a carpenter was to build homes for the wealthy ranchers during the ranch lease era, in the 1880s. His trade as a carpenter connected him to all kinds of different stories and the changing history of the nineteenth century, just because his job was so portable and changeable that he could keep remaking himself to fit. So, as a carpenter, he is building things, but he is also rebuilding himself to fit all these advances and changed economies.

HW In an excellent article on *The Trade*, Katherine Durnin points out that a book like *The Trade* particularly challenges efforts to distinguish between historical writing (history in other words), and historical fiction. Because none of the characters is invented, and because the novel is essentially positing credible scenarios in the gaps in the historical record—for instance, the secret trip that George Simpson makes in the novel to visit Margaret at Fort Carlton—Durnin says that "in imagining a gap in the record as a fabricated silence, Stenson strengthens the argument for historical imagination as a form of possible knowledge, and not mere invention." What do you think about the status of that central gambit of the novel, having Simpson try to force himself upon Margaret and having Margaret's resistance to that coercion being the source of her madness? Do you think that that is a question of being true to the spirit of history and possibly to the letter as well? Given that Margaret was the prettiest woman in the region, and it seems very likely that Simpson would have been attracted to her, and it has certainly been documented that he exploited other women and had a number of country wives, is this a reasonable speculation, and, indeed, might it also actually have happened?

FS The whole business of creating plausible fictional scenarios that fit and fill gaps in the historical record is something that can have a lot of utility for students of history, provided it is understood what you are doing. You can try to be obedient to the spirit of history, or a person might even get very lucky and actually be correct to the letter of history, but I think it is more the former that I aim for. The way I view history is as a kind of a matrix. There are all sorts of things causing all sorts of other things to occur, until what you get is this incredibly dense, interconnected kind of matrix. I am very superstitious about changing any facts that are well corroborated, because I feel that if you were to mess with anything that is actually in its place in that matrix, that was well substantiated, you may feel that you are only changing something at that point, but in fact you are changing everything at every point.

HW So it is sort of a retrospective and anachronistic version of chaos theory.

FS Yes, the reverse. That is how I think you can destroy the credibility of what you do in a million little ways, by making a couple of small shifts. The opposite I also believe to be true, that by leaving things where they are, you get the benefit of all sorts of connections you do not even understand, or you are not even aware of, outside of your own story, and it helps that reader–writer connection in terms of the credibility of the work. I think John Gardner said something about belief being everything in the contract between the reader and the writer; the reader has to believe enough to suspend their disbelief and enter into the work and feel the emotions. I actually think that if the historical fiction is built that way, it does something that is of value to historians, because it is something that historians can't do. Historians can't invent in the gaps, so they wind up just building the structure all full of holes.

HW I would argue that historians do that all the time. Just to give you an example, there is a passage in J.G. McGregor's *John Rowand: Czar of the Prairies*, where McGregor is essentially hypothesizing about John Rowand's reaction on meeting George Simpson for the first time, and he assumes an immediate empathy between these two figures, but one that is, almost by his own admission, totally hypothetical. Yet at the same time he presents it in a fairly mimetic way, as if this is pretty much how it happened.

FS McGregor, and Grant MacEwan too, for example, were popular historians, not academic historians. They worked by a different set of rules, and they did quite liberally suppose things. The academic historians are less likely to do that, whereas, when I do it, I do not have to apologize to anyone or signal my inventions. What a fiction writer can do in a situation might actually be an increase to what more formal historians can do. For example, I was asked by a publisher, University of Calgary Press, to read this book, *Marginal Man on the Blackfoot Frontier*, by John C. Jackson, which is the first biography of Jimmy Jock Bird. I have a blurb on the back, but the one thing that I criticized about the book was the fact that the writer did not seem to take into account the possibility that Jimmy Jock Bird was lying when he said certain things. Whenever he actually found that Jimmy Jock Bird said something, he just took it that that was what he meant. In contrast, I have been able to found a big chunk of a novel on the idea that Jimmy Jock Bird may never have been telling the truth to anyone about what his true motives were, and to write in search of his true motives. The academic historian, who is considered to be creating a more rock-solid truth, may actually be falling farther short of the truth than I am, because he feels that he has to respect the documentary evidence, that he can't cross-examine the documentary evidence unless he has another source that suggests that there is an untruth, or a piece of evidence that allows him to cross-examine, where I can cross-examine the historical record all I want, as long as I instinctually feel that the sum of what I have researched points me in that direction. So there is a freedom to that. Dr. Sarah Carter of the University of Calgary has been using *The Trade* in a Canadian history course, and what she does is ask students to read the book and then she assigns them an essay to take some aspect of it and figure out where the fiction begins and the historical record ends. I think if you can do that with *The Trade* you have a pretty good grasp of the history behind it.

HW Contemporary theories of history, though, are increasingly drawing attention to the way that even the work of the academic historian is incredibly narrativized. So even though academic historians strive to stay true to the historical record and are restrained by the historical record, there is an awful lot of storifying going on: taking a certain figure from the historical record and turning him or her into a kind of character. The process of doing that involves a lot of gestures and techniques that are really kind of fictional.

FS I agree. To use this biography of Jimmy Jock Bird as an example again, the fact that the author has chosen to assume that Jimmy Jock Bird was telling the truth, at certain points in time, implies a belief in and characterization of Jimmy Jock Bird as a truthful man. To me, the fact that Jimmy Jock Bird was known to have double-crossed two companies (and that is a fact) over a bunch of skins and furs in what became Montana suggests to me that he was not.

HW What that illustrates is the way in which academic historical writing is not simply a matter of a kind of mimesis of the past but an interpretive activity that brings with it all kinds of ideological decisions and so on.

FS Where academic history invents as much as I invent as a fiction writer dealing in historical materials is in the matter of characterization. What I do not think an academic historian is as likely to do is to create a fact that no document suggests, and put it in a gap. I am willing to do that and the rules of fiction encourage me to, whereas I think an academic historian has to balk at that point. Certain kinds of historians can say, "Well, it is possible that this sort of thing occurred in that gap." If there is no evidence for it, they are unlikely to even do that much, whereas I am quite happy to, as long as it is plausible and plausible in the sense of arising from character.

HW Also, we are talking about facts of a certain magnitude, because there are many little facts implied in that process of turning a historical figure into a kind of character who acts in a certain way. But what you are describing is something that really sticks out much more in a historical life story, such as, for instance, coercing a woman to have sex. That is a good example of a place where an academic historian or even a popular historian would really balk.

FIGURE 19.
James "Jimmy Jock" Bird,
Blackfoot interpreter. Glenbow
Museum NA-360-21.

FS That brings up a whole other matter of what we have allowed ourselves to say or think about people of importance. I think we have routinely stopped short of assuming or wondering if they would commit certain acts unless those acts are actually somewhere to be found in the historical record. If people are going to invent something, they are more inclined to invent something good; I think they are very unlikely to invent a criminal act. In the case of my vision of the Governor, who is based on George Simpson, I have him attempt a rape on Margaret. I don't think that you will find a historian, academic or popular, who will ever imply such a thing. I thought, "Well, here is a man who is used to having his way; he has power over every single individual who works for, or is in a family that works for, the fur trade in his area, and he has a lot of mistresses." I remember talking about this to people who were descended from people in the fur trade, and a lot of them thought that a young woman would be very flattered. It would probably give her a status that other women did not have, and maybe even gave her family status, which I deal with in Margaret's father's view of the whole situation. But I allowed myself to ask the fictional question of what would happen if one of those desired women said no for the very good reason that she had a man already that she was madly in love with.

HW That strategem, her attempt to offer to trade herself or her body for some kind of concession from Simpson, really dramatizes the difficult position of women in the trade. The novel shows how essential and indispensable they were to the trade on the one hand, and how vulnerable and expendable on the other.

FS I started off with a very inflexible view of what would happen in that scene. I think I had a somewhat Victorian concept originally, that the Governor would want Margaret and she would refuse, and he would try and force the issue. My assumptions were clichéd. The more I struggled with it, the more I thought that I was not giving her enough credit for understanding the situation she was in and understanding how it was going to affect her, Harriott, and her family. I realized that, rather than just being the victim in this *Perils of Pauline* kind of way, she would probably have the courage and understanding to negotiate.

HW How much was Sylvia van Kirk's *Many Tender Ties* an influence? She likewise makes the argument that women in the trade—Native women or white women—were not simply victims. They had a great deal of agency, though it was obviously constrained in various ways.

FS I read *Many Tender Ties* a long time ago for other purposes, and it certainly informed me; it either taught me things or to an extent confirmed my own opinions. I don't think she really entered into the whole issue of sexual politics beyond the concepts of the country wife and the abandoned country wife. I thought, "Well, I want to deal with something else. I want to deal with the possibility that a young couple will love one another in a star-crossed kind of way and that the whole power of the company over their lives will come to torture that love and maybe even ruin their lives over it." The only thing in the historical record and the only thing I really remember in *Many Tender Ties* about the country wife was this idea that there were the callous company men who used these women and dispensed with them when they were done with them, and replaced them with white wives, and then there were the "many tender ties"—that is, there were people who had grown an affection for their country wives and kept them. I thought, "There is a lot more going on. There has to be a lot of transactional sex going on, where people are using their power over other people in the hierarchy and maybe asking for their daughters, almost as a matter of flexing their power." That is the sort of thing we never seem to get at; that is the level at which I think we are still sanitizing our history.

HW I think van Kirk does deal with that to quite a degree in the book, looking back at the role of the more communal and consensual transactions in Native cultures and then at the way in which they get almost commodified within the trade.

FS I feel that what fiction does is it gets down to the level of the individual. It doesn't deal in groups. History tends to deal more in what the pattern is; fiction tends to deal with the exception. So the pattern may have been to accept what Simpson wanted to do, and the exception—and it has to be a plausible exception—is to posit a young couple in love who do not want to play ball. It was bound to have happened, and when something was bound to have happened and yet it is not in the historical record, that is interesting to me.

HW The shift in attitudes towards country marriages that accompanied Simpson marrying an English woman (his cousin Frances), and bringing her to Red River, is really stressed in the novel. What do you think were the implications of that shift? Did it perhaps mark a kind of watershed in the country's colonial history, or at least in the West, perhaps as a kind of retrenchment of imperialist attitudes towards race and towards miscegenation?

FS I think that when Simpson went back to England and got himself an English wife, he really did in a way take an axe to what had been a working social structure in the fur trade since the eighteenth century, which was based on white traders marrying people and at times taking country wives and then perhaps taking different country wives later, which was something that was based quite a bit on the Native approach to marriage. It was not entirely an imposed situation; it was a kind of mutual understanding of how they might deal with this whole matter of marriage and children. Then Simpson comes along and decides that country wives (and he's sort of got his official one, Margaret Taylor, and then his unofficial ones) are just not dignified enough for his exalted position. He is now a much more powerful man than he was in 1822, and he wants to express his power. It really shows a kind of basic racism, for starters. He goes back and gets his white wife and builds the Stone Fort for her at Fort Garry. Then everybody was terrified not to follow suit because (knowing how vengeful and powerful Simpson was) they thought what if—just by retaining their Native or Métis country wife—they might be implying a criticism of what Simpson did, that they might actually suffer in the hierarchy just by staying in their domestic arrangement with a Native wife.

HW It would be seen as an affront to Simpson.

FS As an affront, as disobedience, so people wanted to act preemptively. So they are ditching their country wives and taking furlough in England, looking for white women and bringing them back. It created an angry debate in fur trade society about what was right and what was wrong.

HW It also seems to be a movement from a somewhat more comfortable and mutual cultural transaction to this imperialist and exclusive idea about what civilization is. It seems be a real turning point in deciding what kind of country this is going to be and what the culture of this place is going to be.

FS Not to suggest that the country was not thoroughly racist up to that time—it probably was in many different ways—but it was the embarking on an entirely new level of racism. It really was a move from something that made sense to something that made no sense, for the sake of appearances. It was the introduction of a kind of falsity, the superficiality and disconnectedness of a lot of things we do in the name of civilization. It meant replacing the idea of taking a wife because her father was a very useful trading partner (who had a lot of power amongst his people and would bring you that family's and that tribe's trade) with the idea of taking a white wife because it would look better to Britain. So basically you have a very utilitarian thing replaced by something that had an absence of utility. I put that in the mouth of John Rowand: "What could be more worthless than an English wife?"

HW Simpson also seems to have shifted the trade from a more transactual and bilateral relationship with Native people (I am not suggesting it was an egalitarian paradise) to a more imperial relationship. That is Peter C. Newman's description of it in *Company of Adventurers*. Would you agree with that?

FS I think that as Simpson became more powerful, he became more like a Caesar. Marrying an English wife was not the only thing that he did that made no sense. The building of the Stone Fort was also a completely ridiculous thing to do. It was in the wrong place, it had no trading utility whatsoever, and it actually made everything difficult because everybody who wanted to talk to him and do business had to make an otherwise unnecessary and time-consuming excursion. So he started to do all these pretentious things that did not make sense just because he was powerful enough to do them. In historical terms, and in the novel, what brought him down was that he tried to be inhuman, and yet he was not successful; he was human after all. He could not satisfy or comfort or sufficiently protect his delicate English wife. Their son died. She was broken-hearted. She lost her will to stay there, or found the will to leave is probably more to the point.

HW And he did not have the power to stop her. While he was able to withstand the disapproval of all sorts of people beneath him whom he alienates, he could not withstand her disapproval.

FS The most basic thing he tries to do for himself, within the area in which he is all-powerful, is bring his white wife into it, and she will not stay. She moves to Lachine, and he has to live without her for most of the time. And I think this really began the destruction of him in a way.

HW *The Trade* seems to be part of a revisionist fictional reassessment of the legacy of colonialism, essentially demythologizing the accomplishments of those explorers, traders, politicians, and military officers who have been lionized as part of the traditional narrative of Canadian history. Yet you qualify that critical portrait of the trade by questioning, or having your characters question, the stereotype of the homicidal, racist trader. I am thinking of Rowand's exchange with Robert Rundle, the Wesleyan missionary, or Harriott's comments to the journalists from *Harper's* who come to interview him in Red River. Their defence of fur traders provides an interesting qualification of that revisionism, which often takes the form of a simplistic turning upside down of the relationship between Native people and those figures of colonial authority.

FS Faulkner was often asked whether he was trying to revise the view of the South and he said something to the effect that, no, he was just trying to write books. I know sociologically why I hold certain views, when I am confronted with history, because I have a natural tendency to side with certain individuals. If Peter C. Newman wrote a novel about the fur trade, he would want to be Simpson, right? I think he might. Yet that was not open to me, just because there are certain fictional jobs open to me and certain ones that aren't. Harriott very much appealed to me, for example, because of the few things said about him in the Gladstone memoir. I just thought, "What a fascinating guy; what an able man." He had a genuine affection for and interest in his men, whereas everybody else at his level in the trade was just looking for their next advancement. Certainly it was not easy for Harriott to be the way he was, but that job of being Harriott was open to me. I could have had a go at being Simpson; it was fictionally possible for me. Still, I would have had no interest in seeing the world or exploring the whole terrain through him.

HW Your body rejected the transplant.

FS It is more natural for me to view the history through a guy like Rowand or Harriott or Jimmy Jock. I could not have predicted what would happen, what specific revision would take place. It is more an organic process of discovering things by reliving all this stuff through them (admittedly as invented by me). One of the discoveries I made was what Rowand says to Rundle when the missionary presumes that traders kill Indians: "If you know nothing about fur trading, maybe you know something about farming. Does a farmer kill his milk cow?" Yes, there was killing on both sides, but in any larger sense, the traders would want the Natives to do well; they needed the Natives to want to come to hunt and to feverishly partake in the trade. I don't think that they knew any of the long-term effects of the things that caused Indians to die in a widespread way—the disease and even the alcohol. I think Simpson was capable of some prediction in that way and just would not have cared; he had that kind of callous, imperial mindset, whereas I don't think the average trader did.

HW My point was that you don't simply portray the trade as some kind of homogeneous colonial machine. Your portrait of it is a lot more nuanced, instead of just flipping the portrait from a heroizing and mythologizing narrative—which has been more or less the standard treatment of "the company of adventurers"—to the company of thieves or the company of murderers.

FS The longer I do historical fiction, the more I am starting to have a methodology and an ideology about it—which is to give back complexity. I suppose a lot of my work does amount to championing the point of view of the working class, but all I am doing really is presuming to look through them. I am not actually trying to make them succeed in the story or best the bad guys— that is not really my mission—but that is who I choose to look through. What I am really trying to do in a larger sense is to give back the complexity and the level of detail that is taken away. Most approaches to history seem to simplify those details, make them small, take their complexity away, and use history for some purpose. It is like the argument about whether wilderness has a value if no people are using it. Is its only value in how people can make use of it? I think it is the same thing with history: does history have a value unless history can be put to work? All kinds of people believe that its only purpose is to help lobby for something in the present. I feel that wilderness does have a basic intrinsic value, and I feel the same way about history.

HW And you do a kind of violence to both when you make use of them.

FS There has been way too much scrunching the history down and stripping away all its complexity. I think that when somebody says that the fur trade was evil, they are usually trying to make a point about something in the present. The same thing was obviously true when they were saying the fur trade was good, that it brought Christianity and progress to the Natives, it brought the Industrial Revolution tools to a bunch of stone-age savages, which used to be the way people would talk. So, as you say, a violence was done to the richness of the story. I am attracted by the notion that I could do something to replenish that complexity.

HW An important consideration in the writing of historical fiction that *The Trade* really brings to the foreground is the choice of narrative perspective. Contemporary theorizing about the writing of history has drawn attention to the problems of who is speaking and how, to the problems of the authoritative, omniscient voice that basically pronounces, "This happened." It has also drawn attention to the problems of even focalizing the narrative through the consciousness of a historical figure, which creates the illusion of having access to that figure's experience of the past. Many contemporary writers of historical fiction—and this is true to a degree of your approach in *The Trade*—have resorted to a more dialogic or polyphonic approach, using multiple voices to convey the variety or heterogeneity of perspectives in which the past exists in these traces (in journals, in diaries, in logbooks, other histories, and so on). How important is this choice of narrative voices, and what challenges does it pose to your imaginative engagement with the past?

FS It is easier to be the narrative tyrant if you are functioning through one voice, if you imagine your way into this one historical figure and then view the whole universe of that time through that one experience. Taking a variety of experiences and playing them off against one another prevents you from dominating the story with your own imagining of one experience. If you say, "Well, I am most enticed to view this world through Harriott," then it becomes Harriott's nineteenth century, Harriott's fur trade, whereas if you are also looking at it through Rowand and through Robert Rundle and through Jimmy Jock Bird, it is these points of view struggling with one another, pulling in their own direction, and perhaps you arrive at something more balanced, something more like a truth that exceeds the singular invention.

HW A good example is the distance between how John Rowand sees things and how William Gladstone sees things. Much of the narrative is focalized through Rowand, and that narrative perspective cultivates a certain degree of intimacy with him and sympathy for him; we appreciate the challenges that he faces, especially in trying to protect Harriott without incurring the hostility of Simpson. Yet when you look at the segments that are ostensibly from William Gladstone's diaries, they put Rowand in a much less flattering light.

What did you want to set in motion by having that difference of perspectives in the novel?

FS When I take the point of view of a character, I don't see myself as manipulative or even controlling that process. There is a job to do. I think of writing as being more like acting than any other allied art form, and if I take the persona of Rowand and use everything I know about him to bring about a fidelity in my performance as Rowand, then, if it is actually going to be art, it should actually get beyond what I think. If you ask me to give a capsule biography of Rowand, what I write *as* Rowand should be very different, because there is a different set of responsibilities involved. I think that the more voices you add to the mix in this fashion, the more you give back the complexity to the story and the less that it will be thematized. If I thematize about the trade, it is something I do in the aftermath of having written about it; it is more about understanding what I have done than it is about a planned strategy.

HW Margaret Sweatman uses the analogy of historical fiction being a kind of embezzlement of public property, and I want to take up that idea and ask about your portrait of the Wesleyan missionary Robert Rundle. In two chapters at the end of *The Trade* there are these fictionalized private documents of both Rundle and the artist Paul Kane, who was described as essentially the first tourist to the West. Kane's letters serve in part as a sequel to the section on Rundle, providing reflections on Rundle's relationships with Harriott and with Jimmy Jock Bird. But "The Missionary," which is the section on Rundle, ends with a private, "unofficial" journal that reverses the relative confidence of the historical Rundle's official journal and underlines the brutality, cruelty, and depravity—the Hobbesian world—of the trade. In that section, echoing Harriott's religious skepticism, Rundle writes, "What good to throw a cloak of religion over such an evil core?" What inclined you to give this kind of spin to the figure of Rundle?

FS The Rundle papers, which the Glenbow Museum published a number of years ago, were his official diary, in which you do get the sense that this was written because he felt that what he was doing had historical value. He was the first Methodist missionary to reach Fort Edmonton, Rocky Mountain House; to bring Christianity to the tribes along the Rocky Mountains and to the Blackfoot. He wanted to leave a public record, but at times it veers into what you would put in a personal, secret diary. I think he forgot sometimes what he was about and injected into what he was writing a kind of moan of pain. So I wanted to split those two things and create the idea of a second level, a diary he wishes could be secret from God. Because there was a tangible feeling (and

FIGURE 20.
Reverend Robert T. Rundle.
Glenbow Museum NA-642-1.

again it is the thing that a fiction writer can do that historians have a harder time to do) almost of agony from Rundle. He just could not believe at times how alone, how deserted by God, he felt. What could be worse, if you are a missionary out in this wilderness with people whom you don't really understand, who don't really understand you, and your only companion is God, if you then feel that God has deserted you? That has to be a loneliness more profound than anything. So that kind of agony is what I tried to put into the second document. But in my opinion, there was on several occasions in Rundle's official journal, that literal historical document, a feeling that this was just the tip of the iceberg of some profound pain—that it is about loneliness, failure, and desertion.

HW So it is a matter of bringing out more explicitly something that you feel is present and subterranean in that historical document.

FS Also, I wanted the book to be built like the nineteenth century. At the start of *The Trade* are these secret goings-on that the "civilized" world really doesn't know very much about, and so that world is allowed to function in secrecy. Then, as the century went on, all of a sudden Europe and Britain are providing this pressure to Christianize the Indians. The first people who have nothing to do with the secret economic contract between the Hudson's Bay Company and the Indians (and the Métis as a middle group created by the trade) are the missionaries. Then the tourists start coming: painters, hunters, explorers. So I wanted to build the novel that way, too, so that they enter the story, in just the physical sense of the structure of the book, about where in the century they did arrive. So that was the idea of having a section on the missionary and then a section on the artist. They are not part of what is going on, and they are the first people to see into it from that outside position. They try and make sense of what is there in their terms, because they have not grown up in it like everybody else. So they will find certain things exceedingly strange. Rundle, for instance, just cannot understand the whole dependence on rum, which for Harriott is just common sense, because that is all he knows. Harriott has been in the Northwest since he was twelve.

HW In some ways it is part of coping with the evil that is the brutality of the world of the trade, as opposed to the rum itself, which Rundle sees as being the source of evil.

Jimmy Jock Bird is really an enigmatic figure in the novel, because he has really no voice or little voice in the historical record. Part of Durnin's argument is that you are constrained in the novel by the documents that you have to work with. She makes the point that the creation of those silences is sometimes an act of power; those gaps in the historical record are sometimes there because the powerful do not want certain things to be acknowledged and recorded. She argues—perhaps conversely—that another aspect of the selectivity of the historical record is that the marginalized do not have a textual voice that a historian or a writer can then work with. And if, as she puts it, you are working with an archival premise, then in some ways you are constrained with figures like Margaret, and Jimmy Jock Bird, who is portrayed by George Simpson and by Rowand and more recently by J.G. MacGregor in his biography of John Rowand, as this unreliable turncoat, simmering with resentment over being denied advancement within the company because he is of mixed heritage; and yet Paul Kane, in his diary, finds Jimmy Jock quite affable and genial. In *The Trade*, though, he becomes much more of a figure of resistance, countering the encroachment of whites on the southern plains and in some respects being Harriott's implicit ally against the trade.

FS The few available biographical materials about Jimmy Jock Bird are so contradictory. It gave me this insight: "What if someone understood the power and control you can have over other people if you have no desire to be on the record, to be recognized for your achievements?" In the rest of the world, everybody wants to be remembered, they want to be known to have had power. So all Jimmy Jock had to do (this is my fictional imagining of him) was to resist the urge to be recognized for having done anything. If he can do that, he has tremendous power over all the other people who function by the other method. That was the premise I had for his character, and in archival terms it made sense of all the things that didn't make sense. So perhaps in some forensic kind of way that may be the one time that I actually did create a few ideas and occurrences and attitudes for a fictional character based on a historical figure that may be truer than anything that has been written about him. I think there has been a general failure to understand him. Simpson didn't understand him; Rowand certainly didn't; Harriott perhaps did; Rundle was really mystified by him. In all cases it was also a failure to understand that a man whose genetic ingredients were half Indian and half white would actually choose the Indian half. Such was the absolute basic racism of the time that if you had a choice you would always choose white; that if you had to choose between Indians and the company, you would always choose the company. They kept on believing that with Jimmy Jock, and that belief kept on allowing him to defraud them and double-cross them over and over again. They would go on paying him, because someone who was in charge of the payment (and that is Simpson as far as my book is concerned) could not believe that he was double-crossing him, could not believe that he was actually working on behalf of the Indians; but I really do think he was. Also that story about him murdering Godin, or having Godin murdered, and cutting Andrew Wyeth's initials into his hand as he was dying is true. Jimmy Jock Bird did that. He was an acknowledged, dangerous war chief.

HW You said earlier on when we were talking about revisionist portraits that you are not giving the working grunt the victory in the end. But one thing that Harriott and Jimmy Jock share at the end of the novel is that in some ways they ultimately elude Simpson. Obviously he has done incredible damage to Harriott, but in forcing Harriott's retirement Simpson in some ways delivers to Harriott what he has been looking for, an escape from the trade.

FS We talked about how the trade was this oppressive structure clamped on top of these people, that some people are trying to get out of, while some people are not. Harriott is trying to get out of it and trying to get his wife, and child eventually, out of it, and Jimmy Jock *has* found a way out of it. He is actually the most successful. But Harriott kind of pops out of it by accident by being forced to retire. His victory is that he has actually somewhat preserved his

sanity, preserved his humanity. Jimmy Jock has got out of it in a very mysterious way; and here I may differ a little from Katherine's argument. I did not
feel in any way bothered by my lack of access to Jimmy Jock. I wanted to create the feeling of a lack of access as far as Jimmy Jock is concerned. I want to
feel that all kinds of people are trying to understand Jimmy Jock, including this
novel, and no one can quite do it.

HW So it is not a matter of being constrained by a lack of archival sources so
much as simply a choice of characterization, that you want him to be enigmatic.

FS I want him to elude this whole matter of record and known facts and
known personas. That is how he got out of the company; he has made a very
conscious effort to elude the trade. The key thing is not necessarily caring or
wanting to be acknowledged for anything he has done, which is something I
have him talking about with Paul Kane on their trip back to Edmonton from
Rocky Mountain House.

HW In the opening of your book on Rocky Mountain House, you note that
most people learn history from reading first-hand or second-hand textual
accounts or by watching films or looking at historical photographs, but then
you observe "that the knowledge and appreciation gained in these ways is
good, but something will always be missing until we actually stand in places
where history happened."

FS There is a great difference between what I will write if I have or haven't been
to the place where an event occurred. On the one hand you are really dealing
with the sensory, and on the other you are not. Again, it is a matter of complexity. There is always more complexity if you are writing from the experience of having been to the place, because otherwise you are generalizing, or
you are synthesizing from memory what it is like, for instance, to stand in an
aspen forest beside a river. I think an experience of place enriches all of that.
Somebody who had a tremendous influence on me in this respect was Rudy
Wiebe. His essay about the writing of *Big Bear*, "On the Trail of Big Bear," has
the best analysis of imagining a past reality by synthesizing an experience in
the present and thinking of what things are the same. He talks about the smell
of hot horse piss or the sound of a saddle on a cold day. He addresses what is
added by having some sort of current experience in your own life that relates
to what is to be depicted in the past.

HW I am also wondering whether an engagement with history tends to come
out of an experience of a particular and local terrain, part of that being an
appreciation of the strata beneath the present.

FS Whereas this synthesized history that I was talking about is some people's way of learning a period, my way is to circumnavigate the synthesized history and try to work as much as possible from the primary documents out, so that I am visiting history at its most tangible points, including physical places. In experiential terms, revisiting the landscape in the moment and knowing the landscape from a lifetime of living there are very important primary materials to work through in imagining the history. So rather than deal with it like a synthesized, predigested version of the landscape, if you visit it in the primary form—as with historical documents—your relationship to it is going to be as visceral as it can be, given the immense period of time that has gone by.

The Trade and Lightning are the result of my having made a conscious decision to be a certain kind of writer who lives his whole life in a certain place and writes from that place, knows it from the ground up, knows the landscape very intimately, and knows it at any point. You could slice it anywhere and I would still understand it, so that I could go to an archive and take any piece that I find and know where to put it. Fiction writing is always an experiment, and my version of that experiment is to try and understand the place as a kind of matrix, and the landscape is an enormous part of that. When I was writing Lightning, I would often jump in the car and drive fifteen minutes west and just sit and stare into that valley at Cochrane, where a big chunk of the novel took place. I did a lot of travelling up the North Saskatchewan for The Trade. I walked through Fort Edmonton many a time and walked the river down around Rocky Mountain House and stared at the clearing where the old forts were. I remember suddenly figuring out, from doing that, that in times of continuous use, the clearing around the fort would actually expand as they used all the trees, and in times when it was shut down, the woods would encroach. Just little things like that. So it is always important to study the terrain and imagine the history in terms of the terrain. Furthermore, my way of writing is cinematic, so it is also a matter of having enough information in terms of the landscape and the physical culture of the history to actually have an image in my head that I can then write from.

HW Lightning, I would say, is more of a Western than a historical novel, and yet at the same time there are historical figures in it—the Marquis of Lorne makes a brief appearance, your old friend William Gladstone is there, there are references to Charles Dickens's son, the RCMP inspector Francis Dickens— but beyond that I also get the sense of a certain desire to historicize the Western, to convey a sense of the historical currents shaping the lives of a cowboy like your main character Doc Windham. Would that be fair to say?

FS I would have to argue against that, because I tried to write *Lightning* in the same way I wrote *The Trade*, although over a much more compressed time period. There is one major difference between those two books, and that is that in *The Trade* all the characters, major and minor, are based on historical figures. In *Lightning* only the minor characters are from the historical record. The major figures—Doc Windham, Dog Eye, and Pearly—are invented. So, in a way, I was trying to write a historical novel of a period that has been written about a lot. The result of all that writing is a genre called the Western, but my aspiration was to ignore the genre and write a literary historical novel about that period. Now if a Western resulted, so be it, but the effort was not to really write within the bounds or the conventions of that genre. The genre and the whole popular cultural phenomena that have come out of that period are so strong that I think it is almost impossible to see *Lightning* as other than a genre Western.

HW A lot of what happens in it certainly evokes the tropes of the Western: the lynching and the desire to avenge a lynching, the beleaguered heroine Pearly, and so on. I am not saying that it is a stereotypical Western or even a conventional Western, but in a lot of ways the novel is crossing that same geographical and generic territory.

FS The lynching at the beginning of *Lightning* was based on the fact that I was using an actual historical cattle drive, the Nelson Story Drive, that was diverted from Missouri and wound up going up the Bozeman Trail in Montana in 1866. All the things that happened with the Indians are factual. The time at which the cowboys in the novel arrived at Virginia City was exactly a year after there had been twenty-five lynchings of highwaymen and members of a criminal gang. Vigilante lynchings were becoming the public response in Montana territory to criminal problems or any disturbances of the public peace. So, in a sense, I was doing exactly what I did with *The Trade*. I was going back to historical documents and fictionalizing out of them, but because of the popular culture surrounding the Western, the events that I selected from those primary documents are interpreted as my having chosen things from the Western genre. In fact, it is the other way around; that is how we got the Western genre.

HW In talking about historicizing the Western I was getting at the distinction between the Western as a form of romance, inhabiting a somewhat exotic and unrealistic fictional space, and your novel as a historicized story of a cowboy. In that sense, ultimately we may not be that far apart in how we see the book, but I take your point that the Western is this almost hegemonic term that overshadows what you are trying to do with the novel, which is to write a historical piece comparable to *The Trade*.

FS I was conscious of that right from the beginning of this project. I remember saying to people that in *The Trade* I had the luxury of creating fiction out of historical materials that had not been heavily fictionalized. *Lightning* was absolutely the reverse. I would be trying to use the same process as in *The Trade*, but for the open-range era, so I was conscious of how frequently fictionalized the material had been. The Canadian aspect of that history had not been used in fiction to any degree, and that gave me my hope of building something new and worthwhile.

Pushing Out the Poison
Joseph Boyden

Of Scottish, Irish, and Métis ancestry, Joseph Boyden grew up in Willowdale, Ontario, the ninth of eleven children. During his childhood, the family spent much of their summers in northern Ontario, visiting relatives on his mother's side. After attending high school in Toronto, Boyden, the (self-professed) black sheep of a family of black sheep, spent much of his youth travelling by bus and motorcycle through Canada and the United States, eventually settling in New Orleans. Having studied creative writing at York University, Boyden began an MFA at the University of New Orleans in 1992, which he completed in 1995. He then returned to Canada to take up a teaching position at Northern College in Moosonee, travelling to small Native communities around James Bay, and has since split his time between New Orleans and northern Ontario, which pro-vides the inspiration for most of his fiction. His first collection of stories, *Born With a Tooth*, was published in 2001. In 2005, Boyden published *Three Day Road*, a novel about two young Cree men who serve as snipers and scouts in Belgium and France in World War I. The novel, inspired by the experiences of legendary Ojibway sniper Francis Peghamagabow, was nominated for the Governor General's Award for fiction and won the 2006 Rogers Writers' Trust

Fiction Prize. I talked to Joseph Boyden by telephone in February of 2006 at his home in New Orleans, where he teaches creative writing and Canadian literature at the University of New Orleans.

HW I've read that your interest in military history and in Aboriginal soldiers comes out of your own family background. Can you tell me a bit about that interest and the way that your family background figures into it?

JB Sure. I've always been very fascinated by Canadian military culture and the place of Aboriginal people in that. I come from a very military family. My mother's father was a motorcycle dispatch rider in World War I. He was actually blown off his motorcycle on Nov. 11, 1918, the last day of the war, while he was delivering a dispatch. I used to like to imagine when I was a child that he was delivering news of the Armistice, but there's no way to know.

HW He was blinded then, wasn't he?

JB He was blinded in one eye that day, and then moved to Canada. He was from Scotland and was with the Scottish Regiment. Then he made the decision, while recuperating, to move to Canada. That's what he did and never went back home. He was a fascinating guy, though I never got to know him; he died before I was born. My uncle, my father's older brother, was an infantryman in World War I. He went into the conflict quite late, but served in the war there. My great-aunt Ella, who is on my mother's side as well, was a nurse over in Flanders and France during World War I, and she received a number of medals for her service. And then my father was a lieutenant-colonel with both the Irish Regiment of Canada and the Cape Breton Highlanders during World War II.

HW He was a medical officer, I believe.

JB He was a medical officer serving right in the front lines. He was awarded the Distinguished Service Order. He was actually mentioned for the Victoria Cross a number of times. A General Brown, who knew my father and who was still alive, in his nineties, told my family the story that my father actually won the Victoria Cross, was in Rome to receive it, was up all night in a cantina drinking with one of his buddies, and then he walked out into the morning and saw a British general who had sent a number of my father's troops into a really stupid engagement in which a number of them died. So my father angrily confronted him and ended up getting in a fight and beating him up and therefore lost the Victoria Cross and was given the Distinguished Service Order instead.

HW From what I understand, your father was the most highly decorated medical officer in that war. Is that right?

JB In the British Empire. He went to Buckingham Palace—I still have the invitation signed by King George—in January of 1945, when the war was just moving into Germany. King George pinned the Distinguished Service Order on my father and told him that he was the mostly highly decorated medical officer in the British Empire. So all of these things came to be these legends in my household I've always known about. I think this legend and myth swirling around in my head all these years needed to come out, and so in a big part that's why I wrote *Three Day Road*.

HW So you had family members in both World War I and World War II, and ultimately you ended up choosing to write about World War I. Was that a difficult decision?

JB It was. At first I was definitely going to write about World War II. I've read about it all my life, because my father was involved in it, and he passed away when I was eight, so it was a way of me keeping in touch with him, reading the history of what had happened to him and where he had gone in Italy and Holland and North Africa. So at the very beginning I thought, "Yes, it'll be World War II," but then I quickly realized that everyone was directing movies or writing about World War II. Then I thought that World War I made far more sense to write about because it was a very difficult time for Canadian Natives, while at the same time it was the first modern conflict. There was this clash between the old and the new, and the bourgeoisie versus the proletariat, etc.; all of these world events were going on that were really reshaping us. Also, and especially, there was a quiet war being fought at home, in Canada, during World War I: the Native people were being forced on to reservations, their language taken away, customs taken away, religion taken away, children taken away to residential school. So there was this really insidious battle going on, involving Native people and the government. Also, I had known about Francis Pegahmagabow, the great Ojibway sniper, all my life. Our family spent much of my childhood in and around Wasauksing reserve in Georgian Bay, where he was from, so I knew about him as well. So it just made perfect sense to me that this needed to be a novel about World War I and Native involvement in the war.

HW In your acknowledgments to *Three Day Road* you express the desire to pay tribute to those Native soldiers who fought in World War I, and you add there, "Your bravery and skill do not go unnoticed." In some ways, though, can't we say that they have gone unnoticed, in the sense that those Native soldiers haven't really received the kind of credit that they should have? And, if that's the case, is part of the intention of *Three Day Road* to in some way correct that situation or address that situation?

JB No question. I think my acknowledgements were more wishful thinking than anything when it came to us acknowledging what our Native soldiers have done for us. I think it's one of the greatest overlooked parts of Canadian history that so many of us know nothing about and that shocked and amazed me, especially as I read more and more about how many Natives volunteered. Canada developed the best pension plan for soldiers, after World War I, and all the veterans who returned home got it, except for the Native soldiers, who didn't get any compensation whatsoever. They were made a lot of promises, too, huge promises of land, of the vote, of freedom, and those promises all disappeared immediately on their return home. It's a very sad part of our history, and maybe it's part of our history that we choose not to try to remember because Canadians aren't known across the world as being unfair people. We like to think of ourselves as very fair-minded, and yet our treatment of Native soldiers returning home from World War I and World War II and Korea was horrendous.

HW And, just to pour salt into the wound, there were cases of Aboriginal land being expropriated to give to veterans.

JB That's what is behind the whole blow-up at Ipperwash in Ontario, with Dudley George being shot by the Ontario Provincial Police. That park was Indian land taken away by the government in World War II, and the Ojibway are just simply trying to fight for what had been taken away from them. It evolved into a battle between the police and the Native protesters, and one of the protesters was shot to death, and there's an ongoing inquiry about it. But it's just one example of, I'm sure, hundreds.

I didn't want to go into the novel thinking "I'm going to teach every Canadian about Native involvement in the war," but it was definitely a passion of mine to want to shine a little light on a part of our history that so few know about.

HW As you mentioned earlier, Aboriginal people did enlist in both world wars in proportionately quite high numbers, and it's tempting in some ways to see it as very ironic that they would be eager to enlist to fight in the defence of Canada or Britain, neither of which had been particularly good to them, to say the least.

JB Exactly. It's a fascinating kind of conundrum why they did. Often whole reserves, all of the able-bodied men on the reserves, went off to war. Native men volunteered at far higher rates than any other group, far higher, and I had to wonder why, because they were not being treated well by the Canadian government. I think every man had his individual reasons, but I came up with three main reasons why they did. The first one is why any young man would decide to go to war and fight, and that's for the sense of adventure, for the romanticism, to get away from their little place, to see some of the world.

HW For the sense of camaraderie as well.

JB Yes: "My buddies are going and so I'm going to go too." I think many young men were sucked into World War I thinking about the romanticism. "It's going to be over by Christmas, so I'd better get going" and all of that; I think a lot of men probably did it for that reason. But from a Native perspective, I imagine that a lot of these young men went off because it was a very difficult time for Native people. I think a lot of young Native men felt almost emasculated, like something important had been taken away from them. As I mentioned, many of the residential schools wouldn't allow them to speak their language, practice their religion or customs. And so this was a chance I think for a lot of Native men to—

HW Reassert their warrior identity?

JB Exactly, reassert an identity, and oftentimes that was a warrior identity, that's tied in with the Native thinking. So I think that's another big reason. Then there is a third reason, which is unfortunately again very insidious, and that is that a lot of times Native men were basically lied to. Their Indian agent would tell them they had to go, even though this was before conscription. It was their obligation to go. There was a lot of lying going on.

HW I came across another theory, that at least some of them enlisted not to defend Canada as such but to defend their land, which is an interesting distinction.

JB Exactly.

HW The two main characters of *Three Day Road*, Elijah Whiskeyjack and Xavier Bird, serve with the Southern Ontario Rifles as part of the Second Canadian Division.

JB That's a fictional regiment. I didn't want to be held in by choosing a real regiment. I mean, creatively I would have been held back a little by having to be true to the real regiment, and then I was worried about the historical over-shadowing the creative. I didn't want it to feel heavy-handed in its research, and so I invented my own regiment, which was very typical of many of the regiments at that time, usually labourers, farmers, etc. There were more northern regiments—Pegahmagabow belonged to the Algonquin Regiment, which is a real regiment in Georgian Bay—but I wanted them to travel further. I wanted them to get to the white world, so to speak, to Toronto, so I could really contrast where they come from and where they're heading to.

HW Your research for the novel involved travelling to Europe to visit the sites of quite a few of the battles described in the novel. What was that like and how did it help you to write those scenes?

JB Just amazing. I urge anyone who hasn't been over to go see. It's just awe-inspiring and very sad. I actually wrote much of the novel before I went overseas; I couldn't afford to go overseas until I did. So when I did finally get over there, I was really happy to see that what I noted and what I had imagined and what I had read was very true to the geographics of the place. It's the most beautiful country. It reminds me in many ways of southern Ontario, the farm fields and the forests and the rivers, and so it was almost difficult at first to picture this as being just one mass of mud and trenches. But then it became easier when I got out into the landscape. One of my favorite journeys was renting a bicycle in Ypres. You get a little map from the museum there—which is called In Flanders Fields Museum and which is just amazing—and there's a forty-kilometre bike tour which goes all around the Ypres Salient. You can take your time and stop at different places of importance to the Canadian army and the British army and the German army.

HW I guess that would be a fairly circumscribed area in which all these intense battles took place.

JB Yes, it's not a big area in which so many died. It's unbelievable how small it is. I brought my son there last year, and we actually found a live eighteen-pounder shell near Vimy Ridge, and we found bullets and everything else. It's really a fascinating place. All you have to do is scratch a little bit below the surface and you begin finding relics. Every year still, thousands of tons of ammunition and unexploded shells are pushed up by the earth, as if the earth is trying to rid itself of this poison.

HW *Three Day Road* is inspired by the experiences of a number of Aboriginal veterans in the Great War, and particularly the story of Francis Pegahmagabow, whom you mentioned earlier.

FIGURE 21. Francis Pegahmagabow. Courtesy of the William Hammond Mathers Museum, Indiana University.

JB I'm friends with his relatives, who are amazing people; I was actually at their family reunion in June. I'd known a number of them for many years, and so I was familiar with this incredible story, about this Ojibway sniper sneaking around in the trenches, running up the highest kills of any soldier who was a sniper, in any war, not just World War I. He had a reported 378 enemy kills, which is kind of a horrifying number if you think about it. He was very good at what he did—not that I think that he enjoyed it much, but he certainly was good at it, became recognized for it, became the most highly decorated Native person in World War I, actually.

HW Or perhaps in any conflict.

JB I think so, though I'm not sure about World War II. Tommy Prince and a few others were pretty highly decorated as well, but, yes, it's pretty astounding what Francis Pegahmagabow did. I wonder, though, if he had been a white soldier and had done so much, whether at least a Distinguished Service Order or a Victoria Cross might have been called for. I wonder sometimes if there was a kind of racism that factored into why he wasn't decorated even more highly. You know, the Military Medal is nothing to cough at—

HW But there were a lot of them handed out.

JB There were a lot of them handed out, yes.

HW I get the sense that officers tended to be quite suspicious of the kinds of numbers that snipers ran up while out on their own.

JB And Peggy didn't work with a spotter.

HW So I wonder if that suspicion might not have been intensified in his case because of racist assumptions.

JB I know for a fact that there were a couple of jealous officers who questioned his numbers, but when I think about it, he had no reason to lie. He was a very honest man. There is a very sad story, about when he came back to his reserve at Wasauksing, which is also known as Parry Island, after the war. He decided he wanted to try his hand at raising some horses, so he asked his Indian agent for a loan of three hundred dollars to buy some, and the agent looked at him and said, "No way can I give you that loan. How can I trust you with live animals?" And unfortunately, this was happening to more than just Pegahmagabow. This happened to a lot of Native soldiers coming home.

See, the problem with World War I is that records were not kept very well, especially when it came to Native enlistment and the role of Natives in the war. For example, Pegahmagabow won the Military Medal and two bars, but historians don't even know how he won the second bar to his Military Medal. Paperwork was a bit shoddy at times, so even if historians want to shine more light on this, it's very difficult to do so because there's very little evidence left any more.

HW In *Three Day Road* Peggy is a character, or at least he's there on the periphery of the story. Were you tempted to write more directly about him?

JB I never really was, because his record is there and stands, for those few Canadians who do know about him, and I didn't want to limit myself by basically writing a biographical novel. You know, there's no way Pegahmagabow was a morphine addict or went *windigo* or anything like that at all, but there were themes that I wanted to explore that I knew would just be reined in too tightly if I involved Pegahmagabow more in the novel. I did enjoy having him be a character on the periphery of the story, the one sniper that Elijah needs to try to live up to and to try to beat, in this one-sided competition that Elijah enters into with him. I felt that was fun. But I was a little nervous actually introducing the character of Peggy fictionally into the novel. There's one scene in which he meets Xavier and Elijah in an *estaminet*, a café, behind the lines.

HW I'm curious about that scene, because there is this very palpable ambiguity about it. They meet this Anishnabe man who they think is Peggy, and Elijah assumes he's Peggy, but something the man says—"You must mistake me for someone else"—suggests that he might not be who Elijah thinks he is. So there is a little uncertainty ultimately about his identity at the end of the scene. Was that a deliberate effect?

JB It was definitely deliberate. I was really kind of hoping to play with the idea of identity among Native men who were suddenly surrounded by a culture not their own in a war that is just a mad war. This whole issue of identity plays throughout the novel, for instance with Xavier assuming Elijah's identity at the end, even though it's not his fault. It's something that I'm exploring in this novel that I'm working on now, this whole idea of identity and how easy or how difficult it is to break that identity or to lose your identity. So, yes, I definitely wanted Peggy to serve as a motif in some ways, or as a theme— that issue of who we are and why we are here.

HW One of the things that Anishnabe corporal warns Elijah about in that scene is that once he returns to Canada he's going to be forgotten, he's going to be a nobody, and this is a gesture to, as you mentioned earlier, what was an important part of the experience of the war for Aboriginal veterans: their very disillusioning return to a society that showed very little appreciation for their sacrifice and that continued to discriminate against them and to treat them poorly. Basically they were back to being Indians, when they had hoped to make a different impression.

JB The best experiences of their lives happened during the war, because they were treated as equals by their peers and even by their officers. Their officers treated them as equals, and this was the first experience for a lot of Native men with whites who actually treated them fairly and with respect. I think the trenches were a great equalizer; you could die at any second and there was no special treatment when it came to shells and machine guns. I've read that a lot of Native men thought that it was wonderful and that they were actually going to head back to something good after this. "How could somebody deny me my rights now when I have put my life on the line for my country?" But they did, and unfortunately the same thing happened again in World War II. Native people didn't get the vote until the late 1960s in Canada, and that's another fact Canadians don't know or are willing to recognize.

HW You raise the issue of what it's going to be like for them to return home, just very briefly, in that scene, but the actual narrative of *Three Day Road* doesn't really get into that territory.

JB I felt it was an area best explored on its own in another work. In the bigger picture, what I hope to do is have a triptych, not so much a trilogy but a triptych of novels, dealing with these families, the first one being *Three Day Road.* The second one is the one I'm working on now, which is very contemporary, though with grandchildren of characters in the first novel. For the third one I want to return to where the first one leaves off and look at the life of Xavier and Niska upon his return to the Canadian north.

HW In some ways, just as important to the war narrative of *Three Day Road* are those segments that deal with Niska, Xavier's aunt, who takes him away from the residential school and raises him herself in the bush. Through her character, with her whole family, you're dealing with that momentous transition from life in the bush to life on the reserve. What kinds of dynamics were you trying to capture there?

JB I can't purposely set out to write on some big theme—I just try to let things happen organically—but again this was definitely the time when there was a huge transition in the Native community, their being forced onto reserves and having their children taken away. You know, I also didn't want to romanticize what life was like before the white man. It was never an easy life for the Cree of northern Ontario and Quebec. It was often a brutal existence, and hence the *windigo,* but I definitely believe that a huge amount of injustice went on for a number of years, and factually it's pretty easy to back up with the residential school system. So I wanted Niska to be the last holdout in a way—not that she literally is, because there are Native people I know up north who still don't have much at all to do with white society—but I wanted her to be representative of that very strong will not to have to capitulate. And I like the idea of her being a woman doing it, because the female is so incredibly important to Ojibway and Cree culture. So I wanted her to be a strong woman who was doing this on her own, despite what everyone says about her and despite the toughness of her existence there. She's not going to give it up.

HW There is the shift in dependency too, the transition from the Hudson's Bay Company being dependent on the Cree to essentially setting the conditions so that the opposite comes about.

JB And it was not fictionalized at all, this idea that if you did not bring your children to the residential school, the Hudson's Bay Company would have nothing to do with you any more, etc. The word "insidious" comes up a lot when I think of this kind of three-handed relationship that the Hudson's Bay Company had with the government and the Church. But yes, it's a very fascinating part of our history that is just so rich, and again I don't know how much many of us know about it. I feel very under-read when it comes to it, just because there's such a vast history. However, you know, I've met old women who were in residential school who told me, "Best years of my life. I really enjoyed it." But for the majority of people I've talked to it was the opposite; it was a horrendous experience for them.

HW There is a substantial book called *Shingwauk's Vision* about the history of the residential schools, and there's a very interesting passage in which the author, J.R. Miller, tries to modify that picture of the residential schools having been just a monolithic, unremitting nightmare and points out how those who try to qualify that impression and say exactly that—"You know, actually for me, the experience in residential school was quite positive"—are almost censored, or at least not given any airtime by the media.

JB I think part of that is that it's probably a minority who felt that way. It's very hard to say, though. That's the one thing when you're dealing with the Native community; everyone is so individualistic in that community, as I see with the Cree and the Ojibway, that to get one consensus from all the people is a very difficult thing. They're all strong-willed and very individual thinkers; that's what I see over and over again.

HW Another thing is that, given how bleak and insidious (to use your word) most of that history was, one can see how it would be a hard thing to say, "Well, you know, the residential schools weren't all that bad." Obviously, though, for you in the novel it was important to have the residential school there, as something that specifically shapes Elijah and Elijah's behaviour. Can you comment on the role of the residential school in the novel?

JB I didn't want the residential school to be a huge black cloud over this novel. I wanted to present it in the way it was, as an insidious kind of institution. Xavier ends up getting through the war—not unscathed, by any means, in fact really damaged—but still manages to get through because he has a grounding in who he is and where he comes from, whereas Elijah is raised in the residential school and that in part feeds into what ends up happening to him and what he ends up doing and, ultimately, into his fate. He isn't grounded in his place or culture, and this ends up being very damaging to him. Again, I didn't want to beat people over the head with a big stick, saying, "The residential school is bad and look what we've done." I wanted it to play out in a natural and organic way. Hopefully that's what I did. You know, the school touches everyone. It touches Niska, it affects Xavier, but I think it affects Elijah the most, because he spends the most time in it. It's hard to put a positive spin on the residential schools after talking to people up in Fort Albany and Moosonee and Kashechewan who went to St. Anne's and were just victimized by the place.

HW Moose Factory is quite a prominent focus of your writing. Many of the stories in your collection *Born With a Tooth* are set there, as is a good part of the narrative in *Three Day Road*. You taught, or I think you still teach, in that area.

JB I did teach there and lived a couple of years up that way and I maintain very close friendships there, in those communities. I still get up a number of times a year.

HW Did that experience prompt an interest in the history of the community too?

JB No question. Moose Factory and Fort Albany are the oldest settled communities in Ontario and were really a huge focus for the Hudson's Bay Company fur trade. The word "factory" means a trading place, a place where you come together, and so the British used the term "factory." In many ways, Canada's birth took place right in that area. It's a very isolated area, but it was also in so many ways a kind of political and financial birthplace of what we now know as Canada. So, yes, the place draws me back. It's very remote, it's very beautiful, in a very austere way. The winters are long and very difficult, but the summers are short and beautiful. The people are just amazing. I love the people there.

HW I want to talk a little bit about the cultural context of fighting and warfare in the novel, because there is (again, quite implicit and not beating the reader over the head) a contrast in world views in that regard.

JB Xavier ends up hating what he does, being a soldier and having to hunt other men, basically, whereas Elijah learns to love it. I was worried at times that it was almost too simplistic to set up that kind of dichotomy, but at the same time there's a certain natural power in that kind of conflict. Fiction doesn't always need conflict, but often conflict is a big part of good fiction, and it makes it readable, and that was just a natural thing for me to want to explore.

HW What does it mean to be a warrior in the world that, say, Xavier comes from, and what does it mean to be a soldier on the front in World War I?

JB Xavier goes grudgingly to the war. He's going for the reason a lot of other young men went, because their friends were doing it and they thought, "Maybe I should go too." You see, the Cree aren't known, especially in Ontario, as a warrior society, not, say, like the Iroquois or even the Ojibway, who had to protect themselves from the Iroquois and the Sioux all the time. The Cree had their moments, there's no question. The Iroquois raiding party would come all the way up to James Bay to kick butt, and the Cree battled them at this branch of two rivers and wiped them out. They left one man alive, one Iroquois warrior, and cut the ears off all the rest of the dead Iroquois and put them in a basket and sent that warrior back home, telling him, "Tell your people 'Don't ever come up this way again.'" I think conflict with Native people involves a defence of their land or their area, and so it's an interesting conundrum when you're going to fight as a Native person in a completely different country for reasons that you wouldn't typically fight for.

HW Do you think that there is a different sense of what honour involves and a different motivation for killing?

JB That was a tough one too, because again you can't speak of Native people as one large group. Every band is different, and with every band there are clans that have far different opinions of the world, and so I didn't want to generalize. I think the idea of hunting, though, and all your life not being wigged out by the idea of blood and of skinning and of what it takes to survive, is so a part of them that, for Elijah, translating the hunting of animals to the hunting of humans is not that big of a step; it was kill or be killed, and I think for a lot of soldiers of any race in any of the wars it's the same kind of thing. You have to go to your most basic and brutal instincts and put away all of your civilized thinking about the world. And that's again why World War I was so fascinating. Some of the great philosophical thinkers and poets of the twentieth century were involved in that conflict, some of the most well-educated people as well as the least-educated, and they were all reduced to the same kind of animalistic behaviour while in the trenches. The ability just to be able to pull back from that to go for a few days' break behind the lines and become men again is just startling to me. I think so much psychological damage came out of World War I that we don't know about. The term "shell-shocked" came out of World War I, and I've seen old black-and-white footage of soldiers suffering from it, and it's just horrendous. I wonder how the generation that made it back ever healed from this kind of brutality. Obviously these are huge themes and huge chunks of history that I'm trying to tackle, so I had to do it in as individualistic a way as I could, and that was through the eyes of two best friends who basically go in opposite directions.

HW What prompted that question partly was that there was a sense in the novel that Elijah's obsession with his reputation is in some ways a loss of equilibrium or perspective or perhaps even honour.

JB There is no question that Elijah is a competitive sort. He's very gifted with the English language, and he has a way of putting people at ease around him. You know, his last name is Whiskeyjack, which is Weesageechak, which is the trickster in Cree. There's a little story about how the name Whiskeyjack came about. The Hudson's Bay men, when they first came to Cree country in Ontario, set up camp with the Cree, and as soon as they did these big grey jays would fly in, and if they didn't watch their food they'd jump down and steal it, or they'd steal shiny objects. The Hudson's Bay men asked the Cree, "What's this bird? What do you call this bird?" and they said "Weesageechak. It's Weesageechak, he's a trickster. He's gonna play a joke on you." And the English couldn't pronounce that, so they called him whiskeyjack, and that's where that name actually comes from. Elijah is very much the trickster in this novel in many ways. He loves to play games, he loves to tease.

HW There is that scene where he feeds Xavier some horse meat and tells him it's the flesh of a German.

JB Exactly, and I was hoping that the reader, just like Xavier, would never really figure out whether it was human or not, whether Elijah's joking or not. Elijah likes to play tricks. When they're training in Toronto, and he teaches Xavier the English words to ask Lieutenant Breech if he can get his own sleeping quarters, he knows it's going to get him in trouble but he does it anyway, just because he likes to play the joke on him, try to teach him a little something too, to let Xavier know that he's no different than the others now and has to get by just like the others do. So definitely there's that light side of Elijah, that love of life and that love of communicating with people, but there is also that very dark part of him that comes out and ends up overwhelming him.

HW That dark side in a way is this voracious appetite for kills and, in that sense, literally human flesh. That obviously brings us to what I think is the central motif of the novel, unifying the various layers of the whole narrative, and that's the motif of the *windigo*. How do you see its place in the story and particularly in terms of the war itself?

JB The *windigo* is definitely a big, big motif in this book that pulls together the different generations. Originally, the *windigo* story was told around the campfire. The elders would tell the children about it, sort of as a lesson, as a way of teaching, just as a fable or anything else is. You know, "Be careful, don't become greedy, don't do the wrong thing or the *windigos* are going to come and get you," these thirty-foot-high beasts with claws for feet and hands. It was a bit of a scare tactic, but it was also used as a light story at times as well. I was far more fascinated by the psychological idea of the *windigo* than the legend. I read a brilliant non-fiction book called *Killing the Shaman* years ago, a real-life story of a western Ontario Ojibway clan, and it really stuck with me. Basically it was about a man who was a *hookimaw,* the head of his band, and when they were out in the bush hunting, one of them went mad and then decided to eat human flesh, which is obviously a huge no-no. So the shaman had to deal with him, and the way he dealt with him was by excising him, by literally killing him. And the North-West Mounted Police got word of this—the story of Niska's father is probably one of the things based on what really happened—and the shaman was taken away by the police and died in custody. I realized that this whole psychological exploration of the *windigo* made perfect sense for the World War I subject matter—when you're asked to do horrendous things, how far can you go in doing these things before you break? When are you made a hero for doing what you do, and when does it become a crime? There's a very thin line there, just as I think there's a very thin line with many of us in terms of whether what we do is good for us, or whether we're overdoing it and it's bad for us.

HW It also speaks to the theme of individual selfishness as opposed to communal well-being.

JB I think that's a big part of it. If you're out in the bush, and you have to depend on your skills to survive with a group of people, everyone has to pull their weight, and— this doesn't happen very often, but every once in a while if somebody cracks or goes crazy, everything breaks down. The hunters can't go out hunting for fear that their family will be harmed by this person. The children become scared, and things start to break down. It's a very tight society one has to keep when living this hunting–gathering existence in a brutal climate. So I liked playing with the historical aspect of that, with Niska and her father having to deal with the odd character who goes mad or goes too far. But then when you apply it to the war as well, where is that line between being a hero and being a criminal?

HW That's a recurrent theme in fiction of the Great War.

JB I think so, because that's one of the things that people would have to face all the time, and that's a brutal thing to be forced to face.

HW To be ordered to do essentially insane things—

JB And by men who are miles behind the lines, who have no understanding of the reality of the situation.

HW With the *windigo* there is also the theme of excess that travels very well into the theatre of the war, because the *windigo* is a creature of excess. It's a condition that comes about through a kind of excess, through being greedy, through not honouring or recognizing a sense of balance and moderation.

JB Yes, and I think that's a cross-cultural concern, one that we all have. Ultimately, as humans, the best way we get along is by respecting the earth—it's a very simple thing to say and a cliché thing to say almost—but by respecting other people and not taking too much. The whole Ojibway and Cree view of the natural world is completely opposite to the Western view of the natural world, this idea in the West that we control nature, and we are the masters of our physical universe, and animals are lower than us, and it doesn't matter if we drill for oil everywhere, because we are in control of that environment. But the Ojibway and the Cree believe quite the opposite, which is that we're at the bottom of the totem pole, so to speak. A rock doesn't need us to survive, a moose certainly doesn't need humans to survive, trees don't need humans to survive. Nothing in nature needs humans to survive. But humans need everything in nature in order to survive, and that's why we are lower than most things rather than the ones who control them. You can't control the environment and that's been proven over and over again; look at Hurricane Katrina hitting New Orleans. It's not a possible thing. Some of these conflicting world views are very central to the novel as well.

HW I want to pick up on another motif, and that's the use of morphine in the novel. Quite a bit of the narrative is taken up with how first Elijah and subsequently Xavier become addicted to morphine as a way of coping, not just with the pain but more generally with the trauma of battle. Even though some of the other soldiers—Grey Eyes, for instance—rely on morphine as well, it's hard not to see this as a kind of indirect commentary on the impact of alcohol on Native communities. Is that suggestion there?

JB It would be fair to say that that's there. I had to walk very carefully there, because of the whole stereotype of the drunken Indian, of the addicted Indian, of the weak Indian. There's a lot of unfair cultural weight there. One thing I realized in my reading and research was that every soldier in the British and Canadian army carried a little tin metal case in their packs, and inside were syringes of morphine so that, in case they were wounded in No Man's Land or couldn't get back, they could medicate themselves. So it was a very common thing, the use of morphine, especially for wounds. With the government not really knowing, until too late, that the rate of addiction to it was really scary, there is unfortunately not much written that I have found. Again, I don't think statistics were always so well kept in the First World War. But, yes, I knew I was walking some very dangerous ground by having two of my three protagonists at different points being addicted to a substance. Whereas Elijah gets involved in it voluntarily, Xavier went through what probably hundreds of thousands of soldiers who were wounded went through, and that was the morphine withdrawal, becoming addicted to it for a while and then not being able to get it any more and having to deal with that. So with one character that addiction is voluntary, whereas with the other it is more of a medical thing.

HW The handling of time in the novel is an important feature of its form, its narrative shape, as the narrative moves back and forth between Xavier's return, his experiences in the war, and his life in the bush before the war. The movement between those different temporal levels is very fluid, and the distinction between them is often blurred. What does that strategy say about how you view history?

JB There are different views of history, of course. There is the classic line that if we don't remember our history we're doomed to repeat it, but even more so I think that history is a fluid thing. Especially with Native people, the past is always a part of the present as well as the future. What you do now is going to affect your future, but what you've done in the past is also going to affect your future. That's part of the reason I had Xavier be addicted to morphine, because it's easier for him to blur these lines in a very natural way, because his world is blurry when he's telling the story, remembering his past.

HW He's hallucinogenically both in the past and in the present.

JB Right, and that fed into the way I told the story. I originally wrote the story chronologically, with two young men paddling off through the bush, going through a forest fire, eventually joining the army, going overseas and becoming snipers. Then interspersed with the chapters of these two young men was this old woman's voice—the reader didn't have any idea who she was—telling the story of her life, until about two-thirds of the way through the novel you suddenly realize, "My gosh, this old woman is the aunt of Xavier, and that's why she's here." So I finished a first draft of it and showed it to my French publisher, Francis Giffard, who I trust very much as an editor, as well as my wife, Amanda, and they said, "You're definitely writing about something that hasn't been written about before, but there's something missing with this narrative, and I'm not sure what it is." I didn't know either, until I realized that I was applying a Western storytelling tradition to what is ostensibly a Native story. Once I realized that, the light bulb went on: I needed to tell the story in a circular way. I needed to tell it in a more Native style, in my own style, anyway, which is a more circular kind of telling.

HW As opposed to a more teleological and linear style.

JB Exactly. The linear style would work fine for it, I guess, but it became far better, I believe, when I actually looked back and told it the way I did.

HW I'm also thinking about Niska's visions, in which she essentially is in the future, sees the future. She has recurrent premonitions about the war that the boys are going to go into, and this in a way disrupts and defies that rigorous, chronological unfolding of time.

JB Exactly. I'm fascinated by magical realism, in small doses, and I wanted to apply my own kind of magical realism to this text, but not in a big way. I wanted it to be a small but underlying part of the novel, which is Niska's epileptic fits, though I left it so that these fits are never labelled that. She wouldn't know what that is. But they definitely are a doorway for her to see into the future a little bit, which is part of where her power comes from as a medicine woman, as a healer. What's kind of fun is that in the novel I'm writing now, a great-niece of Niska suffers from epilepsy, but it's labelled epilepsy, because she's living in the modern world. She's living in the contemporary world, but she suffers the same kind of fits that Niska once did.

HW Is she similarly visionary?

JB She sees visions, but they're much more cloudy. The power has been watered down over the generations, so she's not so clear and not so sure of herself as Niska is. She's also quite a bit younger than Niska too. But it's that whole idea of vision and of understanding—again going back to history being fluid—

that the past exists right here beside us just as much as the future is going to be dictated by what we do right now and what we've done in the past. It's the kind of theme that fascinates me, and I think that is partly due to my growing up with a father who was born in 1898 and who was in World War II and an uncle who was in World War I. This history lived around me and still does. Even though they're gone now it's still a very huge part of who I am.

HW [*picking jaw up off floor*] That's really kind of remarkable. I'm older than you by a few years, and my father was what I thought was comparatively old, nearly forty, when I was born, and he was born in 1923, and your father was born a whole quarter-century earlier.

JB Yes, and I'm not an old guy. I'm thirty-nine, now, and have two younger brothers in their mid-thirties. So it's interesting. My father crossed over a couple of generations, and that's really integral to who I am; you can't really escape that—not that I would want to. Certainly this idea of one generation stretching right back into two centuries ago is something that's been quietly amazing to me.

HW There is a strong emphasis, conveyed particularly through the character of Niska, on the relationship between storytelling and healing. Now, I know again this can verge into the cliché, but still, it's quite prominent in the novel as a motif. Do you look at the whole of the novel in this light? In other words, is *Three Day Road* part of a larger process of healing?

JB For sure. I hope in some small way it is. I've heard from so many Native people and white people who have come up after a reading, for example, and said, "I had an uncle in World War II and I've still got his medals" or "I had a grandfather in World War I and he was a sniper as well." People always come and tell me these little stories afterwards and I just love it. It makes me really happy, because I think such a part of understanding who we are, especially who I am as an individual, is knowing where you come from, and other people approach me and I see that they believe the same thing. So, yes, that's huge. I did walk a line; parts of the novel could have appeared to others as very cliché—you know, the storytelling old woman and the silent Indian who has this best friend who is a talkative Indian, and all of this. So I had to handle it very carefully, in a non-clichéd way, and I hope that I did, because it comes from these characters. I let them go. You know, the best advice I was ever given in regards to writing was from my first publisher, Marc Côté. He said, "Don't try to control your characters. Let them go. Let them wander a bit once you know who they are. Don't try to tell them that they have to go from point A to point B to point C. Let them go and see where they go." And I did, and I think some good stuff came out of it for my own writing. Going back to the original question, though, yes, this whole story is kind of like a Matryoshka doll—you know, those Russian dolls that you open up and then there's another inside and then there's another. But the stories in *Three Day Road* are kind of the inverse of Matryoshka dolls; you open up a small one and there's a bigger one in it and then another bigger one and then another bigger one, and really this is just a novel of two people telling stories. It's all it simply is, Niska realizing she has no medicine to give Xavier, who is very close to death, other than feeding him the stories of her life. She remembers her father told her that when in danger, when in trouble, when sick, remember who you are, remember where you come from. There is real strength in that. There's no question this is a war novel, but just as importantly this is a novel about the healing power and love of family and how that can save you, as simpleton as that sounds. It's something that is just as important as the war aspect of it. And I think that's probably why so many women have responded really strongly to it too, because Niska's a strong female character and she stands up for herself. A lot of women have come to me and said, "You know, this is not subject matter I'd ever think of picking up and reading about, but when I did, I got something out of it," and that makes me very happy.

HW Practically all the historical novels that deal with Aboriginal history in Canada are written by non-Natives. I'm thinking about historical novels in the sense of narratives that are working, even peripherally, with actual historical figures and actual historical events, incorporating characters and episodes that are part of the larger historical record in a fictional context. Do you think that we are going to start to see more of such novels being published by Aboriginal writers in the future?

JB Definitely. I think that's already happening. You know, I'm what I call a "Heinz 57." I'm a classic Canadian in that part of my background is Irish, on one side, and the other side is Métis, so I'm a real mix of a lot of different cultures in Canada. What I'm finding now is how rich Native writing is in Canada. I was in Saskatoon last fall for the Anskohk Aboriginal Literature Festival. McNally Robinson put out the first annual award for best Native book, and the authors that I was surrounded by were just amazing. Thomas King is great, Lee Maracle is great, and they're the big ones, but there are so many younger ones coming up and wanting to write and finding their voices. So, yes, I see more Aboriginal people claiming their history, and not being so—I don't know if afraid to do it is the right word—but being willing to share it with others. I see that happening with a lot of young writers.

HW Most of that writing, though, has been preoccupied with contemporary issues.

JB Rather than looking more at historical subjects, as you said.

HW Yes. Think about the kinds of novels that could be written about the residential school experience, or the signing of the treaties, just for starters.

JB I hope there will be; I really hope so. Unfortunately there was a real break for many generations due directly to the residential school system, which makes a lot of people not sure of their own history any more and which is really sad. But I'm hoping, and believing, that those who are coming of age now, who are in their forties and fifties, who are the last survivors of residential school, are going to be able to write about it. And I've seen it already. There's a man named Ed Matatawabin, who's a very good friend, a former chief of Fort Albany. He wrote a novel called *Hanaway*, and it's just brilliant. Here's a great example of a Native man, a victim of the residential school, who turned around and became chief of his reserve and has a beautiful family and has done very well for himself. He is actually speaking historically of his people and of residential school and of the *windigo* as well. So I do see it with some, the ones who are I guess strong enough in some ways, or have the confidence enough, because I think one of the most damaging things the residential school did to so many young people was completely break their confidence.

HW So it's almost a kind of Catch-22—that it's important to recover that history but on the other hand exceedingly difficult, if not impossible, to do so because that chain of oral memory and oral history, in that sense, has been broken or damaged.

JB It has been. The great thing about Ed Matatawabin is that he's never been afraid to say, "I don't give a damn if you don't like what I'm doing. I'm going to do it. I'm going to do it because I know it's healthy and it's the best thing to do." So he wrote *Hanaway* and he did it all by himself and found a little publisher named Trafford, and put out this book, which is just an amazing book. I hope to see much more of that. Thomas King just recently wrote *A Short History of Indians in Canada*—there's the word "history" right there in the title—and the stories are hilarious, but at the same time King is such the trickster himself. He has a real sense of humour while uncovering some very sad things.

HW In many ways he is playing with history but—and maybe I have too narrow a concept of the historical novel—in a way that's generically far from the traditional historical novel and even from something like *Three Day Road,* which is much closer to that form.

JB Yes. I think it takes a certain kind of writer to want to write a historical novel and to do it in a decent fashion. So I think we're talking about a relatively small pool when it comes to our community that both want to, and are able to, and feel they have something to say. As I was saying, I have seen a lot of stories coming out that often do touch on history, and they do touch on legends, or they do touch on family lore. I think we're seeing a real mix of the historical with the contemporary.

HW You said that it takes a certain kind of writer to write a historical novel. What kind of writer does it take to write a historical novel?

JB Somebody who's really in touch with and in love with the past. For example, I think I was able to write this novel because I had a father who was so much older, and as a result I feel really in touch with decades where I wasn't even alive. I think that it takes somebody who is willing to sit down and really grind out some research and then ingest it and then kind of spit it back out properly, or in such a way that it doesn't become overbearing. Someone who's almost living in the past in their own head as much as they do in the contemporary world or maybe really hates the contemporary world at times [*laughs*], not necessarily wanting to go back to a better time, but to a time through which we can try to understand how we ended up here.

In the Lair of the Minotaur
Heather Robertson

Heather Robertson grew up in Winnipeg and after attending Columbia University in the 1960s returned to Canada to pursue a career as a freelance writer, writing for magazines such as *Maclean's, Chatelaine*, and *Saturday Night*, among others. She has written a number of books of non-fiction, including *Reservations Are for Indians* (1970), *Grass Roots* (1973), *A Terrible Beauty: The Art of Canada at War* (1977), *More Than a Rose: Prime Ministers, Wives and Other Women* (1991), *Driving Force: The McLaughlin Family and the Age of the Car* (1995), and her latest book, *Magical, Mysterious Lake of the Woods* (2003). During the 1980s, Robertson published *The King Years*, a trilogy of novels revolving around William Lyon Mackenzie King. *Willie: A Romance* (1983) examines King's years in political exile during World War I, *Lily: A Rhapsody in Red* (1986) looks at King in and out of power between the wars, and *Igor: A Novel of Intrigue* (1989) centres on the atomic spy scandal initiated by the 1945 defection of cipher clerk Igor Gouzenko from the Soviet Embassy. I talked to Heather Robertson at her home in King City, Ontario, in November of 2001.

HW Here you are, you've written this trilogy of novels about Mackenzie King, and I want to try to track you down to interview you, and where do I find you but in King City. Coincidence? I don't think so. How did that come about?

HR No, it is coincidence, total coincidence. It's not named for Mackenzie King at all.

HW You have done a lot of writing about Canadian history in both fiction and non-fiction. I wonder if you could talk a little bit about how that interest came about.

HR Well, I guess it goes back to my childhood. My father was a history teacher when I was growing up in Winnipeg, and when I was about ten, my father decided that he was going to document historic sites in the Red River Valley. As an only child, I tagged along with him. We went down the Red River to St. Andrew's Church, which was the early Anglican church there, where a lot of the early Hudson's Bay, Selkirk settler people were buried. It struck me very strongly, walking around that churchyard through the grass and looking, reading the grave stones and all the little stories that those gravestones told: you know, women dying at the age of twenty-one or twenty-two, and they'd be buried with a child, a lot of children dying, people drowning, being killed in accidents. Those early gravestones told a story about these people, so I was able to get a sense that they were real people. These were real people!

HW So it was a kind of epiphany?

HR A total epiphany at the age of about ten, that these were real people and that they lived and died here, and I was standing here in this very place where they had gone to church and where they had lived, and it just completely sprang alive to me. That distance was lost. All of a sudden history was very, very real to me. Also, growing up in a community like Winnipeg, I had a very strong historical consciousness: the Red River settlers, lots of legends, Riel and the Riel Rebellion, and the fur trade, and the Hudson's Bay Company. It's a very historically rich small place.

HW That sense of history has really been sustained in your work as a journalist and as a freelance writer. You have written a number of non-fiction books on historical subjects, delving into Canadian history with books like *A Terrible Beauty* and your book on prime ministers' wives, so it's obviously very important to you to raise your readers' consciousness about Canadian history.

HR Well, it is really a question of raising my own consciousness, I think, of trying to understand the society, the country in which I lived. I think at that time—and I think it's still very true—history was confused with mythology. It was the Quiet Revolution in Quebec in the 1960s that was a huge shock to us all. I want to go back a little farther than that, actually; it was 1963. This was my second epiphany. I was doing my master's in English literature at Columbia that year, and that was when John F. Kennedy was shot. It was like Sept. 11, the emotional outburst, and New York City came to a complete halt, and there was nothing for days and days except for tolling bells and the funeral, and then Lee Harvey Oswald was shot on television, which I saw. I felt really Canadian; I felt that this was not my president. John Diefenbaker was prime minister of Canada, and it was hard to imagine a politician more different from JFK. As a western Canadian, I was sympathetic to Dief. I was also anti-nuclear weapons, anti-war and, like most young Canadians, passionate about the civil rights movement. I was an outsider, a colonial in an imperialist culture. I felt really alienated, and I thought to myself, "I am not an American. I never will be an American. I am a Canadian, but I don't know who I am." This was happening to people like Margaret Atwood and a whole generation of Canadians who were studying in the United States on scholarships—the whole assumption in the 1950s and early 60s was that we were little Americans in waiting. I thought, if I stayed in the United States, I would have to learn a whole different culture, a culture that was really, really foreign to me. So, when I came back in '64, I was very curious about what Canada really was. All of those assumptions that I and my culture—my middle-class, western Canadian, English-speaking culture—had taken for granted were gone, just gone. I wanted to figure things out because I didn't understand.

HW I am a Canadian and I don't know who I am. I think that should be the national slogan.

HR Well, it was very true at that time, because you had that whole nationalist movement emerging. It was a very radicalizing time, and at that time I wasn't particularly interested in writing fiction, because I was very impatient with writers who didn't engage in some sort of dialogue. Then, when I was writing a lot for *Saturday Night*, I remember interviewing Donald Creighton—and what a character he was—and reading a lot of Creighton and coming across his wonderful phrase about the "Authorized Version" of Canadian history being the Liberal view. That made a big impression on me because, even though Creighton himself was a mythologizer in his own way, he also got through to me the fact that there was more than one version, that there were many interpretations of how we saw ourselves, and how we told our story. And of course Creighton's a very good storyteller. So he got across that idea that you could make history into a story, which of course is what it is.

HW That is of course what you do in the *King Years* trilogy. How did you first become interested in King, and what made you decide to turn to fiction?

HR I got interested in King I think when I moved to Ontario. I spent a lot of time doing stories in Ottawa and got very interested in Ottawa, because it was an attractive little place. It struck me that the only way that I could understand Canada in the twentieth century was to understand Mackenzie King, because he was such a totally dominant figure. Mackenzie King had always been a kind of toad-like figure in our household. He was a troll in western Canada; he was just loathed, hated. He was seen as a troll-like, evil figure, especially in a very CCF household like ours. So, I thought "Well, you've got this person who holds somehow the key to Canada's ambiguity and perhaps our failure." Then C.P. Stacey's book was published, *A Very Double Life*, and it was just brilliant. Here was this exposé of King not only being a spiritualist but having a sex life with prostitutes and God knows who, right? So, it was this huge revelation. And of course Stacey was just excoriated by the historical community.

HW For hanging out the dirty laundry, so to speak?

HR How could he dare do this? How could he dare use a prime minister's private papers, diaries, to write this serious work of history? So, it was Stacey who just smashed that barrier down. He said, "Look, these diaries are here!" There had been a huge conspiracy at some point to destroy them, burn them— but that's another whole story. So there was this huge revelation that this prime minister had a very double life and was a much more interesting guy than we might have assumed. So I read Stacey's book and then something occurred to me: here we have King writing about encountering all these women; what would one of these young women think of him? So the idea for *Willie* just came to me in an image, which was this dark night in Ottawa, by the canal, by the river, or wherever, with King walking along with his silver-handled cane—trip, trap, trip, trap, trip, trap, in his mincing way—and encountering a woman he took to be a prostitute, propositioning her, and then telling that whole story from her point of view, essentially a feminist view. So I thought—and this was very subconscious—to tell this story, this part of Canadian history, from a woman's point of view. So I just found myself with a motherlode of characters that nobody had written about, a whole bunch of really interesting stories, and then Lily just started to speak to me. It's partly my voice, but she's a composite of a lot of women that Willie King knew, because I read those bloody diaries. I did read them all, which took weeks, months, months, months!

HW That must have been a key moment in the writing of this trilogy, when those diaries became accessible, and when you first encountered them. Do you remember your reaction?

HR Amazing, they're amazing. It's a whole entry into this cave with this monster in it. I call him the minotaur. The mind that you enter in these diaries—it's King's own voice that is so extraordinary, because there are such private things, and they're so frank and so bizarre. He provided me with the form, which was the diary. So in *Willie* it's a sort of war of countervailing diaries. I felt, as a non-fiction writer, very comfortable with the diary form. Then I encountered Talbot Papineau. I had done a book, *Salt of the Earth,* of homesteading photographs. We decided we'd follow *Salt of the Earth* with a similar book about the wars and war artists, although it started out to be a book with photographs. While I was reading C.P. Stacey, and poking around with Willie King and Charlotte Whitton, I was also working on this project, and then I discovered Talbot Papineau's letters, and I cried and I cried and cried. I remember just sitting there in the reading room of the archives. There they were, these little pieces of blue paper, the little aeroforms, that he had written with his own hand, his accounts, you know, love letters mostly, to this pen-pal woman in the United States, Beatrice.

HW Beatrice Fox.

HR They were so moving and they were so revealing of his life at the front, and his sense of despair and cynicism, and his own sensitivity, and oh, I just cried and cried. And there were his letters to his mother. I felt so silly—tears were streaming … All of these people were looking around at me.

HW Those passages in *Willie* are extremely moving.

HR So by the time *A Terrible Beauty* was published in 1977, I had these characters, I had my triangle. I had Lily in the middle and I then had Willie, who was such a shit, you know, and sat out the war with the Rockefellers in the States, but Mr. Canada, right? Mr. Canada. Then I had Papineau, who was basically the martyr, who was mostly francophone, and who represented that whole alienated, failed culture too. So I basically could write a story, which was in a sense a story of Canada, but do it through people.

HW When did you hit on the idea of using Papineau as a foil for King? In so many ways in the novel they are opposites and rivals, political rivals and rivals for Lily's affections.

HR I saw Papineau, in a sense, as being the true nationalist, the true Canadian, who was basically sacrificed by the Brits historically (that's my view), and who made a moral decision that, rather than come home and flack for a war that he hated, he would stay on the front line and take his chances there— it's a sort of act of courage and self-sacrifice—and sacrificing his own political career, while King was clawing and grasping, scrabbling to promote himself and to get ahead. That was the basic structure. The resources that were there, the King diaries and the letters, just allowed the story to tell itself.

HW What about the decision to use that material as you found it, because a lot of the material in *Willie* is taken fairly directly from the Mackenzie King diaries and from Papineau's letters? Did you struggle with that?

HR Not really. What I did try to do, I think, was not to change the context or the intent of that material, so, in terms of Papineau's letters to Beatrice, I changed the identity to Lily, but she was almost an equivalent woman. I did the same thing with King writing about young women. His diary was concerned with his amours on the whole with women, like Lily, who were young and dangerous, and not approved by mother.

HW Whose approval was pretty important.

HR Conventionally, he was supposed to be attracted to the blondes, you know, the ones who looked like mother, right? But truly I think he was attracted to women of the night, the working class. Another book that was influential was the H.S. Ferns and Bernard Ostry book, *The Age of Mackenzie King*. It detailed his whole obsession with picking up working girls when he was in Toronto, when he was at university, and then working with the missions and the social agencies, studying their living conditions; but it was always the women he was interested in, you know, the factory girls. That makes a very interesting dichotomy, because you can bring in the whole issue of class. All this material just sort of lent itself. Then, of course, the main thing to remember about *Willie* is that it is a romance and also a comic novel. There is a whole element of comedy in it, based on fact. The Duke and Duchess of Connaught, for instance, are incredibly silly people. So you have these wonderful people like the Duke and Duchess offering themselves up as characters.

HW Almost as caricatures.

FIGURE 22. Talbot Mercer Papineau. Library and Archives Canada C13224.

HR I think, when you do look at Canadian history, a lot of it is comic, because you have these strange people, like the dukes and duchesses and the Prince of Wales, or whoever, who arrive from time to time, and the whole institution of the Governor General, and many others, and there's a lot of pomposity and a lot of foolishness. So, it was a way of having a look at that as well. Another big image that hit me, actually, what really gave me the idea … I remember being in Ottawa one day and seeing this horde of young women coming out of the Centre Block, a horde of them, all secretaries going home, and I thought, "This is a place full of secretaries, and these are the people who are making this country work, all these women in there." So that was what prompted me to make Lily a secretary, because it is a way of getting behind and around and inside.

HW What about going beyond the historical record? One interesting thing about *Willie* is that, on the one hand, so much of it is fairly tied to the historical record, in that you're using more or less direct excerpts or, in some cases, somewhat abridged excerpts, but in a lot of the rest of the novel you're, let's say, taking a pretty free hand with history. You are obviously feeling free to invent some instances. What about that decision?

HR Well, you have to be specific. I borrow a lot here and there. You'd have to cite me an actual historical event that I'd invented.

HW Well, I guess I am thinking of King's relationship with Lily, and especially some of his more aggressive advances, but I guess that would fall under the hypothetical nature of Lily to begin with.

HR A couple of psychiatrists have had a look at King's papers, and I think that King's sexuality, and his personality, and the psychiatric assessment of him as being a borderline psychopath justified that. I felt that this would not be out of character. He was extremely manipulative towards these young women that he courted, and suffered from huge ... well, he masturbated like crazy, eh? Stacey's kind of playing this down, but it's true! [*laughs*] In the diaries, you know, you don't have to be a rocket scientist to figure it out. And Stacey figured out what he meant by going for a stroll.

HW Or when he recorded money as "wasted."

HR Yeah, so masturbation was just a huge part of his life. It was a very huge part of his life. So that's how a lot of this gets incorporated. I wish, I deeply wish, that King's diaries had been properly annotated and published in their entirety, an annotated version. I think that's probably impossible now. That is one reason why I wrote it as a novel, because you can avoid those absences of scholarship. Rather than filling in the scholarly holes, you leap over them and create a fictional version ... that's why I was very careful about calling it a romance.

HW At the same time, I guess a lot of the hypothetical scenes are still extensions of what you see.

HR Of what I read, yes—that masturbation was very much a part of his sexuality. It's sad that his diaries have not been published, because as a human being he is so interesting. He left this record of himself and of the country. There are long, long transcripts of his meetings with all kinds of interesting people, incredibly interesting stuff.

HW And his labyrinthian personal reflections on those meetings, on political decisions, or his personal relationships. It is pretty fascinating stuff—he's a remarkable character.

HR I guess historians all got frightened off after Stacey and have not really gone back.

HW We talked a little bit about how the idea for using Talbot Papineau as a character came from *A Terrible Beauty*, your book on Canadian war art. In the introduction, you talked about the importance of paying tribute to Papineau and to the thousands of other Canadians who gave their lives during the war, and you hoped that "the meaning of their sacrifice rests with our collective national consciousness, our future is their monument." Now in some ways this is the kind of commemoration that underlies a lot of the traditional history that I think you've already voiced a certain amount of skepticism about. I wonder if you can speak to that idea of nationalism and the idea of nationalism as it features quite prominently in *Willie* and in that contrast between those two characters.

HR I was born in '42, and we grew up with absolute silence, except for Remembrance Day, about the war. It was just not there. I think it was partly that Mackenzie King, who was anti-British, anti-war, pro-American, certainly didn't want the war to be remembered, and I think a lot of people didn't want wars to be remembered. It was not a time when it was correct, politically wise, certainly for Canadians, to recognize war. War was obscene. That's how it was seen, and it was and is today. I think there was also the postwar feeling that we won the war, we're prosperous, we're making money, the economy is booming, we're all having babies. Let's get on with it. Let's be happy.

HW Let's put that nightmare behind us.

HR Let's put it behind us and get on and build a good, happy, peaceful life, which is a very commendable point of view, and I was very much a part of that. So I think there were a number of things. Certainly there was the deliberate forgetting by the Authorized Version. The First World War had been deeply associated with the Conservative Party and deeply hurtful to the Liberal Party. It was very contentious in French Canada.

HW So, to come back to that idea of nationalism and Talbot Papineau, I get the sense that your aim is to represent the horrors of the actual experience of soldiers and to do justice to their memory as opposed to having that history buried and moving on.

HR Well, I was thinking that this is a part of our history that it's very important for us to look at. The concept of white space is very important in my view of things. I am very conscious, certainly as a journalist, of what is *not said*, and so I began to look at these blank holes in the historical record. The wars were certainly one. I guess I feel it's useful to pick up those rocks and to explore experience that was uniquely Canadian. The war experience of Canadians was different from the war experience of the British, or the Americans, for God's sake. The whole issue of the Canadian identity emerging at Vimy, I think, is terrible romanticism, but I do admire people like Sam Hughes, who was a son of a gun, but he stood up to the Brits and he said, "I am going to have my own army, my *own* army!" That to me is a huge watershed that was not appreciated at the time, and so I think Canadians perhaps in the long run had a better experience than the Aussies and the Kiwis. You get those who still argue that the sacrifice, even though it was numbering in the thousands, sixty thousand, was worth it, but then you get people like Talbot Papineau who would probably say no. Fiction allows you what history does as well, to explore a kind of argument. Fiction allows you to engage your reader in a much more profound way, because you can get inside people's minds, because they're into the story. If they can get through the book, they've got everything that's in there, including their history lesson, and including all of the complications and the moral, political, and ethical issues that are engaged there.

HW What would you say, in a nutshell, is the lesson of *Willie*?

HR Oh, there's no lesson, I hope there's no lesson. I hope it's just a story [*laughs*]. It's just a story. It did make people think. I mean, my only goal as a writer, ever, has been to make people think. If you write well, you get people really emotionally, intellectually, and psychologically engaged.

HW Reading is a kind of dialogue.

HR It's a dialogue. If you can engage people at that kind of level, ultimately—and I don't claim to have done this—it's possible actually to change the way people behave, you know, as well as the way they think. I think there are some books that have had a profound effect on not only how Canadians think but how we act. One example is *None Is Too Many*, the story about the treatment of Jewish refugees—I think that has really affected the way that people have thought about anti-Semitism and racism in Canadian society—and certainly Pierre Vallières's book *White Niggers of America* did change things.

HW They challenged Canada's image of itself as a haven of tolerance.

HR I do think that *Willie* did—I think I put the stake through his heart [*laughs*]. Attitudes towards Mackenzie King have totally changed; he's now a figure of fun, right? Except to historian Jack Granatstein.

HW That's what I was coming to next—on the topic of intense responses to *Willie*. During a post-*Willie* interview on CBC's *Morningside* (referred to in a piece by Elspeth Cameron), Granatstein took issue with the liberties that you take in the novel. One thing that he said, in so many words, referring to Willie's attempted rape of Lily and the whole idea of King having a secret mistress, was that King's life was interesting enough without all this.

HR Oh, is that what he said? Well, King's life was far more interesting than what I wrote, I'll tell you. No, I was in Calgary actually when Granatstein was on the air, so I never did hear, and I never got a chance to reply, but I guess my feeling was obviously that Granatstein was reading it as history, not as fiction, and you have to read them differently, and that also Granatstein was well known as being a very mainstream Liberal historian, who had always staunchly defended the saintliness of Mackenzie King. So his response was certainly predictable.

HW Well, one thing you said, I guess in indirect response to it, was that historians leave out all the good bits.

HR There's also the prejudice that if you're not teaching at a university you don't know any history, right? But I had read voluminously, I'd read the books, I had read the secondary literature, not only about King but about Bill Herridge, about Laurier, all these other people, and I'd read the diaries, and I probably had read more of King's diaries than any other person in Canada, so I did know what I was basing my book on. Men can be very prudish [*laughs*]; women are a lot more comfortable about writing about sex. It's too bad that, in a sense, historians have left this out, probably all kinds of people have, because it makes people so much more interesting, and history would be more accessible to the public if people could be seen as people, not as icons. But anyway, as I say, it was in a sense a comic novel, because King is such a comic person on one level, and such a deadly serious person on another level.

HW He certainly did have a material impact on the shape of Canada and on so many people's lives, and there's such an interesting tension between the absurdity of the man and his personality that comes through in *The King Years* and his significance.

HR Well, he was just a politician driven by personal need, and I suspect that most of them are. I think if you sliced open Jean Chrétien or Brian Mulroney (Stevie Cameron sort of did him), that you'd find something very similar. You know, not like King, whose problems were, I think, very highly sexual, but perhaps other kinds of problems. This is one way that you can do this fictionally, without being sued, especially if you write about the dead. Certainly one of the great hazards of doing this kind of fiction is that you can't libel the dead—that's very firmly entrenched in Canadian law—but you have to be very, very careful what you say about the living. So a lot of writers don't want to go there.

HW Let's move on to *Lily*. Now, as the title suggests, the focus in this novel swings away from King and tracks Lily's romance with the left, her involvement with the labour movement and some of the principal conflicts of the period between the wars, such as the riot in Estevan, the On-to-Ottawa trek. Willie doesn't get left behind, but he's not quite as prominent. What prompted that shift?

HR I felt that at this point I had pretty well said all I wanted to say about Mackenzie King and that the romance was essentially over, and so Lily became more of a picaresque figure. I wanted to explore—and I don't think I did it successfully at all—the history of the left, which is another huge white space, in a sense, in our collective memory.

HW Why don't you think it was successful?

HR Because it wasn't a romance! I think it lacks the tension. It doesn't have the richness of story to it. It's too much history and not enough story.

HW But there's a lot of great material there. A lot of great characters, people like Communist activist Annie Buller—

HR Yes, Annie's great. Yes, there are, but I still feel that I didn't adequately get inside the material. I think possibly there wasn't the kind of passion and motivation that was in the first book. Writing about the left in Canada is very, very hard under any circumstances.

HW Why do you say that?

HR I feel that I didn't really capture the essence of it, in spite of all the research I've done and in spite of my own Marxist background on my father's side. I think possibly the handicap is the rhetoric, the way these people talk. The story of the left is a kind of saga in itself.

HW Is it a saga or is it a farce?

HR Exactly. There's a kind of unreality to it ultimately. You see it in Tim Buck and all these kinds of people. There's a kind of posturing and—

HW Detachment?

HR Yes, I think. There's a kind of unreality about it. The Liberal Party of Canada is deadly serious. The left is not, so I think this is the great problem. You're telling stories about some wonderful people, but they're all faintly ridiculous. They're all unreal, there's a kind of unreality.

HW On the other hand, that lends itself well to comedy. If you emphasized the importance of comedy in *Willie,* then certainly there's a lot of comedy in *Lily* as well, and a lot of that comedy seems to be provided by the left. The people involved in the founding of the Communist Party, for instance, certainly get spoofed.

HR It didn't do well, it didn't sell well at all, so I think I failed, because I didn't engage the reader, I think partly because the reader wouldn't know that the barn scene—that is, the founding of the Communist Party of Canada—was real or made up, whereas with Mackenzie King they sort of had an image of what was real about Mackenzie King, so I could play against that. But dealing with the left and the Communist Party, it sounds so fictional. I felt that I was writing a story about a story, people who I think were fictionalizing their lives to begin with. It's very, very difficult to write fiction about fictional people, people whose lives are fictionalized. You could do it as classic sort of spy genre, which is the way people tend to look at the Communist party, or at the NDP if you read *The Globe and Mail.*

HW So you wanted to get inside them as people, but it was difficult because what you found there was just a kind of public posturing.

HR That was what was difficult about it. I think that except for Annie Buller, who is really interesting, and I think a very genuine person, it was hard to get a grasp of the rest of them the way I would have liked to, and I think that's still true. You just don't see novels about the left, at least I can't think of one. There are Communists in Margaret Atwood's *The Blind Assassin* and Michael Ondaatje's *In the Skin of a Lion;* however, they are portrayed in a highly romanticized, unrealistic way. But there are possibilities there.

HW I think it's fair to say that your portrait of the left in *Lily,* and particularly those organizers of the Communist Party, is not complimentary, and I get the sense from reading the book that if the left hadn't been so bumbling and incompetent and ideologically muddle-headed that it really might have been able to accomplish something in those years between the wars. Is that so?

HR Yes. I was really coming from a position much closer to what Canadians saw as Stalinism at that time, really in an attempt to be provocative, and engage some sort of rethinking of this, because in many ways the 1930s, certainly in western Canada, were a time of great creative and social activity. Certainly politically, in terms of mainstream politics—R.B. Bennett and these people—

it was repressive, and I think King's whole philosophy of prevention—"Let's not do anything in case we do something"—his whole philosophy of inaction, is really reprehensible.

HW Especially since it was an inaction that worked essentially in the interests of the political and economic establishment.

HR Well, it was, I think, a kind of malaise. One of the handicaps was that it was hard to get a grip on the Conservatives, hard to get a grip on R.B. Bennett. He's quite opaque; he hasn't left a lot in the way of archival material. That's why I call the novel a rhapsody, because I didn't know quite what to call it. It was experimental; it was in a sense a kind of rant [*laughs*]. But it's a time that has defied representation.

HW For me the most intriguing figure of the trilogy—I mean, beyond King, who is obviously more than intriguing—is Jack Esselwein, otherwise known as John Leopold, who I think steals the show in *Lily*. Under the name of Esselwein, Leopold turns out to be a spy, infiltrating the ranks of the Communist Party and working for the Mounted Police—as he's described in *Lily*, "the shortest man in the Mounted Police, the only Jew, and, as far as I know, the only Bolshevik." I made the mistake of assuming that Leopold was completely fictional—I just thought he had to be; he couldn't be real—but it turned out that I was wrong. How did you come across Leopold, and what made you decide to give him such a prominent role in the novel and make him into Lily's lover?

HR I think this probably goes back to *Grass Roots*, my documentary about small towns on the Prairies. In all that reading I discovered the whole story of the Communist Party and Leopold, Esselwein, all of that. So I just followed the crumbs, I think, and quite a lot has been written about the early days of the Communist Party, because they were under investigation by the RCMP. Leopold's role is very well documented in the Gouzenko story, so I just followed it back.

HW What about making him Lily's lover? Where did that inspiration come from?

HR Oh, that was just an inspiration. You have to have something. No, that was sheer fiction. But that's not a shame.

HW He's a very interesting character, in the sense that he seemed to have been on the margins of the force, obviously not really fitting the profile of the Mountie of the time, because of his ethnic background, as well as having to be a spy and not being seen as a valid member of the force.

FIGURE 23. Inspector John Leopold. Copyright © Library and Archives Canada/Royal Canadian Mounted Police collection/PA-210766.

HR Well, the real mystique, the insuperable problem historically here, is that the RCMP records are closed and will apparently be in perpetuity, forever and ever, amen, right? So there's no way that any historian can in fact find out anything more from the RCMP files, about what these people were doing. For a historical novelist, the lack of access to sources is a huge handicap, and it's a huge handicap for historians, and I don't know why historians don't complain about this.

HW One of the key subplots in *Lily* involves the Brownlee case, the scandal over Alberta premier John Brownlee's affair with teenage family friend Vivian Macmillan. In the novel you obviously went to quite an extent to integrate that story into the narrative of Lily's involvement in the labour movement. What was it about the case that made you want to deal with it there?

HR Well, again, I think it was another look at the King and Lily relationship, another revisiting of that sort of power relationship. Remember, we're still talking here about the mid-eighties, when the novel was written. Men and women are still unequal, but they were even less equal then, and so it interested me because, again, it was a way of looking at how powerful people simply appropriate others, in a way. I think really what I'm writing about in those books is power and who has it.

FIGURE 24.
Vivian Macmillan. Courtesy
of the Provincial Archives of
Alberta A.8007.

HW So Brownlee's coercion of Vivian was an extension of some of the political and economic scandals that were going on at the time, consolidating the establishment's—and particularly the Liberal establishment's—power and the Conservatives' as well.

HR I saw it as a metaphor for that, a way of expressing what was happening to the young and the helpless. I guess the difficulty is that the poor never get to write their story, you know? We don't hear the voices of the poor and the marginalized in this country. One of the reasons simply is that their stories don't sell books, and they don't sell newspapers, because people don't want to read about it. The people who buy these products, and the advertisers who advertise in the press, don't want to read about that. So that's another white space.

HW Since I first read *Lily* I've been wondering about the plot against Willie in the novel—the coup attempt in which both Bill Herridge and Bungo (Governor General Julian Byng) are involved. Is that based on historical events?

HR I would think so, yes. King was a deeply hated person, particularly at that time, and again, historical sources are thin, but certainly there's a good deal

FIGURE 25. Rt. Hon. W.L. Mackenzie King visiting Berlin. Library and Archives Canada PA-119013.

of evidence that there was. There was a great deal of fascism around in Canada in the late thirties. Certainly Herridge's participation in these right-wing corporate government models is documented. They were welcomed with open arms in those days. You know, Mussolini was very popular. King was actually enchanted with Hitler and Mussolini, enchanted with them, particularly Hitler. The whole fascist ethic at that time was, in a lot of circles, very, very powerful. So I don't think I've written anything for which there isn't a substantial amount of evidence. Certainly King was loathed by Herridge and by Bungo and by George Drew and by this huge faction of the Conservatives, because he was sort of the Osama bin Laden of his day. He kept popping up. They'd whack at Mackenzie King, and they'd beat him, and he'd be back [*laughs*].

HW You mentioned King's fascination with Hitler, and towards the end of *Lily* Willie is going to visit Hitler. Now in *Igor,* the third novel of the trilogy, rather than picking up the thread where *Lily* left off, you really switch tracks from the first two books, and both Willie and Lily are moved to the sidelines, leaving the stage to your heroine, Jennie Hutchinson, and of course the enigmatic Igor Gouzenko. Also, unlike the first two novels, *Igor* is set more or less in the present, around the time the novel was published, rather than at the time of Gouzenko's defection. What were your reasons for shifting the focus and structure of your representing of history?

HR Well, it was an experiment. I thought, "Do I really want to go through the whole Gouzenko myth?" I came to the conclusion, which I firmly believe, that the whole Gouzenko myth was a lie; it's a deliberate lie.

HW The myth that Gouzenko was the saviour of the Western world?

HR Well, that he was a Soviet defector. I'm completely and totally convinced, and will be until my dying day, that he was in fact an American plant. I'm completely convinced of this, because the evidence is there if you read it very, very carefully—what people have said who've met Gouzenko and saw him, right? He didn't have a whole lot of documents. He didn't! So I thought, "Well, I'm in a real pickle here, because if I do it in a straight-up way, I have to do it as the whole myth, the whole story."

HW Was he alive while you were writing it? Because of course it seems that with Gouzenko there was always the threat of a lawsuit.

HR No, he died in 1982. I wasn't worrying about that. I just thought, "Well, if I get all immersed in the received myth of the Gouzenko story, then that's the myth that I'll be telling," because as soon as Gouzenko appears, walks out and into that newspaper office, you are either on one side or the other; he's either the real thing or he's a phony. So I would have found it a very long-term task to work that through, doing the straight-up historical thing, because the records are not public, the whole Gouzenko file is deep top secret; there is no historical resource there that can tell you really one way or the other. So I thought I'd have a run at it a different way—also because that story, the myth, is so well known. I mean the guy with a bag on his head—

HW And cut-out eyes.

HR Gouzenko himself told his story ad nauseam, which is suspicious in the first place, so by the time I got to it, that version, the authorized version, was very, very firmly set in people's minds. So I decided to have a sideways run at it; it's a different way of writing a historical novel, bringing it a little closer to journalism, where I've always sort of been, and using the journalism model as the model. So, it was very experimental. I liked it. Anne Collins hated it.

HW She certainly did.

HR She tore me limb from limb. And then she went back and even tore *Willie* apart, which she had loved.

FIGURE 26. Igor Gouzenko on TV. Library and Archives Canada PA-129625, courtesy of *The (Montreal) Gazette*.

HW She wrote in that *Saturday Night* review that you sound in it "like not a novelist but a journalist looking for a framework to bolster an untenable theory or two." What do you think of that?

HR Well, it was untenable to her, but I still think I'm right. People don't necessarily believe my version, historians can't, because you can't get at the documents—this is the whole problem. I think the motivation for starting the Cold War was just so huge that it had to be done. I think certainly, looking back, that the only people who gained from the Cold War were the Americans, the only people, making it all up, and now they're doing it again. I like to be provocative. Researching the whole atomic industry was pretty interesting too.

HW A lot of the narrative is taken up with Jennie's efforts researching the story and trying to track down the goods on Gouzenko and the larger background of espionage and intrigue. Is her activity a reflection of your activity in researching the story?

HR Yes. I just decided to have a run at it a different way. I would have hoped that somebody would say, "Let's have another look at Gouzenko, and is there something in it?"

HW But it hasn't happened yet, and maybe this is what you meant, when you made the comment that with *Willie* or with King you won—that is, your version and C.P. Stacey's version, prevailed—but with *Igor* you lost.

HR Well, I'm not sure I lost. There were a number of writers, particularly American writers, in touch with me who'd read the book, who did try to find something really hard, you know, and they didn't, they couldn't find something hard. So it remains a novel; it didn't get translated into a documentary or whatever, which still helps prove my case. Then with the end of the Cold War, the Berlin Wall came down about this time, so everybody said, "Forget about all that shit. We don't care." It's a question of timing.

HW What about making Jennie American? A big part of the novel is Jennie's coming to Canada and trying to understand what Canada is about, and asking that question that we raised earlier, "Who am I?" I'm wondering how you came up with Jennie in the first place and why you emphasized that search for identity, as she is also searching for her father and searching for the real story of Gouzenko.

HR Well, I suppose in a sense it reflects my own return from the States, you know, in '64 when I came home, and it's also in a way another point of view, looking at ourselves from this perspective—from outside rather than from inside.

HW It introduces a very different dynamic, having Americans like Jennie and her husband Jake interrogating what it means to be Canadian.

HR I think I just probably wanted to do it for fun. I like to take risks, and I wanted to have a look at the Americans and see what they were doing at this particular period of time.

HW *Igor* is dealing with a time of hysteria over breached security in North America, and it highlights the breaches of civil rights that that hysteria led to. Are you having a sense of déjà vu these days?

HR Oh, God, yes, and not just there but here. They've just passed this bill, right, that's not going to allow people to demonstrate without being terrorists? This is in Canada. No, I find it very scary, very scary, what President Bush is doing. I mean, military kangaroo courts and I don't know … I guess as a writer, as a novelist, it's always a compliment to be prescient—anybody feels good about that—but I think if you do deal in your work with what's going on, then things will happen.

HW So do you think there are lessons in the Gouzenko affair that really carried through to what's happening now?

HR Yes. I see Gouzenko's role as really an act of politics. It was a political move that was represented as something other than it was, and I think that goes on constantly. We just don't know about it. Obviously journalists should be more suspicious, and they should be more investigative, and they should be less credulous than they are, so that you wouldn't have to do this sort of thing in a novel, you know, to raise a speculation that is immediately dismissed as fantasy. But I'm very serious about it. I'm perfectly convinced, in my mind, that these machinations do change the course of history. Sometimes we learn about them much later, sometimes we don't.

HW One clear issue is the question of sovereignty, and the push to harmonize various arrangements between Canada and the U.S. certainly makes me think of the 1940 Ogdensburg meeting between Franklin Roosevelt and Mackenzie King, which ultimately bound Canada to a joint continental defence policy. This in some way seems to be a replay.

HR Well, I guess my theory is that King was a traitor, basically. That's really Ferns and Ostry's theory as well, that he was essentially treasonous in his inaction. His need to seek approval was so strong—as, again, a man who was so driven by personal obsessions and needs—that they got in the way of people who were entirely driven by realpolitik. So I guess what I was doing with *Igor* was really starting to look at the elephant to the south, right, and in a sense it represents Canada's failure—

HW Failure to stake an independent course.

HR Yes. I just think to be taken in by Gouzenko was so extraordinarily gullible, actually gullible. And I think we're constantly gullible. When I sit down to write, I only have a vague idea of what I'm going to write, and with the Gouzenko book it was a little more directed, because I was convinced that he was an American plant. There is also an implication in the novel that Gouzenko was a double agent, and that his "defection" was arranged and approved by the Soviets. Why? As we now know, the USSR did not have the bomb, but the exposure of a Soviet spy ring suggested that they might indeed have it. This suspicion may have deterred the USA from attacking and invading the USSR. So Stalin may have had the last laugh. Gouzenko was a very public person after his "defection." Had the Soviets wanted to bump him off, it would have been easy to do so. Ultimately, I think all you want to do is tell a good story in a way that is meaningful to people at some level.

HW But also exposes them to their history.

HR Yes, and hopefully a view of history that is provocative.

HW One that doesn't just reinforce the status quo or the establishment version, the authorized version.

HR The authorized version, or the Heritage Minutes version, if I may say so [*laughs*], which you're up against all the time. I have this theory that, in terms of history, you're either a mythologizer or a debunker; you're on one side or the other. There are the mythologizers, like Granatstein, and then there are the revisionists, who come along and say, "Well, you're full of bunk, and this is the way it really was." I think it should be healthy for that debate to be taking place, but what tends to happen in Canada, in the interests of national unity and political correctness and everything else, is that the mythology version is accepted as the true story, and the revisionist versions tend to be pushed to the margins, so that they become underground texts, and there are not that many of them. It's very hard, when people are propagandized to look at history in a certain way, for a revisionist view to get a tiny little piece of their imagination. I don't find that healthy. It's also very boring, and people wonder why history is so boring. I think one of the ways I could deal with these novels was that I was using a sort of feminist voice at a time when that voice was interesting and new, right? But it wouldn't be now; now it would be tedious.

HW Well, I don't know about tedious. One thing that's interesting about *The King Years* trilogy is that it's anticipating a feature that is being used quite a bit more in historical fiction; I'm thinking not just of the voice of women in history, and female narrators telling stories, and history that's focusing on the role of women in history, but even that more specific technique of looking at a prominent male historical figure through the eyes of a fictional amour. What importance do you place on coming at your material in this way?

HR It's the innocent eye. I did my master's thesis on the role of the child narrator in Victorian fiction, and the role was basically to provide that innocent eye. So that I think is the device. It can be a woman's eye, which is kind of an innocent eye. Looking back, Margaret Trudeau must have been a big influence on my books, because there she was in the early 1970s, you know, this flower child, this child bride, married to Pierre and gallivanting around 24 Sussex Drive and smoking dope. Wonderful. That was definitely an influence. If you use the innocent eye, not only is the reader attracted to that, but you can reveal all of this corruption and horror and mismanagement and evilness and so on—all that is not innocent. I think that's where that device comes from, and you could probably use it in other narrative forms as well.

HW It also gives the trilogy—I would say, anyway—a fairly feminist slant.

HR Oh, I suppose. Though I'm not sure about *Igor*. I would hesitate to use the word "feminist" because there's no doctrinaire feminism there, no Gloria Steinem stuff.

HW But feminism doesn't have to be doctrinaire.

HR No, but are you familiar with Maggie Muggins? A storyteller, Mary Grannan, on the CBC, back in the forties and fifties, had this little girl called Maggie Muggins, this terrifically intrepid little red-headed kid who had this high little voice and was always having adventures, and I was totally enchanted by this little girl my own age, because she was strong and she was independent and she had adventures and she didn't get spanked and she didn't get locked up in her room or anything like that. So I think possibly it's that attitude, "I'm free and I'm me and I'm entitled to my opinions." It's not a matter of feminism as much as assertiveness, for people who have been without power or have been subservient, to be able to be assertive, and it's an assertive voice.

HW In Lily's adventures in the political system, whether it is in Ottawa or during her misadventures in the Communist Party, there is a sense that women are considered subordinate and are very often at the mercy of a fairly patriarchal political establishment, and Lily helps us to see that gender imbalance in play, and that victimization, which often takes place along gendered lines.

HR I did want to present an independent woman, a woman who worked for a living, for one thing, just because I was tired of victims, I was really tired of reading about victims, because that's what you tended to get in romance literature, in most literature by and about women, at least at that time.

HW One of the main things that attracted me to the trilogy is that it's extremely funny. The stereotype of Canadian history, of course, is that not only is there little of it but also that it's very dry, and that's really far from the case with *The King Years*. At the same time, you're dealing with some pretty serious stuff over the course of the trilogy. There is the suppression of labour activism, the execution of the Rosenbergs, the start of the Cold War, the thwarting of political independence for Canada, and at times I found myself wondering whether perhaps there wasn't too much levity. Do you think that there's a danger in making history entertaining when you also want people to take it seriously?

HR Oh, I think I'll err on the side of entertainment [*laughs*]. If you can get people to laugh, you can get them to listen; I think that's really true. I think people can laugh with the books, without laughing at the characters, unless, you know, they're obviously meant to be laughed at. You can feel very ambivalent about Mackenzie King; he's very funny, but he's also a figure that greatly haunts us. A lot of people have a black sense of humour, that when things are really bad, the only thing you can do is make a joke or see it in a more humorous light, because it makes it more tolerable. So yes, I don't apologize for that.

HW I'm not asking you to [*laughs*], and in some ways I think a dark sense of humour is a pretty Canadian thing.

HR Yes. I don't have a problem with that, especially not in a novel. It would be hard to write straight history as if it was all a barrel of laughs, but certainly in a novel, when I've labelled them pretty clearly as being fictional, if you want to do a bit of a comic-book approach, then that's okay.

HW In *Willie*, Talbot Papineau comments at one point, when he's making his decision to return to the front instead of working for the War Office, that he would rather make history than write about it. What do you think about that distinction?

HR I wonder if he really said that; he must have. Yes, I think he did say that. Rather make history than write about it? Boy. Well, I think it was Papineau who said that, because he had the choice. But, who knows who makes history, right? What goes in the dustbin tends to be decided long after people are dead.

HW I'm wondering whether there is a distinction between the two.

HR Well, no. If your books do in fact change the way people behave, or the values of your society, then you can in fact make history. I think that's true of Pierre Vallières. A lot of historians, I think, have wasted an awful lot of time writing about politicians, most of whom are very irrelevant and are forgotten about almost instantly. There's this whole trend, which has now gone out of fashion, towards social history, you know, writing about minorities and Chinese railroad workers and all that sort of stuff. It could be ultimately that the obscure Chinese railroad workers—nobody can remember their names—will be remembered long after the then-premier of British Columbia who nobody can remember, right? So it's very much a class thing; who we remember very much reflects the value of the society we live in.

HW There are a lot of Canadian writers who write fiction on historical subjects, and obviously there are a lot of Canadian historians, but as a switch hitter, somebody who's written fiction and non-fiction on historical subjects, you're fairly rare. How well do those two impulses sit together? Are there any differences in how you approach your material, both in terms of research, particularly, but also writing?

HR The research is, I would say, basically very similar. I do my own research; not all writers do that. I really enjoy it; I really love doing it if I'm into it, and

I usually am into the project. I really enjoy the research, and particularly archival work, where you're looking at the real thing, and poking around and finding stuff out that nobody else knows, or you think nobody else knows except the archivists, and that's very satisfying. With my other books—I didn't have a deadline for any of my novels, but I wanted to get them done—I had personal deadlines.

HW So there is a real constraint on the amount of research you can do.

HR There's a constraint, but it's not the amount of research so much as the speed; it has to be much more intensive. I find fiction is just more subconsciously driven.

HW Does it make you look at the material with a slightly different eye?

HR It's more internal. I would have a character or characters from that time, who would be telling the story in their words. So the narrative voice would not be mine; it would be theirs. That's the tricky part to me, to find those voices of those people and organize the historical information around—

HW Their motives.

HR —to allow those personalities to express the historical information, so that the only information that would be included would be information that those characters wanted to share. It would be their revision or their take on their lives. When I do conventional history I put in what I consider to be the most relevant and interesting material, but if I'm doing a novel the material that goes in has to be the most pertinent to the story of those characters.

HW I wonder if there isn't a slippery slope there in the sense that sometimes it might end up working the other way around—that what happens to the character gets driven by the kind of history that you want to address in the book.

HR Oh sure, oh sure. I think that's true.

HW I'm thinking, for instance, of what a well-travelled person Lily is and how she ends up being embroiled in so many historical events.

HR That's why it's not as successful a novel as I would have liked. I think in that case it does work more as history and less as fiction. But again, I was up against problems that I didn't solve. If I could just add, too, that when I was doing it, it was still very experimental; there weren't too many other people out there doing it. So it's very difficult; you couldn't go around and look at six other authors and think "Well, what's this person doing?" Now there's a much larger body of literature that writers have going into this field, right, so it's much easier, there's a body of Canadian work that one can read.

HW Why do you think that's happened? Do you have any thoughts about that proliferation of historical fiction? There is certainly a lot more being published now in Canada than even in the early 1980s.

HR Well, I think, it sells? Well, actually, I don't even think it does sell. It still tends to be rather marginalized. I am an admirer of Rudy Wiebe's historical novels, and Wiebe wins his share of Canadian literary awards, but you don't find him becoming an international celebrity, or his novels being made into movies. And I see Vanderhaeghe's novels more in the tradition of romance, the "horse opera" of cowboy movies. Fred Stenson's *The Trade* was shortlisted for the Giller Prize, but didn't take the country by storm.

HW I can think of a few books that have done pretty well recently. There's *The Colony of Unrequited Dreams.* That's done very well. *Icefields* is quite a good seller, and *The Englishman's Boy.*

HR Except for Vanderhaeghe, I don't think that they're getting recognized as *historical* novels. I don't see any critics coming out there saying, "Oh, we have all these wonderful historical novels," right? They're good novels. They're there, but I'm still not at all certain that it has been recognized as a genre that has respect. It's happening, but there are still very, very few people, and they tend to be regional. Maybe it's easier to handle in a kind of regional way, because if you make your lens fairly narrow, it's easier to deal with.

HW Now that you put it that way—your lens is pretty wide-angle. You obviously wanted to be panoramic in *The King Years,* as evidenced by the title itself. It has quite a historical span, but also it is dealing with so much of the history of the first half of the twentieth century. Was that a conscious objective on your part?

HR Yes, because I felt that King was such an important figure, and as I said earlier, if we could understand him, then we could understand this period of time. I mean, basically I was dealing with that period of time from 1914 until 1945, which is a relatively short period of time, but I moved around a lot. I have a panoramic view, I guess. I haven't thought about that before, but I do. I like to make connections.

HW Lily has an awful lot of connections. It's quite amazing, indeed dizzying, how many people she knows.

HR That was a bit of a Dickensian joke. I've been very influenced by the Victorian novel, the Dickensian picaresque novel. There are a lot of coincidences, you know?

HW There are certainly a lot of coincidences in *The King Years*.

HR But it's kind of fun, because it has that comic edge and it has a satiric quality to it; you can play around with coincidences. I'm not pretending to write fine literature here. There's a lot of melodrama and stuff like that, but then I think it reflects the characters; they're melodramatic people. But it is true in Canada that you're always bumping into somebody. It is absolutely true. The darnedest people turn up, God knows where or why, but all of a sudden, boom, there they are.

HW Would you characterize the trilogy, then, as parody? I would certainly see that with *Igor*, which seems to be making fun of the thriller or the spy novel.

HR Stylistically, yes, I suppose. It's an anti-spy novel, because I rarely read spy novels; I find them so tedious. I've been influenced a great deal by television and radio. I worked in television for about a year and a half, and when you work in that medium it's very different, and you do have more of a panoramic view, and you're also able to cut, to take a kind of documentary approach and cut scenes. You could deal with a large number of people on the screen, and a fairly heavy load of information—visual information, verbal information—all at once, and you could expect your audience to follow. I just decided to do that, and to adapt that type of medium to the printed page, keeping Dickens in mind.

HW D'Arcy McGee once said that "The dead have their rights as the living have. Injustice to them is one of the worst forms of all injustice." Do you think that writers of historical fiction have a certain responsibility to the past?

HR To the past?

HW To the past, to the dead, to history.

HR That's a tough question. I don't know how you define responsibility. As a writer, I have a responsibility to the truth, and how that truth is perceived and expressed can differ from writer to writer. I think that's absolutely crucial to our society, the ability to say that the emperor has no clothes, to challenge the conventional wisdom. I mean the past is made out of the present, and the present is overwhelmingly interpreted by the corporations and by the political parties and by the rich, who own our media, that we need to have public archives and libraries, to preserve the untold story, and so perhaps the greatest responsibility to the past is not to the public persona or perception that is derived from the public domain, but from the private material that people leave behind, like those diaries, and those letters, by golly. Perhaps there is more truth in the perception that someone like Willie King would write in his diary, in the privacy of his study, or what Talbot Papineau would write on a piece of blue paper in a trench somewhere in France. Is there more truth to that than there is to their public persona? I would say yes.

The Iceman Cometh Across
Thomas Wharton

Thomas Wharton was born in Grande Prairie and spent his teens in Jasper. He moved to Edmonton to do a BA in English at the University of Alberta, and subsequently embarked on an MA in creative writing. His master's thesis became his first novel, *Icefields* (1995), a historical novel set in Jasper during the exploration and subsequent commercialization of the Columbia Icefield. The novel won a number of prizes, including the Commonwealth Writers Prize for Best First Book (Caribbean and Canada). Wharton went on to pursue his PhD at the University of Calgary, where he wrote his second novel, *Salamander* (2001), a fantastical, Borgesian labyrinth of narratives set in eighteenth-century Europe and New France. *Salamander* was nominated for the Governor General's Award for fiction. His latest novel is *The Logogryph* (2004), which was nominated for the Dublin IMPAC Award. He now teaches creative writing at the University of Alberta in Edmonton. I talked to Thomas Wharton in Edmonton in June of 2002. He is not at all icy.

HW Your novel *Icefields* traces the history of the Rockies, and particularly of Jasper and the Columbia Icefield over the course of half a century. In *Icefields* you provide these wonderful definitions of geological terms, which serve as chapter headings in the novel, and I want to begin with your definition of a "moraine": "Rock debris deposited by the receding ice: a chaotic jumble of fragments, from which history must be reconstructed." Is that description a reflection of how you see history and the difficulties of reproducing it or representing it in fiction?

TW One of the reasons I write is my fascination with the complexity of life around us at any moment of our lives—all those things happening in our own lives and in the larger world around us—how all these things pass into the past so quickly, leaving us with just traces to hang onto, and that's what we end up having to work with, as writers or historians or whatever, to reconstruct what happened in the past. We pick certain things and we make a narrative out of what we feel is important in the past, worth remembering, and string these things together and try to make something logical or at least rational, or something that we can hold on to …

HW Something coherent.

TW That's the word. I'm fascinated by that fact and what that means. Does that mean that history is a kind of fiction, because it's a reshaping of things? To me, the moraine is a kind of metaphor for that, because geologists will do the same thing; they'll look at this heap of rubble and they'll say "Okay, these pieces obviously came from this layer, and these pieces came from this layer"; they'll reconstruct a mountain out of this rubble.

HW So there is a kind of speculative and, as you suggest, fictional quality to that process.

TW And so much of it just is simply lost. You cannot bring everything together and tell a complete story. It's impossible. It's one of those areas in which writing shades off into those philosophical questions about … where does everything go? Can somehow everything be captured, in this world or another world?

HW And what kinds of things last, what kind of things are left over, and how does that incomplete record shape what we think of as history?

TW And what does it tell us about who we are, right? That's the other thing, too. We use history to try to figure out for ourselves who we are and why we're in this particular place, time, and situation.

HW Let's talk about some of the fragments that precipitated the narrative of *Icefields*. That image of somebody being stuck in a crevasse was, I think, a very early one, and at one point you mentioned one of the episodes out of the tales of Johnny Chinook as being an influence there. Can you talk a little bit about those stories and about the specific tale that stuck in your mind?

TW Well, I can't claim to remember which exact story it was I might have mentioned before, but I know that they were all influential, because at first *Icefields* started out as a collection of short pieces that were going to bring the Johnny Chinook stories into a contemporary style.

HW These were sort of tall tales out of the oral tradition.

TW Yes, there was this ethnographer from the States, who came to Alberta in the 1930s and '40s, and just traveled around and talked to oral storytellers, and he thought, "Here's a gold mine, this culture which is relatively new, and people are still transmitting their history like this." But also, a lot of these were tall tales, and so he collected tall tales—mostly that's what he was interested in—and he invented this character called Johnny Chinook, who's sort of the spirit of storytelling. I read these stories and I enjoyed them, and then I found out from my uncle that my grandfather had contributed a couple of these tales to this collection, although he personally isn't mentioned. And I thought, "this is great, I'm following in his footsteps."

HW Sticking to that same image of somebody being stuck in the crevasse: in the original expedition—I think it was in the Bow Valley—involving Norman Collie, one of the expedition members, C.S. Thompson, who appears very briefly in *Icefields* as a character, fell into a crevasse and was, like Edward Byrne, stuck upside down. Was that also an early impetus for the whole narrative, or that side of it?

TW It was. I wanted to use a glacier in this narrative. I knew that I was going to do that. Living in Jasper and going up to the icefields had made a really deep impact on me—that landscape. I knew I wanted to write about that, and I wasn't quite sure about what I was going to do. I knew that somebody was going to go into the ice, or something was, and that time was going to be involved. And then I started reading the historical accounts, and I read Collie's book, and there was this guy who had this mishap, this Thompson, and the writing started to shift more toward history and fact rather than fantasy and tall tale. Thompson was there fairly early on as a template for what happens to Byrne. Collie then became much more interesting to me, once I'd borrowed this idea of falling into the ice. I think it was Collie who said, "Well,

I'm not married; I'll be the one to climb down and rescue him," and they had this little argument. Collie did make that statement, if I remember correctly, when Thompson was in the ice. And that, to me, was a really fascinating thing for somebody to say. It said so much about who these guys were, and their time and place and all that. So that then became more interesting, and Byrne then developed on his own as a completely fictional character.

HW [*laughs*] I won't bring up trying to find "Edward Byrne: A Life in Ice," one of the sources listed in your acknowledgements.

TW I've been taken to task by a few people about that—"You can't do this! Putting fake entries in a bibliography."

HW In *Icefields* some of the characters are historical figures—Norman Collie, who we just were talking about, Lewis (you call him Lucas) Swift, who lived in Jasper House—whereas others are based on historical figures—Sexsmith, Frank Trask, and Freya Becker. I'm curious about what goes on behind those decisions about whether a character is going to have the same name, or be quite similar to a historical figure, or is going to be a modified version. What makes you feel that you can leave a historical figure more or less intact, and what kinds of things lead you to decide that a character becomes somebody else?

TW It's true that, in writing, these decisions sometimes are difficult to reconstruct, but I do know that when I was writing *Icefields* I was pretty cautious about all this kind of thing. As a general rule of thumb, if I knew that somebody was going to become a major person in the narrative, then I decided I needed to fictionalize him a bit more, because I was wary of claiming all sorts of characteristics for people who really existed, imagining things about them. So there's a rough dividing line, I think, between those I'd given their historical name and tried to be accurate about—they generally were the more minor players—and the ones who were the major characters. They may be based on historical people, but, as I say, once I knew that they were going to be major it was time for a name change and all that kind of thing. That had to do mostly with caution and just feeling my way as a writer, since this was my first book and I wasn't sure what I could get away with.

HW That's also a typical convention of the historical novel, to have the principal historical players on the margins and to concentrate on a fictional character as the protagonist, who is involved in the action.

TW You can see how certain historical writers enjoy that so much. For instance, Tolstoy with *War and Peace;* you can almost feel his delight that he can make Napoleon this minor little person who appears once or twice.

FIGURE 27.
James Carnegie, Earl of
Southesk, 1827–1905.
Glenbow Museum NA-1355-1.

HW The Earl of Sexsmith in *Icefields* is based on the historical Earl of Southesk, an aristocrat who came to the Rockies on a hunting expedition in the nineteenth century. How did Sexsmith come to play such a role in the novel?

TW Well, I was just fascinated by the Earl of Southesk, and I had written about him in other forms, in a short story and so on. So I had this other material, and I thought this would add another layer to *Icefields* that might be interesting, kind of historical, but also it would allow me to introduce mythology into this, Native mythology. So I decided to introduce a fictionalized version of this character that I had written about before.

HW What about the grail motif? The original Earl of Southesk was just interested in hunting and bagging big game, and you added this whole quest for the grail—this vision that he has and desire to find it up in the mountains, in the icefields.

TW I think that was just an offshoot of what I understood of the historical Earl of Southesk. He was a very romantically minded person, really into

Shakespeare, reading by night in the tent, giving these poetic names to things and so on, and I just decided to go further in that direction, and make him somebody who sees the mountains in a very spiritual context, in his own way.

HW It's a very European way, is that what you're getting at?

TW I think so. I think it comes around to my sense of Jasper when I lived there. It was a very British place. There weren't many First Nations people around when I was growing up there. There was a really strong British heritage and I was quite aware of that, and that coloured my sense of the place.

HW That sense of the Earl of Sexsmith in some ways being very Eurocentric in his outlook is really consolidated through his relationship with his servant, Viraj, who is your invention, right?

TW Right.

HW Southesk's original helper was Métis. So, given your interest in the history of Native people in Jasper, which figures fairly prominently in *Icefields*, why make your character East Indian? That's quite an interesting jump.

TW I think it just has to do with the way my mind works as a writer. It's one of those decisions that you can't really rationalize. My mind looks for incongruities, it looks for contrasts, it looks for things that stand out or seem strange, or it invents those things if it can't find them. I had always been interested in the fact that the Aboriginal people here were called Indians, by mistake, and so I decided to weave that into the story as well, to take this person from a very, very humid, hot place, and have him describe his first moment of touching ice.

HW Expose him to a world of ice.

TW Just the contrast in that, and the shock to his system, and so on. It also involves this beautiful woman, too, right? All of that comes together, hits him, at the same time.

HW Plus he's "half-caste," so there's an interesting parallel between him and the Métis.

TW Right. He's almost a character that could have ... there could have been a novel about him. In some ways I always feel frustrated that, in weaving this together, certain characters only became minor players, when they were really fascinating to me in their own right. I've always thought that about Freya especially. There's probably another book there about her adventures, elsewhere.

HW The character of Freya is influenced by a couple of historical figures: Mary Schaeffer, who was supposedly the first European woman to see Maligne Lake, and also Freya Stark, who was a very prominent mountaineer, but not in the Rockies.

TW No, she explored Arabia and other areas around the Middle East and Asia as well. Freya Stark is a wonderful writer; her prose is beautiful, poetic. I don't think in that sense she's too much like Freya in the novel, who is more journalistic and looking for ways to get a good story out of something. I just borrowed the name and the sense of an independent woman going out and doing these things that were sort of shocking for a woman to do. Freya Stark was on her own on many of these travels, and it was so unusual for a white woman to go out alone in these places. So I guess I borrowed some of that for Freya Becker, the fictional character.

HW And of course the name Freya gives that character a certain mythic resonance, as well.

TW It's part of the whole Nordic thing that I'm doing there. My idea was that this book was going to be cold and icy in so many ways, and so I borrowed her name from Norse mythology. It's just one more little nudge in that direction.

HW How do you view the whole history of discovery, particularly in the Rockies? I'm thinking of the portrait of Norman Collie, which I find is somewhat ambivalent in the novel, because on the one hand he's portrayed as a Renaissance man, almost—he's incredibly accomplished and versatile as a mountaineer, as a scientist—but on the other hand he's also a kind of extension of colonial conquest, of the path that Sexsmith is cutting in the narrative, and it made me wonder about your view of the bigger picture of discovery, how you see its role in the history of Canada.

TW A character like Collie becomes ambivalent probably because I feel ambivalent about that whole process of discovery. On the one hand I feel a great deal of affection for people like him and A.P. Coleman, for instance, who came out to the Rockies as a professor of geology, supposedly wanting to write about the geology of the place.

HW He was at the University of Toronto.

TW Right, and he ended up writing books that became very poetic and appreciative of the landscape and the people he met. It's interesting to see the scientist and the—I don't know what you'd call the other half—poet, I guess, in the same person, writing, shifting back and forth between these. So, I have a

FIGURE 28.
A.P. Coleman. Whyte
Museum of the Canadian
Rockies V1-ACOOP-82.

lot of affection and appreciation for these guys, because they were amazing in a lot of ways. But it's true, on the other hand, they were one of the less noxious examples of the awful things that were done in the name of spreading a particular kind of civilization around the world, right? I mean, they were out there, no doubt at least partly, for a similar kind of reason: to expand the knowledge base of what was seen as the centre of civilization, British, European civilization. And so in some ways it's tied into all the other sorts of exploitations and things that happened in North America and all over the place. So I guess as a writer I want to exercise my critical faculties, but I try not to be too judgmental, from my point of view. I want to see if I can present a much more balanced picture of these people. I think Sexsmith tips over into—

HW Satire.

TW But these other guys, these later Victorian explorers and writers, I didn't see them in quite the same way.

HW It strikes me that there's an interesting duality to it, in the sense that mountaineering is a kind of conquest on the one hand, but it's also an aesthetic experience, and that makes these figures very ambivalent. There is a lot to admire there, but it is part of a claiming of territory.

TW "Because we have seen this and we have been here, it now belongs to us," in a sense. But I'm attracted to these characters and these people because part of what they get out of going there is similar to my feelings about the place and having lived there and my feelings towards the mountains and the wilderness. So I feel I can understand them, at least partly.

HW Is it that there's a similar appreciation of the sublime?

TW That's part of it. I guess I mean more in terms of something in their character that makes them come out to these places, the urge to get away from civilization, not so much to be a representative of civilization but to get away from it.

HW That strikes me as a really interesting paradox—getting away from civilization but bringing it with you at the same time—and that's the paradox of tourism, too. In some ways, the patterns of tourism that you're looking at later on in the novel are an extension of what you've described of these earlier explorers.

Frank Trask, the guide and entrepreneur in *Icefields*, is based at least in part on the Brewster family, a family of entrepreneurs behind what is now a substantial tourism operation in the West, and particularly in the Rockies. Can you talk a little about their role in opening up the mountains to tourism and to commercializing the Rockies?

TW Well, they were really crucial. They were there almost from the beginning. There were four brothers, and two of them started up an outfitting and guiding operation in Banff. A lot of what they did was taking people up through the Bow River Valley up towards Jasper, and I think they helped out at least one of Collie's expeditions, if I'm not mistaken. I know that they were involved with many people who came to explore and other people, too, who were out there to draw and sketch and paint and so on. Eventually two other brothers set up an outfitting operation in Jasper, too. So all the way along they were part of that. I've always felt a little guilty about my portrayal of Trask. I guess I just let him be who he was, and it was only afterwards that I thought, "Well, he's not really like these Brewster boys at all," from what I understood of them. They weren't so crassly commercial or materialistic as he was. They had much more of an appreciation for leaving things as they were. Eventually their company got bigger and bigger until they finally—I think it was in the sixties—sold out to Greyhound or something.

FIGURE 29. Brewster tour buses at the terminus of the Athabasca glacier, Columbia Icefield. Whyte Museum of the Canadian Rockies v92-PA64-12.

HW They did, like Trask, develop snowcoach tours up onto the icefields, and that certainly had a great deal to do with the level of penetration of tourism into the Rockies.

TW I guess with Trask I let my imagination run wild, with this diorama business and all of these other things that he wanted to do. I don't think they were really like that, you know. So in a sense he really seems to me to be a complete invention. There never was someone like that. But he was fun to write.

HW Well, he provides some wonderful opportunities for satire of some of the excesses of tourist promotion.

Speaking of Trask, there were a couple of guides, I think, who accompanied the original Collie expedition. One of them was the legendary Bill Peyto, who figures pretty prominently in the history of the Rockies. Is he behind the scenes at all?

TW I think there's a bit of him in Trask for sure, the crustiness and the playing up of the business of being a mountain man. Trask was like that to a certain extent. But there's also a bit of him in Byrne, oddly enough, in that Peyto

FIGURE 30. Left to right: Bill Peyto, Hugh Stutfield, and J.N. Collie, 1898. Whyte Museum of the Canadian Rockies v62-PA-7.

was a guy who really wanted to get away from it all. He was a totally independent person who was happy living in a cabin by himself for months at a time. There's a famous story about how another mountain man, I think it was Jimmy Simpson, came to stay with him for a couple of weeks up in his trapping cabin somewhere, and they hardly said two words to each other for several weeks. They just went about their business, and finally one day Peyto said, "So, when are you leaving?" It was like, "Get out of here!" Yeah, he's a wonderful, fascinating, colourful, romantic figure, and in a sense he was almost too good to use straight up. I felt it would be too easy to just take him and stick him into a book like this, and so I stayed away from him to a certain extent, but I did put something of that nature—going and hiding up in a hut on a glacier—into what Byrne does.

HW That makes for an interesting reversal, because of course Byrne and Trask are really pitted against each other in the novel. In a lot of ways Trask is responsible for interrupting that solitude by promoting the icefields and making a lot of people want to get away from it all there, in the same place, together.

TW I really noticed that the last time I was at the icefields. They built a huge new hotel there, and my wife and kids and I stopped there on the way back from B.C. I was floored by how many people there were that day. The parking lot was just full, and the hotel and the gift shop were packed with people. It had never been like that before, that I'd seen.

HW Had you spent quite a bit of time there as a kid, exploring? How old were you when you lived in Jasper?

TW I lived there from the age of fourteen to … I guess it would have been eighteen, so not that long, and it was all tied up with being a teenager and all that stuff. Often times I just went off by myself because of teen angst or whatever, needing to be alone and think about things.

HW That's right. What great possibilities for being alone.

TW So it's all bound up in my memory of that place, and that time of life and so on.

HW Speaking of Peyto as a colourful figure, there are a lot of colourful figures who populate the history of Jasper and the Rockies—Jim Simpson is one that you mentioned. Were there some interesting stories and figures that it might have been tempting to bring into the book but that never made it? Or do you want to save those up?

TW There are some I may use later. I did have a lot more little nuggets of information in the manuscript at one point, and when I was working on it with Rudy Wiebe, who was my editor with NeWest Press, he said something like, "Put everything you know into the book, not everything you can think of." That was the way he put it. So there were a lot more of these things, and I had to cut some of them out, because they were just there because I found them fascinating, thought I'd just put them into the collage; they just didn't belong, really. They were there like a kind of gossip around the story: "This also happened, too; did you know that?" But there are some wacky stories. The Rockies collected more than their fair share of kooks—

HW And eccentrics.

TW Oh yes. I don't know if you've heard of the story of Operation Habakkuk, but during the Second World War, all these ships were being sunk in the Atlantic by the U-boats, and Churchill was looking for some way to make the supply lines across the ocean more secure, and this person named Jeffrey Pike, who was in a mental hospital at the time or something, suggested, "What about ships of ice?" They would look like icebergs, and they would go by unmolested by the U-boats, right? So they decided, "Well, okay, let's try this. Nothing else seems to work." They set up this operation at Patricia Lake in

Jasper, the town, and it was all hush-hush. And this Jeffrey Pike was put in charge of this and soon found that … you know, he tried to create these chunks of ice and they sank too much, so he invented this stuff he called Pike-crete, after himself; it was wood chips mixed with ice, but it still didn't work. The people who were working with him on the project, the labourers, were Doukhobors, from B.C. or somewhere; when they discovered that this project was actually for the war effort, they put their tools down and quit. So the whole thing was just a farce from beginning to end and was finally scrapped.

HW Going back to A.P. Coleman, whom you mentioned earlier, and the kinds of ideas and experience that he represents: through Edward Byrne, who is a fictional character, you're engaging with a number of Victorian scientists whose geological interests and metaphysical qualms were somehow behind their fascination with glaciers and with mountaineering. I wonder if you could talk a bit about figures like Louis Agassiz, and John Tyndall, and Coleman, and what attracts you about them as figures, and their obsession with glaciers and mountaineering.

TW Originally I was seeking out their books for the sake of information, primarily it was just research, but I really became attracted to their writing, and what drew me towards them as characters was the beauty of their writing about weather, about ice, about rock. All three of them are really lovely, wonderful prose writers, Tyndall especially. His descriptions of clouds and glaciation and so on are really, really lovely, and so that deepened my sense of these people and added a layer to the writing of the book. It added a layer of—I'm not sure what to call it—mountain metaphysics or something. Here we had these people who were ostensibly trying to be very scientific about everything but they were still in an age in history where they were allowed to wax poetic about things in a way that science has kind of completely sealed itself off from. There still are popularizers of science who are very good writers, and so there's still that kind of thing going on, but …

HW It seems to me that there's an element of wonder there that's tinged with religion or metaphysics or something that distinguishes it from popular science writing today.

TW Sure. I think it goes a long way back in the history of writing about mountains, thinking about mountains. For a long time in Europe, mountains were thought of as frightening places; you stay away from them, right? They're just dangerous and awful and scary, and that gradually becomes this notion of the sublime, something that's terrifying and awe-inspiring about nature and that mountains are a very powerful example of. That goes way back, and you can see that in their writing as well. They're allowing themselves to be overcome by that at times. I know, in a sense, that whole thing has been deconstructed as kind of a cultural—

HW Construct.

TW Yes, but at the same time I feel that it's real, too, in a way, that I have felt those feelings, right, before I'd ever heard it—

HW Deconstructed.

TW Or whatever. And so, as I said before, I just have a sense of sympathy with these people, a sort of understanding.

HW You want to retain a sense of wonder, and in some ways there's just too great a degree of cynicism in that elimination of immediacy from one's experience of nature and particularly of the mountains.

TW I think that was one of the main concerns for me, to find a way to write about this place that would avoid clichés of writing about the mountains and would, if possible, somehow be close to that wordless experience of a place. That was the challenge, and that was why the book ended up in the form and style that it did. I've talked many times about trying to mime the landscape in my writing and in the structure of the book, and that's why it is so fragmentary and sparse, because I'm looking for a way to make the language reflect something about this place—the language itself, as a form and as a shape and as a sound.

HW In the novel there seems to be an ongoing comparison between historical time and geological time. There's a real contrast between the—I guess the only word I can think of is glacial—progress of changes in the landscape and the speed with which change is happening in the social and cultural world of the Rockies and the world outside.

TW It goes back to what I was saying before about my fascination with the way things slip into the past, and then we're left with trying to put together bits and pieces that we choose from the past. That then becomes a kind of fascination with time, too; what is time, and how does it flow, and why does it seem to flow at different rates at different times in our lives and so on, and how things do persist—how we consider ourselves living at this particular moment in time but we are also, in some ways, still Victorians, and we are people of earlier eras in certain ways, right, that can be seen when we read books or texts or look at documents from those past eras, and you can make these connections and realize that something has persisted and has cropped up again in us.

HW I suppose there's a tendency to think of progress and evolution as absolutely uniform.

TW Yes, right. I don't believe in that at all. I think that all of the centuries of human development are still in some ways present in the present moment. So I guess I began to see the glacier as a kind of metaphor for that. The ice comes down and covers the landscape, and when it recedes the landscape is changed, and things can be embedded in the ice, pop out later unexpectedly. In a sense, then, that's a metaphor for time covering things over so that we think that they're gone, and then they can somehow come to life again, be extracted or found. It's one of those strange paradoxes that strikes you once in a while, in a particular moment seems very crystal clear; I suddenly realize, "My God, I'm still thinking like a Victorian!"

HW That contrast also—and this is sort of a cliché—is tied up with that sense of awe. Looking at the incredibly gradual rate of geological change in some ways diminishes the importance of human history, I guess, or change in human societies, makes what we think of as historical cataclysms seem very minor and almost ephemeral.

TW [*significant pause, laughter*] Yes, I'd say that. I'm at a loss for what to add to that.

HW I know that one of your main interests is modernism. *Icefields* strikes me as a confrontation with or engagement with modernism, much like Michael Ondaatje's *In the Skin of a Lion* is a real engagement with modernism, but in an urban context, as opposed to *Icefields*, which is obviously dealing with the wilderness, with the mountains.

TW It's true. When I started out writing the book I hadn't really made any kind of a connection between my interest in modernism—in Joyce, in Yeats, people like that—and what I was doing. But at a certain point I realized that I had various motifs that were running through the book and that were recurring; for instance, there's a motif of tea-drinking and hot liquids that keeps cropping up throughout the book. I realized I have sort of organized things to make these connections between these points that don't necessarily seem to be connected at first, and I see that as a very modernist way of approaching a book; in some ways it's a Joycean way. This novel, to me at any rate, doesn't feel at all Joycean in style, but at least in the way it was put together.

Joyce conceived of each chapter of his novel and how certain motifs would crop up again in later parts of the novel but a different riff would be played on them, and that's how I worked there. So in a sense I was supplying, for myself perhaps, a modernist novel that Canada had never had, right, at the actual time high modernism—or whatever you want to call it—was at its peak. There wasn't anything like that in Canada. Canada was still struggling to develop any kind of a literature at that point and there wasn't any experimentation and so on going on. I like to think of *Icefields* as a modernist novel slightly out of its time.

HW But what about its engagement with the modern age—maybe modernity is a better word—the whole idea of progress and the development of what we see as a modern society and all these amenities coming to the Rockies? It goes back in some ways to the idea of civilization penetrating into the wilderness.

TW It allowed me to explore a leading edge of that process happening, and that's part of the reason why I brought myth into it, the story of the girl named Athabasca. Her story doesn't quite make sense; it doesn't click together with what comes later with the Europeans and so on. There's something missing there or something's lost in the translation, and modernity does that because it wants to make sense out of things that don't make sense in the way that it sees the world. Certainly Sexsmith is a kind of prototype of that, not being able to understand, wanting to see things in his own way, to make use in his way of something that to her might mean something entirely different. So that's definitely happening there, but what's also happening is that I, as a writer, am borrowing from myth to inform the book and its motifs and its interests. In a sense, I'm doing something similar to what other modernists might have done, like Joyce taking the Odysseus myth and writing that through the modern world and making parallels and ironic contrasts between the mythic and the modern.

HW But at the same time, there's a certain amount of self-consciousness, or self-reflexivity, in the narrative—such as the description of a moraine that we started out the conversation with—that in some ways affiliates the book with postmodernism as well. Would you go for that?

TW I don't know if I would. I try to stay away from that particular label. It seems to me to have grown to mean just about anything that's come after modernism, right, and so I don't find it all that useful, and it doesn't really help me to understand the process of actually writing, because these things aren't really conscious choices. You don't set out to do something postmodernly, as a writer. That wasn't anywhere in the original impulse. A book becomes, for me ... certain premises are laid down and certain things I want to explore, and then it takes on its own life and its own shape. I think what happens with those moments of self-reflexivity is that what sustains me through the writing of the book is my fascination with character, let's say, or place or landscape or whatever, but also the process I'm going through, but I don't consciously think about that. It's just that the energy of the writing gets diverted at times into comments or statements or suggestions or echoes in the book that are in some way about what I'm doing. But it is often only later that people point them out to me, and then I go, "Oh I see, you're right, that's true. I am kind of talking about what I'm doing."

HW That doesn't have to be a function of self-identification—you know, "I'm a postmodern writer and therefore I write postmodernly"—but in some ways it goes back to history and the historical moment in which this kind of reflection on the activity one is engaged in is becoming quite recurrent and certainly a recurrent artistic motif or conscious strategy. That drawing attention to artifice, which is part of the satire of tourism, at least as I see it, shares certain characteristics with those reflections on the process of writing, on the process of reconstructing or representing the past. But that doesn't mean you have to go around wearing a T-shirt that says "I am postmodern!"

TW That's right. I know that, because I was fascinated by the modernists and reading a lot of theory and criticism and so on, these things probably creep in, but very rarely are they intended. Often when I catch myself doing something like that deliberately, I will edit it out, because—

HW That's not where you want to go.

TW Well, I want to discover it as I go along. One of the main reasons I write is because I'm a reader, and I love reading, and I want to read a book that I haven't read before; I can't find it anywhere, so I have to write it. So I don't like to be too many steps ahead of what I'm writing. I get a lot of my energy from not knowing how it's all going to develop.

HW Going back to this engagement with modernity, that whole idea of progress: what place does the First World War play in that? The First World War is appearing in a lot of contemporary historical fiction, and it plays quite a pivotal and cataclysmic role in *Icefields*, in this history of a world—the mountains—which is really so far removed from it geographically. How did that burst into the narrative? Was it just that that was the era you were dealing with and therefore this was going to be a part of it?

TW I had decided to set the opening of the book at this historical moment in 1898, when Europeans first saw the Columbia icefields, and it was a question then of what was happening in the world at that time. When I got to the early twentieth century, there was no avoiding the First World War, really, at all. I think it also had to do with the Britishness of the place—many of the people who I knew when I was in Jasper, the older people, the parents of friends of mine, who had stories about the past, and their sense of their link with the British Empire, and the feeling that Jasper was part of that; even though it was far away, they were somehow going to maintain certain aspects of Britishness in this far-off place.

And there was an old fellow, who was dead before we moved there—I can't remember his name, unfortunately—but he had been in the First World War, and he had come back home to Jasper, and he became the town eccentric. People thought that maybe something had happened to him there, had affected him in some way. He became famous for all these weird things that he would do. He dug tunnels under his house, going towards his neighbours' houses—they were never finished—and he had assembled all sorts of machines down there, old junk that he dragged down there. Sometimes he'd sit up on his roof, I guess, and play the fiddle, or something like that. So he was always in the back of my mind, and when I was looking for a way to bring the war right into my story, I think that I was borrowing from that and bringing it into the story of Hal.

HW It really seems like an intrusion of history, a certain kind of history, cataclysmic history into this, not idyllic world, but peaceful and remote world.

TW You know, in a place like Jasper, the decisions that were made there were made by people mostly of British heritage, so you see things like, for instance, the mountain that's now known as Edith Cavell, which was Montaigne de la Grande Traverse at one time when the fur trade was going through there, and of course, you know, the name couldn't stay French. It was changed to Fitzhugh, and then during the First World War, there was this huge patriotic indignation about the shooting of this nurse who had helped these Allied soldiers escape in Belgium. So you see that somebody from somewhere, not in Jasper, makes the decision to change the name of this mountain to reflect this patriotic feeling. Somebody of the centre just arbitrarily decides to rename this mountain far away.

HW The railway plays a huge part in the novel, and the railway baron, the character Anton Sibelius, is a bit of a sketch of William Cornelius van Horne, who was a huge force behind the building of the transcontinental railway. Now,

Icefields doesn't strike me as exactly celebrating the railway. It seems to be definitely a kind of intrusion into the wilderness and particularly into the lives of the Native people living in the area, and that comes through in Sara's cold reception of Byrne when he returns to the mountains later. How do you see the railway's role in Canadian history and particularly in the history of the Rockies?

TW I grew up with the National Dream story, the Pierre Berton myth of the railway as this epic, heroic project that sewed the country together, and so, years later, coming to look at this place and write about it, I realized that I needed to deal with the whole story of the railroad. I certainly, by that time, wasn't interested in retelling the same old story, right? And I became aware, in looking at the history of Jasper, that there had been a whole community of people displaced so that this thing could come through, and that to me seemed much more worthy of telling, rather than just retelling the same old story. The building of this railroad is still a magnificent story in its own right but, as I say, there's more to it than that. There are these other little stories that have been buried, and aren't well known, and as a writer I guess I'm looking for those fragments that somebody else hasn't noticed.

HW Because they're all part of the picture, and in some ways it's a righting of the picture, which is distorted in these very epic and celebratory terms. Even though the accomplishment itself is certainly momentous, it's not the whole picture.

TW No.

HW In your portrait of the commercialization of the environment, essentially the opening up of the Rockies to tourism, and in Trask's use of job creation in defence of his development schemes—when he's arguing with Byrne, trying to justify making the region attractive to tourists and knocking down trees and so on—I find that the novel really comes across as highly anachronistic, that is, really speaking of the present as it represents the past. It's addressing pressing ecological concerns of today through the way it seems to be presenting to us a past era. Was that something that was quite conscious on your part?

TW I think the story of Byrne at some point deliberately became a story that was meant to show a development of an environmental consciousness. He stands for that larger movement in history of people becoming aware that maybe civilization isn't all it's cracked up to be, so, rather than just march right into these places that have yet to be developed, we should somehow protect them. I think that over the course of the novel he moves towards what we see today as an environmental, ecologically oriented attitude.

HW The spoofing of some of Trask's development schemes—for instance, when he wants to import penguins and have them swimming in the meltwater pool and his desire to construct this very cheesy facade around his bus terminal—really made me think of the present and the idea that everything is all spectacle, all artifice and simulacrum.

TW Life does imitate fiction there, because they now do have this huge diorama of Athabasca glacier. It's in this new chalet hotel, and it's a huge representation of what you can actually see outside, with little pointers to show you what this and that is, and you can walk underneath it.

HW On that note of Byrne as a proto-environmentalist: at one point Elspeth asks Byrne to take this stone that she has been given by a guest at the chalet, this young boy, to take it back to its place of origin, basically put it back in nature. Is this a metaphor that speaks for your feelings about the natural world, your own ecological attitude—that it's all about leaving as small a footprint as possible?

TW I think in some way I felt like a bit of a plunderer, I guess you could say. I had talked to people in Jasper who weren't too happy to find out that I had fictionalized things. A couple of people complained to me, "We have enough trouble getting the tourists to understand what really happened here. Why are you doing this, changing things around, changing the landscape?" That bothered me and made me a little wary of what I was doing. I was aware that putting that stone back was in some way a gesture that I was trying to make towards the place.

Later, long after I had finished the book, I came across George Steiner's theory of the fourfold aspect of translation, in his book *After Babel*. There are four aspects to translation. There's—I can't even remember the four—there's incursion and extraction, and the last one is reciprocity. That's his idea that a translator has to somehow give something back to the original, and I was delighted by that idea, because I thought maybe in some way I was trying to do that too. My way of somehow giving something back to the wordless place— you know, nature, wilderness—was giving an excess of meaning. There are so many different points of view in this book about what the ice means and what the landscape means, and the story jumps around and looks at this place from different angles and at different time periods. That kind of excess of meaning and excess of ways of constructing, I feel, is a way of leaving it somehow inexplicable too.

HW Inexplicable and less depleted.

TW Yes. The very process of saying "Hey, you can look at this in different ways" also suggests that no one way is the truth, and there is something that is always going to be beyond us or out of our reach in some ways.

HW When you're writing about history or when you're writing about a particular place, there is a tendency for authenticity, for accuracy, to become a bone of contention with readers, particularly as you've just described. How much should a writer be concerned with authenticity, with getting it right, with this responsibility to be true in one way or another to a history, to a particular place?

TW As I said before, a book for me takes on its own life, and in a way I find that what I have to be authentic to is my vision of the book, as opposed to something out of the real world. What I said earlier, about looking at things from different points of view, I guess is my way of dealing with that worry that somehow I'm misrepresenting something. So for me as a writer, the concern isn't so much to make sure that I stick with one particular truth as it is to explore the story around a truth, perhaps, and see that there are other ways of seeing something.

When the book first came out, the first review was by a fellow who lives in Canmore, named Bob Sanford, and he runs an interpretive company there, and I was pretty apprehensive about this—you know, reviews by people who lived there, in the mountains. And his review starts out by saying, "When I first picked up this book I was thinking, 'Oh no, here's somebody who's gone and screwed up the historical record and played with the landscape,'" and I thought, "Oh, no." But as the review progressed he came to appreciate what I had done. He was glad to see that somebody was really trying to see a place in many different ways and really concentrating an artistic vision on a place that was important to him and important to a lot of people. I really, really appreciated that. It confirmed to me that, "Yes, you can go ahead and do these things, and there will be people who don't understand and will be angry, but there will be people who will appreciate it."

HW In the novel, you're portraying Trask as commodifying nature. Are you worried that in turn you are commodifying nature, or history, or even both of them? Is that something you struggled with?

TW No [*laughs*]. Yes, I guess it's a concern but it's not a major one, because in the end I think that the place that I've written about is still what it is, and then there is this book that is about this place, which is like that real place, but it is its own world. It's no longer the real Jasper, and I know that.

HW It's tied up with these questions of wonder and the sublime that we were addressing earlier, trying to get through this impasse of any vision being a kind of social construct. In reading the book I could see that a ready criticism would be that the writer is essentially doing something similar to the activity of a key character in the novel who is being satirized, implicitly criticized. How is your approach to the mountains, in creating a kind of aesthetic experience for your reader, different from what Trask is doing in trying to create a kind of aesthetic experience for the visitor?

TW I guess I just have to reiterate something that I said before, and that is I'm hoping to present a sense of multiple points of view and of multiple ways of seeing something, and some of them are more critical, more judgmental than others. In that way, I guess I am not trying to wrap everything up in a package that totally aestheticizes a place and says, "This is a place of sheer wonder." I think there is more going on there than that, and I know that for me, personally, that's also the case. As I said before, I'm aware that this landscape has been and is constructed in a romantic way and that I kind of buy into that, but I'm not satisfied with just saying that, because I know that there's more to it. But as a writer, I guess, I wanted to have both if I possibly could, to be critical and to maybe make the reader say, "Hey, look, what is it that we're doing when we come to this place, and what should we be doing?" These are the sorts of questions that do get raised.

HW To draw attention to the way that the mountains and wilderness are aestheticized.

TW Yes, and also how, as you said way back at the beginning, tourism becomes a kind of resource extraction, and it is an incursion as well; slowly these activities have a deleterious effect on the wildlife and on all these things, right? So I know that I'm thinking about these things, and I want the reader to think about them, at the same time that I want the reader to have an aesthetic experience. I have had lots of people come up to me and say, "I really felt that, in writing that book, you captured something of the spirit of that place that I had felt too," and I certainly don't want to discount that. I think if people want to make that connection between my work and the feelings they have had, then that's a perfectly valid way to read, and I appreciate that, but I don't think that is completely what is going on when you read it.

HW There's an interesting description of Freya's writing, a reflection of Hal's, and it struck me again as a really important moment of self-reflection in the novel: "If she places herself in the foreground of her narratives it is because she knows this, that her words can only be a transcription of an elusive, end-lessly recurring moment of first contact. In her swift passage through a new world she moves like a bullet. A small violence. Her writing a record of dam-age." So in other words he's drawing attention to her consciousness of the fact that her presence changes a place. I guess it's a variation on the Heisenberg prin-ciple that objects change their behaviour under observation. Can we apply that description to your own writing about history and about place?

TW This is a classic example of one of those things that I hadn't even noticed before somebody pointed it out. I think that it's true that there may not be an "I" in the centre of this story, but there is me writing, and there is me aware that my observations are subjective in some ways. So when I am thinking about a place and trying to write about it and transcribing it, I am looking for those things I didn't know before, or looking to be hit with a realization about something that I hadn't considered before, relating to this place. So there is some way in which that is really quite accurate, and certainly I am aware that I'm damaging certain stories, too, at the same time. There is the myth of the heroic creation of the railways, you know. I am doing a small damage to that heroic story by suggesting there were some less than heroic aspects to it, right? So, yes, I like that a lot.

HW Hal is also admiring a certain kind of honesty in her writing, that she rec-ognizes that intrusion and the effects that it has. It seems to me that quite a bit of contemporary historical fiction and even writing about history itself is really foregrounding that recognition, that there is no objectivity in writing about history, and that the presence of the viewer has an incredible influence on what kind of picture we get of history.

TW I think it's something that I'm still exploring as a writer.

HW I'm really struck by just how different a kettle of … well, stories your second novel, *Salamander*, is. It's just so different from *Icefields*.

TW My editor at McClelland & Stewart had read *Icefields* and liked it a lot, and she was kind of flabbergasted by this complete shift in time, place, you name it. I don't know; I think that for me every book becomes, as I said, its own world, and I'm looking for a book that I always wanted to read, and in the case of *Salamander*, as with *Icefields*, there's a book that I want to read, or wanted to read, or have been looking for, and it wasn't there and I had to write it. *Icefields* is more concerned with looking for a book about a place I've lived that isn't there, whereas *Salamander* is more concerned with looking for a book that I have always been looking for, that isn't there. That's why there is a fairy-tale quality in this book. In the writing of it I was searching back through my history as a reader and how I was always motivated by looking for a book that wasn't there. A particular book might suggest to me something, and then I would go looking for that, and so that's the kind of shape that it took. In some way it's a meditation on reading; it's really a book about reading. So it had to take its own shape, and the shape that it took was really influenced by my whole history as a reader, going back to fairy tales in childhood.

HW That fairy-tale, fabular quality of *Salamander* creates an interesting contrast between the two books. It seems to me that in *Icefields* the fantastical and the magical are hovering on the edge of the historical and the real—I'm thinking particularly of the image of the angel embedded in the glacier—but then in *Salamander* the opposite is the case: we can feel the presence of history—whether it's the conquest of Quebec or the fall of the Ottoman Empire—hovering at the edges of this very fantastic world that Nicholas Flood and his daughter Pica travel through.

TW I guess it was more my impatience with realism, as a reader, primarily—with realism as a strand in history and literature, and one that's fairly recent—than a conscious decision to push history to the fringe. You can see its development and how it has become the central mode of fiction, a kind of decision to ground things in a solid factual basis. The idea of realism is also a construct, too.

HW If the historical is just on the edge of the narrative in *Salamander*, given your reservations about realism, why is it there at all—those historical edges, those historical details that help to situate it in place and time (somewhat anyway), whereas most of the novel is really in the rarified air of the fairy tale?

TW Yes, it is, but everything that happens comes out of something that I was aware of, that was in operation at that time in history, the eighteenth century—the whole fascination with automatons and porcelain, and all the wars going on and all of these things, they are tied to history. I guess I said to myself, as a reader/writer, "I want to let this book go wherever it wants to go and explore reading in whatever way it wants to do it, and I'm not going to look too far ahead. I've chosen this era, and so I'm going to let myself dream an eighteenth century which is somehow tied to history, use history as a base, and just dream my own kind of eighteenth century."

I guess it's a primal impulse that is right there at the heart of writing, too, to have my own world, to make my own world—and whatever psychological or whatever reasons you want to find for that, I'm sure there are some. My mind feeds off historical tidbits, stories, fragments that I find and that I think I can make use of, or that seem to me fascinating and that I want to explore. With this book I just let that process go, completely, whereas with *Icefields* I was much more concerned to be tied to the historical record.

HW How about the fact that the whole series of narratives in this book is framed by this little story, set in Canada, during the fall of Quebec in 1759? Why that particular historical marker?

TW It was like an anchor for me so that, no matter what happened, no matter where I lost my way, I would know that there was something that I could come back to, and in looking at the eighteenth century, and reading about it, and exploring it, there was that crucial moment for Canadian history, so I kept coming back to that and thinking there's some way in which I have to make use of it, if only to give myself a link to Canada, as an idea, so that as a Canadian writer I can say, "Yes, somehow this has something to do with Canada" [*laughs*]. So that I don't get completely lost, right?

HW Going back to the fact that it's a fairly fairy-tale world—despite that, the principal character, Nicholas Flood, is himself a historical figure, or are you pulling my leg again?

TW [*laughs*] Yes, I did the same damn thing. I made up a book to put in the bibliography.

HW I wondered about that, because I read an interview, and somebody said that Nicholas Flood was a historical figure.

TW Yes, I read that too. There was a Robert Flood, who was an alchemist and sort of proto-scientist, in the Elizabethan era, and his work, as far as I understand, is a kind of almagam of mysticism and science, and I think I just borrowed the name. That's about it.

HW So why this predilection for fictionalized bibliographical entries?

TW I think that when I finish a book, I feel like I'm not finished playing fictionally. Somehow I like to have the fiction bleed over into the real world in some small way. I don't why; it's an odd impulse, all right. I guess it seals the book off with a buried statement: don't believe everything you read. I don't know.

HW Keeping that boundary between the fictional and the real nicely blurred.

TW For sure.

HW I was very surprised to see Anthony Henday—supposedly the first European to cross the Prairies to within sight of the Rockies—pop up in *Salamander* as the proprietor of a London coffee house that Nicholas Flood stumbles into at one point. What inspired the injection of him into the narrative?

TW It's similar to that idea of starting the book in Quebec. It is a way to bring my world into this book, the specific place that I live and looking into the history of that time—what was going on here, from a European perspective. It was almost nothing, but then you have this Henday coming here; he was trying to make contact with the Blackfoot actually. He was using the Cree as an intermediary to try to find these people, so that they could trade with him, and when he finally did find them, they were so uninterested. "We have our own way of life. Why the hell should we trap a bunch of animals and haul them north for you guys? What use is that to us?" They just sort of dismissed him, and I've always been interested in that character and maybe will write about him again in some larger story.

HW So just a little cameo here.

TW I guess you could say that. Actually, at the time that the novel happens he would have been here, so I had to depart from the historical record to even have him there at the coffee shop in London, but it's interesting that he did kind of disappear, right? He did his yeoman service for the Hudson's Bay Company and melted into the crowd and was never heard of again. There was some suggestion that he might have been a smuggler, before and maybe after; he might have been in more shady sorts of transactions. There's not a lot that's known about the guy.

HW Now, your first two books obviously in very different ways have been set in the past, so can we expect to see the past in your work in the future?

TW Yes.

The Living Haunt the Dead
Michael Crummey

Michael Crummey is a fiction writer and poet. He grew up in the mining towns of Wabush, Labrador, and Buchans, in central Newfoundland. His earlier books include *Arguments with Gravity* (1996), *Hard Light* (1998), *Salvage* (2002), and the short-story collection *Flesh and Blood* (1998). He received the Bronwen Wallace Award for Poetry in 1994 and the Writers' Alliance of Newfoundland and Labrador Literary Award for Poetry in 1996. His novel *River Thieves*, which deals with the capture of one of the last surviving Beothuk at the beginning of the nineteenth century, was published by Doubleday in 2001. The novel won the Winterset Award and the Thomas Head Raddall Atlantic Fiction Prize. He also published, in collaboration with Greg Locke, *Newfoundland: Journey into a Lost Nation* (2004). His latest novel is *The Wreckage* (2005). I talked to Michael Crummey in Wolfville in October of 2004.

HW Your novel *River Thieves*, which deals with a couple of key episodes in the fate of the now-extinct Beothuk of Newfoundland, is not really your first foray into the past. One of your volumes of poetry, *Hard Light*, is preoccupied with the history of your own family and with your father's experiences in the Labrador fishery. In "Her Mark," a poem from *Hard Light*, which is about one of your ancestors, Ellen Rose, she says, "The day will come when we are not remembered, I have wasted no part of my life in trying to make it otherwise." How does that comment sit with your writing about the lives of your predecessors in *Hard Light*? What do you think about that sentiment, and what does it say more generally about your own preoccupation with the past as a writer?

MC That piece, "Her Mark," grew out of a particular set of circumstances. I was living in Ontario at the time, and I took a leave from work and went home for a summer to write *Hard Light* on my first Canada Council grant. I went home specifically to write about Dad's life—growing up in an outport in Newfoundland, taking part in the fishery—with a real sense that was a time that was disappearing. The way Dad grew up and the world he was part of in the 1930s and '40s (with the exception that they had electric lights and inboard motors and cod traps) was exactly the way people had lived in Newfoundland for almost 250 years, and in the span of his lifetime it's disappeared completely. I had a real sense that Dad was the last living connection to this world, and I went home to try and get some of it on paper.

When I was growing up Dad always talked about Uncle Bill Rose, an old man who lived in the house with them, and it wasn't until I started working on the book that I finally clued in that Uncle Bill was Dad's grandfather. Dad and everyone else in Western Bay called him Uncle Bill because it was a sign of respect for an older man. My second realization was that I had never heard a soul mention Uncle Bill's wife, my great-grandmother. She died at least thirty years before Uncle Bill did, and by the time I came along there was no sign of her. We went to the house that Dad grew up in, which at the time was abandoned, and we found a bunch of legal deeds in a drawer. One of those was a deed of gift from my great-grandmother to my grandmother. She was signing over a piece of land. And I thought, "Who is this person?" There are no pictures of her that I know of. I don't think there's even a headstone; there's a family plot, and she's not there. I was really struck by that. In this project of dealing with what felt like a disappearing world, I came across this woman who had literally—but for this one document—disappeared. Even on that document, the name is written by somebody else and she signed it with an X, because she was illiterate, obviously. It just felt like she was at the centre of the project, emotionally, this person who I was connected to by blood but had never heard tell of before and had just come across this last piece of evidence by accident. So I took that deed of gift and rewrote it as "Her Mark" with my own emotional response built in there. I don't even know if that line was in my head when I started writing it, or if that's where it led me.

HW I am thinking about the contrast of her stance of living in the moment and not being at all preoccupied with posterity and your own very definite pre-occupation with what it was like and in some ways a kind of ethic of preser-vation.

MC The impetus for the project was my sense that this was the last chance to get some of that world down on paper. The flip side of that sense of necessity is admitting that this is the last nail in the coffin. Here is this long-standing oral culture where most people were illiterate, and me wanting to get it down on paper before it disappears is an admission that it's just about gone. There's also an admission, in that piece, that my project is in many ways completely foreign to the people I'm writing about; it's one more way that I'm separated from them.

HW You grew up in mining towns in Newfoundland and Labrador, and espe-cially in your story collection *Flesh and Blood* there is a strong consciousness of the distinctive history of those communities. You write of the dwindling of one of those towns, Buchans, in your essay prefacing Greg Locke's photo-graphs in your new collaborative book, *Newfoundland: Journey into a Lost Nation*. How has that background shaped your sensibility as a writer and your sense of the past?

MC It has become clear to me, over the course of several books, that loss in all its forms is really what I'm interested in—personal loss, cultural loss—and that comes in part from growing up in Buchans, which, by the time I was old enough to be aware of where I was growing up and what was going on there, was very clearly a dying town, with a "glorious" past; people were always talk-ing about how great things used to be in Buchans. I was right there in the middle of the decline, and we left because my dad, who had worked there for thirty years, was laid off shortly before the mines stopped operations alto-gether. All through my early adolescence people were moving away, houses were being boarded up, and it was clear that there was no reprieve. I remem-ber planes flying over Buchans and over the barrens with these torpedo-look-ing things hanging underneath, and they were X-raying the ground, trying to find a new body of ore that would keep the town going, and I felt that there was a kind of weird desperation to that.

HW So you were breathing an almost elegiac air, in a way.

MC I think I'm completely shaped by that. My brothers for some reason were not. It hasn't become a preoccupation in their lives. So obviously there was something in me that really responded to that. Growing up there, at that time, has marked me as a writer, and has become central to just about everything I have written since. Also, Buchans is close to Red Indian Lake, where many of the events in the story of the Beothuk took place. It was just another thing that was in the air, you know; it wasn't really talked about. We had a cabin on the lake, and I spent a lot of time out there as a kid. The local food center had a snack bar that was called the Shanawdithit Snack Bar.

HW Sort of an Aboriginal Avonlea, writ small.

MC Yeah, it was bad. At the Shanawdithit Snack Bar there was a huge mural of an Indian maid, straight out of Hollywood, with the two braids down the side and the feathers at the back of the head. And what did I know? That was my picture of Shanawdithit. I don't remember ever being told about the Beothuk, but I knew that story, or one version of it anyway. I don't why, but when I was thirty-one or thirty-two that story stepped forward and said, "Here's a novel; why don't you try something here?" That historical story inhabits the margins of *River Thieves*. For the European characters, except for moments near the end of the novel, the Beothuk and what's happening to them is very marginal to their lives and concerns. But that loss at the margin was the only reason for me, emotionally, to write that book. The story that becomes the spine of *River Thieves* is like a little soap opera between the European characters. That wouldn't have interested me enough to write a novel without that loss that's happening in the shadows. I wanted to write a story that inhabited some of the same emotional geography as a way of pointing indirectly towards it.

HW In the poem "Finnish Cemetery Revisited," which is in your collection *Salvage*, we have this passage:

It's the living that haunt the homes
of the dead, wanting something
from them we can't articulate,
something we can only gesture dumbly towards

Now that you've written a historical novel on the vanishing of the Beothuk, does that passage resonate any differently for you?

MC It certainly feels more and more true in terms of my own motivation. I do have a real sense that at least some of us need something from our past. The story of what happened to the Beothuk is something that Newfoundland will never get past. Every generation of Newfoundlanders is going to have to ask, "What does this mean for me?" and we are always going to be picking at that scab, never really knowing exactly what we want, some kind of absolution maybe.

HW There's no question that it is a story that Newfoundland writers come back to again and again. There are poems and plays, and in terms of fiction there has been Peter Such's 1973 novel *Riverrun*, Kevin Major's 1989 *Blood Red Ochre*, even *The Colony of Unrequited Dreams*, which is largely about Joey Smallwood, comes back to Shanawdithit at the end of the book, and then a few years before *River Thieves*, Bernard Assiniwi published *The Beothuk Saga*. Is there some impulse here to confront a kind of absence at the very base of Newfoundland's origins?

MC I think so. I think there are pivotal events in a country's or a people's history that they never escape. In the States, for example, slavery is the story that they will never escape, and they will constantly have to be saying, "What was it about us that allowed that to happen? What does it say about us as a country if that's where we started?" In Newfoundland, it's the Beothuk story we're haunted by. There is a very real collective sense of guilt in Newfoundland around what happened to the Beothuk.

HW At one point in the novel, naval officer David Buchan, reflecting much later on his callous treatment of his mother right before he entered the navy, says, "When the dead have been wronged they never leave you quite, even if you might eventually wish it." That certainly jumps out as a sentiment clearly applicable to the fate of the Beothuk as well. But it also raises the issue of whether writing this kind of historical fiction is some sort of consolation or compensation for colonial guilt. Why do you feel that this history needs to be written, or rewritten in fiction? What is driving that impulse?

MC When I decide on a story I don't say, "Well, why am I interested?" I just know that it resonates with me in a way that makes me want to spend some time with it. I have a sense that the story of the Beothuk is central to me personally because of where I grew up, not just in Newfoundland but in that particular geographical location as well. It is something I am haunted by, and I think there is definitely an element in it of trying to provide some sort of atonement or to ease some sort of collective guilt, just by acknowledging "this is what happened."

HW Mary Dalton has written an article, "Shadow Indians: The Beothuk Motif in Newfoundland Literature," about the representation of the Beothuk in Newfoundland literature, in which she talks about the use of the Beothuk as emblems or projections of writers' psyches and desires. As she puts it, "We write shadow Indians, who serve us beyond the grave." The Beothuk are not represented essentially as themselves so much as they serve some kind of function that is, in one way or another, a projection of the writer's needs. Was that an anxiety that you wrestled with while you were writing the book?

MC I think that goes back to my sense of not knowing what I wanted to do when I started the book, except that I knew I did not want to write a book *about* the Beothuk. I had read *Riverrun*. I wasn't actually aware of Assiniwi's book until after I finished *River Thieves*, but that attempt to recreate the Beothuk on the page—to try and say, "What did they feel about what was happening to them?"—to me has always felt completely wrong-headed and beside the point.

HW It really jumps out of the book that you stay at a distance. It is a difficult choice, because on the one hand you have, as you state it, that position of discomfort about presuming to be able to get into that identity, but the other option is to keep them at a distance and essentially almost absent or "other" them.

MC The point to me has always been that we can't know what they thought. That is the point of the whole story: that the loss is so complete that they are completely absent, and trying to pretend otherwise is another affront to them; it is one more awful thing that we can do to the Beothuk today. So what I wanted to do was just to continually point to the fact that all we can know about them is what the white people who survived knew about them. Even when we see Mary in the book, we never know what she is thinking. We are only seeing what the white people around her are guessing she might be thinking, and that is because in the historical record that is all we have. We know the historical Mary March did these things, but that is all we know. Why didn't she want to go back when they were trying to bring her back to her people? We have no idea why; we can only guess. That is a chasm that can't ever be crossed. That's what extinction means.

HW In the prologue, though, initially we see that episode of Mary's capture from her perspective, and in a way that doesn't immediately identify her as Aboriginal. There is an initial deracializing of that incident, as we see it developing from her perspective, and, when towards the end of the prologue John Peyton Jr. is designated as a white man, it's an interesting revelation.

MC The decision to write the scene in that way was more an aesthetic one. I wanted an immediacy to that scene that would bring people into the book quickly, and writing it from that perspective was the most effective way to do that. But it is true that that's probably the only point of the book where I break that rule, and I am inside that woman's head briefly. But even there it remains at the level of sensation, basic emotional response. I never try to guess or suggest what she thinks about what is happening there.

It's also true I very consciously did not want to have a situation where the European characters are the norm in the novel, and everybody else is some racialized "other." Throughout the book people are identified according to racialized categories, but that includes the Europeans. In one scene I might refer to a character as "the Indian man" and a moment later identify a European as "the white man." I didn't want to suggest that there is a norm—white, which doesn't require any mention—and then things that deviate from the norm and require an explanatory term. That was one of the ways I wanted to try to point it out.

HW Your characterization of Mary March in the book seems to be collapsing together the stories of the historical Demasduit, Mary March, and the story of Shanawdithit, the so-called "last of the Beothuk" who stayed with John Peyton for quite a few years. Given that the story of the Beothuk is a foundational story, in some ways so treasured, in Newfoundland, what prompted that departure, and how did you feel about making it?

MC Well, there are all sorts of things you have to deal with when you are trying to write a historical novel. One of them is the historical record. Another is the aesthetic structure of a novel, which has some strictures involved in it. You want a book that is not going to be 1500 pages and also that is going to have a narrative arc to it that holds together. You can't write it exactly as it was, because as a novel that would fail. So there were many places where I had to make decisions that collapsed characters into one another, changed the historical record slightly, to deal with aesthetic, writerly questions like "How do I speed this up? How do I hold these things together?"

HW A good example would be having Mary March and John Peyton essentially paired throughout that narrative. Adhering to the historical record would prevent that.

MC Well, they actually did become quite close. She stayed with a minister in Twillingate, but around the time that they were making these attempts to get her back to her people, John Peyton was the person she looked to as her protector, so that part of it is historically accurate. Having her in the Peytons' household is not, but again that was an aesthetic decision. There were a lot of political issues around the minister being involved in all this in the first place, and he was reprimanded by the church for it, and including all of that started to feel way too messy, too far away from where I wanted this book to go. So I

FIGURE 31. Demasduwit (Mary March), 1819. Library and Archives Canada c-087698.

had to make those decisions. Also, John Peyton was not on that first expedition to Red Indian Lake. He was still living in England at the time, but for the narrative arc of the novel to hold together he and Buchan had to meet earlier and had to be more closely connected. So there were all sorts of places where I messed with the historical record.

HW And how did that make you feel, as the psychoanalysts say? [*laughs*]

MC I think what I wanted was a bottom line. I wanted there to be a spine through the book that I did not fuck with, if I can put it that elegantly. I wanted to think that there was a bottom line for me in terms of what I wasn't willing to mess with, and that for me was the three expeditions down the river. The book is divided into three parts, and in each part there is an expedition. In the first part it's Buchan's expedition where the two sailors are beheaded; the second section has the expedition where John Peyton and John Sr. try to recover their goods; and the third one has the attempt to bring Mary's body back. And even though I put John Peyton on that first expedition, when in reality he was not even in Newfoundland, I would not allow his presence to change anything that happened on that expedition as we have it in the historical record; so all of the Beothuk responses that we have to the presence of these men, all of the things that led up to the beheading of the soldiers, the response of the Europeans on the expedition, are taken directly from the historical record, and I was not going to mess with that. When I read the historical record, of course, I have an emotional response to it, and writing the novel was my attempt to get that on paper. I felt like I was free, outside of those touchstones, to muck with history enough to create a story that resonated emotionally with where those three expeditions touched me.

In many ways, for me, Cassie's story became the heart of the book. I felt like the things that had happened to her and her response to those things were kind of mirror images—maybe a funhouse mirror, I don't know [*laughs*]— of some of the things that the Beothuk may have felt about what was happening to them. The Beothuk response to the European incursions was basically to withdraw. They didn't trust these people, but instead of standing and fighting, they seemed to be incredibly insular and also in many ways very pacifist. They clearly could have wreaked a lot more havoc than they did; there were very isolated European settlers, and the Beothuk could have just walked in at night and killed people whenever they felt like it. But in every story of a Beothuk killing a white person that has any sort of corroboration, the Beothuk are acting in direct response to something that that white person has done. So it seemed that they wanted no truck with violence unless they were forced. Whenever they got their hands on a rifle, they just smashed it up. More than anything they seemed to want—and again this is only a guess—to be left alone. And Cassie's response to some sort of emotional betrayal or trauma is to withdraw and withdraw and withdraw. That is the reason she ends up staying in this place, on her own, in a situation where she knows John Peyton is interested but she is holding him off, and John Sr. is kind of her protector, and she has her own space and feels like that is going to save her. In the end, Cassie realizes that isn't true and has to leave, where for the Beothuk, of course, that was never an option.

HW *River Thieves* is a love story involving a romantic quadrangle between John Peyton Jr., John Peyton Sr., David Buchan, and Cassie—Cassandra Jure. Now, in the historical literature on the Peytons there does appear, very fleetingly, a Mrs. Jure, a widow who was John Peyton, Jr.'s housekeeper while

Shanawdithit was staying with the family. Given that Cassandra Jure is obviously a much more fictional character than the other principal characters,
what made you decide to retain that name, instead of just introducing a whole
new fictional character?

MC Cassie is the one central character of those four who is completely fictional. But writing her, I wanted it to feel that she was possible, plausible.
When you read the historical record of European settlement in Newfoundland,
women are almost completely absent. They're there, but they barely rate a
mention. And I decided from the outset I wasn't going to write a book without any central female characters. And there was this Mrs. Jure, who was a
housekeeper for the Peytons, who was one of the sources for historian J.P.
Howley's Beothuk vocabulary. So clearly there had been a fair bit of interchange between Mrs. Jure and the Beothuk woman who was living in the
house; there had been some back-and-forth, and she had learned some of the
language from this woman. That to me was a very interesting thing. What
would that relationship have been like? How would those things even have
come up? It seems there would have to be a story to that. Maybe it's just that
she was a curious woman and picked these things up. But I decided that I
wanted this character, Cassie, in that household, and I wanted that interchange
to be part of it, so I just stuck with that name.

HW And now you can't go to any Jure family reunions.

MC [*laughs*] Well, I haven't met any Jures since the book has come out, but
I have met a ton of Peytons.

HW John Peyton Jr. and John Peyton Sr. are historical figures whose role in
the fate of the Beothuk is highly controversial, and in *River Thieves* you portray that relationship as a distinctly Freudian competition. Are you consciously
transforming them into allegorical figures, or is this competitive relationship
something that is suggested of them in the historical record?

MC I think in many ways that the relationship between those two men was
the start of the book for me. When I first started reading with a view to writing a book where the Beothuk were central, I was interested in writing a book
about Shanawdithit and the man she did her drawings for, William Cormack.
I felt that there was a book in that relationship. But as soon as I started reading Ingeborg Marshall's book *A History and Ethnography of the Beothuk*, the
Peytons to me *were* the novel. The father–son thing was a real hook; it seemed
like they were in many ways diametrically opposed. John Peyton Sr. was a bastard when it came to the Beothuk. He had no patience, no concern. They were

FIGURE 32.
John Peyton Jr., J.P. The Rooms,
Provincial Archives Division,
Newfoundland and Labrador
A17-105.

an impediment to his undertakings, and he had no compunction about responding with brutal violence to the kind of pilfering and vandalism that the Beothuk used as a way of protesting the fact that they were losing their salmon rivers.

HW And indiscriminate violence too, according to the historical record.

MC Absolutely. There was no sense that there were particular Beothuk that he was after. The first ones he ran across were good enough for him if he was trying to avenge some petty theft or incursion. I think it's important to point out here that there is quite a bit of myth that has built up around the violence that was perpetrated against the Beothuk. You have all kinds of stories about hundreds of them being herded into the ocean and slaughtered at a time when there weren't more than 100 or 150 of them alive. There are stories of people saying, "I've killed my ninety-nine and I want my one hundred." Those are obviously apocryphal stories; they're obviously people bragging. They couldn't possibly have killed that many individually. But when you look at the stories that there is any kind of corroboration for, Peyton and his men come up over and over and over. I think that is partly because the Beothuk had retreated by this point to the River Exploits, Red Indian Lake, and the Bay of

Exploits. They had nowhere else to go, so when Peyton moved in there, and started taking up those salmon rivers, it was fight or die. So that is where most of the violence that we have any kind of corroboration for took place, and John Sr.'s name comes up over and over again. For whatever reason—and nobody knows why; it may have just been guilt over the sins of the father or something along those lines—John Peyton Jr. was involved in just about every official attempt to establish some kind of friendly contact with the Beothuk. There was a very split-personality response to the Beothuk in Newfoundland, even at the time. Many people felt a lot of sympathy for the Beothuk; they thought of them in a very condescending way as poor wretched creatures who were being unnecessarily brutalized. On the other side there were people who felt that the Beothuk were being given too easy a ride, in the courts especially—that if a man was brought to court for violence or depredations against the Beothuk he was automatically considered guilty, and that the townies (basically the people in St. John's) had no idea what it was like out in the real world. In many ways John Peyton Jr. and John Peyton Sr. exemplify that split in the "Newfoundland psyche." If there is such a thing.

HW But there is some skepticism about the motivation of John Peyton Jr. in some historical sources. B.D. Fardy, for instance, suggests at times that his concern might have been more mercenary than humanitarian, because there was always or often a reward involved.

MC Even in the novel John Peyton Jr.'s motivations are not all that altruistic. Basically, he's pissed at his father, who he thinks is sleeping with the woman he's in love with, and so siding with Buchan is his way of getting back at his father. And there's no question during that second expedition in the book, when they go to recover their materials, that they were after a Beothuk, because the reward offered for bringing one of them home would just about cover their losses. And I do think that even for the settlers who were most sympathetic to the Beothuk it wasn't a big deal; it wasn't something they felt like starting a crusade over. It was always something that was happening on the margins of their world. There was no burning desire among people on the northeast shore, as far as I can tell, to do something to help. There was a justice of the peace up there who was very vocal about how appallingly the Beothuk were being treated and how something had to be done, but he was largely ignored. So, I did not want the book to say about Peyton that he was a completely altruistic, humanitarian guy; I don't think he was.

I think also that in the aftermath something happened with Shanawdithit in the house—nobody knows what it was—that affected his sense of what had happened to the Beothuk. I mean, there are all kinds of rumours in New-foundland about what happened between Peyton Jr. and Shanawdithit; there are some people who claim there was some kind of sexual relationship, and other people who would say that it was more a father–daughter relationship. Obviously they became quite close. Also, obviously, John Peyton Jr.'s wife was quite happy to have her out of the house. John Peyton Jr. was not present when William Cormack showed up and said he was taking Shanawdithit.

HW It seemed that there was some tension between Peyton and Cormack that came out of that, because Cormack just whisked her away, and that seemed to sour their relationship.

MC I have no idea what the truth is; we may never know. There is some spec-ulation as well that the Peyton family knows and they are not talking, and this is part of what interested me: the Peyton family has become inextricably linked with the Beothuk but also emotionally inextricably tied to them. There is a very real sense when you talk to some of these people now that they feel some kind of … not just guilt about what happened but some kind of ownership of that story.

HW Some kind of proprietorial sentiment.

MC Not just proprietorial but custodial. When I started writing the book I had a big debate in my head about using historical names, and for a while I thought about calling the Peytons P-a-y-t-o-n instead of P-e-y. I thought for a while about just making up names for these characters, and in the end that seemed (even though I'm mucking with the record so much) completely wrong. These events were happening among this tiny group of people, and there was an odd, and in some way appalling, intimacy to what was happen-ing. The Beothuk, the ones who were still alive at the time, certainly would have known the Peytons and the men who worked for them by sight, and these Beothuk women ended up living with the people who had been basically hunt-ing them. And this sort of Stockholm syndrome thing started happening, where the women attached themselves to these white men as their protectors. I thought that changing the names of those people would lose the bizarre inti-macy of the historical record that I wanted. It would have been completely wrong for the emotional geography of the story that I was really interested in.

HW There comes a point at which it is better to muck with history visibly than to, somewhat dishonestly, keep so many details of the same story but pretend it is not the same story by changing the surface of it.

MC I did feel strongly that there was violation in that. I felt like the book had to acknowledge that somehow, and there is a scene I ended up writing where Peyton has been sitting with Buchan's journal, which he has asked Reilly to steal for him, because he thinks if he gets that information he can somehow protect his family, protect his friends. As he is sitting there, before he has even looked at it, he has this realization that there is no way to protect himself or his father or any of those other people, because they are so intimately connected to what is going on.

HW That is when this phrase appears: "But two hundred years from now, he knew, some stranger could raise his bones from the earth and put whatever words they liked in his mouth. It was a broken, helpless feeling." That just leapt out at me as a kind of *mea culpa*—the awareness of historical fiction, as you are describing it, as almost an act of desecration.

MC I wanted the book to acknowledge that this is not history; this is somebody mucking with history. I felt like I owed Peyton, as well as all of those other characters, that moment, to have them say, "This is not me talking." So a lot of the book points to that sense of the violation of putting words into the mouths of these characters, giving internal lives to these characters, who were real people who lived their own unknowable lives. It encourages readers to recognize that these are different things. It points to the whole project to say, "You can't take this as historical or factual truth. If you do that, you're making a big mistake." In fact, you could say the same thing about history. One of the important contributions of historical fiction is to continually say, "Everything we know about the past is a construction, to a certain extent."

HW We have been talking all along about the historical record and historical accuracy, and yet a lot of your comments, especially that last one, are questioning just what that term means. On that note, I want to come back to the epigraph to the book, where you quote the historian J.P. Howley, who in his 1915 history, *The Beothucks or Red Indians*, essentially gives priority to John Peyton Jr.'s account of the capture of Demasduit. He says, and you repeat it in *River Thieves*, "Various versions of this event have appeared from time to time in our histories and other publications, but as numerous discrepancies characterize these accounts, I prefer to give the story as I had it from the lips of the late John Peyton, J.P. of Twillingate, himself the actual captor of the Beothuck woman." Now on the one hand I get a definite sense of irony here, and yet in a lot of ways John Peyton's version does get a certain primacy in the novel.

MC [*laughs*] Well, it is almost a cliché of historical fiction now that there is no objective truth that we can point to and say this is actually what happened. It's all different versions, and everybody's version has a bias to it, and part of what historical fiction has been doing over the last twenty or thirty years is just setting one version up against another, letting one knock down the other. I think that's why that scene on the ice becomes the turning point in the entire novel. Even among the men who were present, the descriptions of what happened vary so bizarrely and widely as to make you think that they can't possibly have been at the same event. So you then start asking yourself what is behind their version. One of the things that I learned when I was doing research for the book is that my version, what I had grown up with as the story of what happened to the Beothuk, was almost completely false, which stunned me.

HW Can you give a quick summary of what that version was?

MC I grew up with what some people now call the atrocity myth (to say "myth" is overstating it, but I see the point). The story that I grew up with—and I can't point to a source—is what I had in my head when I sat down to write this book, before I started doing research. The Beothuk were a huge group of people, somewhere around fifty thousand (nobody knows now where that number came from—somebody wrote it down once and it got repeated again and again) and they are extinct today because they were hunted down and slaughtered like animals, mostly for sport. That was what I understood to be the story of the Beothuk. Then when I sat down and started doing the research, it was just so obvious that there was almost no truth to that. The Beothuk were a very small group of people and the best guess anthropologists can make is, at the time of first contact, somewhere between five hundred and five thousand, meaning they couldn't possibly have numbered less than five hundred (that is the absolute minimum), and they couldn't possibly have numbered more than five thousand (that is the absolute maximum). The best guess is somewhere between one and two thousand. The extinction of the Beothuk, furthermore, had as much to do with the geography of the island as it did with violence perpetrated by Europeans. I have to be really careful when I talk about the difference in these versions of the story, because people sometimes think I am trying to minimize the events. To me the "real" story is no less horrific and no less tragic; it's just different. There is a lot more grey in there than I ever expected, and that is part of what I wanted the book to reflect. The Beothuk very rarely congregated in large groups, at least as far as we understand it. They wintered inland in larger groups, but during the summers they dispersed into small family groups along pretty much the entire coastline. There were a number of early contacts that were positive, and the Beothuk seemed to be intrigued by these white people. Then there were a couple of awful misunderstandings (and nobody knows how much of this is apocryphal) where the Beothuk seemed to be expecting people who had been there the year before, and different Europeans showed up, saw all these Beothuk congregating, and fired on them. There were one or two other similar situations, and the Beothuk seemed to decide at that point they wanted nothing to do with it and started retreating geographically. This meant that they started losing access to resources. They also were exposed to European diseases that ravaged them, and then, at an incredibly critical juncture, when their numbers were dwindling really quickly, they were also exposed to this horrific violence on the northeast coast that just decimated the numbers they had left. The loss of those last salmon rivers was huge. There also seemed to have been some change in the caribou migration patterns at the time, which meant they didn't have as much food as they needed to survive the winters. The combination of all those factors is what ended the Beothuk. If (and it sounds awful to say it) they hadn't been so insular, if they had decided instead that they would try to make some kind of contact with the Europeans, there's a possibility that things would have ended differently. They seemed to have decided (and I think, psychologically, it makes sense) that something horrific and lethal was happening to them, and it had everything to do with whatever was encroaching, and they wanted nothing to do with any of that.

The funny thing is that the history of what happened to the Beothuk is still changing. You know, my book would be slightly different if I wrote it now than when I wrote it in 2001, just because of some things that are now accepted as truth that at the time weren't talked about or dismissed as unlikely. So it's not like this is a static story.

HW On the topic of plausibility, an important grey area is the possibility that there were two Beothuk men rather than one murdered in that clash on Red Indian Lake in 1819. This is dismissed by a lot of people as just not possible, but it is part of the controversy over the historical Peytons. In *River Thieves* you turn that possibility into the central episode of the narrative. Now, is it fair to assume that this is your conclusion based on the research that you did for the novel, or is it more a case of pursuing in fiction one possibility suggested by the gaps or the contradictions in the historical record?

MC It is my conclusion that were two men killed there and that the version that Peyton tells is a truncated or a modified or a biased version that is designed to protect somebody or some people. Basically they are saying, "We killed one person in self-defence." Completely ludicrous, but that's their story.

HW And an obstinate person, may I point out [*laughs*].

MC Incredibly obstinate. I mean, who wouldn't kill him? Really. Seriously, though, to me it's incredibly poignant that this man walks into the middle of a group of strangers who are holding his wife hostage and stands there and speaks to them, trying to talk them into being civilized, basically, even though they didn't understand a word of what he was saying. He is the more human person in that encounter, and then he is brutally killed when he responds as anybody would respond.

HW This is where we get into that really dangerous territory of postmodern multiplicity of perspective. It is clear that you are emotionally identifying with that reading of Nonosabusut's gesture, of his intervention, and yet we have other historical perspectives, for instance that of Amy Peyton, the wife of one of the Peytons' descendants, who basically argues that what he is doing there is getting agitated by the presence of John Peyton Sr., this notorious opponent of the Beothuk.

MC Obviously, this is my own take on the multiplicity, and that reflects my own bias. Where I end up going in the book reflects where I'm coming from, and that's my right as a writer.

HW On the other hand you could argue that there is also first of all an emotional logic to your reading, and I would say an emotional illogic to Amy Peyton's argument, which is essentially deflecting blame away from the Peytons and in some ways projecting an irrational response onto Nonosabusut.

MC Sure, the savage is basically acting like a savage, in which case there is no rational way to deal with him. Killing him becomes the only available option. Which is an appalling reading of that entire situation. There was a member of the party who wrote a newspaper account years later which I felt rang true, because there was nothing to be gained from his account other than possibly losing friends. The article didn't name the Peytons, but there's no question who the Mr. P. is. And it certainly makes the Peytons look far less innocent. Also, it seemed to me implausible to think that he was making those things up, whereas it seemed very plausible to me that the other stories were shaped deliberately to protect particular people. That is part of the reason that I lean more in that direction in the book. To me that seems like a more plausible story, when I think about those particular men, their histories, what actually happened on the lake, the fact that there are different versions of the story. I am not a nihilist or a complete relativist. I don't think that there is one objective truth that you can know; it's more like there's a dartboard of truth up there you throw darts at, and you can come nearer to or farther from the truth. You can look at darts thrown up by other people and say, "Not even on the board." So part of what I was doing when I was reading all this was saying, "How close can I come to the truth?"

HW So postmodern relativity does not mean the equality of all competing and multiple perspectives.

MC To me, the notion that everything is relative, or nothing is more true than anything else, is just as stupid and useless as the notion that there is one objective truth that you can't veer away from, that is factual and completely knowable. As in all things, the truth seems to lie somewhere in the middle of those two competing perspectives.

HW And also that we have to look with some skepticism and some astute gauging of intentions and interests at the historical documents that are talking to each other, against each other, because there are all kinds of considerations of agency and vested interests and so on.

MC Particularly with the story of the Beothuk, in terms of the historians, there is nothing from the other side that has not passed through the side that is telling the story. Everything we know about the Beothuk has been filtered through a white person. Even stories of Mikma'q violence against the Beothuk (and this is one of the things that I became more aware of after the book came out)—all of that was reported by white people. Every single instance is reported by a white person. John Peyton Jr. talked about it all the time. In one of his letters he is trying to say how awfully these people have been treated by the Europeans and by the Mikma'q, and it seems to have been to try to minimize what the Europeans did, to say, "Well, we're not the only ones." The Mikma'q claim that there was never any violence between the two groups, and they have stuck to that story from the beginning. I found a little pamphlet by someone hired by the government to do something that brought him into contact with the Mikma'q, and he became interested in the story of Mikma'q violence towards the Beothuk. He did his own investigation of the question and claims there is not one single shred of evidence that you could trust, to say that was true. I had this character, Noel Young, a Mikma'q man from whom Buchan gets the story that Joseph Reilly was the one who killed the Beothuk on Red Indian Lake. Noel Young admits to having been violent towards the Beothuk in the novel. But even then I was uncomfortable with it. Buchan talks about having been told that the Mikma'q had been violent toward the Beothuk, and Noel Young smiles at Buchan and says, "You shouldn't believe everything a white man tells you." Again, that was me saying, "You have to know where this is coming from." He does admit to Buchan, "[I]f I hadn't gone after them, they'd have gone after me." But I don't know if I were writing the book now if that is something I would have in there.

HW You talked a little earlier about the Peytons' custodial attitude towards the story. Especially given that, in fictional terms anyway, *River Thieves* is essentially asserting a cover-up at the heart of the incident (and you have said that you subscribe to that theory) what kind of reaction have you had to the novel as a judgment on the role of settlers, and more specifically the Peyton family, in the disappearance of the Beothuk?

MC In general, there has not been any sort of negative response; there has not been any flak. In fact, I have gotten a pretty easy ride, hopefully because of the work I did, but I have gotten a pretty easy ride in terms of historical accuracy as well. That was one of the things I was most nervous about, because I remember Wayne Johnston just got hell over *Colony*. Even Ingeborg Marshall, who I got to meet, said there were one or two small things, but she was really impressed with the historical accuracy of the book. She said, "I have issues with using historical figures as characters in novels," but she added, "That's a different thing; we won't talk about it."

I have met a number of Peytons, including a Mr. Baird, whose mother knew John Peyton Jr. He was in his nineties and sharp as a tack. I was at a literary festival in Eastport, where Mr. Baird has a summer home, and Michael Winter introduced me to Mr. Baird's son, who told me he had given my book to his father. I said, "Oh, what'd he think?" and then I said, "No, never mind; I'd rather not know" [*laughs*]. He said, "You know, Dad inhaled that book; he read it in two days, and I asked him afterwards what did he think of it and he said, 'Mmmm, I don't know.'" He asked me if I wanted to meet his father and I said, "If it's all the same to you, I don't think I do." But the two—Michael Winter and Mr. Baird's son—conspired. I was supposed to pick Michael up to bring him back to St. John's and Mr. Baird was just down over the hill, and they brought me down there, so I sat and talked to this man for half an hour, about his own life but also about the Beothuk and his family's role in that story. He was not at all defensive about what was written in the book in terms of his family's involvement in particular events. There was no sense of him saying, "That wasn't true. You're giving the wrong impression." He did say—I really admired him; he was a real gentleman—"The book offended me." But what offended him was he didn't understand how you could take these real people and write a book and call it a novel.

HW Just that basic premise of the historical novel.

MC Yes. Here is a man whose mother as a young girl knew this man personally, and that was a very freaky moment, to be sitting with him and to have the
sense of touching his hand, and he is touching his mother's hand, and his
mother is touching John Peyton Jr. It confirmed that discomfort I had when
I was writing the book, that there are real people on the other end of the line.

HW And you are not just ruffling the edges of documents.

MC No, and in Newfoundland (I think this is more true in Newfoundland
than anywhere else I have been in Canada) history is not schoolbooks. History is where your grandfather lived, what land your grandmother grew veg-
etables in, where people came from, where they had their summer places. It
is still very physically present for people, and people have a real sense of ownership of the history of the place, which is why Wayne Johnston, for example,
got such a rough ride and part of the reason I was expecting a rough ride. But
I am really grateful to have met Mr. Baird and to have been able to talk to
him.

John Baird, his son, has a house up on the hill, and before we went down
he showed me a musket that had belonged to John Peyton Jr., and also this huge
copper pot that was on the expedition to bring Mary's body back that was
abandoned and recovered years later by Thomas Peyton, John Jr.'s son. And
we went down the hill with the musket—*I don't know why*. Mr. Baird didn't
know who I was at first, we were kind of introduced, but there were a lot of
people around. Finally, it dawned on him and he says, "Oh, bring over a chair.
You sit next to me." And he looks at John and he sees he's got the gun and he
says, "John, what'd you bring that down here for?" And then he says, "Well, if
you're going to shoot anyone, shoot this fella here" [*laughs*], in the nicest possible way. Everybody had a laugh. We talked about various things, including
his wife. They got married very young, lived together for fifty, sixty years. He
said, "You know, I've got a picture of her inside." He called out to his daughter Mickey and said, "Mickey, take this young fella in and show him a picture
of my sweetie." So she takes me in and brings me across the room and shows
me a picture of Shanawdithit. I guess because she knew I was there to talk
about the Beothuk and when he said "my sweetie," she thought this was the
"sweetie" he was referring to. And it just pointed out to me again this strange
intimacy that family has with this story.

HW I'm curious about which way your sympathies lean in the novel. Do you
sympathize or identify more with a settler like, say, John Peyton Jr. or an ostensibly more benevolent colonial official like David Buchan? In the novel's early

going, it seems that Buchan is the Beothuks' protector against the settlers' depredations, but as the novel progresses he seems to be presented in a less flattering light as a somewhat megalomaniacal martinet. Conversely, the settlers—who seem to be … not demonized, but presented as somewhat predatory in the early going—have their concerns, like their expulsion from the French Shore by English soldiers, brought more to the foreground.

MC Part of what I wanted the novel to do was to reflect my own wildly veering sympathies. The more I delved into the historical record, the broader the areas of grey became. Part of the tragedy of the story, part of what is gut-wrenching about what happened, is that it was so unplanned, if you know what I mean. Here are these people, essentially forced and hunted into extinction, and nobody really noticed that that was what was going on. People were just trying to get on with their lives, basically. Even to someone like John Sr., who I had thought of as a complete bastard—as I wrote him and as I became more and more aware of the circumstances he would have come from, to be where he was—there was a level of grey. The more I learned about the England that these people came from, the more obvious it became that they were responding to the Beothuk in the exact same way that the penal system would have responded to petty thieves in England. There was a naval officer, a Captain Pulling, who became interested in the Beothuk and went around interviewing people about them, and there was one settler who said, "Now, what would you do, sir, if somebody snuck onto your boat and went off with materials from the boat?" It was almost a rhetorical question, and he answered it himself, saying of course the officer would have gone after them and that at the very least he would have had them stripped and flogged, if not hung.

HW Because punishments for theft were extremely severe at that point.

MC So it became obvious to me that the way these people were acting—which to my eyes was barbarous and completely indefensible—to them made complete sense. It wasn't that they were—

HW Genocidal.

MC I think they felt, "This is the way the world is." On the other side of that, of course, are all these settlers who came from the exact same circumstances and responded differently. And that is where judgments come into the story, where we have to say, "This is a good person and this is a not a good person." But it's not a question of pure or absolute good and evil. I think the book makes judgments. I think the book asks readers to make judgments. But at the same time I don't think that any of those can be simple or one-dimensional.

FIGURE 33.
Capt. David Buchan. The Rooms,
Provincial Archives Division,
Newfoundland and Labrador
C1-213.

HW It seems to me that this complex portrait is part of a larger process, especially in contemporary Canadian historical fiction, which is a reappraisal of the legacy of colonialism and a demythologizing and critiquing of figures of colonial authority. The obvious temptation is to turn that upside down into this simplistic victimizer–victimized dichotomy, and I think that *River Thieves* is part of a movement towards looking at that process as much more complex. More importantly, it does so not in a way that reduces everything to a problematic equality, seeing all sides to the point that it is essentially politically paralyzing, neutralizing any kind of judgment and responsibility.

MC I'm not sure if this is a correct reading of the history or not, but part of what I found appalling about the story, just looking into the actual historical record, was how incidental the extinction of the Beothuk was. It barely impinges on people's sense of what Newfoundland is, at the time, what the plan was and what they were doing there. And that's part of the reason I chose to have the Beothuk occupy the margins of the book as well, because that's where they were at the time, and that is what, in the end, made their extinction possible. The result of what the settlers were doing was the extinction of an entire race, but while it was happening it was just day-to-day business. And that's part of what is appalling and unforgivable.

That's not to say, by the way, that if an organized policy of genocide was needed there wouldn't have been one. It happened in many other places; if it was necessary to make it possible for Europeans to settle in Newfoundland and fish there, there probably would have been an official policy of some sort, if not outright genocide then the kind of thing we saw in the rest of Canada, where there was appeasement and pushing people out of their land and broken treaties—the same sort of creeping genocide. But that level of forethought and planning isn't what happened in Newfoundland. It was not even in most people's consciousness. There were only a couple of people who made it their business to say, "Look what's happening here," and just about everybody else continued to completely ignore it until it was too late to do anything.

HW In both *The Colony of Unrequited Dreams* and in *River Thieves*, the question of class—as evident, for instance, in the tensions between the colonial authorities and the settlers and dramatized through the figure of the thief Joseph Reilly—figures prominently. Do you think that the history of Newfoundland is marked by more stark class divisions than the history of the rest of the country?

MC I often think that there are several Newfoundlands, when it comes to class. With Wayne Johnston, writing about St. John's, class is a huge thing, and there are obvious striations, and the class you are born into has an enormous impact on your life. Outport Newfoundland is different, although I think there are obviously two very different classes throughout the history: the merchant class and then everybody else. Outport Newfoundland was almost feudal in how it was set up. The merchants basically owned everything. But in an odd way a Newfoundlander who fished for a living was an independent man, not in terms of economics, but certainly in terms of his day-to-day life. His business was his own, and he went out every day and did his work, and I think that there was something appealing in that. I often wondered why the hell anyone would move from Europe to Newfoundland, but that was one of the attractions: you owned your own piece of land, and you owned your own house, and you worked for yourself. Especially around the time that *River Thieves* covers, there were areas of Newfoundland that existed outside of colonial Newfoundland. Colonial Newfoundland was really the Avalon Peninsula and outside of that, except for these rare incursions where, say, the British Navy went to the west coast and removed every Englishman to meet the conditions of a treaty, people felt they were living outside the purview of the Crown. This was true on the northeast shore especially. People like the Peytons felt they were a law unto themselves, and that was part of what attracted them to that part of the world. So it is a very complicated political and social landscape.

Later on in Newfoundland history I think things became a little less polarized. Some of the distinct class and social divisions have been blurred, and there are all kinds of things responsible for that. The end of the merchant truck system, for one. The standardization of education since confederation, for another. I grew up in a mining town, for example, and I was the first person in either of my parents' families ever to go to university. I did a minor in sociology, and I was taking all of these sociology courses where they were talking about class—working-class this, working-class that—and I think I was in third- or fourth-year university when I was in class one day and I thought, "Oh. My. God! I'm working-class!" [*laughs*]

HW Michael Crummey's epiphany.

MC It had never occurred to me that I was working-class, and I think that's partly because in a mining town like Buchans there was an uptown and a downtown, there was an area of town where management lived, but by then the lines were so blurred. All the kids went to the same schools. It just never occurred to me that there was any difference between those people. I have talked to Mom and Dad enough to know that earlier in the town's history there was a huge line there that you did not cross, but when I was a kid it was like I never even noticed it. I don't know if that is true in the outports as well. I think it may be that people all looked at each other as being in the same boat, that there was not the same sense after confederation of that division between the merchant and everybody else. That is just pure speculation on my part.

HW In *Newfoundland: Journey into a Lost Nation*, you observe that "'The Past' is big business in Newfoundland these days," essentially that there's a commodified, nostalgic version of Newfoundland's past "that does a disservice to the people and the place itself." How does literature about Newfoundland's past—I am thinking of the writing of Wayne Johnston, John Steffler, and Bernice Morgan, for instance, as well as your own work—figure into the current preoccupation with the past in Newfoundland and Labrador?

MC Just to broaden that a little bit, I wonder about this whole explosion of historical fiction in Canada. In a way, it seems to be the result of the commodification of historical fiction, and that people are doing it now partly because it's what's selling. I remember somebody accusing Michael Winter, basically, of writing a historical novel because that is where the money is.

HW This is Winter's *The Big Why*, I take it.

MC Yes. I mean, you cannot read that book and think that there is anything in that of a cash grab. It is such a brilliant piece of writing and also in some ways so anti-mainstream. But I do wonder about where I fit in that whole literary commodification of the past. I think that there is a danger in it. There is a certain violation in that process of imagining lives for these real people. It seems to me there is a continuum. On one end there is a sincere engagement with the past that is an attempt to ask, "Where do we come from, and what does that make us now?" And then it goes all the way over to "Here's a way to make a fast buck." You know, you put on the oilskins, you stand in front of the bars on George Street with a dory and get people to pay five bucks to get their picture taken with you. That basically is the continuum and you don't always know where you are standing. It's a question of constantly interrogating your own motives, asking what interests you about this story and why you are telling it. What do you want out of it? I think Newfoundland is in the middle of a sea change. When I think about my dad, he never asked himself those questions, "Where are we coming from? What does that make us?" He basically took the attitude that this is where you were born, this is what you did to make a living, these are the stories you told because they were funny stories or interesting stories or terrifying stories. It was your entertainment. I was among the first generation of Newfoundlanders in which everybody went to school, and a huge percentage went on to university. And that is changing us in a way that means we are going to be different on the other side of it.

HW It is a real cultural threshold.

MC And when you throw the cod moratorium into the mix, it means that people are hyper-aware of the fact that what we were was a particular thing and what we are going to be in the future is something different. Granted there are going to be connections—we are still going to be Newfoundlanders—but what are we carrying with us and what are we losing? And I think the interest in the past in Newfoundland is partly an attempt to say, "Well, all we will have of that time and way of life are these stories." And also, in a way, trying to point forward, saying, "We want to take some of this with us, wherever it is we're going."

Selected Bibliography

The following entries for each writer interviewed include their historical novels and some of their other publications pertinent to history or to the history discussed in the interviews. They also include a selective list of critical discussions of their work, particularly criticism focusing on the historical aspects of their fiction (and, in some cases, poetry). Finally, the entries include selected sources dealing with the history behind these writers' novels or, in some cases, sources that are referred to in the course of the interviews themselves.

Joseph Boyden

Boyden, Joseph. *Born With a Tooth.* Toronto: Cormorant, 2001.
———. *Three Day Road.* Toronto: Viking Canada, 2005.
Gaffen, Fred. *Forgotten Soldiers.* Penticton, BC: Theytus, 1985.
Hayes, Adrian. *Pegahmagabow: Legendary Warrior, Forgotten Hero.* Huntsville, ON: Fox Meadow, 2003.
Miller, J.R. *Shingwauk's Vision: A History of Native Residential Schools in Canada.* Toronto: University of Toronto Press, 1996.
Summerby, Janice. *Native Soldiers—Foreign Battlefields.* Ottawa: Department of Veterans Affairs, 2005.
Steel, R. James. *The Men Who Marched Away: Canada's Infantry in World War I 1914–1918.* St. Catharines, ON: Vanwell, 1989.

George Elliott Clarke

Clarke, George Elliott. *Beatrice Chancy.* Vancouver: Polestar, 1999.

————. "The Birmingham of Nova Scotia: The Weymouth Falls Justice Committee vs. the Attorney General of Nova Scotia." In *Toward a New Maritimes,* ed. Ian McKay and Scott Milsom, 16–24. Charlottetown, PE: Ragweed Press, 1992.

————. *Execution Poems.* Kentville, NS: Gaspereau, 2001.

————. *Odysseys Home: Mapping African-Canadian Literature.* Toronto: University of Toronto Press, 2002.

————. *Saltwater Spirituals and Deeper Blues.* Lawrencetown Beach, NS: Pottersfield, 1983.

————. *Whylah Falls.* Vancouver: Polestar, 1990.

Andrews, Jennifer. "Revisioning Fredericton: Reading George Elliott Clarke's *Execution Poems.*" Forthcoming in *Essays on Canadian Writing* 86.

Henry, Frances. *Forgotten Canadians: The Blacks of Nova Scotia.* Don Mills, ON: Longman, 1973.

MacLeod, Alexander. "'The Little State of Africadia Is a Community of Believers': Replacing the Regional and Remaking the Real with George Elliot Clarke." Forthcoming in *Essays on Canadian Writing* 86.

Moynagh, Maureen. "Mapping Africadia's Imaginary Geography: An Interview with George Elliott Clarke." *Ariel* 27, no. 4 (1996): 71–94.

Wells, Dorothy. "A Rose Grows in Whylah Falls." *Canadian Literature* 155 (1997): 56–73.

Willis, Susan. "Anansi History: George Elliott Clarke's *Whylah Falls.*" *Journal of Commonwealth and Postcolonial Studies* 9, no. 1 (2002): 47–56.

Winks, Robin W. *The Blacks in Canada.* 2nd ed. Montreal: McGill-Queen's University Press, 1997.

Michael Crummey

Crummey, Michael. *Hard Light.* London, ON: Brick, 1998.

————. *River Thieves.* Toronto: Doubleday Canada, 2001.

————. *The Wreckage.* Toronto: Doubleday Canada, 2005.

Crummey, Michael, and Greg Locke. *Newfoundland: Journey into a Lost Nation.* Toronto: McClelland & Stewart, 2004.

Chafe, Paul. "Lament for a Notion: Loss and the Beothuk in Michael Crummey's *River Thieves.*" *Essays on Canadian Writing* 82 (2004): 93–117.

Dalton, Mary. "Shadow Indians: The Beothuk Motif in Newfoundland Literature." *Newfoundland Studies* 8, no. 2 (1992): 135–46.

Fardy, B.D. *Captain David Buchan in Newfoundland.* St. John's, NL: Harry Cuff, 1983.

————. *Demasduit: Native Newfoundlander.* St. John's, NL: Creative, 1988.

Howley, J.P. *The Beothucks or Red Indians: The Aboriginal Inhabitants of Newfoundland.* Toronto: Coles, 1974. First published 1915.

Marshall, Ingeborg. *A History and Ethnography of the Beothuk.* Montreal: McGill-Queen's University Press, 1996.

Peyton, Amy Louise. *River Lords: Father and Son*. St. John's, NL: Jesperson Press, 1987.

Sugars, Cynthia. "Original Sin, or, The Last of the First Ancestors: Michael Crummey's *River Thieves*." Forthcoming in *English Studies in Canada*.

Wyile, Herb. "Beothuk Gothic: Michael Crummey's *River Thieves*." Forthcoming in *Australasian Canadian Studies* 24, no. 2.

Wayne Johnston

Johnston, Wayne. *Baltimore's Mansion*. Toronto: Knopf Canada, 1999.

———. *The Colony of Unrequited Dreams*. Toronto: Knopf Canada, 1998.

———. *The Custodian of Paradise*. Toronto. Knopf Canada, 2006.

———. *Human Amusements*. Toronto: McClelland & Stewart, 1994.

———. "My Treatment of History in *The Colony of Unrequited Dreams*." *boldtype: an online literary magazine* 3, no. 3 (1999). http://www.randomhouse.com/boldtype/0699/johnston/essay.html.

———. *The Navigator of New York*. Toronto: Knopf Canada, 2002.

Bak, Hans. "Writing Newfoundland, Writing Canada: Wayne Johnston's *The Colony of Unrequited Dreams*." In *The Rhetoric of Canadian Writing*, ed. Conny Steenman-Marcuse, 217–36. Amsterdam: Rodopi, 2002.

Berton, Pierre. *The Arctic Grail: The Quest for the Arctic Passage and the North Pole, 1818–1909*. New York: Viking, 1988.

Cook, Frederick A. *My Attainment of the Pole*. New York: Mitchell Kennerley, 1913.

Dragland, Stan. "*The Colony of Unrequited Dreams*: Romancing History?" *Essays on Canadian Writing* 82 (2004): 187–213.

Fuller, Danielle. "Strange Terrain: Reproducing and Resisting Place-Myths in Two Contemporary Fictions of Newfoundland." *Essays on Canadian Writing* 82 (2004): 21–50.

Gwyn, Richard. *Smallwood: The Unlikely Revolutionary*. Toronto: McClelland & Stewart, 1968.

MacLeod, Alexander. "History versus Geography in Wayne Johnston's *The Colony of Unrequited Dreams*." Forthcoming in *Canadian Literature* 189.

Prowse, D.W. *A History of Newfoundland from the English, Colonial, and Foreign Records*. London: Macmillan, 1895.

Smallwood, Joseph R. *I Chose Canada: The Memoirs of the Honourable Joseph R. "Joey" Smallwood*. Toronto: Macmillan, 1973.

Wyile, Herb. "Historical Strip-Tease: Revelation and the *Bildungsroman* in Wayne Johnston's Writing." *The Antigonish Review* 141/142 (2005): 85–98.

Heather Robertson

Robertson, Heather. *Igor: A Novel of Intrigue. The King Years, Vol. III*. Toronto: James Lorimer, 1989.

———. *Lily: A Rhapsody in Red. The King Years, Vol. II*. Toronto: James Lorimer, 1986.

———. *Willie: A Romance. The King Years, Vol. I*. Toronto: James Lorimer, 1983.

Collins, Anne. "Creating Mayhem." Review of *Igor*, by Heather Robertson. *Saturday Night* 105 (Jan.–Feb. 1990): 43–45.

Hewitt, Steve. "Royal Canadian Mounted Spy: The Secret Life of John Leopold/Jack Esselwein." *Intelligence and National Security* 15, no. 1 (2000): 144–68.

Ferns, H.S., and B. Ostry. *The Age of Mackenzie King: The Rise of the Leader*. London: Heinemann, 1953.

King, William Lyon Mackenzie. *The Mackenzie King Diaries, 1893–1931*. Toronto: University of Toronto Press, 1973.

———. *The Mackenzie King Diaries, 1932–1949*. Toronto: University of Toronto Press, 1980.

Sawatsky, John. *Gouzenko: The Untold Story*. Toronto: Macmillan, 1984.

Stacey, C.P. *A Very Double Life: The Private World of Mackenzie King*. Toronto: Macmillan, 1976.

Fred Stenson

Stenson, Fred. *Lightning*. Vancouver: Douglas & McIntyre, 2003.

———. *Rocky Mountain House National Historic Park*. Toronto: NC Press, 1985.

———. *The Trade*. Vancouver: Douglas & McIntyre, 2000.

Durnin, Katherine. "Archives and Truth in Fred Stenson's *The Trade*." *Canadian Literature* 178 (2003): 73–88.

Galbraith, John S. *The Little Emperor*. Toronto: Macmillan, 1976.

Gladstone, William. *The Gladstone Diary: Travels in the Early West*. Ed. Freda Graham Bundy. Lethbridge: Historic Trails Society of Alberta, 1985. First published 1903.

Jackson, John C. *Jemmy Jock Bird: Marginal Man on the Blackfoot Frontier*. Calgary, AB: University of Calgary Press, 2003.

Kane, Paul. *Wanderings of an Artist among the Indians of North America*. Edmonton, AB: Hurtig, 1968. First published 1859.

MacGregor, J.G. *John Rowand: Czar of the Prairies*. Saskatoon, SK: Western Prairie Producer, 1978.

Newman, Peter. *Caesars of the Wilderness. Company of Adventurers, Vol. II*. Markham, ON: Viking, 1985.

Rundle, Robert. *The Rundle Journals 1840–1848*. Ed. Hugh A. Dempsey. Intr. Gerald M. Hutchinson. Calgary, AB: Historical Society of Alberta, 1977.

Van Kirk, Sylvia. *Many Tender Ties: Women in Fur-Trade Society in Western Canada, 1670–1870*. Winnipeg, MB: Watson & Dwyer, 1986.

Margaret Sweatman

Sweatman, Margaret. *Fox*. Winnipeg, MB: Turnstone, 1991.

———. *When Alice Lay Down with Peter*. Toronto: Knopf Canada, 2001.

Fischlin, Daniel. "'As Sparrows Do Fall': Sweatman's *Fox* and Transforming the Socius." *Open Letter* 9, no. 4 (1995): 55–68.

Helms, Gabriele. "Is Difficulty Impolite? The Performative in Margaret Sweatman's *Fox.*" in *Challenging Canada: Dialogism and Narrative Techniques in Canadian Novels,* 125–44. Montreal: McGill-Queen's University Press, 2003.

Howard, Victor, with Mac Reynolds. *The Mackenzie-Papineau Battallion: The Canadian Contingent in the Spanish Civil War.* Carleton Lib. Ser. 137. Ottawa: Carleton University Press, 1986.

Kramer, Reinhold. "The 1919 Winnipeg General Strike and Margaret Sweatman's *Fox.*" *Canadian Literature* 160 (1999): 50–70.

Smith, Doug. *Let Us Rise! A History of the Manitoba Labour Movement.* Winnipeg, MB: New Star, 1985.

Stonechild, Blair, and Bill Waiser. *Loyal till Death: Indians and the North-West Rebellion.* Calgary, AB: Fifth House, 1997.

Wyile, Herb. "'It Takes More Than Mortality to Make Somebody Dead': Spectres of History in Margaret Sweatman's *When Alice Lay Down with Peter.*" *The University of Toronto Quarterly* 75, no. 2 (2006): 735–51.

Jane Urquhart

Urquhart, Jane. *Away.* Toronto: McClelland & Stewart, 1993.

———. *Changing Heaven.* Toronto: McClelland & Stewart, 1990.

———. *The Stone Carvers.* Toronto: McClelland & Stewart, 2001.

———. *The Underpainter.* Toronto: McClelland & Stewart, 1997.

———. *The Whirlpool.* Toronto: McClelland & Stewart, 1989.

Berton, Pierre. *Vimy.* Toronto: McClelland & Stewart, 1986.

Compton, Anne. "Romancing the Landscape: Jane Urquhart's Fiction." In *Literature of Region and Nation: Proceedings of the 6th International Literature of Region and Nation Conference,* ed. Winnifred M. Bogaards, 211–29. Saint John, NB: Social Sciences and Humanities Research Council, 1998.

Eckstein, Modris. *Rites of Spring: The Great War and the Birth of the Modern Age.* Boston: Houghton Mifflin, 1989.

Ferri, Laura, ed. *Jane Urquhart: Essays on Her Works.* Toronto: Guernica, 2005.

Gordon, Neta. "The Artist and the Witness: Jane Urquhart's *The Underpainter* and *The Stone Carvers.*" *Studies in Canadian Literature* 28, no. 2 (2003): 59–73.

Skelton, Isabel. *The Life of Thomas D'Arcy McGee.* Gardenvale, QC: Garden City Press, 1925.

Slattery, T.P. *The Assassination of D'Arcy McGee.* Toronto: Doubleday Canada, 1968.

Sugars, Cynthia. "Haunted by (a Lack of) Postcolonial Ghosts: Settler Nationalism in Jane Urquhart's *Away.*" *Essays on Canadian Writing* 79 (2003): 1–32.

Wyile, Herb. "'The Opposite of History Is Forgetfulness': Myth, History and the New Dominion in Jane Urquhart's *Away.*" *Studies in Canadian Literature* 24, no. 1 (1999): 20–45.

Guy Vanderhaeghe

Vanderhaeghe, Guy. *The Englishman's Boy.* Toronto: McClelland & Stewart, 1996.
———. *The Last Crossing.* Toronto: McClelland, 2002.
Calder, Alison. "Unsettling the West: Nation and Genre in Guy Vanderhaeghe's *The Englishman's Boy.*" *Studies in Canadian Literature* 25, no. 2 (2000): 96–107.
Dempsey, Hugh. "Jerry Potts: Plainsman." *Montana: the Magazine of Western History* (Autumn 1967): 2–17.
Fardy, B.D. *Jerry Potts: Paladin of the Plains.* Langley, BC: Sunfire, 1984.
Goldring, Philip. "Whisky, Horses and Death: The Cypress Hills Massacre and Its Sequel." *Canadian Historic Sites,* 43–70. Occasional Papers in Archeology and History Series, vol. 21. Ottawa: Parks Canada, 1979.
Johnston, Alex. The *Last Great Indian Battle.* Occasional Paper No. 30. Lethbridge, AB: Lethbridge Historical Society, 1997.
Kramer, Reinhold. "Nationalism, the West, and *The Englishman's Boy.*" *Essays on Canadian Writing* 67 (1999): 1–22.
Long, Philip S. *Jerry Potts: Scout, Frontiersman and Hero.* Calgary, AB: Bonanza, 1974.
Sharp, Paul F. *Whoop-Up Country: The Canadian–American West, 1865–1885.* Minneapolis: University of Minnesota Press, 1955.
Twigg, Alan. Interview with Guy Vanderhaeghe in *Strong Voices: Conversations with 50 Canadian Authors,* 270–74. Madeira Park, BC: Harbour, 1988.
Wyile, Herb. "Dances with Wolfers: Choreographing History in *The Englishman's Boy.*" *Essays on Canadian Writing* 67 (1999): 23–52.
———. "Doing the Honourable Thing: Guy Vanderhaeghe's *The Last Crossing.* Canadian Literature* 185 (2005): 59–74.

Thomas Wharton

Wharton, Thomas. *Icefields.* Edmonton, AB: NeWest, 1995.
———. *Salamander.* Toronto: McClelland & Stewart, 2001.
Banting, Pamela. "The Angel in the Glacier: Geography as Intertext in Thomas Wharton's *Icefields.*" *Interdisciplinary Studies in Literature and the Environment* 7, no. 2 (2000): 67–80.
Carnegie, James, Earl of Southesk. *Saskatchewan and the Rocky Mountains.* Edmonton, AB: M.G. Hurtig, 1969.
Fraser, Esther. *The Canadian Rockies: Early Travels and Explorations.* Edmonton, AB: M.G. Hurtig, 1969.
Hepburn, Allan. "'Enough of a Wonder': Landscape and Tourism in Thomas Wharton's *Icefields.*" *Essays on Canadian Writing* 73 (2001): 72–92.
Omhovère, Claire. "The Melting of Time in Thomas Wharton's *Icefields.*" In *History, Literature and the Writing of the Canadian Prairies,* ed. Alison Calder and Robert Warthaugh, 43–62. Winnipeg, MB: University of Manitoba Press, 2005.
Stutfield, Hugh E.M., and J. Norman Collie. *Climbs & Exploration in the Canadian Rockies.* London: Longmans, Green & Co., 1903.

Rudy Wiebe

Wiebe, Rudy. *The Blue Mountains of China.* Toronto: McClelland & Stewart, 1970.

————. *A Discovery of Strangers.* Toronto: McClelland & Stewart, 1994.

————. *The Mad Trapper.* Toronto: McClelland & Stewart, 1980.

————. *My Lovely Enemy.* Toronto: McClelland & Stewart, 1983.

————. *The Scorched-Wood People.* Toronto: McClelland & Stewart, 1977.

————. *Sweeter Than All the World.* Toronto: Knopf Canada, 2001.

————. *The Temptations of Big Bear.* Toronto: McClelland & Stewart, 1973.

Wiebe, Rudy, and Yvonne Johnson. *Stolen Life: The Journey of a Cree Woman* Toronto: Knopf Canada, 1998.

Howard, Joseph Kinsey. *Strange Empire: A Narrative of the Northwest.* St. Paul: Minnesota Historical Society, 1994. First published 1952.

Howells, Corall Ann. "Rudy Wiebe's Art and Acts of Narrative in *The Scorched-Wood People.*" In *Canadian Story and History 1885–1985,* ed. Colin Nicholson and Peter Easingwood, 18–26. Edinburgh: Centre of Canadian Studies, 1985.

Juneja, Om P., M.F. Salat, and Chandra Mohan. "'Looking at Our Particular World': An Interview with Rudy Wiebe," *World Literature Written in English* 31, no. 2 (1991): 1–18.

Kaltembach, Michèle. "Explorations into History: Rudy Wiebe's *A Discovery of Strangers.*" *Études Canadiennes/Canadian Studies* 44 (1998): 77–87.

Keith, W.J. *Epic Fiction: The Art of Rudy Wiebe.* Edmonton: University of Alberta Press, 1981.

————, ed. *A Voice in the Land: Essays by and about Rudy Wiebe.* Edmonton, AB: NeWest, 1981.

Korkka, Janne. "Representation of Aboriginal Peoples in Rudy Wiebe's Fiction: *The Temptations of Big Bear* and *A Discovery of Strangers.*" In *Walking a Tightrope: Aboriginal People and Their Representations,* ed. Ute Lischke and David T. McNab, 351–76. Waterloo: Wilfrid Laurier University Press, 2005.

Mandel, Eli, and Rudy Wiebe, "Where the Voice Comes From." In *A Voice in the Land,* ed. W.J. Keith, 150–55.

Van Toorn, Penny. *Rudy Wiebe and the Historicity of the Word.* Edmonton: University of Alberta Press, 1995.